Essential
Study
Skills

Essential

Study

Skills

THIRD EDITION

Linda Wong

Lane Community College

HOUGHTON MIFFLIN COMPANY   Boston   New York

Director of Student Success Programs Barbara A. Heinssen
Editorial Assistant Shani Fisher
Project Editor Rachel D'Angelo Wimberly
Senior Production/Design Coordinator Sarah Ambrose
Senior Manufacturing Coordinator Sally Culler

Acknowledgments
The author is grateful to the following for granting permission to reprint excerpts from their works:

Andrea, Alfred J. and James Overfield, THE HUMAN RECORD, Third Edition. Copyright © 1998 by Houghton Mifflin Company. Used with permission.

Berko, Roy M., Andrew D. Wolvin, and Darlyn R. Wolvin, COMMUNICATING, Seventh Edition. Copyright © 1998 by Houghton Mifflin Company. Used with permission.

Bernstein, Douglas A., Thomas K. Srull, Christopher D. Wickens, and Edward J. Roy, PSYCHOLOGY, Fourth Edition. Copyright © 1997 by Houghton Mifflin Company. Used with permission.

DuBrin, Andrew, LEADERSHIP, Second Edition. Copyright © 1998 by Houghton Mifflin Company. Used with permission.

Mansbach, Richard W., THE GLOBAL PUZZLE, Second Edition. Copyright © 1997 by Houghton Mifflin Company. Used with permission.

Payne, David G. and Michael J. Wenger, COGNITIVE PSYCHOLOGY. Copyright © 1998 by Houghton Mifflin Company. Used with permission.

Pride, William M., Robert J. Hughes, and Jagdish R. Kapoor, BUSINESS, Fifth Edition. Copyright © 1996 by Houghton Mifflin Company. Used with permission.

Cover Design: Minko T. Dimov, MinkoImages
Cover Illustration: Celia Johnson

Printed in the U.S.A.

Library of Congress Catalog Card Number: 99-71907
ISBN: 0-618-00395-9

1 2 3 4 5 6 7 8 9 - VH - 03 02 01 00 99

Contents

v

PART FIVE: Strengthening Your Test-Taking Skills

Preface

The third edition of *Essential Study Skills*—a text appropriate for all postsecondary students interested in learning effective study strategies and especially helpful for returning adults and at-risk students—presents innovative new features and a regrouping of chapters. This new organization lays the foundation for and allows the development of metacognition, the process of using knowledge about one's own memory system and learning strategies to tackle intellectual tasks. The metacognitive approach used throughout the third edition enables students to assume responsibility for their own learning and to realize that academic success is a product of skills and behaviors they can acquire, customize, and effectively implement. In addition to the step-by-step approach, encouraging tone, clear rationales, and versatile exercises of previous editions, the new features and the revisions of the third edition provide a greater array of practical strategies and exercises. This worktext approach will bring students not only higher grades and a more thorough learning of information, but, ultimately, it will bring increased confidence, self-esteem, and empowerment.

New Student-Oriented Features Enriching the Third Edition

- A **"Quick Start"** section at the beginning of the third edition presents essential study skills that students can implement during the first week of classes. The **Quick Start Checklist** helps familiarize students with registration, campus resources, computer access, textbook organization, syllabi, and other study skills strategies for successfully starting the semester.

- **Computer Applications** in each chapter provide students with suggestions for integrating their computer abilities with essential study skills, strategies, and activities.

- **Web Site Activities** for each chapter are located on the Houghton Mifflin web site—*http://www.hmco.com/college/success* (choose "Students" and "Wong"). Companion web activities include selected surveys, case studies that can be discussed on the Web, additional enrichment exercises, group web-search activities, and links to web sites with related information. Student responses may also be emailed to instructors. A web-page icon is used throughout the chapters to identify companion web-page activities.

- **Portfolio projects** may be used as individual assignments or as a form of assessment throughout the term.

- **LINKS exercises** connect chapter content to skills, concepts, and excerpts presented in previous chapters.

- A **self-awareness writing assignment** is presented on the profile page at the beginning of each chapter, and a **profile writing assignment** for a personal log (journal) is included at each chapter's conclusion.

- More **group-discussion exercises,** many of which focus on case studies, are presented.

- More **informative excerpts** from a variety of introductory-level college textbooks are included.

■ The **answer keys** for the *Chapter Review Questions*, which are given in the Instructors' Resource Manual, are designed so that each answer key can be individually reproduced for easy in-class self-correcting and/or compiled into answer key booklets.

New Chapter Order and Content

The new sequencing of chapters in the third edition provides students with a strong foundation on which they can build solid study skills. The high-interest chapter on learning styles, now positioned at the beginning of *Essential Study Skills*, is followed by material that provides students with knowledge about learning and memory systems. This new opening sequence of chapters, which emphasizes identification of individual learning styles and understanding of the learning and memory processes, supports the metacognitive approach that is woven into the textbook. With this sound foundation, students can learn text-book reading and notetaking skills, can develop their test-taking skills, and can more effectively develop the study and self-management skills necessary for strong academic performance and success as they work through chapters that prepare them for optimal learning. The pedagogy incorporated in *Essential Study Skills* supports contemporary theories of learning and views on student success.

Part One: Understanding How You Process and Learn

Chapter 1—Discovering and Using Your Learning Style

Three Basic Learning Styles, Learning Strategies, Multiple Intelligences

■ **New:** Howard Gardner's "Eight Intelligences" now complements learning styles.

Chapter 2—Processing Information into Your Memory System

The Information Processing Model, Twelve Memory Principles

■ **New:** An added memory-principles inventory facilitates faster comprehension and learning of the twelve memory principles.

Part Two: Preparing Yourself for Optimal Learning

Chapter 3—Managing Your Time

All About You, Using Goals of Time Management, Creating a Weekly Time-Management Schedule, Using Other Time-Management Tips

■ **New:** Time management now gets its own chapter.

Chapter 4—Setting Goals

Goals, Motivation, Procrastination; Kinds of Goals; Steps for Writing Effective Goals; Tips for Reaching Goals; Goal Setting for Studying

■ **New:** This important topic now receives its own chapter and includes goal setting for study blocks, a five-day test preparation plan, and term projects.

Chapter 5— Improving Your Concentration

The Necessity of Concentration, Setting the Physical Stage, Setting the Mental Stage, Dealing with Distractors

■ **New:** Case studies integrate time management, goal setting, and concentration strategies.

**Part Three:
Using Effective
Textbook Reading
Techniques**

Chapter 6—Using a Reading System

The SQ4R Textbook Reading System, Comprehension Strategies

■ **New:** Chapter presents graphic notetaking systems for each of the organizational patterns of paragraphs.

Chapter 7—Working with Textbook Information

Highlighting Your Textbook, Using Other Marking Techniques, Studying from Your Highlighting and Markings, Writing Summaries

■ **New:** Information presented now includes more than highlighting and marginal notes. A discussion of writing summaries from various sources strengthens the concept of *writing across the curriculum.*

Chapter 8—Learning Terminology

Kinds of Vocabulary, Using Your Textbook Glossaries, Making Flash Cards, Studying from Flash Cards, Making and Using Vocabulary Study Sheets, Additional Vocabulary-Building Strategies

■ **New:** Chapter places greater emphasis on writing definitions that consist of three levels of information; expanded sections contain more information on context clues and word structure clues.

**Part Four:
Using Effective
Notetaking
Techniques**

Chapter 9—Making Cornell Notes for Textbooks

Preparing for Notetaking, Following the Five *R*'s of Cornell, Deciding When to Use Cornell Notetaking, Combining SQ4R and Cornell Notetaking

Chapter 10—Using Cornell Notes for Lectures

Understanding Listening Skills, Strengthening Your Listening Skills, Using the Cornell Notetaking System for Lectures, Techniques for Recording Information, Techniques for Organizing Information, Finding Solutions to Common Notetaking Problems

■ **New:** "Developing Effective Listening Skills" now includes an inventory of correlating listening skills with learning styles. Chapter includes effective listening components and strategies, as well as excerpts that reinforce the need to become an effective listener.

Chapter 11—Using Visual Notetaking Systems

Using Visual Notetaking, Making Visual Mappings, Making Hierarchies, Making Comparison Charts, Making Time Lines

■ **New:** Exercises provide more challenging opportunities to learn to create visual mappings, hierarchies, comparison charts (matrices), and time lines.

**Part Five:
Strengthening Your
Test-Taking Skills**

Chapter 12—Preparing for Tests

Preparing for Tests, Performing Well on the Test Day, Learning from the Test, Dealing with Test Anxiety

■ **New:** Emphasizing effective test-preparation skills, this chapter includes a new test-preparation questionnaire and test-taking anxiety indicator, as well as new information on developing the five-day plan, creating summary notes, and predicting and answering test questions. New coverage also includes test-anxiety reduction techniques such as locus of control, systematic desensitization, and self-fulfilling prophecy.

Chapter 13—Developing Strategies for Objective Tests

Taking Objective Tests, Answering True-False Questions, Answering Multiple-Choice Questions, Answering on Matching Tests, Using the Four Levels of Response, Taking Computerized Tests

■ **New:** Strategies for taking computerized tests are now included.

Chapter 14—Developing Strategies for Recall and Essay Tests

Recall Questions: Fill-in-the-Blank Questions, Listing Questions, Definition Questions, Short-Answer Questions; Essay Questions: Preparing for Essay Tests, Understanding Direction Words, Strategies for Answering Essay Questions, Additional Essay Writing Tips

■ **New:** The sections for short answers and essays contain more examples and exercises. In addition, the essay-answers section now features techniques for predicting essay questions and preparing for essays when questions are known, given in advance, or given on a take-home test.

Appendixes

Appendix A—Chapter Profile Materials

Master Profile Chart, Beginning-of-the-Term Profile: Profile Answer Keys, End-of-the-Term Profile

Appendix B—Portfolio Assessment Form

Appendix C—Library Projects

Exploring Your Library, Library Projects

Classroom-Proven Features Continued in the Third Edition

Essential Study Skills, Third Edition, continues to base itself on the premise that each student possesses a unique way of learning. The features from previous editions that have helped students to understand the concept of studying and to master the process of learning have been retained. Through utilizing the following features, students will come to view academic learning as a product of a set of skills and behaviors that they can comprehend, acquire, customize, and implement effectively:

■ **Visual mappings** provide an overview of the chapter, literally at a glance. At the end of the chapter, students—individually or as a class—can expand the mapping to include supporting details that will help them recall the content.

■ **Profiles at the Beginning of Each Chapter** allow students to assess their attitudes and behaviors. Students complete the profile before reading the chapter, score it, and record it on a Master Profile Chart in Appendix A. The profiles are completed again at the end of the term; the result is an "academic portrait" that shows strengths, weaknesses, and progress.

■ **Boxed information** throughout the chapters highlights key points. Students can refer to this information while previewing the text, reading the chapters, and reviewing for tests.

■ **Exercises** in each chapter provide guided practice in applying the skills to material from an array of academic disciplines. Each chapter also includes exercises in critical thinking that promote a higher level of concept development.

- **Chapter summaries** review the main points in succinct lists that students can consult for a quick review.

- **Options for Personalizing the Chapter** encourage students to tailor the chapter information in ways that demonstrate their understanding or strengthen their memory of the skills in the chapter. Students are asked to summarize the results of their chapter profile in personal logs (journals); to expand the visual map for the chapter; to create flash cards or study sheets from the list of vocabulary words; to express their knowledge, understanding, or application of skills through writing assignments; and/or to create a more comprehensive project to add to a personal portfolio developed throughout the term. These options may all be assigned or self-selected.

- **Review Questions** at the end of each chapter assess students' progress in learning the strategies and applying the skills to the course content. Types of questions include recognition, recall, and critical thinking.

Instructor's Resource Manual

Essential Study Skills, Third Edition, is accompanied by an Instructor's Resource Manual. Part I of the IRM provides teaching tips, answer keys for textbook exercises, and enrichment activities that include additional textbook excerpts that may be used to practice textbook, notetaking, or test-taking skills. Part II contains reproducible answer keys for chapter quizzes. Part III contains masters for making overhead transparencies. Part IV provides optional unit tests that assess students' retention and integration of material across the chapters. Answer keys are also included. Part V provides a printed form and the answers for objective test questions that are available on a computer disk. These questions may be used to construct customized tests, modify existing tests, or create midterm or final exams. The questions provided on the computer disk facilitate the process of creating different tests each term.

Acknowledgments

The third edition of *Essential Study Skills* is dedicated to all the teachers of study skills courses who devote tremendous amounts of time, energy, and enthusiasm to guide students along the paths of higher learning.

Appreciation is extended to the following reviewers who contributed valuable ideas to further strengthen the effectiveness of this textbook for college students: Karen A. Becker, Youngstown State University, OH; Kathy Clark, Linn-Benton Community College, OR; Jan Drake, University of North Dakota, ND; Karen Fenske, Kishwaukee College, IL; Vicki A. Johnson, Century Technical College, MN; Lucy MacDonald, Chemeketa Community College, OR; Marilyn K. Newman, Parkland College, IL; Rebecca Owens, Texas Tech University, TX.

The third edition of *Essential Study Skills* includes an exciting web site with exercises, Internet search projects, and many active links. I would like to thank Barbara Heinssen for recognizing the value of online materials and for supporting the development of the web site for this textbook. I am also very grateful to Lucy MacDonald (Chemeketa Community College in Salem, Oregon), who graciously shared her expertise in the area of online activities and online classes, and to Tim Krause for his talent and ability to develop the web site pages.

I applaud the outstanding editorial and production staff that has worked with me through the stages required to develop and produce this book. I extend very special thanks and appreciation to Shani Fisher, Rachel D'Angelo Wimberly, Monica Hincken, and Sarah Godshall for their organizational skills, attention to minute details, team spirit, and dedication.

To the Student

Essential Study Skills is designed to provide you with skills that will unlock your learning potential. By consistently using the skills presented in this book, you will learn information more thoroughly and remember it more easily. This section tells you how to get the most out of *Essential Study Skills*.

How to Start the Term

As soon as you purchase your book (and read this), read the Quick Start Checklist section preceding the text chapters. As you complete each task designed to prepare you for an excellent start to the term, check the item off. Continue through the checklist until you complete all the items.

How to Start Each Chapter

1. Read the paragraph on the first page for a glimpse of the skills you will learn in the chapter.
2. Study the visual mapping on the first page of the chapter. This mapping is a picture form of the main headings or topics in the chapter.
3. Answer the chapter profile questions on the second page of the chapter honestly. This will not be graded; it will be used to show your current attitude, habits, and knowledge of skills that will be presented in the chapter. Write a short response to the self-awareness question on the bottom of the profile page.
4. Score your profile by counting the number of your answers that match the answer key on page 307 in Appendix A. Then chart your score on the Master Profile Chart on page 306 in Appendix A.
5. Prepare your mind for the content of each chapter by *surveying* the chapter before you begin the careful reading. Survey, or preview, the chapter by

   ■ reading the headings and subheadings.
   ■ reading the highlighted boxed information.
   ■ noticing the key words in bold blue print.
   ■ reading the chapter summary.
   ■ reading the chapter review questions.

6. Now you are ready to begin the process of thorough, accurate reading. Read one paragraph at a time and think about what you have read. Your goal should not be to race through the chapter reading quickly; fast reading is not a reading approach that will lead to comprehension or retention of the information.

How to Use the Special Features in the Chapter

Visual Mapping

This overview shows the "big picture" of the chapter, that is, the most important information or ideas that develop the overall topic of the chapter. The chapter title is in the center of the mapping; the chapter headings branch out from the title beginning at the "11:00 position" and move clockwise.

Boxed Information

As you preview, read, and review, pay special attention to the boxes throughout each chapter. Read each box carefully; then read the following text that discusses each point in detail. Review the boxes when you prepare for tests.

Computer Applications

If you have computer skills and access to a computer, select one or more of the computer applications. This feature promotes the use of technology to enhance your study skills.

Companion Web Activities

The web page icon (🖥) used throughout each chapter indicates companion activities and exercises that are online for *Essential Study Skills*, Third Edition. When accessing the Internet and conducting web searches, realize that "surfing the web" can be very time-consuming. Set a time limit for yourself so you do not consume an excessive amount of time on the Internet. Bookmark the following web site for quick access; then click on the chapter you are studying. Go to **http://www.hmco.com/college** and then select "Student Success."

Summary

For a brief list of key points in the chapter, turn to the summary. Read it during your preview and again after you have read the chapter thoroughly. Practice expanding the summary's points by adding additional details you have learned about each point. Use the summaries as review tools to prepare for tests.

Options for Personalizing the Chapter

Several options are given at the end of each chapter:

1. **Profile Chart**   Write your score in your book. For each chapter, answer the self-analysis and insight questions in your personal log (journal).
2. **Chapter Visual Mapping**   As a means of review, expand the chapter mapping by showing key words or important phrases on your map. Pages 45–46 in Chapter 2 provide you with directions for expanding the mapping. Once you have finished your expansion, you can add colors or pictures to help you remember the different parts of the mapping.
3. **Vocabulary Work**   The foundation of any course is knowing the special terms of each chapter. Creating flash cards or vocabulary sheets will help you learn these terms and provide you with valuable study tools for later review. (See Chapter 8 for more details.)

   To make flash cards: Write the vocabulary term on the front of an index card; write the definition or explanation of the term on the back of the card. Use the fronts and backs of the cards to quiz yourself.

   To make a vocabulary sheet: On a piece of notebook paper, draw a vertical line to create a two-inch column on the left. Write the vocabulary word in this column. Directly across from the word, write the definition or an explanation of the term. Leave a space between each new word so your vocabulary sheet is not cluttered. Practice quizzing yourself by looking at and reciting one side of the page and covering up the other side.

4. **Writing Assignments**   The writing assignments will give you the opportunity to express what you have learned in writing. If the assignments are not required by your instructor, completing them for yourself will strengthen your understanding and application of the skills learned.

5. **Portfolio Development**   The portfolio activities are larger-scale assignments that may be used to assess your acquisition, understanding, and application of specific study skills. If your instructor chooses to assess your performance through the use of a portfolio, specific directions will be given in class. Frequently, students are asked to complete a specific number of portfolio activities, save the completed work, and compile all the activities into one portfolio at the end of the term. Portfolio assignments are most successful and representative of your work when sufficient time is allocated to work on and complete the activities. Use your time management skills to plan time for each step of each portfolio project.

Review Questions   The questions at the end of the chapter will help you check how well you have learned and applied the chapter's study skills. You should be able to complete the questions without looking back at the chapter or your notes. Be sure to read the directions carefully before answering the questions.

General Recommendations

1. Strive to have your reading and assignments done on time. You can gain a sense of being organized, progressing, and being in control of the learning process if you complete your work on time.

2. Have an open mind that is willing to try new strategies for learning. Many of the strategies you used in previous years are perhaps not the most efficient or effective. This is your opportunity to discover the excitement, creativity, and benefits of learning new ways to process academic information.

3. See this course as an opportunity to work hard, apply yourself, and push to work closer to your true potential. Your rewards will be a greater sense of accomplishment, confidence, empowerment, and success. You will learn valuable skills that will become your individualized approach to learning.

Your goal is not to learn *about* study skills; your goal is to learn *to use* powerful study skills consistently to enable you to accomplish other goals and achieve success. Learning, after all, is a lifelong process. Each time you are faced with a new learning situation—whether at school, at home, or at work—you can draw upon the skills you have learned in this book. Apply the skills of goal setting, time management, concentration, processing information, strengthening memory, and acquiring new knowledge to any new task at hand. You will be prepared to experience the rewards of success . . . again and again and again.

Linda Wong

Quick Start Checklist for the First Week of Classes

❐ **Register for your classes before the term begins.**

❐ **Obtain a printout of your classes.**

❐ **Become familiar with the campus and the locations of key departments, services, and facilities.**

If campus tours are not available, use a campus map to explore the campus and its facilities. Take time to locate the following areas:

1. Your classrooms and closest restrooms
2. Most convenient parking areas or bus stops
3. Financial Aid office
4. Career Counseling, Counseling/ Advising offices
5. Student Records or Registrar's office
6. Student Health
7. Library
8. Computer labs
9. Bookstore
10. Tutoring centers
11. Student Activities/ Student Government
12. Cafeteria

❐ **Inquire how to access computer labs, an email account, and the Internet.**

❐ **Visit the library.**

❐ **Organize your notebooks.**

Use dividers to set up a three-ring notebook with sections for each of your classes. If you need to use more than one notebook, consider a notebook for the MWF classes or the T/Th classes. In each section of your notebook, organize the following materials:

1. Your weekly schedule of classes
2. The course *syllabus* (which is an outline of the class and the requirements)
3. A list of names and phone numbers of other students in class whom you may want to call to discuss homework assignments or meet for a study group
4. All of your class notes, handouts, and completed assignments arranged in chronological order

❐ **Create a term-long calendar.**

Locate a month-by-month planner or use a regular calendar to record all scheduled tests, midterms, due dates for projects, study-group meetings, conferences, and the final exams. Begin by carefully examining each course syllabus for important test dates, projects dates, and final exam dates. Also, refer to your college calendar for the term for additional dates of importance (holidays, last day to change grade options or drop courses, and special college events). Place the monthly calendar in the front of your notebook. Plan to update it throughout the term.

❐ **Decide on a system to use to record all homework assignments.**

Select an easy-to-use system for recording your homework assignments. While some instructors provide students with daily assignment sheets, most instructors do not. The system you select should provide you with a list of tasks or assignments that need to be done.

One system that works effectively is to title a sheet of notebook paper as "Assignments." Place this Assignments page in the front of each section of your notebook. Use this page *every time* an assignment is given. Write the date the assignment is given, the specific assignment, the date it is due, and a place to check that the assignment is done. Your assignment sheet will look like this:

Assignments—Math 60			
Date	Assignment	Due	Done
10/3	Read pages 110–125	10/5	x
	Do odd-numbered problems on 112, 115, 118, 125	10/5	x
10/5	Study for quiz on Chapter 3	10/7	

A second system involves using a commercial daily or weekly planner that has enough room for you to write assignments and the due dates. Check off the assignments as they have been completed. A week in your weekly planner would show the assignments on the days they were given.

You can create your own weekly planner page using unlined notebook paper. Make six columns (one for each school day of the week and one to list your classes) and enough rows to show all of your classes. Each time an assignment is given, write the assignment on your planner page. Assignments can be checked off after they are completed. Your weekly planner page would look like this:

classes	Mon.	Tues.	Wed.	Thurs.	Fri.
math					
writing					
theater					
psych.					

❒ **Become familiar with your textbooks by surveying each textbook.**

Before you begin attending classes, get a head start by *surveying* your textbooks. Surveying a textbook involves becoming familiar with the features of the book by previewing or looking through specific sections in the textbook before you begin reading. Surveying, which often takes fifteen minutes to a half an hour per book, will enable you to use the book more effectively and more efficiently throughout the entire term. Take time to complete the following six steps to survey your textbooks.

Step 1: Look at the title page, copyright page, and table of contents in the front of the book.

Step 2: Locate and read the introductory information. This section may also be labeled *Preface, To the Teacher,* or *To the Student.* This introductory material often provides valuable background information on the book and the author and clarifies the purpose.

Step 3: Look in the back of the book for an *appendix*. An appendix provides you with supplementary materials that were not included in the chapters. You may find answer keys to exercises; additional exercises; practice tests; additional readings; frequently used charts, formulas, or theorems; maps; or lengthier documents (such as the Bill of Rights).

Step 4: Look to see if the textbook has a *glossary* (a mini-dictionary that defines key terms used in the textbook).

Step 5: Look to see if your textbook has a section in the back of the book that is titled *References* or *Bibliography*. This section provides you with the names of authors and the books, magazines, or articles that were used by the author as sources of information. This list of references can also be used if you wish to research a topic further.

Step 6: The last step of surveying is to locate the *index* in the back of the book. The index is an alphabetical listing of subjects used throughout the textbook. An index can be used to quickly locate page numbers when you want to

1. review a specific topic that was discussed in class.
2. locate a topic for a class assignment or discussion.
3. review specific information for a topic for an essay.
4. clarify information written in your notes.

❑ **Show up the first day of class ready to learn.**

Many students know that the term begins more smoothly when they are in class the first day and are ready to work. This is the day that the syllabus is usually discussed, introductions are made, and class expectations are explained. The following suggestions can help you get off to a good start:

1. Be on time.
2. Sit toward the front of the classroom rather than "hiding" in the back row. You will be able to see better, will concentrate more easily, and will show you are interested in the course.
3. Come prepared with your notebook, paper, pencils, pens, the textbook, and any other materials that you might need.
4. Be friendly! Show others that you are approachable and willing to be a part of the group. Your friendliness can help set a positive tone in the classroom.
5. Plan to listen carefully and be attentive.
6. Use a highlighter to highlight important information discussed on the syllabus.
7. Plan to take notes. Later in the term, you will learn an effective note-taking system. For now, the format you use for notes is not as important as the habit of writing down information as it is presented. Your notes should also include a record of your homework assignments.

 ❑ **Make a commitment to dedicate sufficient time each week to studying.**

One of the most common mistakes students make involves allocation of time. *Time on task,* or time devoted to studying, is highly correlated to academic success. Students who spend too little time reading, studying, memorizing, and applying information in a variety of ways often struggle with the process of learning. In addition to completing reading assignments, written work, papers and problems, some time each week should be dedicated to reviewing information that has been covered. Time management will be covered later in the term, but for now, you can use a time management technique called the *2:1 ratio*. For most or all of your classes that involve textbook reading assignments and written work, plan to study two hours for every one hour in class. Therefore, if one of your classes meets for three hours a week, plan to study six hours a week for that class. The six hours of study time can be spread throughout the week. You can use your weekly planner or schedule to identify the total hours you plan to study during the week for each of your classes. Your classes and study blocks for each class can be planned on the chart on page xxi.

❐ **Plan to ask questions about the class, the expectations, and the assignments.**

Becoming an *active learner* is important. Be willing to show your interest by asking questions in class. Most instructors are very willing to expand directions or give further explanations about classroom or textbook topics. Student questions also help promote interesting classroom discussions.

❐ **Monitor your stress levels.**

Some stress is normal. Normal stress is manageable and can even be a motivator. New or unfamiliar situations are commonly linked to feelings of self-doubt, lower confidence levels, and lower self-esteem. These feelings are a part of the "learning cycle" and weaken or dwindle as you gain familiarity and "settle in" to the new routine, expectations, and tasks to be completed. Chapter 5 introduces you to a variety of concentration and relaxation techniques that will assist you in keeping your stress at a comfortable, manageable level. Chapter 12 will provide you with specific strategies for stress or anxiety reduction that is related to taking tests. In addition, this course itself will reduce stress levels as you gain skills and confidence by learning strategies designed to strengthen your ability to do well academically.

Stressors, or occurrences in the process of life that cause stress, can occur unexpectedly. Most colleges or universities have counselors, support groups, workshops, or courses that can help a person with stress reduction and with periods of transition. Schedule a time with a counselor to explore the resources and options available on your campus.

Class Schedule

Reg.#	Course Name	Time	Location	Instructor

Time	Mon.	Tues.	Wed.	Thurs.	Fri.	Sat.	Sun.
12–6 a.m.							
6–7:00							
7–8:00							
8–9:00							
9–10:00							
10–11:00							
11–12:00							
12–1:00							
1–2:00							
2–3:00							
3–4:00							
4–5:00							
5–6:00							
6–7:00							
7–8:00							
8–9:00							
9–10:00							
10–11:00							
11–12:00							

Discovering and Using Your Learning Style

To be an effective learner, you must be familiar with how your memory works and which strategies support your unique style of learning. Do you remember information presented in pictures better than information you hear? Can you learn by using rhymes or tunes? Do you remember better when you are involved in hands-on experiences? What abilities or intelligences have you developed that could affect the way you study? This chapter introduces you to three kinds of learning styles, eight intelligences, and study strategies that incorporate your learning style preferences and intellectual strengths to boost your ability to remember new information.

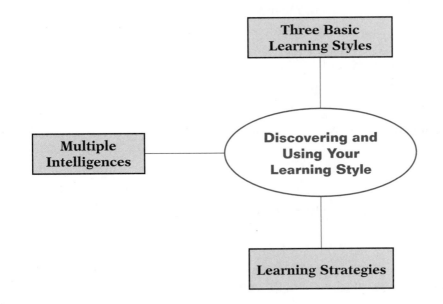

Three Basic
Learning Styles

Multiple
Intelligences

Discovering and
Using Your
Learning Style

Learning Strategies

Name _____ Date _____

 CHAPTER 1 Learning Styles Profile

Do the following profile. Answer each question honestly to show your current attitudes and study habits. Your answers should reflect what you do, not what you wish to do. Check YES if you do the statement always or most of the time. Check NO if you do this seldom or never.

    SCORE the profile. Compare your answers to the answer key on page 307. Star your answers that are the same as the answer key. Count the stars. This is your score.

    RECORD your score on the Master Profile Chart on page 306 in the column that shows the chapter number.

	YES	NO
1. I am aware of my learning style or learning style preference.		
2. I know at least five learning strategies that utilize my learning style.		
3. When I try to learn something new, I incorporate strategies that use a combination of visual, auditory, or kinesthetic skills.		
4. I am willing to try new study strategies to see if they work for me.		
5. I avoid using color-coding when I study or work because it takes too much time or seems inappropriate.		
6. I understand how exaggerated movements, drama, and dance can help some students' learning processes.		
7. I know how to use multi-sensory study tools to assist me in strengthening my memory.		
8. I usually study or learn new information in a straightforward manner without spending time making creative study tools.		
9. I am familiar with common characteristics for each of the three learning modalities (visual, auditory, kinesthetic).		
10. I understand the Theory of Multiple Intelligences and can name all eight intelligences.		
11. I recognize which of eight different intelligences are most developed for me.		
12. I am able to use information about learning styles to better understand people who are different than I am.		

Self-Awareness: Describe how you tend to proceed when learning something new. What approaches do you use to get started? What techniques seem to work best for you?

_____

_____

_____

_____

Three Basic Learning Styles

The term **learning styles** refers to the general way people most easily process, learn, and remember information. Even though the process of learning is very individualized, three commonly recognized learning styles are visual, auditory, and kinesthetic. These three learning styles are also referred to as **learning modalities**. You can lay a strong foundation for learning thoroughly and effectively when you know your learning style and select learning strategies that are based on your learning style (or learning modality) strengths.

Learning Style Inventory

Before you acquire too much information about learning styles that may affect the way you answer the Learning Styles Inventory, complete the following inventory by reading each statement carefully. Check YES if the statement relates to you *all* or *most* of the time. Check NO if the statement *seldom* or *never* relates to you. There is no in-between, so you must check YES or NO. Your first, quick response to the question is usually the best response to use.

Learning Style Inventory

	YES	NO
1. I like to listen and discuss work with a partner.		
2. I learn by hearing my own voice on tape.		
3. I prefer to learn something new by reading about it.		
4. I often write down the directions someone has given me so that I don't forget them.		
5. I enjoy physical sports or exercise.		
6. I learn best when I can see new information in picture form.		
7. I am able to visualize easily.		
8. I learn best when someone talks or explains something to me.		
9. I usually write things down so that I can look back at them later.		
10. If someone says a long word, I can count the syllables that I hear.		
11. I have a good memory for old songs or music.		
12. I like to discuss in small groups.		
13. I often remember the size, shape, and color of objects.		
14. I often repeat out loud the directions someone has given me.		
15. I enjoy working with my hands.		
16. I can remember the faces of actors, settings, and other visual details of a movie I saw in the past.		
17. I often use my hands and body movement when I'm explaining something.		
18. I prefer to practice redrawing diagrams on a chalkboard rather than on paper.		
19. I seem to learn better if I get up and move around while I study.		
20. If I wanted to assemble a bike, I would need pictures or diagrams to help with each step.		

	YES	NO
21. I remember objects better when I have touched them or worked with them.		
22. I learn best by watching someone else first.		
23. I tap my fingers or my hands a lot while I am seated.		
24. I speak a foreign language.		
25. I enjoy building things.		
26. I can follow the plot of a story on the radio.		
27. I enjoy repairing things at home.		
28. I can understand a lecture when I hear it on tape.		
29. I am good at using machines or tools.		
30. I find sitting still for very long difficult.		
31. I enjoy acting or doing pantomimes.		
32. I can easily see patterns in designs.		
33. I need frequent breaks to move around.		
34. I like to recite or write poetry.		
35. I can usually understand people with different accents.		
36. I can hear many different pitches or melodies in music.		
37. I like to dance and create new movements or steps.		
38. I enjoy activities that require physical coordination.		
39. I follow written directions better than oral ones.		
40. I can easily recognize differences between similar sounds.		
41. I like to create or use jingles/rhymes to learn things.		
42. I wish more classes had hands-on experiences.		
43. I can quickly tell if two geometric shapes are identical.		
44. The things I remember best are the things I have seen in print or pictures.		
45. I follow oral directions better than written ones.		
46. I could learn the names of fifteen medical instruments much easier if I could touch and examine them.		
47. I need to say things aloud to myself to remember them.		
48. I can look at a shape and copy it correctly on paper.		
49. I can usually read a map without difficulty.		
50. I can "hear" a person's exact words and tone of voice days after he or she has spoken to me.		
51. I remember directions best when someone gives me landmarks, such as specific buildings and trees.		
52. I have a good eye for colors and color combinations.		
53. I like to paint, draw, or make sculptures.		
54. When I think back to something I once did, I can clearly picture the experience.		

Scoring Your Profile

1. Ignore the NO answers. Work only with the questions that have a YES answer.

2. For every YES answer, look at the number of the question. Find the number in the following chart and circle that number.

3. When you finish, not all the numbers in the following boxes will be circled. Your answers will very likely not match anyone else's in class.

4. Count the number of circles for the Visual box and write the total on the line. Do the same for the Auditory box and the Kinesthetic box.

Visual					Auditory					Kinesthetic				
3,	4,	6,	7,	9,	1,	2,	8,	10,	11,	5,	15,	17,	18,	19,
13,	16,	20,	22,	32,	12,	14,	24,	26,	28,	21,	23,	25,	27,	29,
39,	43,	44,	48,	49,	34,	35,	36,	40,	41,	30,	31,	33,	37,	38,
51,	52,	54			45,	47,	50			42,	46,	53		

Total:_____   Total:_____   Total:_____

Analyzing Your Scores

1. The highest score indicates your *preference.* The lowest score indicates your weakest modality.

2. If your two highest scores are the same or very close, both of these modalities may be your preference.

3. If all three of your scores are identical, you have truly integrated all three modalities and can work equally well in any of the modalities.

4. Scores that are 10 or higher indicated the modality is used frequently by you.

5. Scores lower than 10 indicate the modality is not highly used. It is important to examine why. One reason may be that you have a physical or neurological impairment that makes using the modality difficult or impossible. A second reason, which is often the case, is that you have had limited experience learning how to use the modality effectively as you learn. In this case, learning new strategies can strengthen your use of the modality.

Learning Style Preferences

The Learning Style Inventory indicates your **learning style preference**. This basically means that you would tend to use the learning style or modality with the highest score when you have a choice of how to learn or process new information. For example, if you are in a work situation and your employer asks you to learn a new process on a computer or to learn how to operate a new piece of equipment, you would learn most comfortably if you used your strongest modality. A **visual learner** may prefer to read the manual or learn from pictures, charts, or graphs. An **auditory learner** may prefer to be told how the new process or equipment works. A **kinesthetic learner** may prefer to be shown how the process or piece of equipment works and then be given an opportunity to try each step during the training session.

Learning Style Preferences

1. **Visual learners** learn and remember best by *seeing* and picturing information.
2. **Auditory learners** learn and remember best by *hearing* information.
3. **Kinesthetic learners** learn and remember best by using large and small body *movements* and hands-on *experiences*.

As an adult, you have most likely developed a *preference* for one modality over the others, but you may be able to work in all three modalities if needed. This has not always been the case. Children often begin by favoring one modality. The children who are strongly drawn to books, pictures, colors, shapes, and animation are using the visual modality as their preference. Young children who are nonstop talkers, who ask a lot of questions, and who frequently sing and recite nursery rhymes are using their auditory modality. Young children who explore, have difficulty sitting still, and are often running, jumping, hopping, and rolling, as well as children who enjoy taking things apart and working with their hands, are using their kinesthetic modality. As children mature and as expectations of them are changed (often through education), they begin working with the other modalities. Integration of all three modalities occurs over the years, thus enabling teenagers and adults to function in a variety of situations.

Because the process of learning is highly individualized, it is not surprising to find some adults who have difficulty learning or functioning effectively in one or two of the modalities. Perhaps you or someone you know has difficulty learning or remembering directions or information that is given verbally. Some people may have more than average difficulty understanding a map or a set of directions presented through diagrams or pictures. Others may find they lack coordination skills to do detailed work with their hands or work that requires full body movement. In each of the examples above, difficulties in learning occur when the person is trying to learn through the weak modality. Sometimes the difficulty in learning through a specific modality may be tied to a physical impairment or a neurological impairment such as a specific learning disability. For example, if an individual has difficulty processing spoken information, the person may have a hearing loss. The person may also have a neurological impairment such as an auditory processing deficit that occurs when a person can hear spoken words, but the auditory signals do not travel clearly or efficiently to the auditory interpretation center in the brain. In most cases, the modality often times is weak due to lack of exposure or experience with the given modality. After the person learns effective strategies for the weak modality, the ability to learn in that modality increases.

Fortunately, the ability to integrate the visual, the auditory, and the kinesthetic modalities increases with age and experiences. In this book, you will learn to use learning strategies that focus on your learning style preferences and strengths. However, in order to strengthen your weaker modalities, you will be encouraged to practice and use learning strategies that are based on your weaker modalities as well. You will also learn to use a wide variety of strategies that are *multi-sensory* since they incorporate more than one learning style or modality. The goal is to strengthen and utilize all three modalities so that you can function more effectively in any situation.

Common Characteristics of Visual, Auditory, and Kinesthetic Learners

The following chart shows common characteristics of each of the three types of learners or learning styles. A person does not necessarily possess abilities or strengths in all of the characteristics but may instead "specialize" in some of the characteristics. Some of this may be due to a person's educational background or background of experiences. For example, an auditory learner may be strong in the area of language skills but may not have had the experience to develop skills with a foreign language or music.

Common Characteristics

VISUAL

- Learn best by seeing information
- Can easily recall printed information in the form of numbers, words, phrases, or sentences
- Can easily understand and recall information presented in pictures, charts, or diagrams
- Have strong visualization skills and can look up (often up to the left) and "see" information
- Can make "movies in their minds" of information they are reading
- Have strong visual-spatial skills that involve sizes, shapes, textures, angles, and dimensions
- Pay close attention and learn to interpret body language (facial expressions, eyes, stance)
- Have a keen awareness of aesthetics, the beauty of the physical environment, and visual media

AUDITORY

- Learn best by hearing information
- Can accurately remember details of information heard in conversations or lectures
- Have strong language skills that include well-developed vocabularies and appreciation of words
- Have strong oral communication skills that enable them to carry on conversations and be articulate
- Have "finely tuned ears" and may find learning a foreign language relatively easy
- Hear tones, rhythms, and notes of music and often have exceptional musical talents

KINESTHETIC

- Learn best by using their hands ("hands-on" learning) or by full body movement
- Learn best by doing
- Learn well in activities that involve performing (athletes, actors, dancers)
- Work well with their hands in areas such as repair work, sculpting, art, or working with tools
- Are well-coordinated with a strong sense of timing and body movements
- Often wiggle, tap their feet, or move their legs when they sit
- Often were labelled as "hyperactive"

✎ **EXERCISE 1.1 Discussing Learning Styles**

Break into groups of three to five students. Complete the following directions together.

1. List all the Learning Styles Inventory scores of the people in your group. It is not important to attach names to the scores.

2. Are any two scores the same in your group? _____
   Looking at a variety of different learning style scores emphasizes how unique each person is in terms of how information is processed. Very seldom will you find another person in a classroom with a Learning Styles Inventory score identical to yours.

3. Think about a young child you know. Think about the way the child explores the world and learns new information. Which learning modality is being expressed as a preferred modality by this child? Share your information with the other members of your group.

4. Sometimes it is difficult to remember our own early years. From what you remember, which learning style do you feel was the strongest when you were a child? Explain your answer to the members of your group.

✎ **EXERCISE 1.2 Identifying Your Learning Style**

Refer to your scores of the Learning Style Inventory to answer the questions.

1. What were your Learning Style Inventory scores?

Visual	**Auditory**	**Kinesthetic**

2. Do you agree that the score with the highest number above is your learning style preference? Why or why not?

3. Do you agree that the lowest score above is your weakest modality?
   What are some of the possible reasons that this score is lower than the others?

4. Many people are comfortable using all three modalities, not just the strongest modality. Which of the modalities do you feel comfortable using to learn new information?

5. Think of a recent experience you had in which you needed to learn something new. How do you go about learning? Which modality did you use the most? Was the learning comfortable or did the circumstances dictate which modality was needed for the task? Explain.

✎ **EXERCISE 1.3 Working with Your Visual, Auditory, and Kinesthetic Skills**

Complete each of the following items with as much detail as possible.

1. Most people have a daily routine when they get up in the morning. Close your eyes and try to make a movie in your mind that shows you going through your daily routine. Answer the following questions after you have pictured this routine in your mind.

Was the picture clear? _____

What colors were visible? _____

Name several specific details you saw in your movie. _____

2. Think back to the last conversation you had with a close friend. Answer the following questions.

Can you remember one complete sentence spoken by your friend? _____

If yes, write the sentence: _____

_____

Can you "hear" the tone of your friend's voice? _____

Oftentimes when a person tries to recall information that was processed through the auditory channels, the person looks to the left (toward the ear) to try to recall the words or sounds. Did you look to the left as you tried to recall your friend's words? _____

3. Solve the following puzzle using any method that works. As you search for the solution, pay attention to the strategies that you chose to use to solve the puzzle.

> A parent and a child are standing together on the sidewalk. They both start walking at the same time. Each person begins the first step with the right foot. The child must take three steps for every two steps the parent takes. How many steps must the child take until they both land again on the same foot?

How many steps did the child need to take? _____

Did they both land on the right foot or the left foot? _____

Explain how you solved this puzzle. _____

_____

_____

_____

Which modality did you use the most? _____

Was this modality your preferred learning style? _____

Learning Strategies

Now that you are aware of your own learning style, you can begin to select **learning strategies** that work with your strengths. In the following chart you will find a wide array of learning strategies for you to try; the majority of your strategies will likely come from your area of strength. However, a valuable goal to set for yourself is to strive to integrate all of the modalities into your learning process; therefore, try using several of the strategies for your weaker modalities as well. As you will also notice, some learning strategies will incorporate more than one modality. **Multisensory learning strategies** have the capability of strengthening your memory even more.

Learning Strategies That Utilize Modalities

VISUAL

- Create stronger visual memories of printed materials by highlighting important ideas with different colors of highlighters or by highlighting specific letters in spelling words or formulas or equations in math.
- Take time to visualize pictures, charts, graphs, or printed information and take time to practice recalling visual memories when you study.
- Create "movies in your mind" of information that you read; use your visual memory as a television screen with the information moving across the screen.
- Use visual study tools such as visual mappings, hierarchies, comparison charts, and time lines to represent information you are studying. Expand chapter mappings or create your own chapter mappings to review main ideas and important details in chapters. Add colors and/or shapes or pictures. (Visual study tools are discussed in Chapter 11.)
- Enhance your notes, flash cards, or any other study tools by adding colors and pictures (sketches, cartoons, stick figures).
- Color-code study tools. (Different colors imprint into memory more easily for some students.) Colors can be used to accentuate specific parts of textbooks, notes, or any written materials you work with or you have created.
- Copy information in your own handwriting if seeing information on paper in your own handwriting helps you learn and remember more easily. Practice visualizing what you write.
- Use your keen observational skills to observe people and pick up on clues they may give about important information, emotions, or their general state of being.
- Always be prepared with a pen and notepaper (or a small notepad) to write down information or directions. (Written information is easier to recall more accurately.)

Learning Strategies That Utilize Modalities (cont.)

AUDITORY

- Talk out loud to explain new information, express your ideas, practice information you are studying, or paraphrase another speaker.
- Recite frequently while you study. Reciting involves speaking out loud in complete sentences and in your own words.
- Read out loud. (Reading out loud often increases a person's comprehension or clarifies confusing information that is read silently.)
- Work with tutors, with a "study buddy," or in a study group to have ample opportunity to ask questions, articulate answers, and express your understanding of information orally.
- For lectures, take your own notes, but back your notes up with a tape recorded version of the lecture. (Request approval first from the instructor.) Review only the parts of the lecture that are unclear or confusing.
- When you practice reciting your notes, flash cards, study tools or information from a textbook, turn on a tape recorder. Tapes made in your own voice often become valuable review tools.
- Verbally explain information or processes to someone or to an imaginary person. Explaining verbally provides immediate feedback of your level of understanding.
- Make review tapes to review the most important information (rules, definitions, formulas, lists of information, dates, or other factual information) prior to a test.
- Create rhymes, jingles, or songs to help you remember specific facts.
- Read confusing information using exaggerated expression. The natural rhythm and patterns of your voice often group information in such a way that it becomes easier to understand.
- Use computerized technology (electronic spell checkers, calculators with a "voice," speech synthesizers on computers) to help with the learning process. Access CD-ROM programs and multimedia software that provide auditory and visual stimuli for learning.

KINESTHETIC

- Handle objects, tools, or machinery that you are trying to learn. For example, handle the rocks you study in geology, repeat applications several times on a computer, or hold and use tools or parts of machinery that are discussed in class or in your textbook.
- Create manipulatives (study tools that you can move around with your hands). These may include flash cards or cards that can be shuffled, spread out, sorted, or stacked as a way to categorize information.
- Cut charts or diagrams apart; reassemble them in their correct order.
- Use exaggerated movements and hand expressions, drama, dance, pantomime, or role playing to assist the development of long-term memory. Muscles also hold memory, so involving movement in the learning process creates muscle memory.
- Type or use a word processor. Using a keyboard involves fine motor skills and muscle memory; it may be easier to remember information that you typed or entered into a computer.
- Talk and walk as you recite or practice information. Pacing or walking with study materials in hand helps some people process information more naturally.
- Work at a chalkboard, with a flip chart, or on large poster paper to create study tools. List, draw, practice, or write information while you stand up and work on a larger surface.
- Learn by doing. Use every opportunity possible to move as you study. For example, if you are studying perimeters in math, tape off an area of a room and walk the perimeter.

✎ EXERCISE 1.4 **Relating What You Have Learned to Yourself**

1. Return to the chart of common characteristics of visual, auditory, and kinesthetic learners. Highlight characteristics in all three modalities that you feel are relevant to you and your strengths. Remember, you may not relate to all the characteristics in one specific modality, and you will likely have some characteristics from all three modalities.

2. Look at the learning strategies chart that lists many different learning strategies for visual, auditory, and kinesthetic learners. Highlight the strategies you feel would be advantageous for you to learn to use effectively.

3. Use your own paper to summarize the information you highlighted in the chart of common characteristics and the chart of learning strategies.

✎ EXERCISE 1.5 **Using Multisensory Skills**

Work with a partner. Read each characteristic below. Write V *if the characteristic is most common of a visual learner;* A *of an auditory learner; or* K *of a kinesthetic learner.*

_____ 1. Without looking at the book, the student can see details of pictures that were studied in the book.

_____ 2. Some people may see this learner as impatient because she acts fidgety if she is expected to be still for a long period of time.

_____ 3. The decor of her living room shows her great awareness and appreciation of aesthetics; everything is coordinated, colorful, and neatly organized.

_____ 4. This man amazes his audiences with the graceful, refined movements he performs in his mime show.

_____ 5. This person can actually "hear" another person's voice and remember details of a conversation long after the conversation has occurred.

_____ 6. As a child, this person enjoyed children's books and focused his interest on the colors and details in the pictures.

_____ 7. This person loves the rhythm and sound of words in poetry; she memorizes and creates poetry with ease.

_____ 8. Many music teachers enjoy having this student in class because of his keen sense of melody and rhythm.

_____ 9. This person works best when at an easel or a chalkboard rather than confined to a chair.

_____ 10. As a child, he was known as a "chatterbox," always talking, asking questions, singing, and reciting nursery rhymes.

*The following learning strategies are well-suited for specific kinds of learners. Decide which modality is utilized the **most** in each strategy. Write* V *for visual,* A *for auditory, and* K *for kinesthetic. If two modalities are both used extensively, you may use both letters.*

_____ 1. Find a "study buddy"—someone who wants to discuss what you are studying in class.

_____ 2. In geometry class, you trace the different angles on the top of the desk when you study for the geometry test.

_____ 3. Because you sometimes confuse numbers, you use a "talking" calculator to check your work.

_____ **4.** After you have taken notes, you highlight sections of your notes with different colors to help you see the notes clearly in your mind.

_____ **5.** After you have highlighted your textbook, you reread your highlighting out loud and practice stringing the highlighted sections together in your own sentences.

_____ **6.** You tape the lectures and use the tape to complete your class notes.

_____ **7.** You make movies in your mind to visualize a literature story you just read.

_____ **8.** You create your own flashcards and add pictures and colors whenever possible.

_____ **9.** You enjoy acting, so when you are reciting information for a class, you move around and recite the information with exaggerated expression.

_____**10.** You work with your new vocabulary words by making up a creative story that uses all your words.

Web-site links are available online.

Computer Projects

1. Use your preferred modality or one of your stronger multiple intelligences to plan and implement a computer project based on the contents of this chapter.

2. Use a flow chart or graphics program to reproduce the chapter mapping on page one of this chapter.

3. Locate a CD-ROM program that provides information on learning theory or learning styles. Plan a presentation to the class to demonstrate the use of the CD-ROM program.

4. Use a graphics program to create a poster that uses more pictures than words to show Howard Gardner's Theory of Multiple Intelligences.

Group Web-Search Activity is available online.

Case Studies are available online.

✎ **EXERCISE 1.6 Using Pictures to Clarify and Remember Information**

1. Carefully read the following paragraph about *the greenhouse effect.* The information can quickly be clarified by drawing a picture to show what is stated in words. Below the paragraph, draw a picture that shows the window pane, the inside of a room with furniture, the short-wave solar radiation or rays, and the long-wave radiation.

> A window pane transmits sunlight. It is nearly transparent, and much of the short-wave energy passes through. Only a little energy is absorbed to heat up the glass. However, the walls and furniture inside a room absorb a large part of the solar radiation coming through the window. The energy radiated from the furniture, unlike the original solar energy, is all long-wave radiation. Much of it is unable to pass out through the window pane. This is why the car seats get so hot on a hot, sunny day when all the windows are closed. Try putting a piece of glass in front of a hot object to see how the heat waves are cut off. A greenhouse traps energy in this way when the sun shines and so does the atmosphere.
>
> —*Investigating the Earth,* American Geological Institute

2. In many sociology and cultural anthropology courses, societies are discussed in terms of their *institutions.* Five common institutions, frequently referred to as the *institutions of society,* are *religion, family, education, economy,* and *government.* Inside the following picture frame, draw a picture that shows all five institutions of society. Try to connect them into one meaningful picture. For example, you could have a family entering a church or place of worship.

Multiple Intelligences

Learning styles provide one framework for understanding how people learn. Howard Gardner, a noted psychologist from Harvard University, takes a more detailed look at learning styles, learning strengths, and abilities with a broader theory about cognitive development. In 1983, Howard Gardner presented his theory of multiple intelligences in his book *Frames of Mind: The Theory of Multiple Intelligences.* This theory of multiple intelligences explores the multiple facets of the mind and of human potential by identifying seven different intelligences. In 1996, Gardner identified an eighth intelligence, that of the *naturalist,* and contends that there very likely are additional intelligences yet to be identified.

Howard Gardner's Theory of Multiple Intelligences has impacted the fields of psychology and education. This theory is a direct challenge to the traditional concept of intelligence measured by standardized IQ tests. The traditional IQ (Intelligence Quotient) tests measure aptitudes or abilities in three main areas: verbal, visual-spatial, and logical mathematics. Using Gardner's theory of multiple intelligences, an individual now can be seen as possessing a wider variety of aptitudes or abilities. Another distinction between the traditional IQ theory and Gardner's theory is that Gardner found that intelligences are not static, meaning that they are not determined at birth and are not permanent for life. Because Gardner contends that intelligence can change, grow, and be strengthened, educators became interested in ways intelligence can be taught and learned. The curriculum and teaching methods in many current educational reform initiatives are a direct result of Gardner's theory of multiple intelligences. Educators are exploring practical applications for classroom teaching as well as assessment of student performance based on the understanding that students' abilities are diverse and that students will excel in the areas of academics and personal growth when recognition and nurturing are given to a wider range of talents or intelligences.

The eight intelligences identified by Howard Gardner are: (1) verbal/linguistic, (2) musical, (3) logical/mathematical, (4) visual-spatial, (5) bodily-kinesthetic, (6) interpersonal, (7) intrapersonal, and (8) naturalistic. Gardner also notes "sub-intelligences" under each of the eight main intelligences. For example, there are many different talents and abilities that can be exhibited under the musical intelligence, yet an individual with a high musical intelligence may not possess all of the sub-intelligences in the category of music. Different skills, abilities, and processes are used to sing, play a musical instrument, compose music, conduct music, critique music, or appreciate music. Each intelligence does, however, have common characteristics and can be correlated to common careers that utilize the talents and abilities of each intelligence.

Verbal/linguistic intelligence is composed of verbal and language abilities. People with this intelligence developed have a love of language, a curiosity and fascination with words and their meanings (semantics), and a sound understanding of the structure of language (syntax). They are sensitive to how words are used, how they sound (phonology), and the feelings that words convey. These individuals possess sharp, detailed, vivid memories about written and spoken language and often excel in activities that involve puns and word games such as crossword puzzles. Those who possess effective verbal communication skills may be strong in public speaking, storytelling, debating, teaching, or consulting that involves oral presentations. Those who possess effective written communication skills often express themselves through journals, prose, or poetry. Individuals with high verbal/linguistic intelligences often select careers as authors, journalists, editors, poets, newscasters, television announcers, motivational speakers, playwrights, or politicians.

Musical intelligence is expressed by people with an acute sensitivity to sounds, melody (pitch), and rhythm. Their recognition and reproduction of tones (timbre) and harmony are well-developed. Strong auditory memory, imagination, and creativity enable these individuals to express feelings and images through music. They understand the basics of music theory and the meanings of musical symbols. To no surprise, they also have a strong appreciation or passion for different types and structures of music and may be more aware than others of the power of music to affect emotions and moods. They often enjoy humming, singing, chanting, or drumming. Individuals with developed musical intelligence often become music teachers, composers, conductors, performers, or work in the fields of sound engineering, film making, television, or advertising.

Logical/mathematical intelligence is exhibited through the use of skills involving logic, sound reasoning, problem-solving, analysis, identification of patterns, sequential thinking, and mathematical calculations. Individuals with this intelligence can think both concretely and abstractly about objects and relationships such as cause-effect. They understand and apply abstract numerical symbols and operations and can perform complex calculations. Problem-solving techniques used are often systematic, logic-based, and sequential; the scientific methods of measuring, hypothesizing, testing, researching, and confirming results may be frequently used. They often become math, science, or business teachers; mathematicians, computer programmers, accountants, tax experts, bankers, researchers, or scientists.

Visual-spatial intelligence exists in people who have keen perceptions of the physical world and the creative ability of imagination. They perceive sizes, shapes, textures, lines, curves, angles, and depths with accuracy and precision. They have the ability in one way or another to graphically present their visual or spatial ideas. They possess strong visual imagery or visualization skills, both of which are linked to active imaginations. For example, a gifted chess player can play a challenging game of chess blindfolded, or an architect can picture the floor plans for a building before the floor plans are drawn or the building is built. Individuals with developed visual-spatial intelligence often enjoy fine arts such as painting, sculpting, drawing, and areas such as drafting, photography, or construction. Career choices may include being an engineer, architect, interior designer, fashion designer, landscaper, carpenter, contractor, graphic artist, advertiser, cartographer, artist, or inventor.

Bodily-kinesthetic intelligence is exhibited by a graceful dancer, a record-setting athlete, a talented actor, a sensational guitarist, an inspiring mime artist, or a noted surgeon. Individuals with this intelligence have developed fine and precise body rhythms, body movements, and motor coordination skills that can be used as a form of expression. Those with well-defined gross (large) motor skills are able to judge how their bodies will respond to certain situations, and they have the ability to fine-tune their bodies in order to perform at higher levels. They have an acute sense of timing and body rhythm; they have well-developed coordination, balance, dexterity, flexibility, and possibly strength and speed. Those with well-defined fine (small) motor skills are able to create or modify things with their hands. They have sensitive touch and can "sense" things through their hands. For example, a mechanic may have his or her hands inside an engine and be able to "feel" a problem with the engine without actually seeing the problem; the same could be true for a surgeon. People with a well-developed bodily-kinesthetic intelligence often enjoy physical exercise, sports, dancing, drama, role-playing, charades, inventing, repairing objects, building things, and learning through a "hands-on" approach. In their professional careers you may see individuals with developed bodily-kinesthetic intelligence working as performers (actors, mimes, dancers); instrumentalists (guitarists, drummers, pianists); professional athletes; teachers of dance, choreography, drama, aerobics, gymnastics, or physical education; activity directors; mechanics; artists (painters, sculptors); or surgeons.

Intrapersonal intelligence focuses on personal-growth, self-understanding, intuition, spirituality, and a desire to achieve personal potential. Individuals with intrapersonal intelligence are reflective and use metacognition. They strive to identify and understand their feelings, values, goals, strengths, weaknesses, and personal history. They use life experiences as lessons to change specific aspects of their lives and seek ways to give life personal meaning. Such individuals often project a sense of pride, self-esteem, confidence, self-responsibility, personal control, and empowerment. They are self-motivators and goal-setters. They strive to select, monitor, and control their emotions, reactions, and public behavior. They are able to adapt to a wide variety of surroundings and circumstances. These talents can be used effectively in most fields of work; they are often combined with the next "personal intelligence," interpersonal intelligence. Some career fields that incorporate the intrapersonal intelligence include psychiatry, spiritual and personal counseling, self-help and motivational writing or speaking, philosophy, and biographers.

Interpersonal intelligence emphasizes effective interpersonal communication skills, social skills, and leadership abilities. People with developed interpersonal intelligence are able to participate and work cooperatively in a group, create bonds with diverse groups of people, and feel a sense of global responsibility toward others. They recognize and understand nonverbal clues shown through facial expressions or body language. Active, involved parents frequently utilize the talents and abilities of this intelligence. This intelligence enables individuals to accurately interpret the behavior, motivation, and intentions of others. They enjoy socializing, helping others, tutoring or teaching, and sharing interpersonal skills with others. They are comfortable assuming leadership roles and enjoy being a part of developing positive group dynamics. Individuals with strong interpersonal intelligence often become teachers, counselors, therapists, healers, telecommunicators, social activists, motivational and personal growth seminar leaders, religious leaders, sociologists, anthropologists, and political organizers.

Naturalist intelligence is the eighth intelligence that was introduced by Gardner in 1996. Individuals with naturalist intelligence are sensitive to the environment and are aware of the balance (or imbalance) of plants, animals, and the environment. They are keen observers of the elements of the natural environment and the daily, seasonal, and cyclical changes that occur. Relationships and the balance of relationships in nature are points of great interest. They often demonstrate detailed knowledge and expertise in recognizing and classifying plants and animals. The above characteristics often lead individuals with naturalist intelligence into careers as meteorologists, geologists, botanists, herbalists, biologists, ecologists, naturalpathic and holistic healers, and medicine men. On an every day level, this naturalist intelligence can also be seen in avid gardeners.

Howard Gardner's Multiple Intelligences Theory has opened a new door to understanding individual differences, talents, skills, abilities, and interests. It is important to remember that most people have all of these intelligences to some degree. Some of the intelligences, or the sub-intelligences of specific categories, may be under-developed and under-utilized; however, given adequate training, experiences, and a conducive environment, these intelligences can be strengthened. Some of the intelligences may already be well-developed and are exhibited through one's choice of activities, hobbies, and careers. This theory serves as a reminder that we are all "evolving-beings," who have the capability of expanding our abilities and intelligences to reach greater levels of potential and fulfillment.

✎ EXERCISE 1.7 Discussing Multiple Intelligences

Work with a partner or in a small group to complete the following sets of directions.

1. List any fifteen different occupations or careers.

_____ _____ _____

_____ _____ _____

_____ _____ _____

_____ _____ _____

_____ _____ _____

2. Use the letter codes shown after each of Howard Gardner's intelligences below. Discuss which intelligence you feel is most actively used for people who excel in the above professions. Next to each profession listed above, write the code.

   1. Verbal/Linguistic (VL)   5. Bodily-Kinesthetic (BK)
   2. Musical (M)   6. Intrapersonal (INTRA)
   3. Logical/Mathematical (MTH)   7. Interpersonal (INTER)
   4. Visual-Spatial (VS)   8. Naturalist (N)

3. The Theory of Multiple Intelligences has many implications for education and educational reform. Many teachers are exploring new teaching methods, activities, and forms of assessment that are directly linked to the Theory of Multiple Intelligences. After each educational activity below, use the codes from above to indicate which intelligence is most encouraged by the activity.

   a. Form a group to create a student handbook for incoming freshman students. _____

   b. Act out a scene from a book in a literature class. _____

   c. Conduct four interviews with people who work in the career field of interest to you. _____

   d. Construct and conduct a survey of students on your campus. Analyze the data and present it in a report format to the president of the college. _____

   e. Collect samples of music from different cultural or ethnic groups. _____

   f. Use a computer graphics program to create an eye-catching presentation. _____

   g. Write a poem about your heritage or cultural ties. _____

   h. Create a collage of international flags to hang in the library. _____

   i. Organize a photography exhibit of your best photographs. _____

   j. Write a paper contrasting American English and British English terms for common objects. _____

   k. Roleplay a conflict resolution strategy. _____

   l. Keep a daily journal or log to record your progress in reaching a specific goal. _____

m. Counsel a friend about a personal problem. _____

n. Attend a movie and then write a movie critique to present to the class. _____

o. Design a tee shirt for an organization on campus. _____

⊖⊖ Exercise 1.8 LINKS

The three learning modalities (learning styles) and the Theory of Multiple Intelligences are two theoretical ways to categorize people's strengths, talents, and abilities. In many ways, the Theory of Multiple Intelligences is a more detailed theory that incorporates the three learning styles or modalities (visual, auditory, and kinesthetic). How are these two theories related? Does the Theory of Multiple Intelligences go beyond the three modalities? Use whatever method you would like to explain or show how these two theories are similar and how they are different. Write your answer on your own paper.

SUMMARY

■ Three main learning styles or learning modalities determine how individuals learn most effectively: visual, auditory, and kinesthetic.

■ Most adults have a learning style preference but are able to function using all three modalities.

■ The most effective study tools are those that are compatible with your visual, auditory, or kinesthetic strengths.

■ Weak learning modalities may be due to lack of experience or training or to physical or neurological conditions.

■ Howard Gardner's Theory of Multiple Intelligences proposes that intelligences can be learned and strengthened.

■ Gardner has identified eight intelligences or abilities that people possess to varying degrees: verbal/linguistic, musical, logical/mathematical, visual-spatial, bodily-kinesthetic, intrapersonal, interpersonal, and naturalist.

■ Sub-intelligences are identified for each of the eight intelligences. The sub-intelligences for one category may not be equally developed.

OPTIONS FOR PERSONALIZING CHAPTER 1

1. **PROFILE CHART—PERSONAL LOG** Use a spiral notebook or loose notebook paper, or set up a computer file to begin a personal log that will be maintained all term. After each chapter is completed, make a log entry for that chapter. Answer the following questions for Chapter 1.

   What score did you have on the Chapter 1 Profile? _____

   What is your preferred learning modality?

   Which of the multiple intelligences do you feel are most developed for you?

   What study strategies that utilize your preferred learning style and stronger intelligences have you identified in this chapter that you would like to use?

2. **WORDS TO KNOW** Knowing the following vocabulary terms is important. Make a vocabulary sheet or vocabulary flash cards for the following terms. (Do this for all future chapters as well.) These vocabulary study tools become valuable as the term progresses.

learning styles	verbal/linguistic intelligence
learning modalities	musical intelligence
learning style preference	logical/mathematical intelligence
visual learner	visual-spatial intelligence
auditory learner	bodily-kinesthetic intelligence
kinesthetic learner	intrapersonal intelligence
learning strategies	interpersonal intelligence
multisensory learning strategies	naturalist intelligence
Howard Gardner's Theory of Multiple Intelligences	

3. **WRITING ASSIGNMENT 1** Use your own paper to reflect on your previous school experiences. Discuss how schools helped you develop *each* of the eight intelligences identified by Howard Gardner. If some of the intelligences were not recognized or developed in school, what could have been done differently? How would use of different methods have affected you?

4. **WRITING ASSIGNMENT 2** Briefly describe what you believe are the learning styles and stronger multiple intelligences of a close family member or a friend. Compare your learning styles and stronger intelligences to those of the person you described. How are the two of you similar? How are you different? Describe an interaction where your differences in processing information became very apparent.

5. **PORTFOLIO DEVELOPMENT** Either locate a web site for the topic of learning styles, the Theory of Multiple Intelligences, or Howard Gardner, or select one of the links on this textbook's web site. Print the information you located and then write a reflection paper that compares the information to the information presented in Chapter 1.

CHAPTER 1 REVIEW QUESTIONS

True-False

Carefully read the following sentences. Pay attention to key words.
  Write T *if the statement is TRUE. Write* F *if it is FALSE.*

_____ 1. Visual learners have strong memories for printed material or pictures, diagrams, or charts.

_____ 2. A kinesthetic learning strategy involves some form of movement.

_____ 3. Reciting involves speaking out loud and using your own words.

_____ 4. Questioning, paraphrasing, and participating in discussions are effective strategies for auditory learners and people with well-developed verbal/linguistic intelligence.

_____ 5. Taped information is most beneficial when it is based on selected study and review information.

_____ 6. Most adults are able to work with tasks that require the use of different modalities.

_____ 7. Auditory learners do well typing notes and making pictures or charts of information.

_____ 8. The three modalities are hands-on, visual, and kinesthetic.

_____ 9. Many study strategies actually utilize more than one modality.

_____10. Intrapersonal intelligence is exhibited by people who work well with others and show leadership skills.

Multiple-Choice

Choose the best answer *for each of the following questions. Write the letter of the best answer on the line.*

_____ 1. A kinesthetic learner who also has strong visual skills needs to learn thirty new vocabulary words and their definitions. This learner would benefit by using the following strategy:
  a. On notebook paper, make a list of the words and their definitions.
  b. Read the definitions of the words into a tape recorder.
  c. Practice writing the words several times on a chalkboard.
  d. Write the words and definitions on chart paper and then add colored pictures.

_____ 2. An auditory learner could study dates and events for history by
  a. reading the dates and reciting the events for each date out loud without looking at the text or notes.
  b. reading the events and reciting the dates for each event out loud without looking at the text or notes.
  c. reviewing from a tape that was made that gives the dates and the events.
  d. all of the above.

_____ 3. A student needs to learn ten different math formulas and the steps required to use the formulas to solve problems. This student makes a set of cards and practices using these manipulatives on the top of the desk to play a game of concentration. This student is using
  a. visual skills.
  b. visual and kinesthetic skills.
  c. auditory skills.
  d. kinesthetic skills.

_____ **4.** Converting written information into large colorful mappings to show key points and then reciting the different levels of information uses
   a. visual-spatial intelligence.
   b. auditory skills and verbal/linguistic intelligence.
   c. kinesthetic skills.
   d. all modalities.

_____ **5.** Howard Gardner's eighth intelligence refers to the ability to
   a. reflect on one's own values, beliefs, and personal growth issues.
   b. perceive the harmony and relationships of the environment.
   c. use intuition and creativity.
   d. keep accurate, detailed records and analyze data.

Short Answer—Critical Thinking

1. After each of the following learning strategies, indicate which of Howard Gardner's eight intelligences will be exhibited by using the strategy:

Highlighting printed materials _____   Making movies in your mind _____

Reciting often   _____   Creating rhythms and tunes _____

Using CD-ROMs with voice   _____   Making manipulatives   _____

Using a word processor   _____   Using drama or dance   _____

2. The Theory of Multiple Intelligences is based on the premise that traditional IQ tests were too limiting. What intelligences were added to expand the concept of intelligence to include a wider range of talents and abilities?

3. Briefly describe some type of information that you need to learn for another class. Discuss ways you can learn this information by using multiple intelligences or a multi-sensory approach.

Processing Information into Your Memory System

The workings of the human mind have fascinated people for centuries. What is involved in learning new information? Are you sometimes certain you've learned new information only to find you can't recall it? Do your study techniques give you feedback to let you know how you are doing? Do you remember main ideas or details more readily? How do you organize information for your memory? This chapter shows you ways to strengthen your ability to process and recall important information.

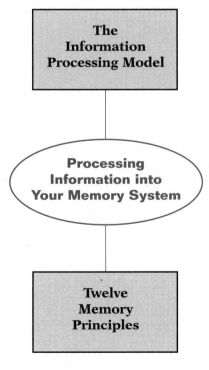

The
Information
Processing Model

Processing
Information into
Your Memory System

Twelve
Memory
Principles

CHAPTER 2 Information Processing Profile

DO, SCORE, and **RECORD** your profile before you read this chapter. If you need to review the process, refer to the complete directions given in the Profile for Chapter 1 on page 2.

	YES	NO
1. I use study methods that give me feedback so that I know whether I am learning.	_____	_____
2. I have problems studying new information when it is not an area of genuine interest to me.	_____	_____
3. I am usually motivated to study, and I am willing to put forth the effort that is required.	_____	_____
4. I have problems identifying and pulling out the information that is important to study.	_____	_____
5. I rearrange information into meaningful units or clusters so that it is easier to learn.	_____	_____
6. I wait until close to test time before I practice the information that I previously read.	_____	_____
7. I talk out loud to myself as I study because reciting seems to help me learn.	_____	_____
8. I use the same method of learning information for everything I need to study.	_____	_____
9. I spend almost all my studying time trying to memorize specific details exactly as they were presented in the book.	_____	_____
10. I make movies in my mind about the information I am learning.	_____	_____
11. I take time to relate or associate new information to information I already know.	_____	_____
12. I use methods to concentrate when I study.	_____	_____

Self-Awareness: Describe your current feelings about your memory. Is it weak or strong? Does it vary from one situation to another? What kinds of problems do you have with memory in school and outside of the school setting?

_____

_____

_____

_____

_____

The Information Processing Model

Psychologists frequently use the **Information Processing Model** to help explain how we receive, process, and learn information. The Information Processing Model consists of six main parts. While each part has its own distinctive functions, the parts do not work independently. Each part has an important role to move information through your memory system as you learn. Refer to the following diagram of the model as you read about each of its parts.

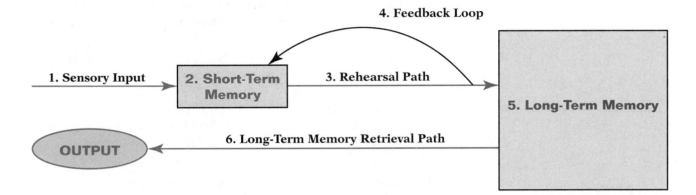

The Information Processing Model

1. Our senses take in information, or sensory input.
2. Our short-term memory receives the information and holds it briefly.
3. We rehearse the information we want to learn.
4. If we get feedback that we aren't learning what we rehearse, that information goes through the feedback loop.
5. Information that is adequately rehearsed moves into our long-term memory, where it is permanently imprinted.
6. Information stored in long-term memory is accessed through long-term retrieval, and the output shows that we have learned.

Sensory Input

We receive information through our five senses (sight, sound, smell, taste, and touch); this information is called **sensory input**. Such input comes in the form of **sensory stimuli**, which can be letters, numbers, words, pictures, and sounds.

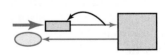

Short-Term Memory

Short-term memory (STM) is a temporary *storage center* that is very limited in time and capacity (up to seven items at one time). Sensory input first moves into short-term memory and remains there for a few seconds. Within that short time, a "decision" is made by the person receiving the stimuli to dump the information and process it no further. This decision may be made consciously or subconsciously. If attention is not given to the stimuli, the automatic response will be to "dump" it. Information that does not move to the next stage is dumped. On the model above, draw a trap door on the bottom of the short-term memory box. Imagine that this trap door opens and simply discards the unwanted or unattended to information. The following examples show how short-term memory works:

■ On your way to school today, you probably passed many different cars. However, you probably cannot accurately remember how many black cars you passed; there was no reason to remember such information. This is true for a vast amount of information taken in by your senses. Information that seems unimportant simply dumps out of short-term memory.

■ You begin to leave for the grocery store with a short list of groceries in mind. Two members of the household call out a total of eight more items for you to pick up at the store. If too much new information is given rapidly, your short-term memory overloads; you forget some of the items by the time you reach your car.

■ At school, you ask for someone's phone number. As you walk toward a phone, you are interrupted by a question from another student. By the time you reach the phone, you have forgotten the number.

■ At the end of class your instructor says, "Be sure to review page 10 because it will be on the test Friday." You vaguely heard the information because your thoughts were elsewhere; chances are good that the information was dumped.

Important points to know about short-term memory:

1. Pay attention to sensory input. You must consciously decide which information is important to learn. This requires you to be alert and ready.

2. Take a positive attitude toward incoming information. A negative attitude can shut down the learning process and the information gets dumped.

3. Remember that short-term memory is limited in capacity. Avoid overloading this memory system by trying to take in more than seven items rapidly at one time.

4. Recognize that the information you identify as important to learn will begin its journey along the rehearsal path.

Rehearsal Path

Once a learner decides that particular information must be learned, that selected information moves on to the **rehearsal path** or stage. The learner now selects effective learning techniques to move the information into long-term memory. This is an *active path* where practice, understanding, and actual learning take place. This path carries the sensory stimuli that are encoded in one of three codes that will be recognized by the long-term memory. The type of **encoding** is based on the type of information that is being transmitted. **Linguistic coding** (also called *semantic coding*) carries verbal information. **Visual coding** (also called *imaginal coding*) carries visual images such as pictures or diagrams. **Motor coding** (also called *physical coding*) carries messages that are related to muscle movement, such as riding a bike, typing, or driving a car.

The rehearsal path is an extremely important part of the information processing model, for the way a person rehearses will affect how clearly, effectively, and efficiently the information will be placed in the long-term memory system. One way to rehearse information is to use **rote memory**. Rote memory involves repetition, lots of repetition, to learn the information in the *exact form* that it was received. Rote memory often does not involve thoroughly understanding the information, its purpose, or its relationship to other things. While rote memory can be useful at times, such as memorizing a new phone number, a spelling word, an interesting quotation, or your social security number, it often is ineffective for learning academic material. Rote memory does not provide you with adequate comprehension of the information to be able to apply it in different ways or to different situations. The results are simply too limiting.

A second way, and a much more powerful way, to rehearse information is to use **elaborative rehearsal**. Elaborative rehearsal involves active thinking processes. Time and effort are given to understanding the information, seeing how it relates to other information, recognizing how it can be used, associating or linking it to information you know, and using multi-sensory approaches to learn the information accurately and thoroughly. When you learn information through elaborative rehearsal, you will be able to explain it, show you understand it, and apply it as needed.

The following example shows how rehearsal works:

■ To learn five new math formulas, you make flashcards for each formula. You practice and recite the information out loud. You check your accuracy. You then match the formulas to different kinds of problems. A pattern is identified so you know when to use each formula.

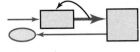

Important points to know about the rehearsal path:

1. Your choice of rehearsal strategies is important. Select strategies that use your strong modalities and abilities.

2. Use a variety of rehearsal techniques. You are more likely to recall information when you have practiced it in more than one way and you have included more than one sensory channel.

3. Emphasize understanding what you are practicing by using elaborative rehearsal. Avoid rote memory, in which little meaning is attached to the information.

4. Recognize that the rehearsal stage involves practice. Time and effort are required to learn the information accurately and thoroughly.

5. Feedback should be included so you know whether or not you are readily learning the information. This self-quizzing helps ensure that you are creating a clear imprint in long-term memory. Feedback can include reciting, writing, discussing, drawing, or otherwise demonstrating understanding.

6. Pay attention to the feedback you receive. If you don't know the information, do not skip over it or move on. Try a different method for rehearsing the information. If you know the information, it has moved into your long-term memory.

7. Avoid doing the same learning activity again and again; you may wind up recycling through the feedback loop without showing any progress. Vary your approach to rehearsing.

Feedback Loop

When you rehearse and find out that you do not understand or know the new information, you receive feedback that more rehearsal or practice is required. The information "zips" through the **feedback loop**, which is nothing more than a quick path back to short-term memory.

Important points to know about the feedback loop:

1. The feedback loop is an *inactive path*. It does nothing but immediately send the information back into short-term memory for further rehearsal.

2. An easy image to associate with the feedback loop is the suction duct that is used at banks to send deposits or withdrawals from the teller to the car that is in a lane away from the building. The driver of the car puts his or her

money into a container and sends the container through a suction duct that drops the container at the teller window. The feedback loop works in a similar way.

Long-Term Memory

Long-term memory (LTM) is an enormous *storage system* that "files away" information. So that new information can be located when it is needed, long-term memory often stores it in clusters of related information called **schemas.** (As an interesting note, with advanced technology, brain scans can actually show which sections of the brain are activated when a person learns specific kinds of information.) When you start to learn something new and unfamiliar, the learning process at first is challenging, frustrating, and full of errors. The initial learning process of an unfamiliar topic or information may be difficult because you are just beginning to construct a new schema for this knowledge. Later, after you have learned this information or skill, learning additional information is easier and smoother because a schema for that subject already exists. This concept of schemas helps explain why learning is so much easier and sometimes effortless when there is an interest, a background, and perhaps even some expertise in a specific field.

Another way to look at long-term memory is to think of your brain as a filing system with many different files and many different drawers filled with different kinds of information. When information is carefully placed in the file cabinet, it can be located when it is needed in the future. If any drawer is opened and the file is stuffed in without organization or logic, the file may be difficult to find at a later time. Elaborative rehearsal organizes information carefully and logically, so it is easier to locate in long-term memory at a later time.

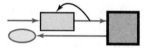

Important points to know about long-term memory:

1. Information that has been processed along the rehearsal path is carried to long-term memory by neurological impulses, or neurotransmitters.

2. Information that enters long-term memory is **imprinted** in your brain. The impact of the impulses marks the place in the brain in which the information is stored.

3. Because information is imprinted, long-term memory is considered to be permanent memory.

4. Long-term memory is a storage facility with unlimited capacity. It never runs out of space to store new information.

5. New information is linked or imprinted in existing schemas.

Long-Term Memory Retrieval Path

Long-term retrieval is the process of accessing, or finding, information stored in the long-term memory system. When information is retrieved along this *active path,* you are then able to show what you have learned through some form of "output." Output may mean that you are able to respond correctly by talking, explaining, writing, drawing, demonstrating, or applying the learned information in one or more ways. Practice keeps information accessible. By reviewing information on a regular basis, you strengthen the retrieval path so that you can use the information you worked hard to learn.

Learning a foreign language is a good example of the necessity to practice retrieval. You spent time learning a foreign language but have not practiced it for many years, so you probably no longer speak that language fluently. You may remember the sentence structure, but you have probably forgotten the vocabulary needed to express your ideas. If you do not retrieve information for years at a time, you will no longer have access to that information in memory.

However, by "brushing up" with a few lessons, the vocabulary may return to you fairly quickly. You will definitely "relearn" the language faster than you learned it the first time.

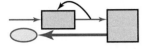

Important points to know about the long-term memory retrieval path:

1. To readily access information stored in long-term memory, you must review that information regularly and frequently.

2. When you search your memory for information that you have learned, if you can't immediately locate the information, think about related categories. Through the process of association, you can often link information until you locate the information being sought.

3. Practice retrieving information by several methods. This can include reciting, summarizing, drawing, or reproducing it or by seeing relationships it has with other learned information.

4. Information that was initially well-organized, firmly attached to existing schemas, and imprinted clearly and accurately will be easier to retrieve. However, time and practice retrieving will still be required in order to access this information over time.

Output

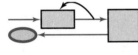

Output is the end result or the "proof" that learning has taken place. Output occurs when each part of the Information Processing Model functions effectively. There are many ways to show outcome. Positive results on a test show that specific kinds of learning occurred. Being able to express new concepts, to argue a point of view with specific details to back up your comments, or to connect ideas together smoothly in a paper or an essay all demonstrate information that has been learned. Being able to apply information, such as constructing an electronics board, tuning an engine, or using a formula to solve a math problem also demonstrates positive output.

Your knowledge of the Information Processing Model can now be used to assess your own learning progress. Examine the techniques you are using to study. Are you alert to incoming sensory stimuli? Are you rehearsing effectively? Are you using techniques to give you feedback as you study? Are you organizing the information clearly around schemas? Are you taking time to practice retrieving information? With your knowledge about how learning occurs, you can now adjust your methods and fine-tune your approach to processing and learning new information.

Important points to know about output:

1. Output is the proof that learning has taken place.

2. Output is a demonstration of accuracy; your answer or your product works correctly and is logically correct.

3. Output can be shown verbally, in writing, or through completion of a product.

Name _____ Date _____

✎ **EXERCISE 2.1 Understanding the Information Processing Model**

Without referring to your notes, draw and label the six parts of the Information Processing Model that result in output. Two methods for drawing this model are provided:

1. Draw the model in the order the parts were presented in this chapter. Label all the parts.

2. Draw the small and the large storage centers. Draw the path going into short-term memory. Draw the other two paths (one into and one out of long-term memory). Draw the feedback loop. Draw output. Label all the parts.

✎ **EXERCISE 2.2 Discussing Case Studies**

Work with a partner or in a group of three or four people. Read the following situations carefully. In each case, the student has problems learning because she or he is not using one part of the Information Processing Model efficiently. Identify which part is not being used. Write your answer on the line.

_____ **1.** Manuel has twenty new vocabulary words to learn. He reads through them quickly and is surprised to find he can't remember any of the definitions.

_____ **2.** Teresa spent many hours studying her biology notes for a test that was scheduled three weeks later. She got involved with many other activities and did not review before the test. She figured that she had already learned the information; her test scores showed that she hadn't.

_____ **3.** Leon repeated several math formulas again and again. He is good at rote memory. On a test, he was not able to answer questions about the formulas because they were presented differently from the way he had memorized them.

_____ **4.** Cindy needed to associate fifteen writers to the time periods in which they produced their work. She practiced matching the writers to their works. On the test, she could recall which author wrote which book but not in which period.

_____ **5.** Kim made flash cards for all the important terms she had to know in her psychology class. She recited the information on her cards. If she missed some definitions, she continued on until she could find ones that she knew.

EXERCISE 2.3 Memory Principles Inventory

You will soon learn about the twelve principles of memory that are used to enhance the learning process. First, complete the following inventory by answering YES or NO to each question below. The letter in the upper left hand corner of each box will be explained later.

S		YES	NO
1. Do you spend a lot of time studying but seem to study the "wrong information" for a test?		_____	_____
2. Do you get frustrated when you read because everything seems important?		_____	_____
3. Do you tend to highlight too much when you highlight a textbook?		_____	_____
4. Do your notes seem excessively long and overly detailed?		_____	_____
5. Do you avoid making study tools such as flashcards because you are not sure what information to put on the study tools?		_____	_____

A		YES	NO
1. Do you tend to memorize facts or ideas in isolation?		_____	_____
2. When you try to recall information you have studied, do you sometimes "feel lost" because there is no direct way to access the information in your memory?		_____	_____
3. Do you feel that you are memorizing numerous lists of information but don't really understand what they mean or how they are connected?		_____	_____
4. Do you "go blank" on tests when a question asks for information in a form or context different from the way you studied it?		_____	_____
5. Do you lack sufficient time to link difficult information to familiar words or to pictures?		_____	_____

V		YES	NO
1. When you finish reading, do you have difficulty remembering what paragraphs were even about?		_____	_____
2. Do you have difficulty remembering information in the form of a chart that was presented on the chalkboard or on a screen?		_____	_____
3. Is it difficult for you to get a visual image of printed information?		_____	_____
4. When you try to recall information, do you rely mainly on words rather than pictures?		_____	_____
5. Are the notes and study tools that you create done with only a pencil or one color pen?		_____	_____

E		YES	NO
1. Do you sometimes take "the easy way out" or look for shortcuts when you study?		_____	_____
2. Do you feel that doing problems or creating study tools that were not assigned is a waste of your time?		_____	_____
3. Does the term *studying* mean to basically "do the assignments" and then studying is over?		_____	_____
4. If extra credit projects or options are available, do you tend to skip doing them?		_____	_____
5. Do you choose not to spend time studying with another student or attending a weekly study group?		_____	_____

C		YES	NO
1.	Do you easily get distracted or find your mind wandering?	_____	_____
2.	Are there so many interruptions when you study that you are not quite sure what you accomplished at the end of a study block?	_____	_____
3.	Do you miss important information during a lecture because your mind tends to wander or daydream?	_____	_____
4.	When you are reading, do you find it difficult to keep your mind focused on the information in the textbook?	_____	_____
5.	Do you study with the television, radio, or stereo turned on?	_____	_____

R		YES	NO
1.	Do you have weak auditory skills?	_____	_____
2.	Do you have difficulty expressing your ideas on paper?	_____	_____
3.	Do you have difficulty clearly explaining textbook information to another person?	_____	_____
4.	Does your current method of studying lack techniques that give you feedback about whether or not you know the information?	_____	_____
5.	Do you feel awkward or uncomfortable talking out loud to yourself?	_____	_____

I		YES	NO
1.	Do you label the class or the textbook you are using as boring, dumb, useless, or a waste of your time?	_____	_____
2.	Do you dislike going to class?	_____	_____
3.	Once you are in class, do you resent being there and tend to tune out whatever is going on?	_____	_____
4.	Do you find it difficult to complete homework assignments because you just can't get interested in the subject?	_____	_____
5.	Is it difficult to understand why you have to take specific courses when they don't seem to be related to your career field?	_____	_____

B		YES	NO
1.	Do you have problems finding the main idea even though you are able to understand the individual details?	_____	_____
2.	Do you understand general concepts but oftentimes have difficulty giving the details that are related to the concept?	_____	_____
3.	Do you need to make a more concerted effort to take the time finding the relationships between concepts and details?	_____	_____
4.	Do your lecture notes capture main ideas but lack details?	_____	_____
5.	Do your notes include running lists of details without a clear method of showing main ideas?	_____	_____

F	YES	NO
1. Do you use tests as your main means of getting feedback about what you have learned?		
2. Do you keep taking in new information without stopping to see if you are trying to learn too much too fast?		
3. When you are rehearsing, do you "keep on going" even if you sense that something is not clearly understood?		
4. Do you tend to use self-quizzing only when you are preparing for a test?		
5. Do you sometimes cram for tests?		

O	YES	NO
1. Does the information that is presented in class or in the textbook seem disorganized?		
2. Do you have difficulty remembering the sequence of important events, steps of a process, or details in general?		
3. When you try to do a "memory search" to locate information in your memory, are you sometimes unable to find the information?		
4. Do you spend most of your time trying to learn information in the exact order that it is presented?		
5. Do you feel unsure about rearranging, reorganizing, or regrouping information so that it is easier to learn and recall?		

T	YES	NO
1. Do you often find it necessary to cram for tests because you simply run out of time?		
2. Do you get tired when you study because you are trying to study too much at one time?		
3. When you study, do you change to a second subject as soon as you complete the assignments for the first subject?		
4. Are some of your study blocks more than three hours long?		
5. In at least one of your courses, do you spend less time studying that subject than most other students in class?		

On	YES	NO
1. Once you have completed an assignment, do you put it aside until close to the time of the next test?		
2. Do you have problems remembering or recalling information that you know you learned several weeks earlier?		
3. Do you need to add more review time to your weekly study schedule?		
4. Do you study less than two hours per week for every one hour in class?		
5. Do you sit down to study and feel that you are all caught up and have nothing to study?		

About the Inventory

*The letters in the upper left-hand corner of each of the boxes above represent one of the principles of memory. In the first box, finish the name of the principle by writing **S**electivity. Continue to finish labeling each box as follows:*

	Concentration	**F**eedback
Association	**R**ecitation	**O**rganization
Visualization	**I**nterest	**T**ime on Task
Effort	**B**ig and Little Pictures	**On**going Review

Now, look at your answers. A NO answer indicates you are already using the principle of memory when you study. If any box of questions above has all five answers as NO, you are already using this principle of memory effectively. YES answers indicate that yes, you will benefit by learning to use this principle of memory more effectively when you study. The more YES answers you have, the greater the need is to add this principle of memory to your learning strategies or study techniques.

Twelve Memory Principles

Learning, as you have seen, is a complex process. Many mental processes are involved in moving information into long-term memory and then retrieving that information when it is needed. The following **twelve memory principles** can help you process information more efficiently through all the stages of information processing. These principles, when used consistently throughout the learning process, result in a stronger, more efficient memory. The memory words **SAVE CRIB FOTO** will help you remember all twelve principles; each letter in the words represents one of the memory principles.

Twelve Memory Principles (SAVE CRIB FOTO)

1. **S**electivity involves selecting what is important to learn.
2. **A**ssociation involves associating or linking new information to something familiar.
3. **V**isualization involves picturing in your mind the information you are learning.
4. **E**ffort on your part is essential for learning.
5. **C**oncentration is necessary when you study.
6. **R**ecitation involves repeating information verbally in your own words.
7. **I**nterest, if it doesn't exist, must be created.
8. **B**ig and little pictures involves recognizing levels of information.
9. **F**eedback in the form of self-quizzing checks your progress.
10. **O**rganization involves logical reordering of information.
11. **T**ime on task refers to the time dedicated and scheduled for learning.
12. **O**ngoing review promotes practice retrieving information from memory.

✎ Exercise 2.4 Learning the Basics

Before you begin reading the details about each memory principle, try learning the basic labels for each of the twelve principles of memory. This will help you "set up the schema" for the information you will be reading. Use the short clue below each line and the initial letter of the word to help you list the twelve principles of memory. Try to complete this without looking at the list on page 34.

S _____   **C** _____   **F** _____
   (Picking and choosing)   (Focusing)   (Self-quizzing)

A _____   **R** _____   **O** _____
   (Linking ideas)   (Explaining out loud)   (Structuring logically)

V _____   **I** _____   **T** _____
   (Seeing it in your mind)   (Enjoying)   (Using minutes and hours)

E _____   **B** _____   **O** _____
   (Trying hard)   (Concepts and details)   (Repeated practice)

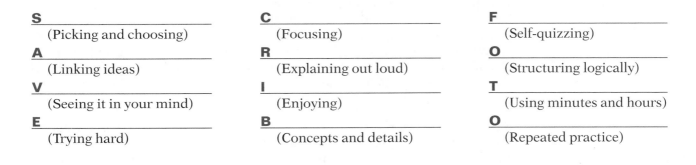

Selectivity

SAVE CRIB FOTO

Selectivity is the process of separating important main ideas and details from a larger body of information. Learning everything—every detail, every example, every word—is not possible and certainly is not reasonable. You as the learner must continually evaluate the importance of information and strive to pick out only that which is significant. Parts III and IV of this book help you improve your selectivity skills as you learn to select what to survey in chapters, what to highlight, what to write in notes, and what importance to place on various study tools. In each case, you will be honing your skills in identifying and pulling out main ideas and supporting details. The process of learning is greatly simplified when you reduce the amount of information that needs to be placed in your memory system *and* you place appropriate information into memory.

Association

SAVE CRIB FOTO

Association is the process of linking two or more items together. The long-term memory system is organized around schemas or clusters of related information. This system of organization is based on interconnections or associations. Sometimes when you try to recall something from memory, you can go straight to the information and have an immediate answer. More frequently, however, a **memory search** involves thinking your way to the information by associating or linking ideas together. One idea serves as a **retrieval cue** for another idea.

In Exercise 1.6, you drew a picture that represents the *institutions of society*. The picture is your retrieval cue for naming the five institutions. First you think of the picture, then you link the word associated to each part of the picture, and finally you name the five institutions. This linking of information during a memory search can be seen as jumping from one stepping stone to another until you arrive at your destination.

In the above example, a specific list (the five institutions) was linked to pictures. Other kinds of links are also used during association. Words can be used to associate ideas together. The mnemonic (memory trick) for the twelve principles of memory is an association that uses three words, SAVE CRIB FOTO, to link to a list of twelve separate items. These memory principles would not be learned as quickly if this association were not used.

Another form of association involves taking the time to link the new information to information that is already known or familiar. Intentional effort is made to associate the new information to existing schemas. This can be done by taking the time to ask yourself questions such as the following:

What do I already know about this subject?

How is the new information similar to or different from something I already know?

Frequently, information that you are studying is already paired so the association is automatic. For example, if you are studying a list of vocabulary words and their meanings, an automatic pairing exists. After sufficient rehearsal, when you name one of the words, the word works as a retrieval cue for the definition. Reverse rehearsal should also be done. When you see or hear the definition, the definition should work as a retrieval cue to the vocabulary word. Recognizing and studying this association will make the learning of new vocabulary words, or any paired information, much easier.

Visualization

SAVE CRIB FOTO

Visualization is the process of making pictures in your mind. It is a valuable skill for several reasons. Information that is mentally pictured is easier to comprehend and recall. Long-term memory is strengthened when two sensory channels (such as auditory for reciting and visual for visualizations) are processing information. Also, mental pictures are stored in one side of the brain (the right hemisphere) and words in the other (the left hemisphere). Using visualizations to aid in processing information activates your entire brain. The result is better memory skills.

The process of visualization can be used to visualize both printed words and pictures or graphic information. Some visual learners have the ability to recall or picture information in the form of printed words. These visual learners can visualize "in their mind's eye" the textbook page, the specific flashcard, the line of notes, or the information written on a screen in the classroom. The information is recalled in the form of words, numbers, or letters such as in formulas. This printed form of visualization can be strengthened even further by adding colors to the words, letters, or numbers. It may be strengthened even further by associating the information with pictures or graphics.

Visualizing images in the form of objects, scenes, or complete story line sequences, such as seeing "movies in the mind," is a valuable skill that can be learned. As mentioned, both comprehension and recall can be improved by consciously using visualization. If you are just beginning to learn to visualize what you read, begin by *visualizing individual objects*. Examine the object closely; pay attention to size, color, shape, and position. Then, close your eyes and try to "see the object on the inside of your eyelids." Open your eyes and compare your visual image to the actual object.

Now, practice *visualizing larger pictures*. Use the technique described above to visualize a larger picture such as a photograph, a map, a graph, or a chart. Focus on visually memorizing the main features or the "skeleton." Once the skeleton image is clear, "zoom in" to work on remembering the smaller parts or details. Each time you encounter visual materials in your classes, take the time to work with creating the visual image of the material in your mind.

The final form of visualization is to *create movies in your mind*. This process works with units of information that are processed through time. Many good readers automatically start the "cameras rolling" when they begin reading. The story unfolds on the movie screen in their minds. This is the same process that should be activated when you read textbooks. The movie may not be as action-filled as a movie in the mind that is created when reading a novel, but the movie will serve as a retrieval cue for information at a later time. For some people, visualizing during the reading process is not automatic; effort and intention are required to create the visual images. Time spent creating movies in the mind and rerunning the movies as a way to review is time well-spent.

Effort

SAVE CRIB FOTO

Effort, driven by motivation and determination, is needed throughout information processing. Taking information in, rehearsing it, and retrieving it all require effort. Many of the study tools you will use to help you boost your memory will not necessarily be seen by teachers or be graded. You are the one who decides whether such study tools will help you learn; you create your own learning activities for yourself, not because they are "required."

To avoid losing information during the learning process, consciously make the effort to learn and retain information. You will be rewarded with more thorough learning, a greater sense of satisfaction, and better grades.

Concentration

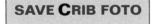

SAVE CRIB FOTO

Concentration, the process of focusing the mind on only one task or item, results in uninterrupted thought processes and more efficient learning. You will learn important techniques for setting the physical stage and the mental stage for good concentration (see Chapter 5). Being able to control your concentration enables you to create the ideal setting for receiving sensory information and moving it through the stages of information processing. Your mind has to be alert and focused on the task at hand. Internal and external distractors should be blocked out or eliminated. Concentration is an essential mental discipline that enables you to make optimum use of your valuable time.

Recitation

SAVE CRIB FOTO

Recitation is the process of verbalizing what you are learning or have already learned. When you recite, remember to use your own words to speak in complete sentences to explain the information as clearly as possible. Imagine that you are trying to explain the information to a friend who is not familiar with the subject. Pay attention to areas that seem a little "fuzzy." This is feedback to you that you need to go back to the sources of your information to check for accuracy and additional details.

Some students are uncomfortable with reciting because they are not used to talking out loud to themselves and so feel that others will think they are "weird." Nevertheless, an increasing number of teachers and students recognize the value of reciting and encourage this process of verbalizing. Reciting is valuable in studying because it provides you with immediate feedback so that you know whether you are really understanding information. As you recite, you activate your auditory channel, which strengthens the path to your long-term memory. Reciting keeps you actively involved; active learning leads to better concentration and comprehension. And as you recite in your own words, your focus is on understanding rather than on rote memory. You are personalizing the material.

Students who have difficulty expressing their ideas in class or expressing their ideas on paper will especially find value in reciting what is being studied. Frequently, all that is needed is the opportunity to put ideas together coherently when there is not a time element involved such as occurs during class discussions or tests. Practice expressing ideas in complete sentences prepares students ahead of time and increases the level of familiarity with information prior to the class discussion or test.

Interest

Interest is exhibited through feelings of curiosity, fascination, enthusiasm, and appreciation. Learning new information about areas that you "love" is usually easy; you have genuine interest working for you. Unfortunately, you will be required to take some courses in which you have no natural interest. Your task,

SAVE CRIB FOTO

then, is to generate an interest so that your learning is more enjoyable and less stressful.

You can create an interest by looking for a value or a purpose in knowing the information, by using new study techniques to learn the information, or by asking another student or several students to join you in a study group so you can learn together. You can also locate someone who is knowledgeable or works in the field that you are studying and ask that person what draws him or her to this field. Checking out books, videos, or cassettes that are related to the topic you are studying may give you a new, more appealing perspective on the topic.

On a more personal level, you may wish to examine your attitude toward the subject to see if your dislike or lack of interest is related to a previous experience or past incident in the class. Take time to identify what you *do* like about the subject. Emphasize and strengthen the positive aspects rather than focusing on the negatives.

The Big and Little Pictures

SAVE CRIB FOTO

Big and little pictures is based on the understanding that learning requires the use of at least two levels of information. One level is the "big picture," which is the general concept or category of information. For example, the subject of concentration is a big picture. To really understand the concept of concentration, however, you need to know another level of information, the specific details, or the "little pictures," that together create this concept. These details include a definition, the uses of concentration, its effects, how it works, and specific strategies.

To get a sense of these two levels of information, draw a circle in the center of your paper. This circle represents the main idea or the general category of information. (This is a schema.) Surround the circle with details that are related to the topic in the center of the circle. Then categorize information into lists with the category (big picture) at the top of the list.

This principle of big picture–little pictures is sometimes also referred to as the "forest and the trees." If you focus only on seeing the forest, you miss the meaning and the beauty of the individual trees. If you focus on only a few individual trees, you do not see that all the trees create a much larger group, the forest.

Learning new knowledge is similar to the idea of the forest and the trees. If you place too much emphasis on the details, you may fail to see their relationships to each other and to larger concepts. If you focus on only finding the main ideas, you are left without the specific details that support or prove the main idea.

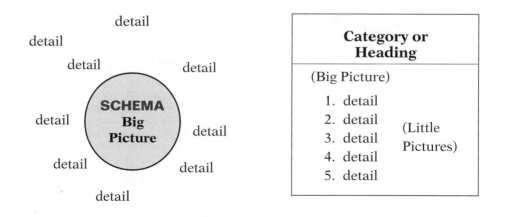

The principle of Big picture–little pictures is used frequently when you study. Each time you highlight, take notes, rearrange information, or make mappings, hierarchies, or outlines, you are using this important principle of memory.

Feedback

[SAVE CRIB **F**OTO]

Feedback is the process of verifying you have learned or of recognizing that you have not learned specific information. The most useful feedback occurs when you use self-quizzing or self-checking when you study. If you are involved in marathon studying or cramming, you do not have sufficient time for feedback. The main feedback from cramming comes *after* you have taken a test. Feedback should occur frequently *before* test time.

Several study techniques can provide feedback as you are learning. *Reciting* is the most frequently used form of feedback. Reciting can be used after you read a paragraph, underline, take notes, practice from flash cards, or use other visual study tools. *Writing summaries* can be effective feedback. At the end of a section in the chapter and at the end of the entire chapter, practice writing a summary of what you have read (and highlighted or placed in your notes). For this to be true feedback, attempt to write your summary without looking at your notes or your book. Then check your accuracy by comparing the summary to your notes or the book.

You can also *draw mappings or pictures* without looking at your notes or the book. Compare your drawings to the original ones. Check your accuracy, and add any details you missed when you drew from memory. This same process can be used to reproduce the visual mappings found at the beginning of each chapter in this book. Finally, as you work through a chapter, *write your own test questions*. Once you have finished with the chapter, quiz yourself. This gives you feedback that is similar to the feedback you receive during tests. If the chapter has chapter questions, sample exercises, or quizzes, complete these sections even if they are not assigned. This extra effort will provide you with feedback that can help you focus your attention on areas that need additional work.

Organization

[SAVE CRIB F**O**TO]

Organization refers to a meaningful, logical structure or arrangement of ideas. Organization as a principle of memory does not refer to organizing furniture, a study area, notebooks, or assignments.

If you sit at a computer keyboard and begin punching in random commands and information, the computer may not accept what you have entered. The mind works in much the same way. The information you want to put into your long-term memory must be organized in a meaningful, logical way if you want to access it later. When you try to retrieve information from long-term memory, your mind searches through the different "files" of information you have stored. If you "threw everything into your memory" without filing it properly, or without associating it with clusters of information, you would have difficulty locating the information you thought you learned.

This principle of organization explains why rote memory of small, individual facts is not a very reliable memory. Rote memory involves repeating a fact or detail in the exact words each time. Information learned through rote memory may be in your long-term memory but may be difficult to find. If a teacher asks you a question that is stated differently from the way you memorized the information, you will not be able to use the memorized detail effectively. You may not even recognize that the question and what you learned are related.

The order in which information is presented in a textbook or in a lecture may not be the most logically organized way to study the information.

Elaborative rehearsal often involves *rearranging* the information into more concise and more logical ways. The following six ways are often used to rearrange information for more effective studying:

1. Place the information in **chronological order** to show the sequence of events over a period of time.

2. **Categorize** the information. Look for logical groupings within the information you are studying. Rewrite the information into lists.

3. Place the information **alphabetically** into lists or groups.

4. Rearrange the information into a **visual graph** or **visual study tool.** This may include organizing the information into a visual mapping, a hierarchy, a time line, a comparison-contrast chart, or a flow chart.

5. Organize the information around a **visual graphic,** which may be any kind of picture. The picture becomes the point of focus. The words are used as labels for the visual graphic.

6. Organize the information into a set of **Cornell notes,** outlines, or flash cards. Flash cards will be discussed in Chapter 8. Cornell notes will be explained in Chapters 9 and 10.

Time on Task

SAVE CRIB FOTO

Time on task refers to the amount of time you spend involved in the learning process. There is a high correlation between the amount of time spent studying and the grade earned in a course. Students who spend too little time studying, for whatever reason, tend not to do well in the class. Students who spend ample time on the task of studying tend to show greater success. Chapter 3 discusses time management strategies; however, one strategy that is valuable to know at this time is the **2:1 ratio**. The 2:1 ratio states that for most college courses, sufficient time on task will occur if you study two hours for every one hour in class. If your class meets for three hours a week, study six hours a week for that class.

HOW you spend time on task is also important. If you overload your memory system by trying to study too much information at one time or for too long of a time period, the ability to comprehend and remember what you have read decreases. An ideal study block for adults is a fifty-minute period of concentrated studying. Then, if you wish to study for more than one hour, take a ten minute break. Avoid studying for more than three hours in a row. **Marathon studying,** also known as **massed studying,** occurs when you try to study for more than three hours in a row. Marathon studying in most cases is ineffective. **Distributed practice,** or distributed studying, is much more effective; with this method, studying is done in several different study blocks spread throughout the week.

Ongoing Review

SAVE CRIB FOTO

Ongoing review, or practicing what you have stored in long-term memory, makes information much more accessible and easier to retrieve quickly. The 2:1 ratio is recommended because this ratio usually provides you with "extra" time to use each week to review previously studied information. You should never be idle during a study block or be able to say, "I have nothing to study." When you apply ongoing review, information remains active and fresh in your mind, and you can avoid last-minute cramming.

✎ **EXERCISE 2.5 Using the Memory Principle of Association to Create Acronyms**

Acronyms *are words made from the initial letters of key words of items you need to learn. Acronyms use the Principle of Association. Once you have the acronym memorized, associate each letter of the acronym to the word it represents. SAVE CRIB FOTO is an acronym. Use this acronym to name the twelve principles of memory.*

_____ _____ _____

_____ _____ _____

_____ _____ _____

_____ _____ _____

A classic acronym is the word *HOMES* to name the five Great Lakes. Try naming the five Great Lakes below.

H _____ O _____ M _____

E _____ S _____

Use these steps to create and use an acronym:

1. Make a list of the first letters of key terms. Use only one letter per item.
2. Be sure that you have at least one vowel and that you do not have to list the items in order.
3. Look at the letters available. Rearrange the letters until you create a word.
4. Memorize the word and practice "translating" the word by reciting what each letter represents.

Now try making an acronym for each of the following:

When a child has the stomach flu, feed the child **bananas, rice, applesauce,** and **toast.**

Acronym: _____

The four voices in a quartet are the **alto, bass, tenor,** and **soprano.**

Acronym: _____

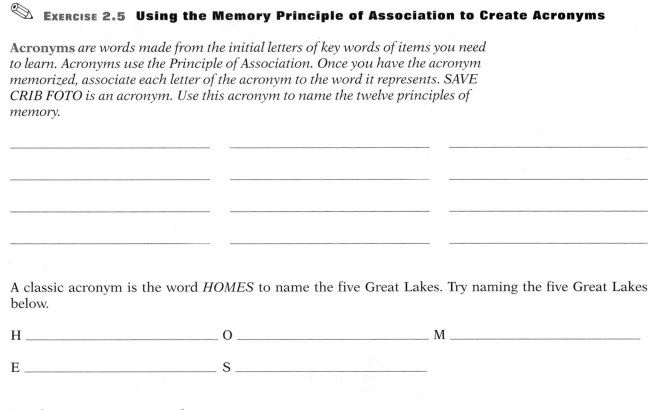 **More acronyms can be found on the web page.**

✎ **EXERCISE 2.6 Critical Thinking**

1. Draw and label the Information Processing Model.

2. Use the numbers below for each of the twelve memory principles. Place the numbers on the Information Processing Model in all locations where you believe that memory principle is *actively used.* Numbers may appear in more than one place.

1. Selectivity	**5.** Concentration	**9.** Feedback
2. Association	**6.** Recitation	**10.** Organization
3. Visualization	**7.** Interest	**11.** Time on Task
4. Effort	**8.** Big and Little Pictures	**12.** Ongoing review

3. Review the information about the Principle of Big and Little Pictures (page 38) and the Principle of Organization. Use this information to organize Howard Gardner's Theory of Multiple Intelligences in a meaningful, logical way. The Principle of Visualization (page 36) can then be used by adding pictures and color to your work.

✎ **EXERCISE 2.7 Principles of Memory Checklist**

The following checklist can be referred to any time you wish assess your study strategies. Ask yourself the following questions:

PRINCIPLES OF MEMORY

SELECTIVITY
ASSOCIATION
VISUALIZATION
EFFORT

CONCENTRATION
RECITATION
INTEREST
BIG AND LITTLE PICTURES

FEEDBACK
ORGANIZATION
TIME ON TASK
ONGOING REVIEW

1. *Before a test:*
   Am I using all the principles of memory to study and prepare for this test?

2. *After a test:*
   Which principles of memory did I use consistently and were they beneficial? Which principles of memory did I not use? How did they perhaps influence my grade? How can I work them into my study strategies?

3. *Throughout the term:*
   How can I modify or personalize my approach to studying by incorporating more of the principles of memory or by using them in a different way?

Memory Checklist

_____ Selectivity: I carefully select the important ideas and supporting details. I spend my time studying this information.

_____ Association: I take time to associate the new information to the information I already know. I look for ways to link two pieces of information together.

_____ Visualization: I make pictures and movies in my mind of the information I am learning. I practice seeing these pictures without looking.

_____ Effort: I willingly apply effort to the process of studying and learning.

_____ Concentration: I use concentration techniques when I study. I strive to keep my attention focused on the material I am studying.

_____ Recitation: I practice information by saying the information out loud and in complete sentences. If I am not able to recite, I use this feedback to study the information further until I can explain it in my own words.

_____ Interest: I take the responsibility to make the information I am studying interesting. If I have no genuine interest in the subject, I create one.

_____ Big and little pictures: I actively look for big ideas, categories, or concepts. I also focus on little pictures, the details that together support the big picture.

_____ Feedback: I use feedback in my study methods by questioning and quizzing myself as I study to be sure that I really understand the material.

_____ Organization: I rearrange or organize information chronologically or categorically so that it is easier to understand. I may also make notes, flashcards, lists, mappings, and tapes or create mnemonics.

_____ Time on task: I use my time management skills so that I am able to schedule enough time for studying, rehearsing, and making appropriate study tools.

_____ Ongoing review: I take time to continually review information that I have previously learned. I actively practice retrieving information from memory.

EXERCISE 2.8 Discussing Case Studies

In the following examples, students in a psychology class are successfully learning new information. Examine the techniques used in each situation. Identify at least one major memory principle being used in the study technique. Explain specifically why you chose this technique.

1. Marsha is learning that different regions in the brain receive information from different senses. The occipital lobe receives visual information. The temporal lobe receives auditory information. The parietal lobe takes in information from the skin. Marsha drew a picture of the three lobes and paired the pictures with pictures of eyes, ears, and skin.

   Principle: _____

   Explain: _____

   _____

   _____

2. Damon knows he learns best when he can discuss information with others. A midterm is scheduled in two weeks. Damon asks other students in class to join him in a study group. Because of his enthusiasm and enjoyment of the subject, many students ask to be a part of the study group.

   Principle: _____

   Explain: _____

   _____

   _____

3. Elena has found that using flashcards helps her tremendously. She writes psychology terms on one side and definitions on the other. She works with all her cards for the course at least once a week. She very conscientiously sorts the cards by the ones she knows and the ones she needs to study further.

   Principle: _____

   Explain: _____

   _____

   _____

4. Curt has a thirty-page chapter that needs to be read by the end of the week. He knows a class discussion is planned, and he wants to be prepared. He also knows that he does not comprehend well or retain information well if he tries to do all the reading and studying the day before the class. Curt makes a schedule for the week and plans sufficient time to read one section a day and study that section thoroughly. His plan also includes a time Friday morning before class to review his notes for each section of the chapter.

   Principle: _____

   Explain: _____

   _____

   _____

✎ EXERCISE 2.9 **Discussing Application**

Work in groups of three or four. Each person needs to select any textbook that he or she is currently using in another class. Open the book to one specific chapter and discuss with the group the following topics:

1. How can you apply the Twelve Principles of Memory to studying from this book?

2. How can you use the rehearsal path, feedback loop, and retrieval path effectively when you study for this course?

3. How can you use your preferred modality to study for this course?

4. How can you make use of your multiple intelligences and multi-sensory learning strategies in this given course?

✎ EXERCISE 2.10 **Expanding Chapter Mappings**

You can create a visual study tool by expanding the chapter mapping found at the beginning of each chapter. Visual mappings are a creative *study tool that can be developed many different ways and still be "correct." Follow these steps to expand a chapter mapping:*

1. Look at the basic structure or "skeleton" of each chapter mapping. Notice that the chapter title is in the center of the mapping. Each box that extends from the center of the mapping is a main heading. For Chapter 2, the two main headings are "The Information Processing Model" and "Twelve Memory Principles."

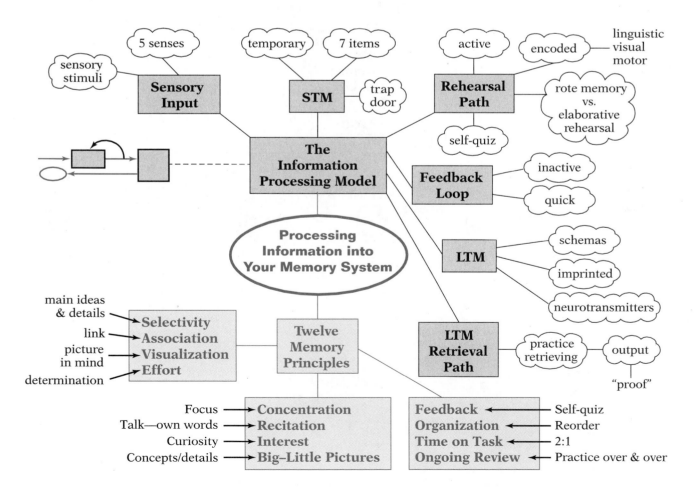

2. Your role in expanding this mapping is to begin by adding all the *subheadings* to the main headings. The subheadings are in the left-hand margin and are printed in bold, black print and are underlined with a blue line. To do this, place the subheadings around the headings. Connect them to the headings with lines. You may arrange them in a variety of ways and place them inside any shape that you wish.

3. Then add any additional *key words* or *short phrases* that serve as retrieval cues to remind you of important concepts related to the subheading.

4. Personalize the mapping by adding colors and, if you like, pictures.

5. A more detailed explanation of visual mappings is discussed in Chapter 11.

Expand the Chapter 2 mapping using your own creative ideas. If you have a graphics program or spreadsheet program on your computer, you may want to experiment creating the mapping on the computer.

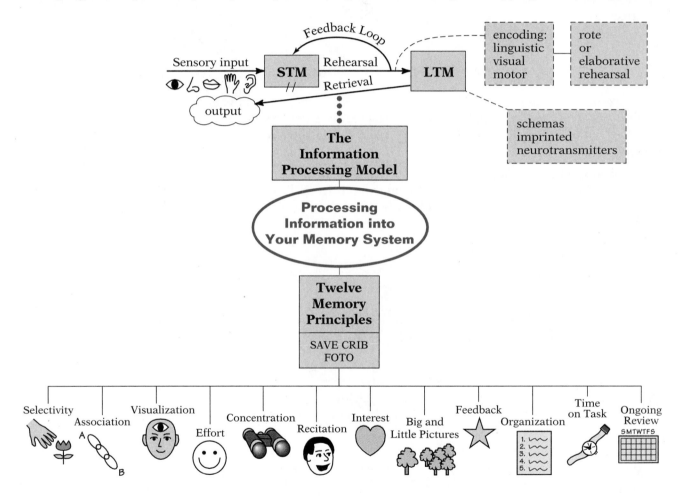

Web-site links are available online.

Computer Projects

1. Use your computer to create an attractive poster that shows the twelve memory principles. Add graphics and color if they are available.
2. Use your computer to expand the chapter mapping by using a flow chart, graphics, or spread-sheet program.
3. Use a tables program or columns to create a vocabulary study sheet for the important terms to know in the chapter.

Group Web-Search Activity is available online.

Case Studies are available online.

SUMMARY

■ The six-part Information Processing Model explains how information is learned.

1. Sensory input is received from stimuli in the environment.
2. Short-term memory briefly stores the information.
3. Information moves along the rehearsal path, where it is practiced.
4. Information that is not yet learned is rerouted through the feedback loop.
5. Effectively learned information is imprinted and stored in long-term memory.
6. When learned information is needed, it is pulled out of long-term memory and moved along the retrieval path.

■ The memory phrase *SAVE CRIB FOTO* is a way of remembering the twelve principles that can be used to strengthen your memory.

1. Selectivity
2. Association
3. Visualization
4. Effort
5. Concentration
6. Recitation
7. Interest
8. Big picture–little pictures
9. Feedback
10. Organization
11. Time on task
12. Ongoing review

OPTIONS FOR PERSONALIZING CHAPTER 2

1. **PROFILE CHART—PERSONAL LOG** Answer the following questions in your personal log. (Refer to page 24 in Chapter 2.)

    What score did you have on the Chapter 2 Profile? _____

    Do you see yourself actively using the rehearsal and the retrieval paths when you study? Explain your answer by giving specific examples or details.

    Which memory principles do you frequently use when you study? Give examples as to how you use them in other courses.

    Which memory principles have you under-utilized in your approach to studying? Explain ways you can incorporate them more consistently in your study methods.

2. WORDS TO KNOW

Information Processing Model	schemas	concentration
sensory input	imprinted	recitation
sensory stimuli	long-term retrieval	interest
short-term memory (STM)	output	big and little pictures
rehearsal path	twelve memory	feedback
encoding	principles	organization
linguistic coding	SAVE CRIB FOTO	time on task
visual coding	selectivity	2:1 ratio
motor coding	association	marathon studying
rote memory	memory search	massed studying
elaborative rehearsal	retrieval cue	distributed practice
feedback loop	visualization	ongoing review
long-term memory (LTM)	effort	acronyms

3. **WRITING ASSIGNMENT 1** You have learned a great deal of information in this chapter about the process of learning. Look back on your previous school history. How did your lack of knowledge about the way people (and you) learn affect your success in school? How do you predict this new knowledge will affect your learning outcomes this term and in the future? In other words, is this information valuable and can it be applied to your academic world?

4. **WRITING ASSIGNMENT 2** Discuss ways the memory principles are used outside of the academic world. What are everyday applications? Be creative and explore a variety of applications. Include sufficient details to explain your thoughts.

5. **PORTFOLIO DEVELOPMENT** We truly are on the frontier of understanding the capabilities of the human brain. Almost weekly, new discoveries are made about the brain's functions, malfunctions or disorders, capabilities, chemistry, and much more. Conduct an electronic search in the library for three or more magazine articles that discuss some aspect of the human brain, learning, or memory. Select articles that have been published within the last five years and articles that are related to the same general topic. Locate the articles and read them carefully. Decide on the method that you would like to use to present the information you located. The method of presentation should reflect your preferred modality or one of your stronger intelligences. The following articles may be of interest to include in your search:

"Total Recall," *GQ*, October, 1996
"Wired for Miracles," *Psychology Today*, May/June, 1998
"Brain Food: How to Eat Smart," *Psychology Today*, May/June, 1996

CHAPTER 2 REVIEW QUESTIONS

TRUE-FALSE

Carefully read the following sentences. Pay attention to key words.
Write T *if the statement is TRUE. Write* F *if it is FALSE.*

_____ 1. Short-term memory holds all sensory stimuli until they are learned.

_____ 2. The feedback loop is used to practice retrieving information from long-term memory.

_____ 3. Practice is needed in the rehearsal and the retrieval stages.

_____ 4. Information that is well organized in long-term memory is believed to be organized around clusters of related information.

_____ 5. The principle of ongoing review is needed on the retrieval path of the Information Processing Model.

_____ 6. The principle of effort is used in more than one stage of the Information Processing Model.

_____ 7. Self-quizzing should be included in study strategies used on the rehearsal path.

_____ 8. The memory principle of organization refers to having an organized work area, notebook, and class notes.

_____ 9. Relating new information to old information involves the principle of association.

_____ 10. The principle of time on task recommends that you use distributed practice when you study.

_____ 11. Marathon studying is different from mass studying because mass studying always lasts longer.

_____ 12. The principle of organization is used when information is rearranged in a meaningful, logical way.

_____ 13. If a person reads rapidly and doesn't remember what was read, the short-term memory system may have been overloaded.

_____ 14. The memory principles of time, effort, interest, and association are used during elaborative rehearsal.

_____ 15. When you do a *memory search,* retrieval cues in the form of words or pictures can assist you in locating information in long-term memory.

Fill-in-the-Blank

You may refer to the list of "Words to Know" on page 48. Write one word on each
line to make an accurate and complete sentence. Do not use any word more than
one time.

1. Sensory _____ carry messages into short-term memory.

2. _____ carry information into our memory systems through the form of neuro-logical impulses.

3. When the 2:1 ratio for studying is used effectively, a student should have time each week to use the

   memory principle of _____ on _____ .

4. _____-_____ memory has a limited capacity and duration (length of time).

5. _____ memory occurs when understanding or meaning are not attached to information as it is memorized.

6. _____ coding carries verbal information into the long-term memory.

7. The _____ _____ is an inactive path that returns information to short-term memory.

8. _____ _____ occurs when study blocks are spread throughout the week.

9. The memory principle of _____ is used when information is rewritten into categories, visual mappings, or chronological order.

10. The memory principle of _____ is used when a student ignores the ideas and details that are not essential for understanding the big picture.

Short Answer—Critical Thinking

1. Give several reasons why some sensory input never reaches long-term memory.

2. Explain the differences between rote memory and elaborative rehearsal.

3. Give at least three reasons why recitation is a powerful memory-boosting strategy.

Managing Your Time

Time management, perhaps the most essential of all study skills, is an organized method for planning the use of your time to reach goals. Does a lack of time create stress in your life? Do you have too little time for family or friends? Does time control you, or do you control time? Do the patterns of your weekday and your weekend make you feel as if you are on a roller coaster? Do you have to cram to get ready for tests? This chapter teaches you strategies to manage your time and create a more fulfilling balance in three important areas of your life: school, work, and leisure.

CHAPTER 3   Time Management Profile

DO, SCORE, and **RECORD** your profile before you read this chapter. If you need to review the process, refer to the complete directions given in the Profile for Chapter 1 on page 2.

	YES	NO
1. I schedule specific times to study during the weekend.	_____	_____
2. I often choose to spend time with friends instead of studying.	_____	_____
3. I try to make each scheduled day different so that I don't get bored.	_____	_____
4. I recognize the times during the day when I am the most mentally alert.	_____	_____
5. I include review time in my study blocks each week.	_____	_____
6. If my assignments are done, I use my study time for social activities.	_____	_____
7. I use a weekly schedule to organize my studying, work, and social life.	_____	_____
8. Friends or family members often interfere with my plans to study.	_____	_____
9. I study for more than three hours in a row.	_____	_____
10. I study my least liked subjects late at night.	_____	_____
11. For most three-credit classes, I study six hours a week for each class.	_____	_____
12. I avoid time management because I prefer to be spontaneous and do things when they need to be done.	_____	_____

Self-Awareness: What is your current attitude toward time management and scheduling time for one-week time periods? What past experiences may have influenced your current attitude? _____

_____

_____

_____

_____

_____

_____

_____

_____

_____

_____

All About You

Pie of Life

As a student, you need to continually balance three main areas in your life: school, work, and leisure. It is not likely (or desirable) that your **Pie of Life** will be divided into three equal sections. How the pie is "sliced" will differ from one person to another. Your goals, needs, and interests will shape your choices in each of these areas. Feeling confident, challenged, satisfied, fulfilled, happy, and in control can be signs that you have done well in balancing the three main areas of life. Frequent bouts with negative feelings, emotional responses, and resentments can be signs that the three areas of life need to be examined and rebalanced

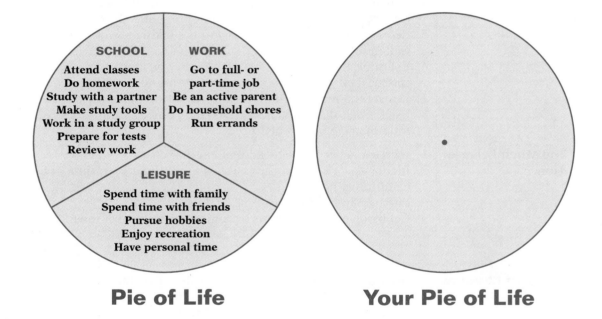

Pie of Life   **Your Pie of Life**

Draw your current Pie of Life in general terms. Divide your pie into three sections to show approximately what percentage of your waking hours you spend in the three main areas of school, work, and leisure. Is the amount of time in each area satisfactory, too much, or too little?

You have only so many hours in a day. If one of your areas of life does not have enough time, you need to take time from somewhere else in the pie. If you have too much time in an area, you need to use time differently or give it away to one of the other areas of the pie. This time-management technique is called the **increase–decrease method**. A chart following contains suggestions for balancing your pie more satisfactorily.

Once you have identified areas that could be adjusted for a better balance in your life, the questions then become How do I get started? Where can I find time to do all these new things? If you are willing to be flexible and to try some new strategies, this chapter has strategies that can help you gain control of your time.

USING THE INCREASE–DECREASE METHOD TO BALANCE YOUR PIE

PROBLEM	*POSSIBLE SOLUTIONS*
Too Little Time for Family or Friends	1. Reduce the amount of time spent on other leisure activities. 2. Explore reducing or changing work hours if possible. 3. Reduce the hours doing chores by seeking more help from other members in the household or by using goal setting to do chores more efficiently. 4. Reduce school hours by taking fewer classes. 5. Reduce time spent studying by learning more efficient study techniques.
Too Little Time for School	1. Reduce social time; make school a greater priority. 2. Maintaining some social time is important, but consider creating more "meaningful" or "quality" social time and eliminating the less significant time spent with friends or family. 3. Reduce work hours, if possible, to make more time for studying. 4. Consider applying for scholarships, financial aid, grants, and/or loans to replace income if the hours at work are reduced. 5. Reduce the number of classes you are taking so you have enough time to do well in fewer classes. 6. Examine the combination of classes you are taking; consider alternative classes if all your classes have heavy reading or writing requirements. 7. Learn time-management techniques so you make better use of your time. 8. Use the self-discipline needed to study during study blocks allocated on your time-management schedule.
Too Much Leisure Time	1. Increase school time by adding another class. 2. Increase work hours, if possible, or volunteer your time at a local agency or community program. 3. Pursue new hobbies or set new goals. 4. Get involved with campus or community organizations.

Circadian Rhythms

Circadian rhythms are the daily cycles or patterns of your body. They are tied to sleep, low energy times (slumps), medium energy times, and high energy times (peaks). Even though clocks work at a consistent rate on a twenty-four-hour cycle, your body does not. People have natural body cycles—times during the day when they are more alert and times when they are in a "slump." Being familiar with your own circadian rhythms is knowledge that can be put to good use when you begin to construct your weekly time-management schedule.

Many studies have been conducted on circadian rhythms. These studies show that most people fall into certain circadian rhythm patterns. However, no circadian rhythm pattern fits all people. Individual differences are involved and individual patterns occur that are a result of modifications imposed by other circumstances, such as a graveyard shift job. You very likely already have a sense of your circadian rhythms. Exercise 3.1 will examine your own cycle further. Once you know your patterns, you can try to arrange tasks on your time-management schedule so they are compatible with your "peaks" and "slumps."

✎ **EXERCISE 3.1 Discovering Your Peaks and Slumps**

The chart on the right shows typical hours of a day. Below is a list of activities. Decide when during the day you prefer to do each activity. Write the activity **number** *on the chart in the correct time slot. You may place an activity in more than one time slot.*

When would you prefer to

1. concentrate on memorizing
2. work on hard math problems
3. sit and relax
4. take a nap
5. do creative writing
6. do household chores
7. sit and talk with a friend
8. write a speech or plan a class presentation
9. exercise or work out
10. do easy review work
11. do problem-solving kinds of homework
12. type or copy notes
13. move around; too restless or sleepy to sit
14. eat
15. organize your notebook, notes, or study materials

5:00 A.M.– 7:00 A.M.
7:00 A.M.– 9:00 A.M.
9:00 A.M.–10:00 A.M.
10:00 A.M.–12:00 noon
12:00 noon–1:00 P.M.
1:00 P.M.– 3:00 P.M.
3:00 P.M.– 5:00 P.M.
5:00 P.M.– 7:00 P.M.
7:00 P.M.– 9:00 P.M.
9:00 P.M.–11:00 P.M.
11:00 P.M.– 1:00 A.M.

Looking for Patterns

Follow the directions below. Place a symbol on each number in the chart that you completed above.

On your chart, **STAR:**	**1, 2, 5, 8, 11**	These activities require peak alertness and concentration. These times are good times for you to do the "serious studying."
On your chart, **CIRCLE:**	**10, 12, 15**	These activities require a lower level of concentration.
On your chart, **BOX IN:**	**3, 4, 6, 7, 9, 13, 14**	These activities can be done without much concentration. These hours are your "slump" hours for studying; try to avoid putting study blocks at this time of day.

Now look for patterns in your time chart. If a time block has all stars or stars and circles, this could be an excellent study time block for you. If a time block has all boxes, this is not a good study time. If you have time blocks that have mixed symbols, these could still be used for effective studying IF you use concentration strategies that keep your mind focused and keep you away from the "other tendencies" you might have at that time.

For the Record

1. What are your best times for high concentration? _____

2. What are the times for medium concentration? _____

3. What are the times for low concentration? _____

4. Do you think you will be able to use the high concentration and medium concentration times for

   studying this term? _____ Explain:

✎ **EXERCISE 3.2   Estimating How You Spend Your Time**

Down the left-hand side of a sheet of your own notebook paper, make a list of all the general categories of activities you do in the course of an average week. For example, you might have these kinds of activities on your paper: fixing meals, shopping, kids' soccer, TV, talking on the phone, laundry, a hobby, family time, volunteer work, job, errands, church, classes, studying, sleeping, eating, household chores, yard work, fun reading, painting, bowling, listening to music, and so on.

After you have your list made, ESTIMATE the amount of hours you spend on each activity during the course of a week. When you finish, total up your hours; your total should be 168 hours for a week. Be careful not to count one activity in two different categories. Make a right-hand column. Write Good *if the amount of time spent in that area feels about right to you. Write* Too Much *or* Too Little *if those are your feelings. This information will help you see areas that need "balancing" or areas that have surplus time that could be transferred to an area that needs more time. Your paper should look like the drawing on the left.*

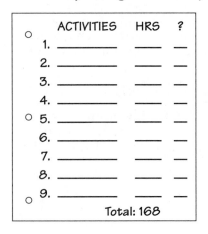

Using Goals of Time Management

The goal of time management is to become a more effective time manager. Knowing how to be a time manager will enable you to monitor and regulate your hours and your activities. Your schedule will be your guide to provide structure to your week, to help you make the best use of the hours in a day, and to help you achieve the goals that you value. Making a commitment to time management will result in less procrastination and more time for your friends, family, and leisure. Your life will have less stress and be more rewarding. You will have greater self-confidence and self-esteem. Yes, all that can really happen when you become *your own* time manager.

The following goals are valuable goals for time managers to use as they begin the process of planning their time.

Goals of Time Management

1. Strive for balance.
2. Create strong patterns in your schedule.
3. Include time for your goals.
4. Establish good health habits.

Strive for Balance

As you develop a weekly schedule for studying, check that you have included enough time for work/chores and leisure/social activities. Your schedule should show a commitment to important goals, such as school, but it should also reflect the need for social, recreation, and leisure time.

Create Patterns

Your schedule will be much easier if it follows consistent patterns. Instead of having each day of the week be different, you might try creating some similarities among the days. The following examples show several kinds of consistent patterns that make following a schedule easier:

1. Study for a specific class the same time each day or the same time on alternating days (MWFS).
2. Plan peak-energy times as study periods every day.
3. If you are on a Monday/Wednesday/Friday and a Tuesday/Thursday schedule for classes, try to have M/W/F look the same and T/TH look the same.
4. When possible, include similar time blocks each day for family, exercise, hobby, other goals, meals, and sleep.

Include Time for Your Goals

Whenever you make a time-management schedule, give some thought to your goals. List your goals for school; schedule sufficient time to better assure you will reach your goals. Also, pay attention to your personal goals and work/chores goals. Your commitment to your goals should be reflected in your schedule. Techniques for goal-setting are presented in Chapter 4.

Establish Good Health Habits

To keep your energy high and emotions positive, do not neglect your health. Remember to include time for health-related areas such as nutritional meals and adequate sleep. Plan to go to bed early enough each night so that you can get the amount of sleep you need. Schedule time to slow down, relax, and enjoy three nutritious meals. Plan time in your schedule for exercise. Adequate sleep, meals, and exercise all contribute to a healthier, well-functioning body.

Creating a Weekly Time-Management Schedule

Each Sunday spend a few minutes planning your schedule for the upcoming week. Keep this schedule in the front of your notebook. Refer to this schedule whenever you wish to make new plans or set up appointments. By using the following steps to create your **weekly schedule**, you can feel confident that you will have a more balanced weekly routine.

> ### Creating a Weekly Time-Management Schedule
>
> 1. Write in all your fixed activities.
> 2. Write in your fixed study times for each class.
> 3. Add several flexible study blocks.
> 4. Add times for specific goals and other responsibilities.
> 5. Schedule leisure, family, and social time.

Write in Fixed Activities

Fixed activities are activities that do not change from week to week or are special appointments that cannot easily be rescheduled. Class times, work, meetings, meals, and sleep are all fixed activities. Begin your weekly schedule by filling in all your fixed activities. Look at the time-management schedule shown on page 60 to see how fixed activities are written on a weekly schedule.

Add Fixed Study Times

Due to work schedules, family schedules, and other obligations you may have, finding sufficient time to study sometimes seems to be a difficult task to do. However, in learning about the memory principles of *time on task* and *ongoing review,* you understand the importance of planning a study schedule with **fixed study times** that allot enough time to complete the reading and writing assignments, create study tools, and use elaborative rehearsal and retrieval strategies.

The **2:1 ratio**, which recommends studying two hours for every one hour in class, is a sound planning formula for most classes. There are some classes that truly do not require use of the 2:1 ratio; there are other classes in which the 2:1 ratio will be too little. *If you choose not to use the 2:1 ratio for a specific class, you should be able to clearly justify your reasoning.* When you first begin using the 2:1 ratio, you may think the ratio gives you too many study hours per week. This is especially true if you interpret studying to mean "just get the reading or the homework done." However, as the term progresses, you will likely find that the 2:1 ratio does indeed provide the study hours needed to do well in the course. If you sit down to study and you have completed all the reading or all the written assignments, *use the time to review, review, review.* You can review the work you just finished, and you can review the work from previous weeks. Use the time for self-quizzing and to make personal study tools to use for later reviews.

Consider incorporating the following suggestions in your weekly time-management schedule when you start to schedule your study blocks.

1. Study during your alert times of the day whenever that is possible. Concentration is easier to achieve during these times, and you tend to be more task-oriented or productive.

2. Study your *hardest* or your *least-liked* subjects early in the day. Often the tendency is to delay studying for these classes until the end of the day when you are likely to be more tired and less interested or motivated.

3. If possible, study right *before* a class in which you are expected to discuss, debate, or participate, such as a foreign language class. Study right *after* a class in which you take a lot of lecture notes or have "problem sets" such as

math classes so that you can work with your notes or start on assignments while the information from class is still fresh in your mind.

4. Plan to study *one subject* for about a fifty-minute time block. If you study for a shorter amount of time, you don't have the advantage of getting very involved with the material. If you study for more than fifty minutes, your comprehension, concentration, and recall or retrieval abilities may begin fading. After fifty minutes, *take about a ten-minute break.*

5. Try to have at least one study block *every day of the week.* Balancing your Pie of Life is easier if there is some studying, some working, and some leisure time every day of the week. Spreading the studying blocks throughout the week, also known as **distributed practice**, promotes stronger memory and recall of the information you are studying.

6. Avoid **marathon studying**, which is also known as **massed practice**. Marathon studying refers to studying for more than three hours in a row. You will be more productive and effective if you study for two hours, even three hours, and then leave to do something else for an hour or two. When you are not studying, often times your mind is still working with the information and processing what you worked on earlier. There are a few circumstances, however, in which marathon studying may be effective. When you are involved in tasks that involve *creativity,* such as painting, constructing a model, or writing a research paper, it may be difficult to leave for a few hours and them come back and "step back" into the same level of creativity. So, if the creative juices are flowing, stay with the task.

With these suggestions in minds, you will need to give thought to available hours that can be designated as study blocks. *Label the study blocks* by identifying which class you will study in each study block. By designating study blocks for specific classes, you can verify that you have planned to use the 2:1 ratio and that you will be creating the habit of spending at least fifty minutes with one single subject. Look at the time-management schedule on page 60. Note how the study blocks are labeled and how they identify which class to study at that time.

Add Flexible Study Blocks

In addition to your regular study blocks, schedule a few study blocks that say "flex." These are safety nets to use in case you have an unexpected assignment or you have underestimated the amount of time needed to study. You can use this **flex time** as needed. If you do not need it for schoolwork, convert the flex-time into free time.

Note: Before scheduling goals, responsibilities, and leisure activities, all of which may vary each week, you may want to photocopy your schedule showing fixed activities, study blocks, and flextimes so you don't need to redo the first three steps each week when you make a new time-management schedule.

Add Time for Goals and Other Responsibilities

Schedule time to work on any goals you have that are not school related. If you have a goal to clean the garage, exercise three times a week, do leisure-time reading, and so forth, plan time to work on these goals. If you don't have time set aside, you will probably not find the time to work on these goals. If you have any other responsibilities, such as household chores, schedule time to complete these tasks. Your schedule can show specific times for the chores that you need to do.

Include Leisure/Family/ Social Time

You can schedule all the remaining time blocks for friends, family, and yourself. Write specific plans or events on your schedule. Having social and leisure time is important; if you do not have enough time on your schedule, look for ways to reduce other areas so that you can find a comfortable balance.

WEEKLY TIME-MANAGEMENT SCHEDULE

For the week of _____ *Oct. 10–15* _____

Time	Mon.	Tues.	Wed.	Thur.	Fri.	Sat.	Sun.
12– 6:00 A.M.							
6– 7:00 A.M.	←——————————————— SLEEP ———————————————→						SLEEP
7– 8:00 A.M.	←————————— WAKE UP, EAT, COMMUTE —————————→					SLEEP	EAT, GET READY
8– 9:00 A.M.	←——————————— STUDY PSYCHOLOGY ———————————→					LAUNDRY, HOUSE-CLEANING	
9–10:00 A.M.	PSY. CLASS	STUDY PSY.	PSY. CLASS	STUDY PSY.	PSY. CLASS		CHURCH
10–11:00 A.M.	COMPUTER CLASS	COMPUTER LAB	COMPUTER CLASS	COMPUTER LAB	COMPUTER CLASS		
11–12:00 NOON	←————————————————— LUNCH —————————————————→					FREE	BRUNCH
12– 1:00 P.M.	←——————————— ALGEBRA CLASS ———————————→					LUNCH	
1– 2:00 P.M.	STUDY ALGEBRA	P.E.	STUDY ALGEBRA	P.E.	STUDY ALGEBRA	FREE	
2– 3:00 P.M.	COMMUTE	CLASS		CLASS		FREE	GO FISHING
3– 4:00 P.M.	REVIEW ANTHRO.	HOOPS	FLEX	HOOPS	FLEX	FREE	
4– 5:00 P.M.	EARLY DINNER	←——————————— SHOOT HOOPS ———————————→				STUDY ALGEBRA	
5– 6:00 P.M.	COMMUTE	←————————————— DINNER —————————————→				FLEX	DINNER
6– 7:00 P.M.		←——————————— FAMILY TIME ———————————→				DINNER	STUDY ANTHRO.
7– 8:00 P.M.	ANTHRO. CLASS	TV		TV			
8– 9:00 P.M.			BOWLING LEAGUE				FLEX
9–10:00 P.M.	TV	STUDY ANTHRO.		STUDY ANTHRO.	SOCIAL TIME	SOCIAL TIME	PLAN WEEKLY SCHEDULE
10–11:00 P.M.	TV	SLEEP		SLEEP			SLEEP
11–12:00 A.M.	←————————————————— SLEEP —————————————————→						SLEEP

✏️ **EXERCISE 3.3 Discussing Key Features of a Weekly Time-Management Schedule**

Work with a partner or a small group to answer each of the following questions
about the weekly schedule shown on page 60.

1. One goal of time management is to create a lifestyle that has balance. Balance occurs when the three parts of the Pie of Life are balanced for the individual. Only that individual truly knows if the pie is balanced or not. However, a time-management schedule can be analyzed and general statements can be made about its effectiveness.

   Devise your own system for "counting hours." Decide how many hours on the weekly schedule are shown for each of the areas of the Pie of Life. Refer back to the Pie of Life chart on page 53 to see the types of activities that fit under each category.

   _____ hours for school   _____ hours for work   _____ hours for leisure
   Do you think this is an effective balance? _____ Why or why not?

2. Schedules are often easier to follow and to make habitual when they consist of some consistent patterns for the week. These patterns work as anchors to stabilize the other activities of the week. Identify at least five different patterns you see in the weekly schedule.

3. As a review, define the term **flexible study times:** _____

   _____

   How many flex times are on this weekly schedule? _____

4. Identify and list the classes this student is taking this term. Then count the total number of hours studying for each class. Write your findings below.

Classes	*Hours*	*Classes*	*Hours*
_____	_____	_____	_____
_____	_____	_____	_____

   Is the 2:1 ratio used for each class? _____ Explain.

✎ EXERCISE 3.4 Taking a Closer Look at the 2:1 Ratio

Select any one of your classes this term for this exercise. On your own paper, write today's date. After the date, briefly name or list ANYTHING that you did TODAY to study or prepare for the class that you selected for this exercise. If you did not do any work for the class this day and/or if you did not plan to do any work for the class this day, that is fine. Simply write the word Nothing. *Keep this log running for three full weeks. Remember each day to jot down quick notes to tell what you did for the selected class.*

At the end of three weeks, analyze your notes. Write a short reflection paper (a paper with your observations and reactions) about the amount of time spent for this selected class. Did you in fact use the 2:1 ratio? If not, why not? Did you need more hours or did you use fewer hours? Did you have enough time to do more than just the assignments? If yes, what type of elaborative rehearsal or study strategies did you use? (If you are developing a portfolio for this class, you could continue monitoring your work for this course for the rest of the term.)

✎ EXERCISE 3.5 Creating Your Weekly Schedules

A time-management form is on page 63. Make several copies of the form before you create your first weekly schedule. Follow each of the steps below. Work first in pencil as you may need to adjust the schedule before you are completely done.

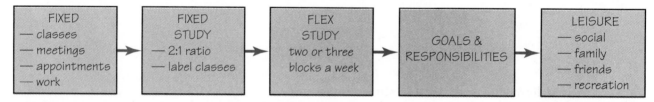

1. Mentally walk through each day on your schedule. Is your schedule realistic? Have you allotted enough time between activities so that they can happen on time? Have you allowed time for commuting? Have you included consistent patterns from day to day and week to week so that your schedule will be easy to learn? If you cannot "see" yourself getting through the day as you have it scheduled, adjust your schedule before you begin the week.

2. Use color-coding on your weekly schedule. Specific activities and the overall patterns on your schedule are more apparent when items are color-coded. Use a color-coding system that makes sense to you. You may want to use one color for all your leisure activities, one for your household chores, one for employment, one for time in class, and one for study blocks.

Experiment with a time-management schedule for three weeks. During the first week, record your successes of "staying on schedule." Place a star on the time blocks that were spent as you had planned. Circle the blocks of time during which you did not do what you had planned to do. At the end of the first week, look for times in which you did not stay on schedule. Figure out why this occurred. If you placed specific kinds of activities in time blocks that simply were not compatible with the task you planned to do, use this information to modify the schedule for the next week. Create a second and then a third time-management schedule. Each week you should see increased successes "living your schedule." Remember, to make time management work, it is important to make the commitment to be flexible and willing to try this new system. Three weeks is usually enough time to learn to use this system and to see the benefits it brings.

WEEKLY TIME-MANAGEMENT SCHEDULE

For the week of _____

Time	Monday	Tuesday	Wednesday	Thursday	Friday	Saturday	Sunday
12–6 A.M.							
6–7:00							
7–8:00							
8–9:00							
9–10:00							
10–11:00							
11–12 NOON							
12–1:00							
1–2:00							
2–3:00							
3–4:00							
4–5:00							
5–6:00							
6–7:00							
7–8:00							
8–9:00							
9–10:00							
10–11:00							
11–12 A.M.							

Weekly Time-Management Checklist

This checklist can be used by you or by someone else to evaluate your weekly time-management schedule and to strengthen it by adding any items that may have been overlooked. Write Y for Yes or N for No.

Study Blocks

_____ Do you have enough study blocks set aside to study for each class? (Use the 2:1 ratio when it is appropriate.)

_____ Do you specifically label "Study" and name the class?

_____ Are your study blocks spread throughout the week?

_____ Are you spending some time studying on the weekends?

_____ Do you avoid marathon studying so that you do not study more than three hours in a row?

_____ Do you avoid studying late at night?

_____ Do you include flextime in your schedule?

Fixed Activities

_____ Do you schedule time for three meals each day?

_____ Do you schedule sufficient time to sleep each night?

_____ Do you keep a fairly regular sleep schedule throughout the week?

Balancing Your Life

_____ Do you plan time specifically to spend with your family and friends?

_____ Do you plan time for exercise, hobbies, or special interests such as clubs, organizations, and recreational teams?

_____ Do you plan specific time to take care of household chores and errands?

_____ Do you plan time to work on specific goals?

Will the Schedule Work?

_____ Can you "walk through each day" in your mind and see that your schedule is realistic and possible?

_____ Are your peak energy times used wisely?

_____ Do you feel that your life will be more balanced if you follow what you have planned on your weekly schedule?

Other

_____ Have you used color codes in the schedule?

_____ Have you referred to the term-long calendar for special deadlines or events?

_____ Are you also using a daily planner or a To-Do List?

EXERCISE 3.6 Final Time-Management Project

Complete this assignment after you have developed and "lived" three weekly time-management schedules. Plan to turn in all three schedules with the answers to the following questions. Write the answers on your own paper. Include sufficient details in your answers to show how much you have learned or gained from this time-management chapter.

1. When we first started this chapter on time management, you were asked to draw your own Pie of Life (page 53). In the circle on the left, draw your original Pie of Life. Then in the circle on the right, draw your current Pie of Life to reflect how you spend your time NOW.

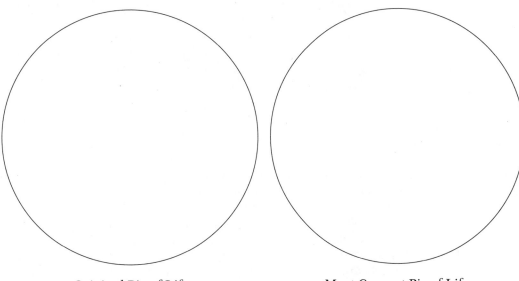

Original Pie of Life   Most Current Pie of Life

2. What changes have occurred in your Pie of Life? Are there differences between the two pies? If yes, which boundaries were shifted? How did you make those shifts? If there are no differences, is that the way you want it? If not, what changes still need to be made?

3. What times were the most difficult times to "stay on schedule"? Why do you think these times were difficult? Did you show improvement over the three weeks with staying on schedule during these difficult times? What still needs to be done?

4. Discuss the effectiveness of your study blocks. Did you use the 2:1 ratio? Was the ratio you used enough to do the assignments *and* review previous work? Did you ever need to use the flex blocks? Were you studying at your most alert times of day?

5. Discuss ways time management has affected your life and the people in your life.

6. Will you continue to create weekly time-management schedules and use them for the remainder of the term? Explain why or why not.

Using Other Time-Management Tips

Time-management is a highly prized skill in the work force and in the academic world. Learning to manage time effectively is a skill that will help you achieve goals, be productive, and achieve success in many different avenues of your life. The following tips help time management work even more effectively.

> ## Useful Time-Management Tips
>
> 1. Inform others of your time-management plans.
> 2. After three weeks with a schedule, use trading time to deal with unexpected events.
> 3. Use daily planners to list specific tasks for each day.
> 4. Each week, refer to your term-long calendar for specific deadlines or events.
> 5. Seek solutions to your individual scheduling conflicts.
> 6. Commit yourself to using time-management techniques for independent study courses, telecourses, and distance learning.

Inform Others of Your Plans

Family members, roommates, partners, or friends should be informed about your goals to organize your time more effectively. Members of your household are often more supportive if they are aware of your goals and priorities and see how you plan to allocate your time. Posting a copy of your schedule on the refrigerator door helps them know when you are available and when you have set special time aside just for them. Involving family members in the creation of your schedule each week can also add structure to the week and strengthen communication about activities and events that are important to include for each person. Developing a weekly schedule in their presence often becomes motivation and incentive for them to create a schedule as well.

Using Trading Time

At first your schedule may seem difficult to follow because it is new and may require a type of self-discipline that you have not used in the past. Try to use your schedule for at least three weeks.

After you have tried following your time-management schedule for three weeks, you can occasionally trade time. **Trading time** means that you can switch activities. For example, if an unexpected social event appears, but you had planned to study, look at your schedule for that day, choose another time that was scheduled for social or leisure, and trade times. By trading time, you are still able to meet the commitment of studying and enjoy the company of friends; the two activities simply exchange time slots. Trading time gives flexibility, but it must be used with caution. If you begin trading time too frequently, you will no longer have a schedule, and you will not be strengthening your self-discipline to say "no" to every appealing activity that comes your way.

Use Daily Planners

Many kinds of **daily planners** are available in your bookstore or local stationery store. If you wish to extend your time-management planning to include daily planning, select a daily planner that appeals to you. Before you go to bed each night, take a few minutes to make a list in your daily planner of the tasks or goals you need to accomplish the next day. This **To-Do List** can list specific tasks you plan to accomplish in each study block, but it does not need to be limited to study times. If you plan to do household chores or run errands, a prioritized list of chores or errands can be listed on your daily planner. Be as specific as you can so your day is well-planned and you begin the day organized and ready to go. If you do not want to purchase a daily planner, a To-Do List can be made just as easily on an index card or sheet of paper. See the example of the daily To-Do List on this page.

TO DO WED:

8–9:00 A.M.   Study Psy.
              Read & notes for
                pages 95–116

CLASSES—Regular schedule

1–3:00 P.M.   Study Algebra
              —Redo Ex. 6 #2–5
              —Do Ex. 7 odd numbers
              —Make study flashcards

3–5:00 P.M.   —Start laundry
              —Grocery shop
              —Read mail
              —Finish laundry

Refer to the Term-Long Calendar

The Quick Start Checklist at the beginning of this textbook encouraged you to create a term-long calendar (see the frontmatter). Each week when you make your weekly schedule, check this calendar for any special events or deadlines. When special assignments, projects, events, or appointments are scheduled, also remember to update your **term-long calendar**.

Seek Solutions

Some students find that their lives have specific circumstances that make creating a weekly time-management schedule difficult. Be resourceful and seek solutions to your scheduling conflicts. Discuss your circumstances with your teacher or with other students; frequently they will be able to suggest solutions. The following problems and solutions are ones commonly presented by students who are learning to create weekly time-management schedules.

1. *Rotating work schedules.* If your work schedule varies each week, you should not have a problem since you are developing a schedule each week. Write your work schedule first as a fixed activity. Adjust your study blocks and other goals and responsibilities around your work schedule.

2. *Different sleep–awake patterns.* Before you photocopy the weekly time-management schedules, block out the times that are shown in the left-hand column. Write in the times that will fit your awake hours. This is a common situation for people who work swing shifts or graveyard shifts.

3. *Young children at home.* Young children require and deserve your time and attention. Their schedules are important and you should accommodate them when you create your schedule. Consider changing your sleep

patterns by getting up earlier in the morning before they are awake. If your children attend child care, consider extending the child care an hour or two. Stay on campus to study during that time. Use all available time between classes to complete as much studying on campus before you leave so that more of your time at home can be devoted to your children's needs.

4. *Not on campus five days a week.* Students who attend classes only two or three days a week have the intention to study on the days they are not on campus, but many times they find they are not as productive as anticipated. Consider coming to campus even on days that you do not have classes. You will probably study more effectively and have access to instructors, tutors, the library, computer labs, and other resources. If you chose your classes so you could have two or three days off from school, next term consider registering for class on all five days of the week. The days at school for classes will be less intense and you will have more time and energy to prepare for classes if they are distributed more effectively over five days.

Use Techniques for Independent Classes

The same time-management techniques emphasized above also need to be used for independent study courses, telecourses, or distance learning courses. These courses, which do not have the structure of regular class meetings, demand a sincere commitment on your part to work with the course material on a regular basis. Many students initially like the idea of these types of courses; however, they soon find out how easy it is to procrastinate and to not have the course work finished in a timely manner or by the end of the term.

Strictly abiding by the time-management techniques already presented will result in completion of courses that require independent study. The first important technique is to use the 2:1 ratio for studying for distance learning and telecourses. Write the study blocks on your weekly schedule and adhere to the schedule. Also, commit to specific hours you will sit down to view the telecourse or distance learning lessons each week. This viewing time should be seen as "class time." Do not allow yourself to procrastinate or push the viewing time into a different time block. Treat this viewing time as if it were an actual class time, just as if you were preparing to participate in a class. If you are taking an independent course that does not use videos or online instruction but only requires that you read and learn the content of books on a reading list, use a 3:1 ratio. This 3:1 ratio compensates for the lack of actual class time. Be aware that "self-learning" many times is more difficult because you do not receive the steady feedback from class discussions, ideas are not clarified as they are in class, and you do not have a sense of whether or not you are learning the information seen as "the most important."

On your term-long calendar, write in the due dates for tests, papers, or projects. Refer to these deadlines when you make your weekly schedules. *You need to remind yourself of the deadlines so that you can pace your reading and studying accurately enough to meet the deadlines.*

One last recommendation is to "map out" or plan the whole term. Look at the course syllabus. If the syllabus doesn't give you "benchmark dates" to have specific parts of the course completed, make your own benchmarks. Break the assignments out by weeks. Write the weekly goals on your term-long calendar. Remember that you are assuming the role of both the planner (teacher) and the student; your planner/teacher role is to organize the materials chronologically and realistically so that you will be able to complete the course on time. Your student role is to commit the time, effort, and energy to learning the information through an independent approach. You will be required to demonstrate that you truly are an organized, responsible, and independent learner.

Web-site links are available online.

Computer Projects

1. Use a weekly planner program to create your weekly time-management schedule. Use color-coding or shading to indicate the categories of activities for the week.
2. Create a weekly or daily "To-Do List" form that you can use to prioritize the tasks that need to be done.
3. Complete Exercise 3.6 on the computer.
4. Use a monthly planner program or tables to create your term-long calendar on the computer.

Group Web-Search Activity is available online.

Case Studies are available online.

SUMMARY

■ Learning to become a time manager can reduce or eliminate worrying, procrastination, and cramming. Managing time also leads to greater self-discipline and a more balanced, enjoyable life.

■ The Pie of Life represents the three areas of life that need to be balanced: school, work, and leisure.

■ Being aware of your circadian rhythm (body's cycles) can assist you in planning activities that are compatible with your alert and "slump" times.

■ Creating balance, strong patterns, time for goals, and time for a healthy lifestyle are objectives of time management.

■ Sharing your time-management plans, trading time, and using daily planners and term-long calendars are valuable time-management tips to use.

■ You can organize your time by creating weekly time-management schedules.
  1. Write your fixed activities.
  2. Write fixed study times. Use the 2:1 ratio and follow the recommended strategies for studying.
  3. Add flex study times in case you need more time.
  4. Add time to work on specific goals, chores, or responsibilities.
  5. Schedule leisure, social, and family time.

■ Your level of commitment can be demonstrated by seeking solutions to problems and pacing yourself to complete independent study courses.

OPTIONS FOR PERSONALIZING CHAPTER 3

1. **PROFILE CHART—PERSONAL LOG**   Answer the following questions in your personal log.

    What score did you have on the Chapter 3 Profile? _____

    What skills from Chapter 3 do you plan to include in your studying system in order to strengthen your ability to be a time manager?

    Discuss your willingness or your resistance to becoming a time manager.

2. WORDS TO KNOW

Pie of Life	marathon studying
increase–decrease method	massed practice
circadian rhythms	flex time
weekly schedule	trading time
fixed activities	daily planners
fixed study times	To-Do List
2:1 ratio	term-long calendar
distributed practice	

3. **WRITING ASSIGNMENT 1**   Time-management skills are valued in many different careers and in the world of academics. Interview two or more people to learn the needs of time management in their fields of work. Ask them for specific time-management tips that they have found to be useful. Summarize the information you obtained from your interviews. In your summary paper, remember to identify the individuals and describe their fields of work. (Secretaries and support staff at your school may be used for the interviews.)

4. **WRITING ASSIGNMENT 2**   Since time management is such a highly-valued skill, many magazine articles have been written to provide readers with tips for using time more effectively. Use your library and electronic searches to locate an article in a magazine (periodical) that provides you with time-management strategies or tips. Locate the article and photocopy it. After you have read the article carefully, write a summary paper that summarizes its contents. You may be asked to share this information in class. If you have difficulty finding articles, you may use one of the following:

"193 Ways to Save Time," *Woman's Day,* Feb. 1, 1994
"30 Things You Can Do to Save Time Today," *Women in Business,* March/April, 1992
"Doing Too Much? 10 Sneaky Shortcuts," *McCalls,* May, 1993
"The Custom-Made Day Planner," *Inc.,* February, 1992
"Create More Time," *Parents,* March, 1993

5. **PORTFOLIO DEVELOPMENT**   Expand the Chapter 3 visual mapping on page 51. After you have expanded the mapping, write a summary paper using the mapping as your guide. In your summary paper, write the first paragraph or two about the first main heading on your mapping. Include the details for that heading in your summary. Continue to summarize each of the headings and the important details for each heading. This expansion of the visual mapping and the summary writing may be continued for additional chapters covered this term.

CHAPTER 3 REVIEW QUESTIONS

True-False

Carefully read the following sentences. Pay attention to key words.
Write T *if the statement is TRUE. Write* F *if the statement is FALSE.*

_____ 1. The three areas of the Pie of Life that need to be balanced are social, school, and leisure.

_____ 2. The 2:1 ratio refers to the number of hours you should attend class each week.

_____ 3. The purpose of the Increase-Decrease Method is to provide a more productive and rewarding balance for you in your Pie of Life.

_____ 4. Planning consistent times during the week for specific activities results in a schedule that is easier to follow because it contains structured patterns.

_____ 5. Trading time allows some flexibility and a method of dealing with special, unexpected events.

_____ 6. A well-planned time-management schedule includes time to review previously studied material.

_____ 7. Distributed practice is the practice of spreading study blocks at different times throughout the week.

_____ 8. Circadian rhythms exist mainly in people who have well-developed musical talents.

_____ 9. Massed practice is beneficial because it results in massive amounts of information covered quickly and efficiently.

_____ 10. When possible, it is best to schedule a study block right before a class that involves an hour of lecturing.

_____ 11. If you decide to use the daily planner method of time management, it is best not to use the weekly schedule system for planning your time.

_____ 12. Flex study blocks are "safety nets" because they provide you with reserve time to complete unfinished assignments or study a subject beyond the 2:1 ratio time that was planned.

_____ 13. It is acceptable to use marathon studying in situations that involve creativity.

_____ 14. Social or leisure time should be scheduled first on your time-management schedule because everyone needs to have time to relax and have fun.

_____ 15. If you finish your assignments before a fifty-minute study block is over, the remaining time should be spent getting started on the assignments for a different class.

Short Answer—Critical Thinking about Case Studies

Read each situation carefully. Answer the questions by providing specific details.

1. Bob and Molly are both taking a 10:00 A.M. college reading class on Monday, Wednesday, and Friday. Molly's fixed study times for this class are on Wednesday and Friday from 7:00 A.M. to 8:00 A.M. and from 10:00 A.M. to 3:00 P.M. on Saturday. Bob chose different fixed study times. He chose to study from 7:00 P.M. to 9:00 P.M. on Mondays, Wednesdays, and Sundays. Which schedule has the potential to be more effective? Give several reasons to support your answer.

2. Cindy always seems to be caught off-guard. She is surprised when she arrives in class and hears that a specific assignment is due that day. She seldom has her assignments done on time. Sometimes she doesn't remember them and other times she runs out of time. She prefers to do all her studying on the weekends, so when something is due in the middle of or at the end of the week, she never has it done. What suggestions could you give to Cindy so she could modify her approach to her assignments?

3. Raymond is frustrated by being in college. He is used to an active life that includes a variety of activities with his friends. None of his friends are going to college, so they just don't seem to understand. Raymond doesn't feel like he has time for the things he really loves doing. This frustration is affecting his overall attitude about school. What strategies could help Raymond?

4. Lydia is a night-owl. She is busy during the day taking classes and working thirty hours a week. She arrives home each day at four o'clock and tends to the needs of her three young children. By the time everyone is fed and tucked into bed, it is ten o'clock at night. Too many nights she finds herself falling asleep on her books. She is behind in all her classes and has no energy left for studying or for herself. How could Lydia use the Increase-Decrease Method to examine ways to solve some of these issues?

5. Michael and his sister are both college students, yet they are quite different in their approaches to school. Michael feels much more successful and in control when he plans and manages his time. His sister, on the other hand, believes she operates best under crisis even though she knows this often results in her throwing assignments together at the last minute. She claims she wants to be "free" and flexible because spontaneity is a part of her personality. What three benefits of time management could Michael use in his argument to convince his sister to try a schedule for three weeks?

Setting Goals

CHAPTER

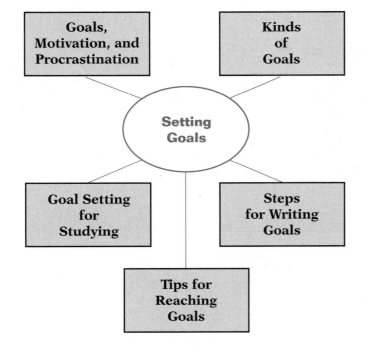

Goal setting involves a systematic plan designed to help you achieve a desired outcome or goal. Reaching goals involves more than just desire. Have you ever made a promise to yourself to reach a goal, but the goal was never reached? Have you ever started on a goal only to find yourself wander off course, run out of time, or lose interest in completing the goal? Do you find yourself frustrated by not getting the things done that you know need to get done? In this chapter, you will learn to use four basic steps for effective goal setting, which will result in completion of more goals plus a greater sense of accomplishment, control, and productivity.

CHAPTER 4   Goal Setting Profile

DO, SCORE, and **RECORD** your profile before you read this chapter. If you need to review the process, refer to the complete directions given in the Profile for Chapter 1 on page 2.

	YES	NO
1. I set goals for myself each week.	_____	_____
2. I write goals, but I leave the time lines open-ended so I can work on the goals when I have time.	_____	_____
3. It is difficult for me to know specifically what goals I want to reach.	_____	_____
4. I use visualization to see myself achieving the goals I really want to reach.	_____	_____
5. I break term-long assignments into smaller steps and set time lines for each step.	_____	_____
6. I have achieved many goals by using a goal-setting system.	_____	_____
7. I am a procrastinator about studying.	_____	_____
8. I am a procrastinator for tasks I don't want to do around the house.	_____	_____
9. I sometimes lack sufficient motivation to follow through on goals that I set.	_____	_____
10. I identify a reward for myself when I reach a goal, and I deny myself the reward if I don't reach the goal.	_____	_____
11. I always plan my goals in my head and don't feel a need to write them down.	_____	_____
12. I use a five-day plan to prepare for major tests or final exams.	_____	_____

Self-Awareness: Describe your attitude toward goal setting. Is this a process you are comfortable with and use, or is it a process you dislike for one or more reasons? Discuss your attitude and support it with details or examples.

_____

_____

_____

_____

_____

_____

_____

_____

_____

Goals, Motivation, and Procrastination

Goals are well-defined plans aimed at achieving a specific result. Students, teachers, athletes, and businesspeople commonly set goals. Successful goal setters:

1. Want to obtain specific results.
2. Design plans to help them reach goals.
3. Are willing to put effort into their plans.
4. Know when they have successfully accomplished a goal.

Motivation—the feeling, emotion, or desire that moves a person to take action—is a key to successful goal setting. Motivation helps you make changes, learn something new, perform at a higher level, and end procrastination. Motivation can also help you stick to a goal even when you feel frustrated or discouraged.

Procrastination is the process of putting something off until a later time, and it deters a person from accomplishing goals. Procrastination is a learned behavior that can be unlearned by replacing it with goal setting. Sometimes procrastination is a form of resistance or a way to avoid doing something that is not seen as pleasant, fun, meaningful, interesting, or essential. In such cases, an adjustment in attitude and recognition of the importance or purpose are required to move away from procrastination and into action. Sometimes the size or the complexity of a task is the reason for procrastination. Breaking the task into smaller, more manageable steps can move a person out of a rut and into action. Procrastination may also be related to the fear of failure. A normal reaction to learning something new is a concern about one's ability to succeed. Rather than fail, procrastinators choose to make excuses for not trying. A final cause of procrastination for some individuals is the result of living and reliving old patterns without having effective strategies for modifying behaviors and making changes. The goal-setting strategies in this chapter will replace procrastination, regardless of its origin, with productivity and accomplishments and provide a new, energized desire to take on new challenges and create new goals.

Kinds of Goals

Goals may be categorized in a variety of ways. In business and in athletics, **performance goals** are frequently used to identify a performance level to achieve. Reaching a specific sales level or enrolling a specific number of new members by a given date are examples of performance goals in business. Athletes may set performance goals to increase weight room performance by ten percent by a given date or to reach a specific time in a track and field or swimming event. Students may also set performance goals such as achieving a specific GPA each term or achieving a specific score on a test. **Task-oriented goals** narrow the focus to completing a task and all its steps by a specific date. Task-oriented goals may be written for everyday tasks that need to be completed or for specific assignments that must be completed by a given date.

Long-Term Goals

Goals also vary in length. Long-term goals, goals that require more than a year to complete, are based on a series of short-term goals that have been sequenced or linked together to accomplish the larger goal. When the individual steps are identified for a **long-term goal**, each step is given its own timeline for completion. Each step serves as a *benchmark,* a checking point to assess accomplishment or completion of the step. Long term goals can be overwhelming; breaking long-term goals into individual steps and working through the steps one at a time as short-term goals makes the process more manageable, instills confidence, and provides motivation to move to the next steps.

Short-Term Goals

Any goal that takes more than one week but less than one year to achieve is called a **short-term goal**. Goals to write a term paper on time, prepare for a mid-term or final exam, or complete a class project all vary in length but are referred to as short-term goals. Performance goals and task-oriented goals may be short-term goals. The goal-setting steps that are used for short-term goals are also the same steps used for immediate goals.

Immediate Goals

Goals that can be done in a few minutes, a day, or up to a week in time are referred to as **immediate goals**. These usually are task-oriented goals and are based on things that "must be done *now.*" Reading an assignment, completing a set of math problems, cleaning out the kitchen cupboards, painting a room, or tuning a car are examples of everyday immediate goals. Once the motivation and the planning steps are in place, immediate goals can be achieved in remarkably little time. Frequently, more time is spent procrastinating about doing immediate goals than is needed to complete the task!

✎ EXERCISE 4.1 Your Long-Term Academic Goal

On your own paper, discuss the following questions:

1. What is your long-term academic goal? What certificate or degree do you hope to obtain?

2. What, if any, skills do you need to acquire before you begin your degree program?

3. What are the requirements of your degree program? Locate a printed page of a catalog or obtain a brochure from the counseling department that shows the sequence of classes and requirements to complete your goal.

4. Do you predict the need to modify the program in any way? If yes, explain the foreseeable needs and discuss your plan of action to make these modifications.

5. Make a two- to five-year outline of the steps you will need to complete in order to reach your goal.

Steps for Writing Effective Goals

Many people have good intentions and a strong desire or motivation to achieve success by reaching goals; however, many of the same people are unable to make their goals a reality. Frequently the missing element is the lack of a process or a strategy. The following **four steps for writing effective goals** are to use with long-term, short-term, and immediate goals.

> ### Four Steps for Writing Effective Goals
>
> 1. Be **S**pecific, clear, and realistic.
> 2. Set a specific **T**arget date for achieving the goal.
> 3. Identify the individual **S**teps involved in reaching the goal.
> 4. Plan a **R**eward for yourself when you reach the goal.

Be Specific   When your goal is clear, specific, and realistic, you have an exact picture of what you wish to achieve. To simply say, "I will do better" or "I want something new" results in vague goals whose achievements are not easily measured. To say, "I will be a millionaire tomorrow" is not realistic for most people. Before you commit to a goal, evaluate if the goal is clear, specific, and realistic for you.

Set a Specific Target Date   Procrastinators (people who put off doing something) seldom achieve goals. You can reduce or eliminate procrastination by setting a specific target date (deadline) and even a specific time to finish the steps involved in reaching your goal. The target date works as a form of motivation to keep you moving forward and on time.

Identify Steps   Careful planning of the steps involved in achieving a goal makes it possible for you to allocate enough time for each step to complete it. Take time to think through the individual steps required. List these steps on paper. If several steps are involved, list specific target dates for completing each step. When you use this method of breaking one large goal into smaller ones, a goal that extends over a long period of time can be treated as a series of smaller goals to be accomplished on their own time lines.

Plan a Reward   You can celebrate the completion of a goal with a reward. You can also use that same reward as an incentive—a motivation—to meet your goal. There are two kinds of rewards you can include in your goal setting plan: extrinsic rewards and intrinsic rewards.

Extrinsic rewards are material things or activities that you will give yourself after you reach your goal. The following rewards are examples of extrinsic rewards: buy a tape, buy a new shirt, go to a movie, go out to dinner, plan a short trip.

Intrinsic rewards are the emotions or feelings you know you will experience when you reach a goal. Many people can be motivated just by recognizing that when the goal is reached they will enjoy feelings such as increased self-esteem, pride, relief, joy, higher confidence, or immense satisfaction.

A reward is a strong motivator only if you use it *after* you reach the goal. You must also withhold the reward if you don't reach the goal. For rewards to work as motivators, select rewards that truly represent what you *want* and can look forward to receiving.

Web-site links are available online.

Computer Projects

1. Create affirmation cards to place around your house and in your notebook. Use graphics, interesting fonts, and attractive borders for your affirmation cards.
2. Create a short form to use to set study-block goals each time you begin a study block.
3. Use a time-planner program to create a five-day study plan for your next test.
4. Use a flow chart or graphics program to expand the chapter mapping.
5. Use columns or tables to create a vocabulary study sheet for the important terms to know and their definitions.

Group Web-Search Activity is available online.

Case Studies are available online.

✎   **EXERCISE 4.2 Applying the Steps for an Immediate Goal**

This exercise will give you the opportunity to complete a small task that you would like to have done but have put off doing (repairing something, organizing your desk, washing windows, cleaning a closet, changing the oil in the car, weeding a garden, mending clothes, organizing a notebook, and so on). Complete each step below.

1. Name a specific, clear, and realistic goal.

2. Give a specific target date and time to have this goal completed.

3. Identify the individual steps that need to be done to complete the goal.

4. What will be your reward (intrinsic or extrinsic)?

5. After you have passed your target date, answer the following questions:
   Did you achieve the goal? Explain.

In what other kinds of situations could you apply these four steps for setting goals?

Tips for Reaching Goals

Have you ever started working toward a well-planned goal with great enthusiasm and conviction only to find yourself quitting before you reach the goal? Many distractions and options can become barriers for reaching goals. The following tips can help keep you motivated and get you back on track when you begin to encounter difficulties achieving your goals.

> **Tips for Reaching Goals**
>
> 1. Evaluate your goals from time to time.
> 2. Visualize yourself reaching your goals.
> 3. Make affirmations to strengthen your convictions.
> 4. Break larger goals into a series of smaller goals.
> 5. Ask for help, guidance, or suggestions when needed.
> 6. Tell your goals to others when this seems appropriate.

Evaluate Your Goals If you are having difficulty with a specific goal, examine whether it is still important or relevant. Goals can become outdated. If the goal is no longer of value to you, abandon it. Do not abandon a goal because it is more difficult than you thought it would be or because you feel frustrated or doubt your own ability to reach the goal. If you truly still desire the end results, do not throw the goal away; use the following techniques to help you continue to move toward your goal.

Visualize Your Goals **Visualizing** is the process of picturing or imagining information or events. Close your eyes and try visualizing yourself achieving your goal. How do you feel? How are others affected?

If you have great difficulty visualizing yourself achieving the goal, this particular goal may not be realistic or right for you. Ask yourself, Who actually set this goal? Why did I choose this goal in the first place? Am I trying to do this for myself or to please someone else? Is this really what I want? Again, if you can explain why this goal is no longer appropriate for you, abandon it.

Use Affirmations **Affirmations** are positive statements used as motivators. Many psychologists believe affirmations help change your basic belief systems and your self-image. When you write affirmations, use the following guidelines:

1. *Use positive words and tones.* Avoid using words such as *no, never, won't.* Say, for instance, "I complete my written work on time," not "I will never turn in a late paper again."

2. *Write in the present tense.* Present tense in verbs gives the sense that the behavior already exists. When you think and believe in the present tense, your actions begin to match your beliefs. Say, for example, "I am a nonsmoker," rather than "I will stop smoking soon."

3. *Write with certainty and conviction.* Say, for instance, "I exercise for thirty minutes every day," not "I want to exercise more each day."

4. *Keep the affirmation short and simple.* Brief, simple affirmations are easier to remember and repeat.

Break Large Goals Down Any time a goal seems too overwhelming, think about it as a series of individual steps. Focus on completing one step at a time. As you accomplish one step, motivation increases to begin on the next. This "chunking technique" is discussed further in Chapter 5.

Ask for Help You do not need to reinvent the wheel. If you have difficulties with part of your goal or feel stalled, seek help and information from knowledgeable people or books. Be resourceful; asking for advice is an effective shortcut.

Tell Your Goals to Others If there are some people in your life who would be supportive of your desire to reach a certain goal, tell them about it. They can help motivate and encourage you to stay on track.

✎ **Exercise 4.3 Discussing Goal Setting**

Work with a partner or in a small group to answer the following questions:

1. What was the last goal that you set and that you achieved? What motivated you to complete the goal?

2. What was the last goal that you set but did not achieve? Why do you think you did not achieve this goal?

3. Write the four steps for writing effective goals:

   a. _____

   b. _____

   c. _____

   d. _____

4. Can these steps be done in a different order and still bring success? Explain your answer.

Goal Setting for Studying

The four steps for goal setting can readily be applied to studying situations. In the first two goal-setting applications for studying, the goals are immediate goals and can be accomplished in one study block or within a five-day period. The third application is a short-term goal that may span over several weeks or over the entire term.

> ### Goal Setting for Studying
>
> 1. Set a study-block goal.
> 2. Set a goal for a five-day study plan to prepare for a major test.
> 3. Set a goal for a term project.

Study-Block Goal

Each time you begin a study block, take a minute or two to identify specifically what you need to do and what you want to accomplish for the fifty-minute study block. This is your **study-block goal**. Use the four steps for goal setting to plan your study time.

1. *Be specific and realistic.* What previous work do you want to review? If you are beginning a new chapter, how much of it do you want to preview? How many pages do you plan to read or to develop into notes or study tools? What problems or writing assignments must you complete? What review work do you want to accomplish? Taking the time to set your focus on what you want to achieve will eliminate wasted time in getting started and will provide you with the incentive to achieve your goal.

2. *Set a target time.* This is easy. In most cases, a target time will be the fifty-minute study block. If you do a back-to-back study block, it may be for a two-hour study block with a ten-minute break between the hours.

3. *What are the steps involved?* Refer to step one and prioritize the tasks. If the task will take the entire study block, you will have only one step to work through. If the task is shorter, you may have two or more steps to complete in the course of the fifty-minute study block.

4. *Decide on an intrinsic or extrinsic reward.* Doing something social with family or friends, having a snack or dessert, watching a favorite television program, listening to music, playing a guitar, or going for a run are examples of motivational extrinsic rewards that may await you upon completion of your study-block tasks. Feelings of confidence, productivity, relief, self-esteem, or preparedness are examples of intrinsic rewards that may also work as powerful motivators to complete a study-block goal.

Five-Day Study Plan

The goal of creating a **five-day study plan** prior to a major test or a final exam combats procrastination and the need to cram. This plan promotes distributed practice and review of the material for the test. Recall or retrieval of information will be higher, and the stress level prior to the test day will be lower. The four steps for writing effective goals, modified slightly for the five-day study plan are:

1. *Be specific and realistic.* Begin by making a list of all the topics that will be included on the test (chapters, classroom lectures, assignments, or projects). Group them into meaningful units or chapters for studying. Remember, you have only five days for this review process. If you have been using ongoing review all term, this review process can move smoothly and efficiently, for you will *not* be rereading entire chapters or reworking all the problems.

2. *Set a timeline.* Plan to use days one, two, three, and four for review of the above groupings of information. Day five should be reserved for a final review of special summary notes that have been compiled on days one through four. When you know you will need to create a five-day study plan to prepare for a test, include this information in the development of your weekly time schedule. These study blocks should be reserved for test preparation. They should not be used for other ongoing assignments. Your study-plan sheet may look like this:

Day 1:	Day 2:	Day 3:	Day 4:	Day 5:
(8–9:00 A.M. and 3–4:00 P.M.) Review Ch. 1	(8–10:00 A.M.) Review Ch. 2	(8–9:00 A.M. and 3–4:00 P.M.) Review Ch. 3–4	(8–10:00 A.M.) Ch. 5 and Review film notes	(7–9:00 P.M.) Review summary notes for all topics

3. *Identify the steps involved.* Now is the time to use the varied study skills you have learned to make review work interesting and personalized. Be specific. For each day and each set of chapters or topics, list your plan for review. You can list these steps or tasks on the study-plan sheet that is shown above.

Day five will be devoted entirely to reviewing the summary sheets or summary flash cards that you prepared during the study-plan days one through four. Notice how a vast amount of information has been reviewed and narrowed down to much more manageable and specific topics when this five-day plan is used.

4. *Plan a reward.* Allow yourself a little "down time" to relax, take in a movie, have a special dinner out, play tennis, or do something special that you were not able to do during the five-day plan. Extrinsic rewards at the end of a five-day plan often times are greater motivators than intrinsic rewards. However, the choice of rewards is yours.

Term-Project Goal

Some instructors assign a project at the beginning of the term that is not due until the middle or the end of the term. Many students get a false sense of time; rather than start right away, they begin the assignment too close to the due date. Unnecessary stress is added, plus study times for other classes often have to be neglected so that the project can be finished. As soon as you are assigned a term-long project, begin planning a schedule for that project. Use the following steps to create your **term-project goal**:

1. *Break the assignment into specific tasks.* What are the actual tasks you will need to work through from the beginning of the project to the end? Analyze the project carefully until you can identify all the individual tasks involved. List these steps on paper.

2. *Estimate the time needed for each task.* Estimate the number of hours you feel will be necessary to complete each task. Base this estimate on your past experiences with similar projects.

3. *Double the estimated time needed for each task.* You do not want to run out of time. To avoid any tendency to underestimate the amount of time you will need, double your estimate. In that way, you are giving yourself extra time in case you run into unforeseen problems or find that you have to change directions.

4. *Record due dates on a calendar for each task.* Use a calendar that covers the term. Consider the amount of hours needed for each task and the study-block times (and flextimes) you have available on your weekly schedules. Set a goal to complete each task by a specific date. Each week when you make your weekly schedule, check this term calendar. Add due dates for tasks to the weekly schedule, too.

   If you finish a task ahead of schedule, it is because you did not need the "doubled time" you allocated. Begin the next task immediately. If you finish your project ahead of schedule, you will have time to revise it again if you wish, and you will be able to breathe a sigh of relief!

5. *Begin right away.* Do not waste time procrastinating.

⛓ Exercise 4.4 LINKS

Explain the relationship between each pair of items in the following box.

Pair of Items	How These Two Items Are Related
goal setting and time management	
time management and procrastination	
procrastination and motivation	
motivation and goal setting	

SUMMARY

- Goals are well-defined plans to achieve a result. Motivation is a key to successful goal setting.

- Procrastination is a learned behavior that can be unlearned by using goal setting.

- Goals can be set for various periods of time (a few minutes up to five years). Long-term goals, short-term goals, and immediate goals are defined by the length of time to reach the goal.

- An effective goal-setting strategy involves four steps: (1) identify a specific goal, (2) identify a target date, (3) identify the steps involved, and (4) establish a reward for yourself.

- Rewards used upon completion of a goal may be intrinsic or extrinsic.

- Tips such as evaluating goals, visualizing, making affirmations, or breaking large goals into smaller steps assist you in reaching your goals.

- Goal setting may be used to establish a set of goals for each study block.

- Goal setting can be used to create a five-day plan to prepare for major tests.

- Goal setting can be used to plan a term-long project so that it will be completed early or on time.

OPTIONS FOR PERSONALIZING CHAPTER 4

1. **PROFILE CHART—PERSONAL LOG**   Answer the following questions in your personal log:

   What score did you have on the Chapter 4 Profile? _____

   What information in this chapter on goal setting was new or of special interest to you? Explain.

   How do you plan to implement the techniques presented in this chapter?

2. **WORDS TO KNOW**

goals	four steps for writing effective goals
motivation	extrinsic rewards
procrastination	intrinsic rewards
performance goals	visualizing
task-oriented goals	affirmations
long-term goal	study-block goal
short-term goal	five-day study plan
immediate goals	term-project goal

3. **EXPAND THE VISUAL MAPPING FOR THE CHAPTER**   On your own paper or on the introductory page of this chapter, expand the chapter visual mapping by adding details that include the subheadings and other important details for the main chapter headings (shown in boxes). You may personalize your mapping by adding colors and pictures.

4. **WRITING ASSIGNMENT 1**   Use your library to conduct an electronic search of magazine articles about goal setting. Locate an article, photocopy it, and read it carefully. Write a summary of the article that tells your reader the main points or highlights of the article. You may be asked to present the information in class.

5. **WRITING ASSIGNMENT 2**   Reflect on at least three different times that you set goals but things happened that "prevented" you from reaching the goals. Discuss each situation. Examine ways you could possibly have dealt with the barriers that existed so that you could have reached the goals. Apply the strategies that you learned in this chapter.

6. **PORTFOLIO DEVELOPMENT**   Choose *one* of the following options:

   Option A: Make specific goals at the beginning of *all your study blocks for one week.* These goals do not need to be highly detailed. At the end of each study block, discuss the success or lack of success in reaching the goals. Discuss the reward system you used. Turn in all your goal sheets along with a summary page about the effectiveness of this approach to study-block goals.

   Option B: Use the five-day plan prior to your next major test. Save and organize all the planning charts and summary notes that you made as part of this five-day plan. Include a summary page that explains your process and discusses its effectiveness or ineffectiveness. On your paper, be sure to identify the name of the course and the instructor that you prepared this five-day plan for.

CHAPTER 4 REVIEW QUESTIONS

Multiple-Choice

Choose the best answer *for each of the following questions. Write the letter of the best answer on the line.*

_____ 1. Both motivation and procrastination
   a. can influence whether or not a person successfully completes a goal.
   b. are feelings that move a person closer to achieving a goal.
   c. can be accomplished by using the four steps to goal setting.
   d. all of the above.

_____ 2. Goals involving term-long projects
   a. use basically the same steps as short-term projects or immediate goals.
   b. expand the target-time step by suggesting the estimated time be doubled.
   c. encourage the use of a term-long calendar for planning.
   d. all of the above.

_____ 3. Goals that seem too large, intimidating, or overwhelming
   a. should be put aside until you have more time.
   b. can be broken into small steps so each step can become a goal.
   c. should be extended over more time so they fit your schedule better.
   d. all of the above.

_____ 4. The steps for writing goals are
   a. self-motivation, time, steps, and review.
   b. short-term, tell, self-motivation, and reward.
   c. specific, time line, steps, and reward.
   d. start, take action, use self-talk, get results.

_____ 5. Which of the following is an example of a well-written goal?
   a. I will clean out the drawers of my desk next week.
   b. I will try to find someone to help me change the spark plugs in my car this weekend.
   c. I will put dividers in all three notebooks and organize all my notes by noon on Sunday.
   d. I hope to find time to pay my bills no later than Friday night.

_____ 6. Which of the following is an example of a well-written affirmation?
   a. I am very capable of understanding the chemistry lectures.
   b. I want to eat less fats and sweets so I can lose more weight.
   c. I have studied and hope I don't blow the test.
   d. I won't miss any more classes.

Short Answer—Critical Thinking

Complete the following chart. In the left column, identify the four steps of goal setting in order. *In the middle column, write the* advantages or benefits *you gain by doing each step. In the last column, discuss the possible* outcomes *or nega-tive results that might occur if you skip using this step in your goal planning.*

Steps	Benefits by Doing	Outcomes If Omitted

Improving Your Concentration

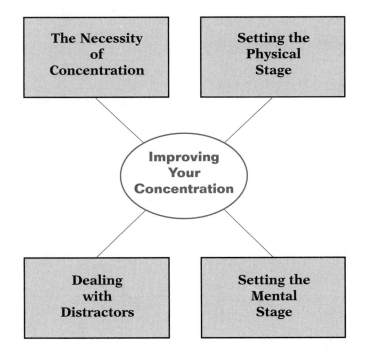

The Necessity of Concentration

Setting the Physical Stage

Improving Your Concentration

Dealing with Distractors

Setting the Mental Stage

Concentration is a mental process of directing your thoughts to one subject or issue at a time. Does your mind wander when you read textbooks or listen to lectures? Can your concentration be easily broken by people, things, or events around you? Do you waste precious study time trying to start concentrating? Is your attention span short? This chapter helps you train and discipline your mind so that your level of concentration and the length of your attention span can be increased to produce better results.

CHAPTER 5 Concentration Profile

DO, SCORE, and **RECORD** your profile before you read this chapter. If you need to review the process, refer to the complete directions given in the Profile for Chapter 1 on page 2.

		YES	NO
1.	I study in a location that has two or more sources of lighting.	____	____
2.	I often feel tense and unable to relax.	____	____
3.	My study area is often cluttered or disorganized.	____	____
4.	I am able to picture myself successfully concentrating while I study.	____	____
5.	I have all the necessary supplies readily available at my place of study at home.	____	____
6.	I know what distracts me, and I use techniques to reduce distractions.	____	____
7.	I use a system to let others know when I do not want to be interrupted or disturbed.	____	____
8.	Concentration for a fifty-minute study block is often difficult for me.	____	____
9.	I know how to use positive self-talk.	____	____
10.	I am often distracted by thoughts of tasks that I feel I have to get done.	____	____
11.	When I feel overwhelmed, I break large tasks down into smaller, meaningful units.	____	____
12.	I turn on the radio, the television, or the stereo when I study.	____	____

Self-Awareness: How do you feel about your current ability to concentrate when you are studying? What methods do you use to block out distractions?

_____

_____

_____

_____

_____

_____

_____

_____

_____

The Necessity of Concentration

Concentration is the ability to focus the mind on one item or task. Concentration is a flighty process; you can concentrate one minute and lose that concentration the very next second. Concentration is a mental discipline that is essential for good studying. It is so important that it is one of the memory principles that help move information more readily through the information processing model.

The focus of this chapter is on strengthening your ability to concentrate while you are studying. When you have difficulty concentrating while you are reading or studying, identifying the source of your poor concentration is one way to begin the process of strengthening your ability to keep your mind focused. Common sources of poor concentration may be stress, worries, lack of interest or motivation, or the presence of disrupting influences in the environment in which you are trying to concentrate. Once you identify the sources as internal or external, you can begin to use concentration strategies to remove the barriers to concentration.

Setting the Physical Stage

Careful attention should be given to the place you choose for studying because your physical environment can directly affect your ability to concentrate. The **ideal study area**, whether at school or at home, has few or no distractions to break your concentration. Begin your search for an ideal study area at school or at home that has as many of the following qualities as possible.

The Ideal Physical Stage

1. The noise level is appropriate for concentration.
2. The table and the chair are a comfortable size.
3. The work surface and surrounding walls are uncluttered.
4. Two or more sources of lighting are present.
5. Necessary supplies are readily available.

Noise Level

Studying, comprehending, and thinking critically are activities based on thought processes. A physical environment filled with noise conflicts with thought processes; concentration is easily disrupted.

How much noise is acceptable without being distracting? The level of tolerable noise varies from person to person. People with attention span deficits often need a very quiet and motionless environment. Individuals with fairly strong concentration skills are able to stay completely focused even with minor noises or movement in their physical environment.

Many students do not consider music to be noise; however, music that contains words or frequent variations in rhythm does interrupt the brain's thought processes and wave patterns. For students who "need" to have music playing while studying, there's a solution. Research has shown that certain kinds of music actually promote a state of relaxation and receptivity to learning new information. Soft, classical music and instrumentals without words (especially Baroque music) are conducive to learning; brain wave patterns (alpha waves) are positively altered to assist the learning process. You can experiment with this by checking classical or Baroque tapes out of your library or by purchasing them in a music store.

While there is a solution for music, there is no solution for television. Turning the television on while studying for many students is a matter of habit. The visual and verbal effects of the television force the brain to tune in, tune out, tune in, tune out to the point that you do not truly retain the entire content of either the television program or what you are reading or studying. A better alternative is to save television as an extrinsic reward to enjoy fully after studying has been completed.

When you are selecting a place to study, begin by considering the amount of noise (and movement) present. On campus, look in the library, lab areas, student areas, or even empty classrooms to find a suitable location for studying. Reserve the lounges, lawns, cafeterias, and coffee shops for relaxation, coffee breaks, and socializing. Seldom do these locations have the qualities of an ideal place to concentrate and study.

Furniture

A cozy couch, an overstuffed chair, or a bed is not conducive to effective studying; they tend to be too comfortable and induce naps. In addition, holding a book, taking notes, or writing papers is extremely awkward, if not impossible, with this furniture. Studying is work, and it requires an appropriate work environment. The starting point is a supportive chair, a table or a desk with an adequate work surface, and enough room to spread out your books, notebook, paper, and necessary supplies.

If you are studying at home, use a table or desk reserved only for studying, if possible. Each time you sit down at this table or desk, your mind associates the location (the table) with the task (concentrating to learn). If you are using a kitchen table or area that serves dual purposes, remove all the items unrelated to studying. This breaks the association with that location and its other purpose (for example, a kitchen table associated with meals). You will spend many hours in your study area, so give careful consideration to its location and organization.

Few Surrounding Distractions

Clutter on your work surface or on the walls surrounding you can easily become distractions. Interesting pictures, objects, a stack of someone else's materials, or a pile of bills can send your mind in a whole new direction. Remove unrelated items, and select places that have limited visual stimuli.

Two or More Sources of Light

Proper lighting is important in any study area. If you have too little light, your eyes can easily become strained and tired. Some lighting can create shadows or glare on your books. To avoid many of the problems created by poor lighting, have two sources of light in your study area. This may include an overhead light and a desk lamp or two lamps in different locations. Two sources of lighting may seem like a minor detail, but sometimes ignoring small details leads to big problems.

Necessary Supplies

Having all the necessary supplies with you when you study at school is often difficult. However, think ahead and plan to have basic supplies with you.

At home, you can give more attention to equipping your study area with necessary supplies; you do not want to interrupt your schoolwork to look for these supplies. Organize your study area at home by using file folders for important papers and small boxes or trays for other useful items.

✎ **Exercise 5.1   Creating Your Perfect Study Area**

*Use your own paper to expand the following chart with details related to your
current study area at home. Describe the current physical environment; then
identify ways it could be improved.*

	Currently Exists	**How Could This Be Improved?**
Noise		
Furniture		
Desk/Walls		
Lighting		
Supplies		

Setting the Mental Stage

After you have set the physical stage for concentration, you can turn your attention to setting the **mental stage**. Since concentration is a mental process, you have to let the mind know that it is time to begin serious work. Your attitude and intent should be firmly established at the beginning of your study block. Your mind and body should be in a relaxed state, open and ready to receive new information to process. The following techniques can help you achieve the ideal mental stage conducive to successful learning.

The Ideal Mental Stage

1. Monitor and reduce your stress levels.
2. Create a positive mental attitude.
3. Create a mindset ready for studying.

Monitor and Reduce Stress Levels

Concentration is difficult to achieve if your body is tense and your mind tends to jump from one subject to another. Identify the sources of stress. Are they related to school, work, family, finances, relationships, or the future? How can you be resourceful and pro-active to reduce or eliminate the sources of stress? Many colleges have classes for stress reduction; counselors may also be available to help you deal with the problems or situations. An abundance of books and stress management tapes are also available at most bookstores.

A small amount of stress is normal, and at times it is even beneficial. Stress that is under control can provide you with the incentive to succeed, the motivation to work hard, and the adrenaline to move forward and persevere. However, when you sense your stress level is out of control, take the responsibility to seek out solutions. Seek the help of counselors and learn to use relaxation techniques and other stress reduction techniques to get your stress level under control and working *for* you rather than *against* you.

The following warning signs are common signs that you need to seek ways to reduce your stress level. Monitor yourself by being aware of the presence of some of these warning signs.

_____ irritability		_____ loss of appetite	
_____ digestive problems		_____ increased use of alcohol, drugs, smoking	
_____ urge to fight			
_____ lack of motivation		_____ loneliness	
_____ tense muscles		_____ mood swings	
_____ obsessive worrying		_____ fatigue	
_____ headaches		_____ depression	
_____ sleep problems		_____ anger, self-pity	
_____ urge to flee		_____ suicidal thoughts	

Relaxation techniques can be used effectively to reduce stress levels. The goal behind relaxation techniques is to create a state of mind and body that perhaps can best be described as "Ahhhhhh." In this state, the body is not tense and the mind is not wandering; you are open and ready to receive new information or expand upon previously learned information. Relaxation techniques are effective with a wide variety of emotional situations: when you feel anxious, nervous, tense, stressed, apprehensive, hyperactive, restless, defeated, frustrated, or overwhelmed.

The following relaxation techniques are easy to learn and require only a few minutes of your time:

1. *Soothing Mask*   Close your eyes. Place your hands on the top of your head. Slowly move your hands down your forehead, down your face, and to your neck. As you do this, picture your hands gently pulling a **soothing mask** over your face. This mask removes other thoughts, worries, fears, or stresses from your mind. Keep your eyes closed for another minute. Feel the soothing mask resting on your face. Block out thoughts or feelings that are not related to your soothing mask. As you practice this technique, you will be able to do it without using your hands. Your imagination can take you through the same process of pulling the mask over your face.

2. *Relaxation Blanket*   Sit comfortably in your chair. Close your eyes. Focus your attention on your feet. Imagine yourself pulling a soft, warm blanket up over your feet. Continue to pull this blanket up over your legs, lap, and chest until the blanket is snuggled around your shoulders and against your neck. Feel how your body is more relaxed now that it is covered with the blanket. This **relaxation blanket** feels as if it is a security blanket keeping you warm, confident, and comfortable. Keep your eyes closed for another minute as you enjoy the warmth and comfort of the blanket.

3. *Breathing by Threes*   This technique can be used with your eyes opened or closed. Inhale slowly through your nose as you count to three. Gently hold your breath as you count to three. Exhale slowly through your nose as you count to three. Repeat this several times. Often you can feel your body begin to slow down and relax when you are **breathing by threes**.

4. *Deep Breathing*   Take a deep breath to fill your lungs. You may think your lungs are full, but there's room for one more breath of air. Inhale once again. Now slowly exhale and feel your body relax. Repeat this **deep breathing** several times. If you feel lightheaded or dizzy after trying this exercise, you may want to select one of the other options.

5. *Perfect Place*   This technique combines breathing with your imagination. Breathe in slowly. As you breathe in, start creating a **perfect place** in the world where you feel relaxed, confident, safe, happy, and comfortable. Breathe out slowly and keep imagining this perfect place. Continue the process of breathing and imagining for a few minutes. The goal of the technique is to get your emotions relaxed and your mind in a positive state. When you have achieved that goal, whisper a friendly "farewell" to your safe place ("later," "thanks," or "bye"). Now that your mind is in a calm state, you are ready to begin working.

6. *Deep Muscle Relaxation*   Stress is often felt in one or more of these muscle groups: shoulders, arms, lower back, legs, chest, fingers, or face. Take a minute to notice the amount of tension you feel in the various locations throughout your body. Then make a clenched fist tight enough that you can feel your fingers pulsating. Breathe several times and feel the tension in your fingers and your hands. Then breathe slowly and uncurl your fists until they are totally relaxed. Pay close attention to the different sensations as you go from tense to relaxed. Continue this with other muscle groups of your body. Let the feelings of **deep muscle relaxation** and the feelings that the tension is washing away spread throughout your body. Feel the difference!

Create a Positive Mental Attitude

Negative emotions hinder the learning process and become a source of procrastination. The attitude you hold toward any task can affect the outcome. Trying to study with a negative attitude is self-defeating. An ideal mental state requires a positive attitude, which at times may require an "attitude adjustment" before you begin the process of studying. Three techniques can be used to create this positive attitude:

Emotional *E* Words   Many motivational words begin with the letter *e: effort, enthusiasm, excitement, energy, eagerness,* and *effectiveness.* Reminding yourself of these **emotional *E* words** can refocus your mind and adjust your attitude to bring you more productive results.

Positive Self-Talk and Affirmations   Self-talk, the little comments you say to yourself quietly, can be positive or negative. When you hear yourself using negative talk about yourself, quickly turn the statements around so you give yourself positive self-talk. A statement such as, "I know I am going to fail this test," can be turned into a positive statement: "I am ready to do well on this test." **Positive self-talk** involves statements that show optimism, confidence, determination, and a sense of control. A personal goal you may want to set is to use positive statements frequently, not just when you need to counteract a negative statement. Chapter 4 discussed **affirmations**, short positive statements that are repeated frequently to alter your belief systems. Consistent use of affirmations reduces the frequency of the use of negative self-talk.

Seeing Success   Visualizing involves using your imagination to create a picture in your mind. **Seeing success** involves visualizing yourself working on a task with complete success. Picture yourself working at your desk, reading your textbooks, and comprehending what you are reading. Picture yourself in total control of the learning process, concentrating without distractions, memorizing, reciting, and remembering what you are studying. Visualizing yourself as successful moves you along the path of achieving your vision.

Create a Mindset for Studying

Many demands are made on our minds. Creating a mindset for studying shifts the focus of the mind from daily events, activities, and entertainment to the more serious task of mental discipline that is required for studying. The following three strategies create a strong mindset for shutting out the other aspects of your life and concentrating on the tasks at hand:

Create Study-Block Goals   Time is saved and motivation is higher when **study-block goals** are clearly identified. Take a few minutes at the beginning of your study block to identify the tasks that need to be done and the time line that is available. Prioritize the tasks so you begin with the most pressing or most important. Then plan an intrinsic or extrinsic reward for yourself. Refer to Chapter 4 to review goal-setting strategies.

Do Warm-Ups to Get Started   *Reviewing* and *previewing*, referred to as **warm-ups** for studying, can be used effectively to begin your concentrated studying. These activities create a "mindset" and ease you into thinking about the topic you are to study. *Reviewing* involves returning to information you have already studied. Look over your last set of class notes. Glance through homework that was returned. Look at the summary or review work from the last chapter. *Previewing* involves skimming or looking through the new information you are planning to learn. If you are going to read a new chapter, glance at the content of the entire chapter first. (This process of surveying will be covered in Chapter 6.) If you are going to work on a writing assignment, glance over the entire assignment and the directions or notes from class. Even though reviewing and previewing activities last only five or ten minutes, they are important strategies that help you shift your mind into the study mode.

Create a Study Ritual or Routine   The mental stage for effective learning may also include establishing a personal **routine or ritual** to use each time you sit down to study. Once the routine is habitual, you can save time and confusion by getting started quickly and getting your mind in the conducive mindset for studying. Your routine should not require much time. For example, first you could do a short relaxation technique, then identify your goals for that study block, visualize yourself working through the goals successfully, then do some warm-ups with the material. You may vary the steps of your ritual; the important point is that you create a personal ritual that signals you are ready to focus on the task at hand.

✎ **EXERCISE 5.2 Discussing External and Internal Distractors**

EXTERNAL	INTERNAL
_____	_____
_____	_____
_____	_____
_____	_____

Work in a group with three or four people. On your own paper, write the names of the people in your group.

1. List as many external distractors as you can. If you run out of ideas, think of a time when you were trying very hard to concentrate but "things" going on around you broke your concentration. Add these distractors to your list.

2. List as many internal distractors as you can. If you run out of ideas, think of a time when you were studying alone, but you just couldn't concentrate because of things going on "inside you." Add these distractors to your list.

3. Circle all the distractors on your lists that frequently break your concentration. These are your personal distractors. As you work through this chapter, pay extra close attention to techniques that can help you control or eliminate your personal distractors.

Dealing with Distractors

Distractions (also called *distractors*) are any occurrences that break your concentration. **External distractors** are caused by things around you (noises, people, television, weather). **Internal distractors** are disruptions that occur within you (daydreams, worries, depression, sickness, hunger, any other emotions). The first step in improving your concentration is to recognize your own common distractors.

Techniques for Reducing External Distractors

Distractions caused by elements in the environment can destroy the opportunity to stay focused on any task at hand. When the task involves mental processes and critical thinking, external distractions can leave you feeling like nothing was learned, little was accomplished, and your study time was wasted. The following techniques can help you deal with external distractors:

Techniques for Dealing with External Distractors

Technique	How It Works
Physical Stage	Use the techniques previously described for establishing an ideal **physical stage** conducive to studying.
Red-Bow	Place a large **red bow** (or any item that serves as a signal) on your door when you are studying. This signals to people in your home that you need privacy and want to work without being disrupted.
Take-Charge	When the people or the environment around you are too disruptive and outside of your control, **take charge** and move to another location or remove the distractor when possible. You can take charge by refusing to answer the phone, by refusing to turn on the television, and by refusing to blame others for your inability to concentrate in a specific location.
Say-No	Family and friends may frequently ask you to participate in activities at times when you planned to study. Keep focusing on your priority and telling them "no." Let them know other times when you are available to join them. This same kind of assertiveness and ability to **say no** can be used to tell yourself "no" to distractors such as snacking, television, or using the phone.
No-Need	Concentration is often interrupted by giving attention to minor noises in the environment even when you know the source of the noise. Train yourself not to give attention to minor movements or noises around you that are familiar. Keep your eyes on your work, and tell yourself that there is "**no need**" to look up; quickly get your mind back on task.
Checkmark	Each time you lose concentration, make a **checkmark** on a "score card" placed on your desk. At the end of the study block, count the number of checks you received. Set a goal each time you sit down to study to reduce the number of checkmarks or distractions that occur.

Techniques for Reducing Internal Distractors

For many students, internal distractors cause more challenges and frustrations than external distractors. Internal distractors can relate to negative emotions: stress, worries, anger, self-doubt, anxiety, low self-esteem, procrastination, nervousness, boredom, fears, and more. They can also, however, stem from positive emotions: anticipation of an upcoming event, falling in love, daydreaming, or remembering a special time. Some internal distractions are linked to a physical condition: sickness, fatigue, pain, insomnia, addiction recovery, side effects of medication, or feeling cold, hot, or hungry. If you experience low concentration that may be related to your physical condition, visit a physician to discuss your situation and seek medical assistance or advice. The following techniques can effectively be used to help you reduce or eliminate the effects of internal distractors that occur while you attempt to study.

Techniques for Dealing with Internal Distractors

Technique	How It Works
Mental Stage	Monitor and reduce your stress levels and use emotional *E* words, positive self-talk, affirmations, seeing success, goal setting, warm-ups, and study rituals that were previously discussed for establishing an ideal mental stage.
Mental Storage Box	Before you begin studying, identify any concerns, worries, or emotions that might interrupt your concentration. Place them inside an imaginary box. Put the cover on the box and mentally shove the box aside for the time being. Your internal distractors are safely put in the **mental storage box** until you find a more appropriate time to deal with the issues.
Tunnel Vision	Picture yourself at the beginning of a tunnel that has a yellow line running right down the middle. You want to walk on the line down the middle of the road so you don't bump against the walls. As soon as your mind begins to wander, flash the picture of the tunnel in your mind and tell yourself to get back to the middle line. Picture yourself quickly bringing a halt to the wandering mind by getting it back on course and moving in the right direction. This is **tunnel vision**.
To-Do List	Make a **To-Do List** of chores, responsibilities, or tasks that you keep thinking about because you feel you need to get them done. Once the list is made, it is easier to put it "out of your mind" for the time being. When you finish studying, set a time to deal with the items on your list.
Chunking	Analyze the task that needs to be done and break it into smaller units. **Chunking**, which was mentioned in Chapter 4, can be used to combat the feelings of being overwhelmed, panicky, or frustrated. Smaller tasks can be seen as smaller goals; as each small step is completed, confidence builds and the self-doubts or negative feelings diminish.
Checkmark	The same checkmark technique used for external distractors can be used successfully for internal distractors. Strive to reduce or eliminate the number of checkmarks (which means the number of times your mind wanders due to internal reasons).

Active Learning	**Active learning** (the opposite of passive learning) means you are actively involved in the learning process. Many internal distractors such as feeling sleepy, bored, uninterested, or unmotivated can be combated by becoming more of a participant in the learning process. Rather than reading without remembering what you have read, or working in a mechanical way, active learning promotes critical thinking, multi-sensory learning, and greater comprehension. All of the following learning strategies are activities used by active learners: 1. Have a pen in your hand when you study. Take notes, write questions, or jot down lists of information you need to learn. 2. Make flash cards to work on the vocabulary in each chapter. 3. Talk out loud (recite) as you study to activate your auditory channel and improve both concentration and comprehension. 4. Use markers to highlight important information in the textbook or in your notes. 5. Write summaries or make other kinds of study tools such as visual mappings, hierarchies, time lines, or comparison charts. 6. Quiz yourself on the material you are studying. Write or recite questions and answers.
Relaxation Strategies	Relaxation techniques can be used to reduce many internal distractors and to create the state of mind most conducive for learning. Use the **relaxation strategies** previously discussed (soothing mask, relaxation blanket, breathing by threes, deep breathing, perfect place, and deep muscle relaxation).

Web-site links are available online.

Computer Projects

1. Create a study-block ritual for yourself. Make a poster that shows this ritual. Place the poster in your study area as a constant reminder.
2. Create a form that you can use for the checkmark technique each time you study. Graph your progress at reducing the number of checks with each study block.
3. Use a flow chart or a graphics program to expand the chapter mapping.
4. Use columns or tables to create a vocabulary study sheet for important terminology to know.

Group Web-Search Activity is available online.

Case Studies are available online.

✎ **EXERCISE 5.3 Learning to Relax**

Select one of the relaxation techniques presented in this chapter. In the privacy of your home, try using the relaxation technique several times. Be ready to discuss your experience and results with the rest of the class. Did you feel your muscles relax? Did you feel stress or tension fade away? Do you think there was any change in your heart rate or blood pressure level?

Exercise 5.4 LINKS

Discuss the following case studies with a partner or in a small group. Read each case study and discuss the problem areas. Then identify strategies or specific techniques (by name) that would be solutions for the problems. You may use specific techniques or strategies you learned in Chapter 3 (Managing Your Time), Chapter 4 (Setting Goals), and this chapter (Improving Your Concentration).

1. Bill gets started on his homework late at night. It usually takes longer than he planned. Consequently, he ends up sleeping late during the day and sometimes ends up missing his first class. He is then frustrated and becomes even less motivated to study the next night.

2. Jennine has a good time-management schedule. However, her real problem is her lack of interest and motivation to study. She sits down to study, but she just can't seem to get going. She spends a good part of her study block trying to decide where to start and "what she feels like doing."

3. Mary insists on studying with the radio on full blast. She doesn't understand why other people can't study with their favorite music playing. She claims she simply cannot concentrate when the room is silent. Her biggest complaint is that she can't seem to remember anything at the end of the study block. She says it is because the book is so poorly written and the class is so useless.

4. José has a lot of friends and enjoys a wide variety of activities outside of school. He was an excellent student in high school, but now he is finding that it is harder to do well in college. No one told him how much more demanding college would be. His friends come by often to see how he is doing. They usually end up inviting him to go out for a while, and he goes. He tries studying when he gets home later at night.

5. Lynn tries to study at the kitchen table since it is the largest work surface in her apartment. She takes a long time getting short assignments done because of all the annoying disruptions and distractions. The humming sound of the refrigerator bothers her as do the sounds that come from outside. Every time she gets distracted, she feels compelled to get up, move around, get something to drink or to snack on. As long as she is up and around, she often stops to throw some laundry in the washing machine or to empty the dishwasher. Needless to say, she feels like she is getting nowhere fast.

6. Jake has several required classes this term that he really doesn't like. He rushes through the work to get it done. Sometimes he gets two or three classes "done" within a one-hour study block. He knows that he is passing because he goes to classes even though he doesn't want to go. He finds them boring and annoying. Jake spends more time telling his friends how horrible the classes and the teachers are than he spends studying for the classes.

7. Jeremy is always telling his friends about the things that he is going to do. On the surface, he seems like a sincere goal-setter. However, Jeremy never seems to follow through on any of his plans or his goals. His friends have stopped listening to his great plans for accomplishments. Jeremy doesn't understand what is happening because he really is interested in reaching his goals. Unfortunately, it just doesn't happen.

8. Sandra loves to read. She always has a book in her hands. She can read a paperback novel in about two days. She also likes to read her textbooks. She is fascinated with all the information and the new subjects she is studying. Sandra doesn't understand how she can be such an avid reader and not remember the information she reads in her textbooks. She is beginning to think that maybe she doesn't have what it takes to be a successful college student.

✎ **EXERCISE 5.5 Applying Techniques**

On your own paper, list four distractors that frequently disrupt your concentration level while you are studying. After each distractor, identify if it is an internal or an external distractor. Then, for each of the distractors you listed, discuss two or more specific concentration strategies that you can use to reduce or eliminate the distractors.

SUMMARY

- Concentration requires that you set a positive mental and physical stage conducive to maintaining a mental focus.

- A positive physical stage includes an ideal study area that deals effectively with noise level, furniture, clutter, lighting, and supplies.

- A positive mental stage includes monitoring and reducing stress, emotional *E* words, self-talk, visualizations, setting goals, doing warm-ups, and creating a ritual.

- Both internal and external distractors can interrupt concentration. Techniques to combat both kinds of distractors can be used to reduce or eliminate poor concentration.

- Select concentration techniques that will help you increase your concentration while studying:

Red-Bow	Take-Charge
Say-No	No-Need
Checkmark	Mental Storage Box
Tunnel Vision	To-Do List
Chunking	Active Learning

- Relaxation techniques can be used to reach the relaxed *Ahhhh* state of mind.

OPTIONS FOR PERSONALIZING CHAPTER 5

1. **PROFILE CHART—PERSONAL LOG**   Make a personal log entry that answers the following questions:

   What score did you have on the Chapter 5 Profile? _____

   Describe typical situations in which your ability to concentrate is low. Identify the source of the distractions.

   Which strategies in this chapter do you feel will be beneficial for you to learn in order to increase your ability to concentrate for longer periods of time?

2. **WORDS TO KNOW**

concentration	positive self-talk	take charge
ideal study area	affirmations	say no
mental stage	seeing success	no need
soothing mask	study-block goals	checkmark
relaxation blanket	warm-ups	mental storage box
breathing by threes	routine or ritual	tunnel vision
deep breathing	external distractors	To-Do List
perfect place	internal distractors	chunking
deep muscle relaxation	physical stage	active learning
emotional *E* words	red bow	relaxation strategies

3. **EXPAND THE CHAPTER VISUAL MAPPING**   In your book or on separate paper, expand the chapter visual mapping. Add details to each of the headings that are already given on the mapping. Personalize the mapping by adding pictures or colors.

4. **WRITING ASSIGNMENT 1: WRITE A CHAPTER SUMMARY**   Use the expanded visual mapping as the guide to writing a summary. While looking only at the chapter visual mapping, write a summary that includes each of the chapter main headings and the important details that explain each heading. After you have written a draft, proofread your spelling, grammar, and sentence structure.

5. **WRITING ASSIGNMENT 2**   Psychologists and researchers agree that we use only a very small portion of our mental abilities or potential. Excluding the concentration strategies you learned in this chapter, summarize as many other strategies or methods you have encountered that could be possible keys to unlocking more of our mental abilities. Consider a variety of sources for this information: reading, television, documentaries, health and nutrition reports, alternative medicines, and any other relevant source of information.

6. **PORTFOLIO DEVELOPMENT**   Design a concentration monitoring system that you can use for three weeks each time you study. Begin by identifying a goal you wish to achieve that focuses on strengthening or lengthening your concentration span. Describe the strategies you plan to implement to achieve your goal. Keep records. After three weeks, write a summary paper about your concentration project. Include any data or information you used to monitor your progress. Evaluate the effectiveness of your three-week plan.

CHAPTER 5 REVIEW QUESTIONS

Multiple-Choice

Choose the best answer *for each of the following questions. Write the letter of the best answer on the line.*

_____ 1. Poor concentration may stem from
   a. stress about personal relationships, worries, or fears.
   b. lack of motivation.
   c. internal and external distractors.
   d. a noisy studying environment.

_____ 2. Mood swings, lack of motivation, depression, muscle tension, and sleep problems may all be
   a. stress signals.
   b. tied to obsessive worrying about life.
   c. internal distractors that affect your ability to concentrate.
   d. all of the above.

_____ 3. External distractors can include
   a. sunshine, noises, and lighting.
   b. smells, noises, and worries.
   c. negative self-talk, clutter, and people.
   d. the checkmark technique, the red-bow technique, and framing.

_____ 4. When you hear yourself involved in negative self-talk, it is best to
   a. calmly listen to it and add other reminders of past disappointments.
   b. replace it with positive statements or affirmations that recognize your good qualities.
   c. turn on the television, radio, or stereo to distract your thought processes.
   d. all of the above.

_____ 5. The ideal physical stage for studying includes
   a. a cleared work space, two sources of lighting, and necessary supplies.
   b. absolutely no noise, one bright light, and a comfortable chair.
   c. minimum noise interferences, a desk lamp, and a hard-backed chair.
   d. stereo for background noise, a couch or soft chair, and an overhead light.

_____ 6. Turning on the television while studying
   a. is a habit that needs to be changed.
   b. results in broken thought patterns and reduced levels of concentration.
   c. is discouraged, but the television can be used as an extrinsic reward later.
   d. all of the above.

_____ 7. Which of the following techniques would work well for a student whose history of difficulties in school has resulted in self-doubt and a poor self-image?
   a. Use seeing success to picture him- or herself concentrating and learning.
   b. Use positive self-talk to combat the negative talk based on "old tapes" and experiences.
   c. Use any of the techniques that emphasize a person's positive qualities and abilities.
   d. Use emotional *E* words and short, positive affirmations written in the present tense.

_____ 8. Which techniques would work best for a student who wants to stop wasting the first half hour of a study block trying to "get started" on studying?
   a. Warm-ups, chunking technique, and setting goals
   b. Perfect place, framing, and red-bow technique
   c. Breathing by threes and relaxation blanket
   d. Tunnel vision, soothing mask, and take-charge

_____ **9.** If a student is upset, nervous, tense, or stressed, the following concentration techniques could be used to calm the student:

    a. mental storage box, deep breathing.

    b. perfect place, relaxation blanket.

    c. positive self-talk, breathing by threes.

    d. all of the above.

_____ **10.** Active learning

    a. occurs when you use a lot of energy reading a textbook nonstop for several hours.

    b. requires that a person be walking, pacing, or moving around while studying.

    c. is a type of passive learning in which learning becomes automatic.

    d. requires the learner to take an active role in the process of learning.

Short Answer—Critical Thinking

Carefully read the following student situations. Analyze each student's concentration problem; then list three or more different concentration techniques that the student could use to increase concentration. Briefly explain how the technique is related to the problem. Write answers on your own paper.

1. Sherrie has always been a somewhat emotional person. She laughs hard, plays hard, worries extensively, and "stresses out" easily. She often feels like her emotional roller coaster is interfering with her desire to do well in school. What do you recommend?

2. Mel spends a lot of time studying, yet he doesn't understand why it doesn't feel like he's learning. He lives in a small apartment and feels the best place to study is on the floor where he has room to spread things out. If he needs to sharpen a pencil, get a calculator, or locate any other supplies, they are usually within close reach in his bedroom or kitchen or on the shelves in his living room. Because he spends a lot of hours studying, he often finds himself drifting off or reclining for short naps to "recuperate." After hours of studying, he often tosses his books aside because he doesn't feel he remembers anything he studied over the last several hours. What do you recommend?

3. Pamela is always in a hurry; no one doubts that she lives a hectic life as a single mother of two children. She also works part time and goes to school full time. To compensate, when she sits down to study, she opens her book and begins reading in a rather frantic, rapid-paced manner. She knows she has to cover as much as she can before her teenagers interrupt or start playing their stereo full blast. Sometimes Pamela gets started quickly and feels confused and overwhelmed, only to later find out she spent her precious time on the wrong assignment. What do you recommend?

4. Eli has real problems with motivation. He says he wants to be in school, but many of his actions do not support his words. Many times when he does sit down to study, within a matter of minutes either the phone rings or his friends stop by to pick him up to go out. He invariably decides to go and come back to study later. When he does return, he has trouble getting started. His mind wanders to his friends or to the next activity they plan to do together. He gets sleepy, puts his head down, and the "study block" is over. What do you recommend?

Using a Reading System

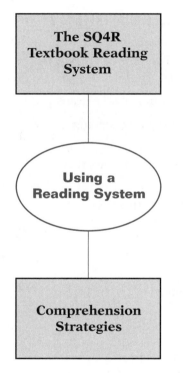

The SQ4R
Textbook Reading
System

Using a
Reading System

Comprehension
Strategies

The process of reading college textbooks requires you to comprehend and learn large amounts of information. Does the amount of information in some chapters overwhelm you? Do you sometimes spend time reading and then not know what you have just read? Do you want to know how to condense the information into notes? Do you skip over some words because they are unfamiliar? Do you have difficulty finding the important main ideas to learn? This chapter provides you with a six-step reading system and techniques for improving your comprehension and remembering larger amounts of information.

Name _____ Date _____

CHAPTER 6 Textbook Reading Profile

DO, SCORE, and **RECORD** your profile before you read this chapter. If you need to review the process, refer to the complete directions given in the Profile for Chapter 1 on page 2.

	YES	NO
1. When I begin reading a new chapter, I open the book to the first page and read straight through to the end of the chapter.	_____	_____
2. I read the chapter review questions and the summary before I start reading the chapter.	_____	_____
3. I write my own study questions for each heading and subheading in the chapter.	_____	_____
4. I read all the information under one complete heading before I stop to think about what I've read.	_____	_____
5. I often finish reading a chapter only to find out that I remember very little of what I have just read.	_____	_____
6. After I read a short section, I stop to highlight, underline, or take notes.	_____	_____
7. When I study, I am quiet because I do all my practicing or reviewing in my head.	_____	_____
8. I skip over unfamiliar words as long as I understand most of the other information.	_____	_____
9. When I don't understand a paragraph, I skip it and hope the next paragraph is easier.	_____	_____
10. I look for the topic sentence in each paragraph.	_____	_____
11. I visualize what I read.	_____	_____
12. I use a consistent system for reading textbook chapters.	_____	_____

Self-Awareness: Describe the system, methods, or approaches you currently use to read a new chapter that has just been assigned. Give sufficient details so your process is clear to your reader.

_____

_____

_____

_____

_____

_____

_____

The SQ4R Textbook Reading System

One of the first textbook reading systems, SQ3R, was developed by Francis P. Robinson in 1941. This system acquired its name by using the first letter of each step in the system: survey, question, read, recite, and review. Other systems have been developed for reading textbooks, but they all basically contain the same essential steps found in SQ3R. The **SQ4R system** in this chapter is based on SQ3R with a fourth R added for the "record" step. The SQ4R system thus becomes a six-step approach to reading and comprehending textbooks.

The Steps of SQ4R

1. *Survey* the chapter.
2. Write *Questions* for each heading and subheading.
3. *Read* the information one paragraph at a time.
4. Select a form of notetaking to *Record* information.
5. *Recite* the important information from the paragraph.
6. *Review* the information learned in the chapter.

Step One: Survey the Chapter

When you first open the book to read a new chapter, do not dive right in and begin reading from the beginning of the chapter straight to the end. Instead, learn the process of **surveying**. Surveying means to "look through," preview, or get an overview of the introductory material, the main body of the chapter, and finally, the specific sections at the end of the chapter.

Surveying the complete chapter gives you "the big picture" of the entire chapter. For most chapters, surveying takes less than twenty minutes. The benefits are many, so surveying the entire chapter is highly recommended. However, sometimes it makes more sense to survey only part of a chapter. If the chapter is too long, you will not be able to survey it in less than twenty minutes, and there may be so many sections to the chapter that you are not able to "see the big picture." When you are dealing with long chapters, survey only the amount of information that you feel you will be able to cover in one study block. If only a portion of the chapter was assigned, then focus most of your surveying on that section of the chapter. For the complete chapter survey, look at the following parts of a chapter.

Introductory Material   The **introductory material** consists of the title for the chapter, the introduction, and the chapter objectives. Read the chapter title carefully and take a moment to relate this topic to previous topics and chapters and information you already know about the topic.

Chapter Headings   The **headings** (and **subheadings**) appear in a larger, bolder, or italic print. Begin moving through the chapter by glancing over the headings and the subheadings. These show you the "skeleton" structure of the chapter. Later, if you want, you can use the headings and subheadings to make an outline or a mapping.

Visual Aids and Marginal Notes   Graphs, charts, drawings, and photographs are all considered **visual aids**. Sometimes visual aids also appear as **marginal notes**. The marginal notes may be brief explanations, short definitions, shortened lists of key points, icons, or pictures used to draw your attention to a key idea or study questions.

Terminology   Most textbooks contain terms and definitions that are important to the content. Words that you should know how to define are often shown in color, in bold print, in italic print, or in underline. Glance at the terms, but do not stop to read the definitions. If you stop to read the definitions, your surveying will become lengthy, and you will be moving into the reading process itself.

End-of-the-Chapter Information   The special features found at the end of chapters vary from textbook to textbook. However, two common features are *chapter review questions* and a *chapter summary.* The **end-of-the-chapter information** is very important to read carefully, for it will summarize for you the most important concepts (main ideas) and supporting details that you should understand after you read and study the chapter. When you begin the reading process, you will have some foresight on the key points; you will also begin setting up your memory system for more thorough learning.

Surveying works to your benefit in several ways:

1. Surveying is a *warm-up activity* that gets your mind focused and prepared for serious work. You will not waste time procrastinating or stumbling through your books and notes trying to find a starting point.

2. It *increases your motivation, interest, and confidence* in learning new information. You may find areas in the chapter that look interesting, stimulate your curiosity, or make you realize that the chapter is not going to be as difficult as you first thought.

3. It helps you *set goals and manage your time.* You will get a general idea about the level of difficulty of the material and the length of the chapter so that you can set goals for the amount of material to cover in a study period.

4. It stimulates the learning process by *laying a foundation for comprehending the chapter.* You will gain insight as to how the chapter is organized and how information is grouped.

Step Two: Write Questions

During the **question step**, formulate a question for each heading or subheading in the chapter. Use the words *which, when, what, why, where, how,* or *who* to turn each heading or subheading into a question. Writing the questions will improve your comprehension as you read and will provide you with valuable study questions to use when you review the chapter. Because the process of learning should be tailored to strategies that work best for you, several options for the question step are available to try and select your preference:

■ *Full Chapter Questions in the Book:* Create the questions and write the questions in your book next to each heading and subheading.

■ *Full Chapter Questions on Paper:* On your own notebook paper, draw a line down your paper to make a 2½-inch margin on the left side of the paper. Write your questions in this margin. Leave several lines between questions so you will have room to write the answers to your questions on the right side of your paper after you have finished reading.

■ *Partial Chapter Questions in the Book or on Paper:* Use the same methods given above, but create questions only for the portion of the chapter that was assigned or the portion you will read during one study block.

■ *Alternating Writing Questions and Reading:* Write a question for a heading or a subheading, read that section carefully, and then write a new question before you begin the next heading or subheading. This is a nontraditional way for this question step, but if you prefer this method, it can be used.

Writing your own study questions has several advantages:

1. The questions give you a *purpose for reading*. Natural curiosity then leads you to read so that you can answer your questions.
2. Your *curiosity can help you concentrate* on what you are reading.
3. With increased concentration, you gain *increased comprehension*.
4. Your questions help *prepare you for future tests*. You can prepare for a test by answering your own questions during the review step of SQ4R.

Step Three: Read Carefully

Some students feel that they should be able to "read fast" to get through the chapter. Others read the chapter only to find at the end of the chapter that they don't remember much of what they have just read; consequently, they find it necessary to reread at least one more time. The **read step** of SQ4R encourages you to read *carefully*. For most textbooks, you should read *one paragraph at a time* and stop so that you can concentrate and comprehend each paragraph. With careful reading, you will not need to spend valuable study time rereading chapters.

If the textbook is written on an easy-to-read level and does not contain large amounts of details in each paragraph, you can read more than one paragraph at a time before you stop for the next step. For a very difficult, technical textbook, you may find that you need to read and stop after several sentences rather than at the end of the paragraph. Reading carefully requires this flexibility; the amount you read at a time should be determined by your reading skills and the level of difficulty of the material.

Reading carefully helps you in several ways:

1. Your *mind stays focused* on the information. Reading too quickly or carelessly puts your mind into "**automatic pilot**," where little or no information registers in your memory.
2. By keeping a stronger focus, you can attain accuracy and higher levels of concentration. The result is *better comprehension*.
3. This approach gives your *memory time to process new information* before you start demanding that it take in even more information. You also have time to think about information and understand it with greater accuracy.
4. It *promotes critical thinking*, an essential skill for college students.

Step Four: Record Information

Reading comprehension involves finding main ideas and recognizing important supporting details. This chapter and the next show you how to locate this information. After you read a paragraph carefully, it is time to use the **record step** by taking notes of the important information you will need to learn. You have five basic choices of notetaking or recording systems to use for the important information:

- Underlining or highlighting (see Chapter 7)
- Writing notes in the margins of the book (see Chapter 7)
- Using the Cornell format to take notes on paper (see Chapter 9)
- Making hierarchies or visual mappings (see Chapter 11)
- Making notes on flash cards (see Chapter 8)

After you learn to use all five options, you may find that you prefer one or two of them. If the textbook you are reading is not too difficult, usually one form of notetaking is sufficient. You may find, however, that you prefer to use a combination of two or more systems to help you study and learn. Your goal is to learn how to use all five options and apply them as you feel is most appropriate for the situation.

Recording can benefit you in several ways:

1. It gives you a *reduced or condensed form of the information* that you need to learn.

2. Because writing is involved, you are *actively involved* in the learning process. Your automatic pilot, a passive form of studying, does not have the opportunity to work.

3. The *writing process* also involves fine motor skills, which form another channel into your memory system.

Step Five: Recite

Before you move on to the next paragraph, stop and use the **recite step**. Recite the information you wrote in your notes. Speak out loud and in complete sentences.

Once you have finished reciting the information just covered, continue to move through the chapter by reading the next paragraph (or section) carefully, recording main ideas and important supporting details, and reciting the new information. As you move through the chapter with this method, your reading is thorough, detailed, and accurate. Your mind is alert, challenged, active, and focused. By devoting time and effort to this careful method of reading, you do not need to reread the chapter. When you have completed this cycle for the entire chapter, move on to the final step of SQ4R.

Reciting, one of the twelve memory principles, is valuable for these reasons:

1. Reciting requires you to *explain the information clearly.*

2. Reciting provides you with *important feedback.* If you are not able to recite the information, then you know that you did not understand it very well. Glance back at your notes for clues.

3. Reciting leads to *active learning,* which increases your level and length of concentration.

4. Reciting *activates the auditory channel* to your brain. The more senses you can use in the learning process, the stronger the paths will be to your memory.

5. Reciting in your own words helps you *avoid rote memorization.* You are giving meaning to the information by using your own words.

6. When you finish the **read-record-recite cycle** for the paragraph, you have the *paragraph's ideas fresh in your memory.* You can then connect these ideas to the new information that you will be taking in as you read the next paragraph.

Step Six: Review

After you have finished surveying, questioning, reading, recording, and reciting, you do the last step—reviewing. The **review step** can be accomplished in a variety of ways. The following activities are helpful for immediate review and ongoing review:

■ Answer any questions at the end of the chapter.

■ Answer the questions that you wrote in the question step.

■ Study and recite from the notes that you took in the record step.

■ Write a summary of the information in the chapter.

■ Personalize the information by asking yourself additional questions: How can this information be used? How does the lecture from class fit in with this information? Why is this important to learn?

■ Create additional study tools such as vocabulary flash cards, study tapes, or visual mappings.

Reviewing is a vital step for several reasons:

1. An immediate review of information *summarizes what you just learned.* It provides you with the "big picture" supported by important details.

2. The process of memory involves putting information into your long-term memory and being able to retrieve it from this memory storage when needed. To be able to *retrieve information efficiently,* you must practice it by reviewing it frequently.

3. Frequent ongoing review *keeps information fresh in your memory.* You have less need to cram or feel unprepared for tests.

4. When information is reviewed and understood clearly, you can more easily *associate new information* with information already in your long-term memory schemas.

5. Making time for immediate and ongoing review *builds confidence* and creates a sense of satisfaction for *being prepared* and *managing time* efficiently.

✎ **EXERCISE 6.1 Knowing the Six Steps**

The following chart shows the steps of SQ4R. Fill each box with the name of the step. Then, with a partner, take turns practicing explaining each step of the process. Include as many details as you can remember without looking back in the book.

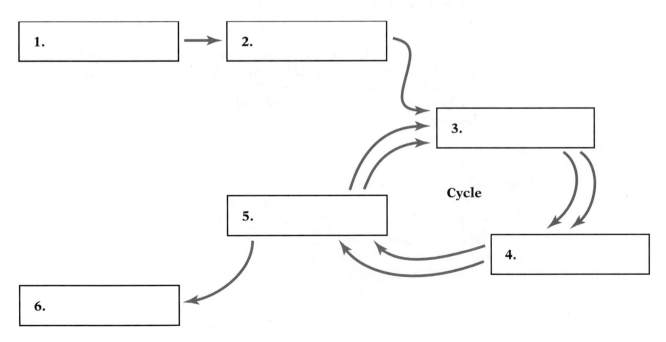

✎ **EXERCISE 6.2 Adjusting Your Reading Methods**

In the Self-Awareness writing at the beginning of the chapter, you discussed a typical approach you use to reading a new chapter. On your own paper, discuss the steps of SQ4R that you included in your previous way of reading a new chapter. Then discuss the changes in your reading approach that will occur when you begin to use the six steps of SQ4R.

Comprehension Strategies

If you are not able to understand what the author is saying, taking notes and reciting are impossible. Before you begin college-level courses that require extensive reading, first assess your reading skills.

College-level reading requires strong decoding skills (reading multisyllable words), comprehension skills, vocabulary skills, and critical thinking skills. If you find reading college textbooks to be difficult, you may need to strengthen your reading skills. Check with your school's developmental education department, study skills department, or reading programs. If reading courses are offered, seriously consider enrolling in one. A struggle with reading can be reduced through reading skills instruction.

If you answer *yes* to one or more of these questions, you would benefit from reading instruction:

■ Do you find that many of the words in your textbooks are unfamiliar?

■ Do you often skip words because you can't read them?

■ Do you have difficulty sounding out longer words?

■ Do you read word-by-word rather than phrase-by-phrase?

■ Do you frequently have difficulty figuring out what the author is saying?

Comprehension is essential for any textbook you are reading. You will be faced with reading assignments in which you read the paragraph but don't immediately understand its contents. The following comprehension techniques will help you break down a paragraph and more fully understand it. Use these techniques consistently as you read:

Comprehension Strategies

1. Read the paragraph out loud.
2. Visualize or create "movies in your mind" about what you are reading.
3. Substitute familiar words for unfamiliar words.
4. Find the topic sentence with the author's main idea.
5. Identify the organizational pattern used for the supporting details.

Read Out Loud

Active reading can be enhanced by reading the information out loud. By saying the words and hearing the words, you give yourself extra assistance in understanding a difficult paragraph. When you read out loud and when you speak, you usually group information into natural phrases, which makes the information easier to understand. When you use this technique, read out loud slowly, enunciate clearly, and concentrate on hearing the words.

Visualize

Weak comprehension sometimes occurs when a person reads too quickly for the information to be processed effectively and accurately. Taking the time to picture the information and create a "movie in your mind" carries a stronger image into your memory system. Some readers automatically visualize as they read; others need to apply more effort and intention to activate the visualization process. When you are having difficulty comprehending (or remembering) what you are reading, evaluate your approach to see if you are taking the time necessary to create the visual images. If pictures were not created, try reading the paragraph more slowly and force the visual images to develop as you read.

Substitute Words

Many readers with comprehension problems have the tendency to skip over unfamiliar words. If you skip some words or read words but do not know their meaning, your weak comprehension of the paragraph may be tied to its vocabulary. Specialized or course-specific vocabulary may be unclear, or words that are not set off in special print may be the source of the problem. Watch carefully for unfamiliar words as you read. Use the glossary in the textbook, a dictionary, or an electronic spell checker with a dictionary to locate a familiar word that has a similar meaning. In the text above the unfamiliar word, write the common or familiar word; then read the paragraph with the common word. This technique converts formal, textbook writing into the vocabulary level that is familiar and comfortable for you. The following example shows how this technique of substituting words adds clarity and improves comprehension of a difficult paragraph.

Few if any philosophies are as enigmatic [*puzzling*] as *Daoism*—the teachings of the Way (Dao). The opening lines of this school's greatest masterpiece, *The Classic of the Way and* Virtue [*morality*] (*Dao De Jing*), which is ascribed to [*associated with*] the legendary [*famous*] Laozi, immediately confront [*challenge*] the reader with Daoism's essential paradox [*contradiction*]: "The Way that can be trodden [*walked*] is not the enduring [*lasting*] and the unchanging Way. The name that can be named is not the enduring and unchanging name." Here is a philosophy that purports [*claims*] to teach *the* Way (of truth) but simultaneously [*at the same time*] claims that the True Way transcends [*exceeds beyond*] human understanding. Encapsulated [*Contained*] within a little book of some five thousand words is a philosophy that defies [*resists*] definition, spurns [*rejects*] reason, and rejects words as inadequate.

Andrea, *The Human Record,* p. 93.

Find the Topic Sentence

The subject of a paragraph is called the **topic**. The topic is usually one, two, or three words. Begin by asking yourself: In one, two, or three words, what is this paragraph about? If you still do not know the topic, look for a word or phrase that appears a number of times in the paragraph. This word or phrase often is the topic.

Once you have determined the topic, you can now look for a broad sentence that contains that topic word. By definition, a paragraph is a series of sentences grouped together to develop one specific main idea. The **main idea** tells the important point the author wants to express in the paragraph; it is expressed in the topic sentence. In textbooks, the topic sentence is often the first sentence. To find the **topic sentence**, ask yourself these questions:

- Does this sentence have the topic word?
- Is this what the author is trying to get across?
- Does everything else in the paragraph relate to this one idea?

The topic sentence is like an umbrella. It needs to be broad enough that all the other information or details in the paragraph relate to the large "**umbrella sentence.**" If the sentence you select as the topic sentence does not in some way include or relate to some of the details in the sentence, you did not find the true topic sentence.

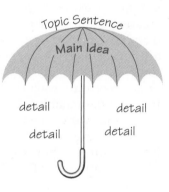

You can use this strategy to locate the main idea:

1. Check the first sentence, since the topic sentence is often placed at the beginning of the paragraph in textbooks.
2. If the first sentence does not seem to be the "umbrella sentence," check the last sentence. Sometimes details are presented and then summarized in the last sentence as a topic sentence.
3. If the last sentence doesn't reflect the main idea of the paragraph, carefully examine the sentences within the paragraph.
4. If none of the sentences work as the "umbrella sentence," you may be working with a paragraph with an implied main idea.

Sometimes writers do not directly state the main idea anywhere in the paragraph. They use an **implied main idea**. The assumption with an implied main idea is that you will be able to state the main idea clearly in your own words after you read and think about all the supporting details. If you cannot find a topic sentence, ask yourself:

- What is the author saying in this paragraph? Answer the question in one sentence in your own words.
- Is there a sentence that says basically this same thing? If the answer is *no*, the topic sentence may be implied.

**Discover the
Organizational
Pattern**

Some readers are able to identify supporting details, but they still have difficulty seeing how the details are related or why they belong in one paragraph under one topic sentence. Discovering the pattern used to organize the details in the paragraph so that they support the main idea can help with comprehension. Although there are many possible **organizational patterns** an author can use, the five most common patterns used in textbooks are discussed in this section.

You will encounter these five organizational patterns not only in reading classes, but also in writing classes. Being familiar with the characteristics of these organizational patterns will strengthen not only your reading skills, but also your writing skills.

The five common patterns are shown below. Following each pattern is an example of a visual form that could be used to show the relationships between two or more items in the paragraph. While there are many ways to pictorially show the information, the examples given are excellent starting points.

Chronological Pattern   If you look carefully at the details, you may notice that they are presented in a logical time sequence called *chronological order.* Chronological order is often used when a story is being told (a narrative) or when a procedure or process is being explained. The **chronological pattern** indicates that the details happen in a specific, fixed order to get to a conclusion or a result.

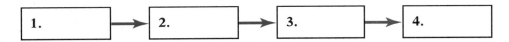

Clue words that are used in this pattern: *when, then, before, next, after, first, second,* and *finally.*

Comparison or Contrast Pattern   When two or more objects or events are being discussed, a **comparison pattern** is being used. This pattern can include both likenesses and differences. However, if only differences between two or more objects are being discussed, a **contrast pattern** is used. After you are able to identify the comparison or the contrast pattern, you will more easily understand what is being said about each subject.

Features	A	B

Clue words that are used to signal likenesses: *also, similarly,* and *likewise.* Clue words that are used to signal differences: *but, in contrast, on the other hand, however, although,* and *while.*

Definition Pattern   Many textbook paragraphs simply explain the meanings of terms. If the term being used is a vital key to comprehending more complex information, an entire paragraph may be devoted to helping you grasp the meaning of the term through the use of explanations, negations, analogies, or examples. A **definition paragraph** often has the term to be defined in bold letters in the first sentence of the paragraph.

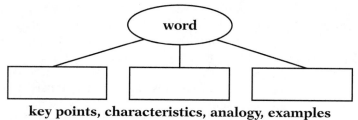

key points, characteristics, analogy, examples

Clue words used in this pattern are: *means, is, can be considered,* and *is defined as.*

Examples Pattern   In the **examples pattern,** once an important idea, term, or theory is presented, the author expands your understanding by giving you clear examples of the theory before moving on to new information.

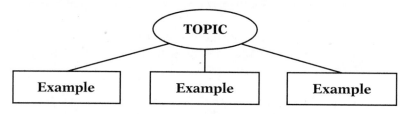

Clue words for this pattern are: *for example, another example, an illustration of this.*

Cause/Effect Pattern   Often the relationship between two items shows that one item caused the other item to happen. Sometimes one cause can have more than one outcome or one effect. In other cases, several causes can produce a given effect or outcome. Whenever there is a relationship that shows that one item caused or made the other happen, a **cause/effect pattern** is being used.

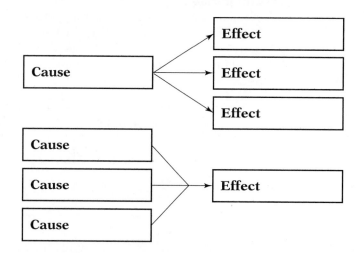

Clue words for this pattern are: *because, since, so, therefore, caused by,* and *result in.*

These six organizational patterns can help you follow the author's thinking and the purpose of each paragraph. (See the following chart.) It is important to realize, however, that one paragraph may use more than one organizational pattern. For example, a definition paragraph may use examples to help explain the definition; a cause/effect paragraph may also use chronological order. If you are able to identify more than one pattern working, you are reading carefully and thinking about the details as they are presented.

Summary Chart for Organizational Patterns

Pattern	Purpose Is to Show:	Clue Words
Chronological	logical time sequence	when, then, before, next, after, first, second, finally, while, since, until
Comparison	likenesses or differences	also, and, similarly, likewise, but, in contrast, on the other hand, however, although, while
Contrast	differences	but, in contrast, on the other hand, however, although, while, yet, whereas, nevertheless
Definition	the meaning of course-specific words (terminology)	mean, is, can be considered, is defined as
Examples	examples that clarify an idea, term, or theory	for example, another example, an illustration of this, similarly
Cause/Effect	relationship between two items that have a cause and an outcome/effect	because, since, so, so that, therefore, caused by, result in, consequently, as a result

Web-site links are available online.

Computer Projects

1. Set up columns for Step 2 of SQ4R. Write your questions in the left column. When you are ready for the review step, write your answers in the right column.
2. Make vocabulary study sheets by working in columns. Write the vocabulary word (terms to know) in the left column. Write the definitions in the right column directly across from the vocabulary words.
3. Write your notes (record step) on the computer.
4. Use a graphing or flow-chart program to expand the visual mapping.
5. Scan a difficult textbook page into the computer. Highlight unfamiliar words. Check their meaning in your computer thesaurus program.
6. Use a graphics program to make visual representations of the organizational patterns for the passages in Exercise 6.6.
7. Use a tables program to complete Exercise 6.7.

Group Web-Search Activity is available online.

Case Studies are available online.

✎ **EXERCISE 6.3 Discussing Visualizations for Passages**

Locate a paragraph or a short passage from one of your textbooks that can be used to practice the skills of visualization. Read the passage and visualize the information unfolding. Create a "movie in your mind" of the information. Bring the passage to class. With a partner, exchange passages. Read your partner's passage and create a "movie in your mind." Verbally describe the movie to your partner so the two of you can compare the images that were created through visualization.

✎ **EXERCISE 6.4 Substituting Common or Familiar Words**

For some students, the words in italics in the following paragraph maybe unfamiliar and lead to poor comprehension. Above each italicized word, write a common word that has the same or very similar meaning. Then read the paragraph out loud using your substituted words.

From Germany to the Balkans, hostility is again breaking loose among the *mosaic* of ethnic minorities that live cheek by *jowl*. The *enmities* are the same as those that *enfeebled* the Austro–Hungarian and Ottoman Empires and helped start World War I in 1914 and that Hitler manipulated in the years leading up to World War II in 1939. Such enmities will continue to threaten world peace in the twenty-first century. A *corollary* of this is the changed nature of war. Formerly war was an interstate affair in which organized armies met in combat. Today, *ferocious* civil war is the norm. The military historian Martin van Crevald writes: "The characteristics of the new kind of warfare, of which Bosnia is an example, are that sophisticated modern weapons play little role. . . . But although sophisticated weapons are scarcely used, these new wars tend to be very bloody because there is no distinction between armies and peoples, so everybody who gets in the way gets killed."

Mansbach, *The Global Puzzle*, p. 17.

✎ EXERCISE 6.5 Finding Topic Sentences

Read each of the following paragraphs carefully. Use a highlighter to highlight the sentence you believe is the topic sentence. Highlight only one sentence in each paragraph. If you find a paragraph with an implied main idea, use your own words to write a main idea next to the paragraph.

1. Global politics, then, has many kinds of issues. Some, such as U.S.–Russian arms negotiations or Syrian–Israeli peace negotiations, involve the quest for security. Others, such as negotiations on trade barriers, focus on economic questions. Still others, such as controversies about acid rain, are about threats to the environment. In other words, the enormous range of issues in global politics covers diverse topics. Increasingly, the global agenda is attracting nontraditional issues that either produce cooperation or necessitate collaboration if disaster is to be avoided.

   Mansbach, *The Global Puzzle*, p. 19.

2. Identities help determine whom people consider to be friends or foes. People have loyalties to numerous groups and identify with them—government, gender, employer, church, ethnicity, and so on. A person in France might identify with a feminist group seeking gender equality, a farm association trying to hold on to agricultural subsidies, a consumer who would like to reduce such subsidies and so lower food prices, the Catholic Church seeking state funds for parochial schools, or even a right-wing political party seeking to expel France's immigrant population. In complex societies, multiple identities are common.

   Mansbach, *The Global Puzzle*, p. 163.

3. Many outdoor trainers and participants believe strongly that they derived substantial personal benefits from outdoor training. Among the most important are developing greater self-confidence, appreciating hidden strengths, and learning to work better with people. Strong proponents of outdoor training believe that those who do not appreciate the training simply do not understand it. Many training directors also have positive attitudes toward outdoor training. They believe that a work team that experiences outdoor training will work more cooperatively back at the office.

   DuBrin, *Leadership*, p. 237.

4. Man probably used his own voice to produce the earliest music, and music through the ages has developed with reference to the voice. It seems likely that primitive human beings, discovering that their voices were capable of certain timbres and pitches, would have had a natural interest in similar sounds encountered by accident; a plucked bow string, wind blowing across the reeds in a brook. This natural tendency to relate new sounds to the human voice makes the voice the most fundamental of musical sounds.

   Wink/Williams.

5. The main forms of plant and animal life may at first glance appear chaotic, but the biologist sees them in a high degree of order. This order is due to an elaborate system of classification. All life is first grouped into a few primary divisions called phyla; each phylum is in turn subdivided into small groups called classes; each class is subdivided into orders; and so on down through the family, the genus, the species, the variety. This system brings order out of chaos, enabling the biologist to consider any plant or animal in its proper relationship to the rest.

   Rorabacher.

EXERCISE 6.6 **Identifying Organizational Patterns**

1. Find the topic sentence. Highlight it. If the main idea is implied, write the main idea in the margin.

2. Analyze the way the details in the paragraph are organized. On the line, *write the letter from below* to indicate which organizational pattern is the most important or dominant pattern used in the paragraph.

a. chronological	**b.** comparison/contrast	**c.** definition
d. examples	**e.** cause/effect	

_____ **1.** The word *civilization* is derived from the Latin adjective *civilis,* which means "political" or "civic." No matter how else we define civilization, an organized civic entity, known as a state, stands at the center of every society we call civilized. A state is a sovereign public power that binds large numbers of people together at a level that transcends the ties of family, clan, tribe, and local community and organizes them for projects far beyond the capabilities of single families or even villages and towns.

   Andrea/Overfield, *The Human Record,* p. 5.

_____ **2.** Some of the world's earliest civilizations have left written records that we cannot yet decipher and might never be able to read. These include India's Harappan civilization, which was centered in the Indus valley from before 2500 to some time after 1700 B.C.E.; and the Minoan civilization of the Aegean island of Crete, which flourished from roughly 2500 to about 1400 B.C.E.; and the African civilization of Kush, located directly south of Egypt, which reached its age of greatness after 800 B.C.E.; but with much earlier origins as a state. For many other early civilizations and cultures we have as yet uncovered no written records. This is the case of mysterious peoples who, between approximately 6000 B.C.E. and the first century C.E., painted and carved thousands of pieces of art on the rocks of Tassili n'Ajjer in what is today the central Saharan Desert. It is also true of the Olmec civilization of Mexico, which appeared around 1200 B.C.E.

   Andrea/Overfield, *The Human Record,* p. 34.

_____ **3.** To understand leadership, it is important to grasp the difference between leadership and management. We get a clue from the standard conceptualization of the functions of management: planning, organizing, directing (or leading), and controlling. Leading is a major part of a manager's job, yet the manager must also plan, organize, and control. Broadly speaking, leadership deals with the interpersonal aspects of a manager's job, whereas planning, organizing, and controlling deal with the administrative aspects. According to current thinking, leadership deals with change, inspiration, motivation, and influence. In contrast, management deals more with maintaining equilibrium and the status quo.

   DuBrin, *Leadership,* p. 3.

_____ **4.** Why does a new product fail? Mainly because the product and its marketing program are not planned and tested as completely as they should be. For example, to save on development costs, a firm may market-test its product but not its entire marketing mix. Or a firm may market a new product before all the "bugs" have been worked out. Or, when problems show up in the testing state, a firm may try to recover its product development costs by pushing ahead with full-scale marketing anyway. Finally, some firms try to market new products with inadequate financing.

   Pride/Hughes/Kapoor, *Business,* p. 401.

_____ **5.** The human brain in late adulthood, however, is smaller and slower in its functioning than the brain in early adulthood. This reduction is thought to be caused by the death of neurons, which do not regenerate. Neurons die at an increasing rate after age 60. The proportion of neurons that die varies across different parts of the brain. In the visual area, the death rate is about 50 percent. In the motor areas, the death rate varies from 20 to 50 percent. In the memory and reasoning areas, the death rate is less than 20 percent. The production of certain neurotransmitters also declines with age.

   Payne/Wenger, *Cognitive Psychology,* p. 359.

⊖⊖ Exercise 6.7 LINKS

For this critical thinking exercise, identify any two principles of memory that are used in the *survey step of SQ4R*. Explain how each principle is used during the survey process. Continue in this manner to identify each of the steps of SQ4R, and discuss two principles of memory that are actively used in each step. Do not repeat any one principle more than two times in your answer. You may create a chart for your answers, or you may write your answers as a short paper with one paragraph used to discuss each of the steps of SQ4R.

SUMMARY

- The goal of the SQ4R reading system is to comprehend information as you work through the chapter of a textbook so that you will not need to keep rereading the chapter to learn information.

- Careful, thorough, and accurate reading results when you use the six steps of the SQ4R reading system.

  1. Survey the sections of the chapter.
  2. Write questions for each heading and subheading.
  3. Read paragraph-by-paragraph.
  4. Record notes after you read each paragraph.
  5. Recite important information.
  6. Review information frequently.

- Use one or more of the five comprehension strategies as needed to understand difficult paragraphs.

  1. Read out loud.
  2. Visualize what you read.
  3. Substitute familiar words.

  4. Find the topic sentence.
  5. Identify the organizational pattern.

- The topic sentence can be identified by:

  1. Finding a sentence that contains the topic word (subject).
  2. Determining if the sentence states the main point the author is making.
  3. Checking that the sentence works as an "umbrella sentence."
  4. Using information about frequency of locations in the paragraph for the topic sentence: first, last, middle, implied.

- The following organizational patterns are used to arrange supporting details within a paragraph.

  1. chronological
  2. comparison/contrast
  3. definitions
  4. examples
  5. cause/effect

OPTIONS FOR PERSONALIZING CHAPTER 6

1. **PROFILE CHART—PERSONAL LOG**   Answer the following questions in your personal log.

   What score did you have on the Chapter 6 Profile? _____

   How does the SQ4R system differ from the methods you discussed using in the Self-Awareness sections at the beginning of the chapter?

   What advantages do you see in using the SQ4R system for reading your textbooks?

2. **WORDS TO KNOW**

SQ4R system	marginal notes	record step
surveying	end-of-the-chapter information	recite step
introductory material	question step	read-record-recite cycle
headings, subheadings	read step	review step
visual aids	automatic pilot	topic

main idea	organizational patterns	definition paragraph
topic sentence	chronological pattern	examples pattern
umbrella sentence	comparison pattern	cause/effect pattern
implied main idea	contrast pattern	

3. **EXPAND THE CHAPTER VISUAL MAPPING**   In this chapter, there are only two main headings. On your own paper or on page 103, expand each of these main headings by adding the subheadings and any other details that are important supporting details.

4. **WRITING ASSIGNMENT 1**   Use all six steps of the SQ4R system for any chapter from another textbook. Explain how you applied each step.

5. **WRITING ASSIGNMENT 2**   *Metacognition* involves understanding how you learn and applying that knowledge to the strategies that you use when you approach a new task. SQ4R provides the learner with options for writing the questions (step 2), recording information (step 4), and reviewing the information (step 6). Explain the options you prefer to use in steps 2, 4, and 6. Explain why you prefer to use those options.

6. **PORTFOLIO DEVELOPMENT**   Select any chapter from any textbook to use the SQ4R system. Complete each of the steps below. Your work may be done by word processing. Your final project should clearly demonstrate your ability to use all six steps of SQ4R effectively.

   a. Write one or more paragraphs that tell how long surveying took, how many pages you surveyed, and what you learned about the chapter by surveying.

   b. Write your questions in your book or on paper.

   c. Write one or more paragraphs that tell how you read and used the read-record-recite cycle.

   d. Include your notes or photocopies of the highlighting that you used for the record step.

   e. Write answers to each of the questions you composed in the question step.

   f. Write one or more paragraphs that tell how you reviewed the material.

CHAPTER 6 REVIEW QUESTIONS

True-False

Carefully read the following sentences. Pay attention to key words.
Write T *if the statement is TRUE. Write* F *if it is FALSE.*

_____ **1.** Writing study questions for headings and subheadings provides a purpose for reading, improves concentration, and results in study questions for review.

_____ **2.** A paragraph may use more than one organizational pattern for organizing the details.

_____ **3.** Reciting is important because it includes the auditory channel and provides feedback for understanding.

_____ **4.** The topic sentence is always the first sentence of a paragraph.

_____ **5.** When you read, you should be able to define general vocabulary words and specialized vocabulary words.

_____ **6.** For most textbook reading, you should usually stop reading after one paragraph so that you can take notes and recite.

_____ **7.** Surveying should always be done for the entire chapter before you begin reading.

_____ **8.** Comprehension often improves when you use a dictionary or a thesaurus to substitute common or familiar words for words that you do not understand.

_____ **9.** Clue words such as *because, since,* or *therefore* frequently appear in paragraphs that use a chronological pattern.

_____ **10.** If you read through a chapter without stopping to record or recite, you are using a passive form of studying.

Multiple-Choice

Choose the best answer *for each of the following questions. Write the letter of the best answer on the line.*

_____ **1.** The SQ4R system is
   a. a four-step system used to read textbooks.
   b. a textbook reading system that involves six different steps.
   c. a reading system that should be used only for very difficult textbooks.
   d. a reading system that uses only the rehearsal path of the memory system.

_____ **2.** Which of the following is *not* true about the first step of the SQ4R process?
   a. The skeletal structure or outline of the chapter can be seen through headings and subheadings.
   b. Marginal notes, insert boxes, and chapter study questions should be read carefully.
   c. Surveying can be skipped if you plan to read the entire chapter carefully.
   d. Surveying can lead to greater motivation, interest, confidence, and comprehension.

_____ **3.** When you use the review step of SQ4R,
   a. you should plan to complete the step in fifteen to twenty minutes.
   b. you can return to and answer the questions created in step 2 of SQ4R.
   c. you will want to reread the chapter one more time, paragraph by paragraph.
   d. it only needs to be the day right before a test.

_____ **4.** The topic sentence in a paragraph occurs in this order of frequency:
  a. Implied, first sentence, middle sentence, last sentence.
  b. Last sentence, first sentence, middle sentence, implied.
  c. Middle sentence, first sentence, last sentence, implied.
  d. First sentence, last sentence, middle sentence, implied.

_____ **5.** Which of the following is *not* true of supporting details of a paragraph?
  a. They will be presented using one or more organizational patterns.
  b. They can be facts, definitions, examples, or reasons.
  c. They support the topic sentence of the paragraph.
  d. They will always provide definitions for terminology or unfamiliar words.

Short Answer—Critical Thinking

1. Brandon tells you about his system of reading a textbook. He says, "I open the book and read for as long as I can . When I get tired or bored, I put the book down for about a half an hour. Then I continue to read. When I am done with the chapter, I decide whether or not I understood what I read. If I didn't understand, I read the chapter one or two more times—if I have time." Critique your friend's approach to reading a textbook by answering the following question: Which steps of SQ4R should Brandon learn to use to correct the weaknesses in his current approach to reading a textbook?

2. Katrina uses the steps of SQ4R. She has good vocabulary and understands the meanings of most words she encounters. However, when she tries to restate what was said in a paragraph, she goes blank because she doesn't know how to pinpoint the author's main idea or explain how the idea was developed. Provide a list of suggestions that would help Katrina understand main ideas and the order of details.

Working with Textbook Information

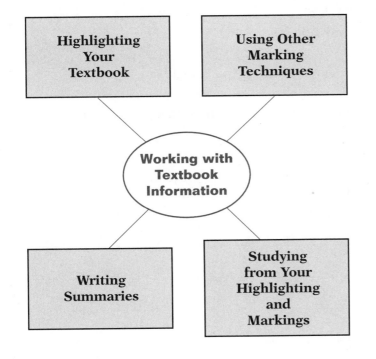

Contrary to what you may have been told most of your life, you should write in your books—especially in your textbooks. What you write or highlight should be done to help you learn and study more efficiently. Do you know how to highlight effectively or do you tend to highlight too much information? Do you use a special technique for the terminology? Do you make good use of available margin space? Do you practice expressing the information in writing prior to a test? This chapter shows you methods for selecting the important information to highlight, ways to mark and create marginal notes, and how to write summaries to use for review later.

CHAPTER 7 Working with Textbook Information

DO, SCORE, and **RECORD** your profile before you read this chapter. If you need to review the process, refer to the complete directions given in the Profile for Chapter 1 on page 2.

	YES	NO
1. I reread chapters at least three times when I am preparing for a test.	_____	_____
2. When I read a chapter, I am usually able to pick out the important details to study.	_____	_____
3. When I highlight, I highlight most of the paragraph.	_____	_____
4. After I have read a paragraph, I can usually find the topic sentence with the main idea.	_____	_____
5. I circle words I know I will have to define.	_____	_____
6. I make brief notes in the margins of my books.	_____	_____
7. I use introductions, special print (bold, italic, or colored), and numerals, and I number words to help me identify supporting details.	_____	_____
8. When I study from my highlighting, I concentrate only on what I marked as important; I try not to read the information I didn't mark.	_____	_____
9. I recite and write summaries by stringing the key ideas and supporting details together to make my own sentences.	_____	_____
10. I use rote memory to recite the exact words and phrases that I highlighted in my notes.	_____	_____
11. All the details in a paragraph seem to be important, so I tend to highlight all of them.	_____	_____
12. I know how to use punctuation and word clues to identify definitions of key terms.	_____	_____

Self-Awareness: Describe a typical way you write in or mark textbooks. Have you established some kind of system to use? Explain your methods and assess their effectiveness.

_____

_____

_____

_____

_____

_____

_____

Highlighting Your Textbook

An effective reader of textbooks must discover how to identify the information that needs to be learned. Chapter 6 discussed the beginning point: finding the main idea of each paragraph. The next step is to identify the details that support the main idea; this information can then be highlighted. Highlighting reduces the amount of information that needs to be studied. When it is time to review the information in a textbook, your study time should be spent focusing on the information that you highlighted and not on rereading entire chapters.

Highlighting involves the use of light-colored highlighter pens to mark the important information to learn. Selectivity is essential. Overmarking a paragraph defeats the purpose of highlighting. Strive to highlight 30–40 percent of the paragraph. Some students prefer to underline important information with a pencil or a pen; however, highlighting is more highly recommended as the colors clearly separate the important information from the less important.

Two levels of information will be highlighted in each paragraph. The steps are shown below:

Steps for Highlighting

1. Locate the topic sentence (the main idea) and highlight it completely.
2. Identify and highlight key words or phrases that support the main idea.

Step One: Find the Topic Sentence

After you have read a paragraph, find the **topic sentence**—main idea—and underline it completely. (You practiced this in Chapter 6.) When you study, a clearly marked topic sentence helps you keep your focus on the author's main point. This is the *only* sentence in a paragraph that should be completely underlined or highlighted. Remember that the main idea or topic sentence must serve as an "umbrella sentence." It must be broad enough that all the other information in the paragraph "fits" under this sentence. Notice how the main ideas underlined in the following passage capture the main point of each paragraph.

(Networking)   In the job-getting process, networking refers to developing a group of acquaintances who might provide job leads and career guidance. The term has been used so much recently that it has perhaps become a buzzword, but it is still an important job-getting tool. Everyone—from the most recent college graduate to the president of a Fortune 500 firm—has a network on which to draw in searching for a job.

Your initial network might include friends, family, professors, former employers, social acquaintances, college alumni, your dentist, family doctor, insurance agent, local business people, your minister or rabbi—in short, everyone you know who might be able to help. Ideally, your network will combine both personal and professional connections. That's one benefit of belonging to professional associations, and college isn't too early to start. Most professional organizations either have student chapters of their associations or provide reduced-rate student memberships in the parent organization.

Step Two: Find the Supporting Details

By finding the topic sentence, you know the main idea or main point of the paragraph. Now you need to identify the important details that support this topic sentence. If you were asked to explain the topic sentence or "prove" the point made in it, which key words, phrases, definitions, facts, statistics, or examples would you use in your explanation? Locate these **supporting details** or key words and mark them. You can skip over words such as *to, and, with, also,* and *in addition* because they are not key words. If a key word is used several times, mark it only once. As you are looking for key words, take note of lists, **bullets** (dashes or dots), and marginal notes. All these may indicate important supporting details.

Once you identify specific supporting details, you need to ask yourself whether or not the details are important to learn. Some details, such as extended explanations of examples, help you understand a concept but are not details you are expected to know. Selectivity is essential so that you do not highlight too much unnecessary information. Because you are selecting details that will serve as triggers or associations for *your memory,* you may select key words or phrases that other students may not feel are necessary. As long as you are targeting the essential details, do not be concerned if your highlighting is not exactly the same as another student's highlighting. Generally speaking, supporting details you will be highlighting include the following:

- specific facts such as names, dates, places, or statistics
- definitions
- reasons or expanded explanations
- causes or effects
- examples

Notice which supporting details are underlined in the following example. Are these the same details you would choose to underline?

> Global politics, then, has many kinds of issues. Some, such as U.S.–Russian arms negotiations or Syrian–Israeli peace negotiations, involve the quest for security. Others, such as negotiations on trade barriers, focus on economic questions. Still others, such as controversies about acid rain, are about threats to the environment. In other words, the enormous range of issues in global politics covers diverse topics. Increasingly, the global agenda is attracting nontraditional issues that either produce cooperation or necessitate collaboration if disaster is to be avoided.
>
> Mansbach, *The Global Puzzle,* p. 19.

Most paragraphs that you read will have a topic sentence and supporting details. However, on occasion you may encounter a paragraph that does not seem to have any new information. This may be a **transition paragraph**; the information in it does not need to be marked. Transition paragraphs

- Are designed to help ideas from one paragraph flow smoothly into the next paragraph.
- Are usually short.
- Do not contain strong main ideas or new details.

If the paragraph you are reading is more than a few sentences long and contains new terminology or new ideas, it is not a transition paragraph. Do not skip over it; read more carefully to find the important information to highlight.

✎ **EXERCISE 7.1 Highlighting Main Ideas and Supporting Details**

Return to the following exercises. Identify and highlight the main ideas and the supporting details that you feel are important. Compare your work with the work of another student. Remember, it is very likely that you and the other student will not have selected exactly the same key words or phrases to highlight.
      Go to Exercise 6.5 (page 117) or Exercise 6.6 (page 118).

Using Other Marking Techniques

Selecting and highlighting the main ideas and the important key words or phrases for the supporting details are the basics of marking a textbook. However, additional techniques can be used to refine the process of marking your textbooks. Each of the following techniques should be used when appropriate to clarify or organize the information more effectively:

Other Marking Techniques

1. Circle important terminology.
2. Add numbers to label steps or lists of information.
3. Add brackets with abbreviations for larger sections of important information.
4. Add marginal notes.

Circle Terminology

More than 60 percent of most test questions are based directly on knowing and understanding specialized terminology (vocabulary words). For this reason, it is important to identify and mark the terms you need to define. Words that are underlined or printed in bold, italic, or colored print are usually terms to know. *Circle key terms to make them stand out.* Then mark the main points of the term's definitions.

   In the following example, notice how the main idea is underlined, key words and phrases are underlined, and terms to know are circled.

> **Decisional Roles** As you might suspect, a (decisional role) is one that involves various aspects of management decision making. The decisional role can be subdivided into the following four specific managerial roles. In the role of (entrepreneur,) the manager is the voluntary initiator of change. For example, a manager for Coca-Cola who develops a new strategy or expands the sales force into a new market is playing the entrepreneur's role. A second role is that of (disturbance handler.) A manager who settles a strike is handling a disturbance. Third, the manager also occasionally plays the role of (resource allocator.) In this role, the manager might have to decide which departmental budgets to cut and which expenditure requests to approve. The fourth role is that of (negotiator.) Being a negotiator might involve settling a dispute between a manager and a worker assigned to the manager's work group.
>
> Pride, *Business*, p. 185.

Frequently the definitions for special terminology (vocabulary words to know) are given within the paragraph. Two kinds of clues that are used to draw your attention to the definitions are summarized following:

Summary Chart

Punctuation Clues			Word Clues
commas	,	,	also, defined as, is, are, called,
dashes	—	—	means, known as, referred to as, to
parentheses	(	)	describe, which is, or
colon	:		

The first kind of clue involves **punctuation clues**. *Commas, dashes, parentheses,* and *colons* are forms of punctuation that signal a definition. The definition is often found between the commas or dashes, inside the parentheses, or following a colon. Notice how the punctuation clues in the following examples signal the definition.

The use of a (quality circle) *a group of employees who meet on company time to solve problems of product quality,* is one way that auto makers are implementing this strategy at operations level.

Instead, Aristarchus propounded the (heliocentric theory)—*that the earth and the planets revolve around the sun.*

Credibility problems can occur from improper or careless (enunciation) (*the way you articulate and pronounce words in context*).

An (empirical formula) is the simplest formula for a compound: *the formula of a substance written with the smallest integer subscripts.*

The second type of clue that signals definitions is the **word clue**. The following words are used frequently to link a vocabulary word to its definition:

also	defined as	referred to as	known as	called
is/are	to describe	mean/means	which is	or

Often, the term is presented first and then followed by the definition. However, the order can be reversed; the definition may be given first followed by the naming of the term. Notice how these word clues are used in the following sentences to signal the definitions:

A (dialect) [is] *a particular speech pattern associated with an area of the country or a cultural or ethnic background.*

When we talk about (culture) *we* [mean] *the customary traits, attitudes, and behaviors of a group of people.*

Add Numbers

A topic sentence that uses words such as *kinds of, reasons, advantages, causes, effects, ways,* or *steps* often has a list of supporting details. **Ordinals,** or "number words," such as first, second, or third, may point you in the direction of individual details. Use a pen to write the numerals (1, 2, 3) on top of the ordinals. Also watch for words such as *next, another reason,* and *finally,* which are **place holder words** used to replace ordinals. Read carefully and write a new numeral on these words as well.

Sometimes ordinals are not used. A clue may be given, however, as to the number of details you should find. For example, saying that there are "five reasons" for something lets you know that you should find five details. These details can be numbered clearly. With a pen, write *1* where the first item in the list is discussed, write *2* where the second item is discussed, and so on until each supporting detail is numbered. Your final number of details should match the original clue (five reasons).

Summary Chart: Signals Used to Guide Numbering in Notes

Topic Sentence Words:	kinds of, reasons, advantages, causes, ways, steps . . .
Ordinals:	first, second, third . . .
Place Holders:	next, also, another, finally . . .
Number Word Clues:	<u>five</u> reasons, <u>four</u> ways, <u>six</u> steps . . .

In the following example, notice how the main ideas (topic sentences) are completely *underlined* and the key words of supporting details are also underlined. Numbers are added to show lists of items. A few marginal notes have been added in the margins to summarize the information.

Consumerism

<u>Consumerism consists of all those activities that are undertaken to protect the rights of consumers in their dealings with business.</u> Consumerism has been with us to some extent since the early nineteenth century, but the <u>movement came to life</u> only in the <u>1960s</u>. It was then that <u>President John F. Kennedy</u> declared that the <u>consumer</u> was entitled to a new "<u>bill of rights.</u>"

The Four Basic Rights of Consumers

Consumer rights =
1. Safety
2. Informed
3. Choice
4. Be heard

<u>Kennedy's consumer bill of rights asserted that consumers have a right to safety, to be informed, to choose, and to be heard.</u> These <u>four rights</u> are the <u>basis</u> of much of the <u>consumer-oriented legislation</u> that has been passed during the last twenty-five years. These rights also provide an effective outline of the objectives and accomplishments of the <u>consumer movement</u>.

Add Brackets and Abbreviations

After you have read a paragraph carefully, several sentences may seem extremely important because together they provide an important explanation or include many important terms. To avoid too much marking, draw a *bracket* next to the information instead of underlining or highlighting.

IMP.

1. The bracket reminds you to study the entire marked section.
2. You can use abbreviations in the margins to indicate the content inside the bracket.
3. Common abbreviations used include:

    EX. for example

    DEF. for definition

    IMP. for important

    ? for information you don't understand
4. Use brackets sparingly. Overuse reduces the effectiveness of marking your textbook.

Add Marginal Notes

Marginal notes are written by you in the margins of your textbook. Marginal notes are most effective in textbooks that provide ample space to the left of the text. Marginal notes must remain brief so the page is not cluttered and the notes are easy to read. Marginal notes can include brief:

■ Summaries of the paragraph.

■ Lists of ideas in the paragraph.

■ Key words or words that you will need to be able to define.

■ Short comments or questions.

Marginal notes can be used several ways depending on the complexity of the information you are reading. If there is a lot of new information in the paragraphs, you may first want to mark the paragraphs and then make marginal notes. If the paragraphs are relatively easy to read and do not contain large amounts of information, you may find that the only notes you will need are marginal notes.

Note how marginal notes help clarify the following passage.

Sign mind

— logical

— controls

— judges

— strangles creativity

Design mind

— creative

— imagination

— artistic

— curious

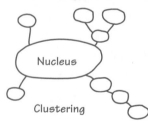

Nucleus

Clustering

In her book *Writing the Natural Way*, Gabrielle Rico explains the method she devised to help her students get in touch with the creative, inventive part of themselves. Rico calls the part of ourselves that is always trying to be logical and put things in the right order the "Sign mind." The other creative part of ourselves that is longing to express our well-hidden imagination and artistic ability she calls the "Design mind." Rico's Sign mind . . . controls, judges, and supervises. To get out from under this watchdog, who tends to strangle our creative impulses in their early stages, Rico suggests the strategy she calls clustering as a way of giving your playful, curious Design mind free rein to generate ideas.

IMP:
Begin with a nucleus word circled on an empty page. Then go with any connections that come into your head, writing each down in its own circle. Connect each new word or phrase with a line to the previous circle. "As you cluster," Rico warns, "you may experience a sense of randomness or, if you are somewhat skeptical, an uneasy sense that it isn't leading anywhere. . . . Trust this natural process, though. We all cluster mentally throughout our lives without knowing it; we have simply never made these clusterings visible on paper."

✎ **EXERCISE 7.2   Practicing Highlighting and Marking Passages**

Photocopy one page from one of your textbooks. Select a page that begins with a heading or a subheading. Practice highlighting and marking the page. Bring your work to class to share.

✎ **EXERCISE 7.3 Applying What You Have Learned**

Use the highlighting and marking techniques you have learned from this chapter to show the main ideas and important supporting details in the following passage.

Maslow's Hierarchy of Needs

The concept of a hierarchy of needs was advanced by Abraham Maslow, a psychologist. A **need** is a personal requirement. Maslow assumed that humans are "wanting" beings who seek to fulfill a variety of needs. He assumed that these needs can be arranged according to their importance in a sequence known as **Maslow's hierarchy of needs**.

At the most basic level are **physiological needs,** the things we require to survive. These needs include food and water, clothing, shelter, and sleep. In the employment context, these needs are usually satisfied through adequate wages.

At the next level are **safety needs,** the things we require for physical and emotional security. Safety needs may be satisfied through job security, health insurance, pension plans, and safe working conditions.

Next are the **social needs,** the human requirements for love and affection and a sense of belonging. To an extent, these needs can be satisfied through the work environment and the informal organization. But social relationships beyond the workplace—with family and friends, for example—are usually needed, too.

At the level of **esteem needs,** we require respect and recognition (the esteem of others), as well as a sense of our own accomplishment and worth (self-esteem). These needs may be satisfied through personal accomplishment, promotion to more responsible jobs, various honors and awards, and other forms of recognition.

At the uppermost level are **self-realization needs,** the needs to grow and develop as people and to become all that we are capable of being. These are the most difficult needs to satisfy, and the means of satisfying them tend to vary with the individual. For some people, learning a new skill, starting a new career after retirement, or becoming the "best there is" at some endeavor may be the way to satisfy the self-realization needs.

Maslow suggested that people work to satisfy their physiological needs first, then their safety needs, and so on up the "needs ladder." In general, they are motivated by the needs at the lowest (most important) level that remain unsatisfied. However, needs at one level do not have to be completely satisfied before needs at the next-higher level come into play. If the majority of a person's physiological and safety needs are satisfied, that person will be motivated primarily by social needs. But any physiological and safety needs that remain unsatisfied will also be important.

Maslow's hierarchy of needs provides a useful way of viewing employee motivation, as well as a guide for management. By and large, American business has been able to satisfy workers' basic needs, but the higher-order needs present more of a problem. They are not satisfied in a simple manner, and the means of satisfaction vary from one employee to another.

Pride, *Business*, pp. 270–271.

Self-realization needs

Esteem needs

Social needs

Safety needs

Physiological needs

Maslow's Hierarchy of Needs

Maslow believed that people seek to fulfill five categories of needs.

Studying from Your Highlighting and Markings

The process of highlighting and marking is only the beginning step in learning. You must now *use* these markings to help you learn important information.

How to Use Marking

1. Reread only the marked information.
2. String the marked information together to make sentences.
3. Recite using your own words.

Reread

Read what you have highlighted; include any numbering that you added. Do *not* let yourself reread the information that is not marked. Review these notes slowly to allow time for your mind to absorb, connect, and associate the information. You may want to read out loud to help your concentration and increase your comprehension. During this step, your reading will sound broken or fragmented. However, you will be reading all the main ideas and the key words of selected details.

String Ideas Together

Look at the marked information again. Instead of just reading, string the words, phrases, and sentences together by using some of your own words to connect the ideas together in full sentences. As you begin **stringing ideas** together, include the main idea and the important supporting details. This is an ideal time to turn on a tape recorder if you would benefit from having a review tape to use for studying. In addition to verbalizing the ideas, you can practice picturing or visualizing the information in the paragraph. Practice stringing the ideas together in your own words helps you *personalize* what you are reading. You are, in fact, converting textbook language into your own, more common form of language. In doing so, you are practicing expressing information in a more familiar form of language—your own.

Refer back to the excerpt about the "Sign mind" and the "Design mind" (page 130). When you look only at the marked information, this is what you'll see:

- Gabrielle Rico explains the method she devised to help her students get in touch with the creative, inventive part of themselves.
- logical, right order—"Sign mind"
- other creative part, imagination and artistic ability—"Design mind"
- "Sign mind" controls, judges, and supervises
- strangle our creative impulses
- strategy, clustering
- playful, curious "Design mind," generate ideas
- Begin with a nucleus word circled on an empty page.
- natural process—we all cluster mentally

As you see in the next example, all the marked information is used, but the markings are connected with additional words, your own words, that you add so your sentences make sense. When you string the foregoing information together into your own sentences, the result may sound like this:

> Rico uses a method to get in touch with the creative, inventive part of people. The logical part of our minds that tries to put everything in a right order is called the "Sign mind." The other creative part of our minds has imagination and our artistic ability. This part is called the "Design mind." The Sign mind always tries to control, judge, and supervise our thinking. It strangles our creative impulses. Rico has a strategy called clustering that helps the playful, curious Design mind to generate ideas.
>
> Clustering begins with a nucleus word circled on an empty page. New words that are related to the nucleus are written down and connected to the nucleus. This is a natural process. We all cluster mentally.

Recite

After you have practiced stringing ideas together, you are ready to try **reciting** the same information out loud in full sentences and without looking. You will be **paraphrasing**, putting the information in your own words. If you were to recite word for word exactly as it was printed in the book, you would be emphasizing rote memory, a type of memory that is not as effective as thorough learning. After you have recited from memory, look back at your book to check your accuracy. Use your marginal notes and other markings as feedback to accuracy. If you made some mistakes, practice saying the information correctly.

Reciting reinforces the information you are learning and imprints the information more firmly in your long-term memory. As you remember, reciting is a principle of memory. It is powerful and it works! If you are an auditory learner, turn on a tape recorder while you are reciting. By recording yourself paraphrasing what you have read, you will create an excellent study tape that you can listen to for reviewing.

✎ **EXERCISE 7.4   Stringing Highlighted Information Together and Reciting**

Return to Exercise 7.3. Reread only the information that was highlighted. Remember, your reading will sound broken or fragmented at this point. Then go back and string the ideas together by adding your own words to connect the highlighted information. Look away. Recite the information about Maslow's hierarchy. Refer back to the passage to check your levels of detail and your accuracy. Practice this several times until you feel prepared to recite the information to a partner, a group, or the class.

✎ **EXERCISE 7.5 Forgetting Theories**

1. *Read the following passage carefully. Then, find the main idea and high-light it completely. Identify and highlight key words and phrases that are supporting details.*

2. *Read the highlighted information. String the ideas together in complete sentences; add your own words as necessary.*

3. *Practice reciting the information in this passage without looking at the printed page.*

Theories of Forgetting

Even when the twelve principles of memory are used, some information may be forgotten. The following five **theories of forgetting** are offered by psychologists to explain some of the reasons information can be "forgotten." The *Decay Theory* applies to short-term memory. It is possible that some stimuli, when received, are too weak. The information simply decays or fades away before it can be sorted or processed. Since this information is never processed, it was never really "learned." The second theory, *Displacement Theory,* also occurs in short-term memory. The Displacement Theory states that if too much information comes into short-term memory too rapidly, some of the information already in short-term memory is shoved aside or displaced. Adequate time was not given to process the information that was displaced; such information, therefore, also was never really "learned." The *Interference Theory* applies to confusion that takes place in long-term memory. One type of confusion occurs when the new information you are learning interferes with your recalling or retrieving information that was previously learned. For example, if you once knew how to speak Portuguese, but are now studying Spanish, words that you once knew in Portuguese may be difficult to locate in memory because your newly acquired language skills in Spanish are interfering. This type of forgetting occurs more frequently when the new and the old information are similar in nature. A second type of confusion occurs when old information interferes with learning new information. The old infor-mation is so thoroughly imprinted that it is recalled or retrieved instead of the new information that you are trying to learn. The *Incomplete Encoding Theory* applies to information as it is rehearsed. Some information is only partially learned or learned inaccurately. When a person tries to recall this information, "forgetting" occurs. The information cannot be remembered because it was not completely processed or imprinted in the memory system. The *Retrieval Failure Theory* occurs when information has been learned, but it cannot be "found" in the memory bank. Failure to locate information in memory may be attributed to a weak organizational system for storing or "filing" information or to lack of use. The information learned was not firmly attached or associated to well-developed schemas or on-going review to practice accessing the information did not occur. Thus, as has been shown above, information can be "forgotten" during several different stages of the Information Processing Model. Effective strategies for taking in information and processing, storing, and rehearsing it can reduce or eliminate the effects of the five main theories of forgetting.

⊕⊕ Exercise 7.6 LINKS

1. The power of pictures and visualizing was discussed in Chapters 1 and 2. If you had difficulty remembering all five theories of forgetting, adding pictures to your memory and recitation work may enhance your ability to recall the information. Under each of the following pictures, name the forgetting theory.

5 Theories of Forgetting

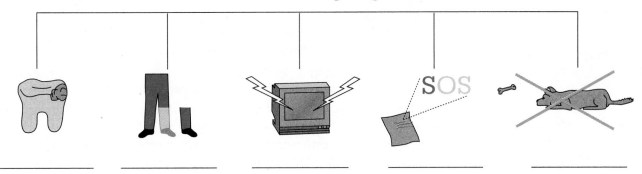

2. *Acronyms* can sometimes be used to strengthen remembering a list of items. Since the forgetting theories do not need to be learned or listed in a specific order, an acronym could be made. Write the five forgetting theories below. Select *one letter* for each theory. Write the letters and then look to see if you can rearrange the letters to create an acronym.

List the Five Theories	Write the Letters	Create Your Acronym
1. _____	_____	_____
2. _____	_____	
3. _____	_____	
4. _____	_____	
5. _____	_____	

3. Draw the Information Processing Model. On the model, show where each theory of forgetting occurs. Organize your work in a way that is easy to read and understand.

Writing Summaries

Summaries are paragraphs that present only the highlights of the information you read. A summary will definitely include the main ideas. A summary should briefly mention (summarize) the most important supporting details. Not all details will be expanded in depth. Minor details, such as examples that were used to develop a point, do not need to be in the summary. Too many minor details will not result in a concise summary. Too few details will not provide you with much information when you later want to use your summary to review the information or prepare for a test.

Summary writing is valuable for several reasons:

1. Many students learn and remember information more readily if they have the opportunity to write it or type it on a computer.

2. Individuals with strong visual print memories can more readily recall the information when it is seen in a shortened or condensed form.

3. Students who have difficulty expressing ideas on paper, especially during essay tests, have the opportunity to practice organizing and expressing ideas on paper *before the test.*

4. Summary writing has many of the same values as reciting. If you can express the information in your own words in a logical, clear manner, you know it.

5. Summaries with the main ideas and most important supporting details are excellent study tools to use for ongoing review of previously discussed chapters and for test preparation.

There are many methods that you may find helpful for structuring your summaries. Three common methods shown below are excellent methods to begin the practice of writing summaries:

Methods for Writing Summaries

1. Record on paper the same information that you speak when you "string ideas together."
2. Develop a chapter mapping. Use the mapping to guide your summary writing.
3. Use chapter features or a chapter outline to guide the structure of your summary.

Summary from Stringing Ideas

When you string highlighted information together, you are basically creating a verbal summary. This same information, when written on paper, becomes a written summary. This summary should state the main ideas and connect the important supporting details by using some of your own words. A written summary for the "Decisional Roles" passage (page 127) may appear as follows:

> A decisional role is one that involves various aspects of management decision making. There are four specific managerial roles that are part of the decisional role. The first is the role of the entrepreneur where the manager becomes the voluntary initiator of change. The second decisional role is that of a disturbance handler in which the manager deals with specific kinds of disturbances. The third role is the resource allocator. The manager in this role makes decisions regarding budget expenditures to approve. The fourth role is that of negotiator; the manager assumes the role of settling disputes.

**Summary from
Chapter Mappings**

Chapter mappings are visual pictures of the topic of the chapter, its main points (headings), and important subpoints (subheadings). After a chapter mapping has been developed, write your summary by discussing each of the branches that stem from the center of the mapping. Your mapping will only show key words, so you will need to use your own words to string the words together into meaningful, organized sentences. In most cases, each heading can be written as a paragraph. Your summary of a chapter will consist of several paragraphs.

**Summary from
Chapter Features
or Outlines**

Some textbooks include chapter features such as summaries that can be the "skeleton" or the structure for summary writing. If the chapter summary is written as a list of important points, expand the list with additional details. Look for meaningful ways to combine the chapter summary points into full paragraphs.

If the textbook does not give a **chapter outline**, you can create your own outline by listing the main headings on paper. Then list the subheadings under each main heading. You may add one or more additional levels of information to include some of the key supporting details of the chapter. Use this outline to guide your summary writing. Include each point in the order that it is presented. Add your own words so the information flows together smoothly. For this chapter, the outline would look like this:

Working with Textbook Information

A. Highlighting Your Textbook
  1. Find the topic sentence
  2. Find the supporting details
B. Using Other Marking Techniques
  1. Circle terminology
  2. Add numbers
  3. Add brackets and abbreviations
  4. Add marginal notes
C. Studying from Your Highlighting and Markings
  1. Reread
  2. String Ideas Together
  3. Recite
D. Writing Summaries
  1. Summary from Stringing Ideas
  2. Summary from Chapter Mappings
  3. Summary from Chapter Features or Outlines

✎ EXERCISE 7.7 Writing Summaries

Select one *of the following options to practice summary writing.*

Option 1: Use your highlighting and markings as guides to write a summary for *each* of the passages in Exercise 7.2.
Option 2: Use your highlighting and markings as guides to write a summary for Maslow's Hierarchy of Needs in Exercise 7.3.
Option 3: Use your highlighting and markings as guides to write a summary for the Theories of Forgetting in Exercise 7.5.
Option 4: Expand any chapter mapping (except Chapter 2) and use the mapping as your guide to writing a chapter summary.
Option 5: Use a chapter outline for any textbook as your guide. Write a chapter summary. Photocopy the chapter outline from the book and turn it in with your summary.
Option 6: Begin with a chapter summary found at the end of each chapter. Expand this summary by adding details.

✎   **EXERCISE 7.8 Programs for Coping with Stress and Promoting Health**

Use your highlighting and marking skills on the following section taken from a psychology textbook. Look for a topic sentence in each paragraph and highlight it. Selectively highlight the important supporting details. Use any other marking system (circling terminology or adding numbers) and marginal notes that would make studying this section easier.

Developing Coping Strategies   Like stress responses, strategies for coping with stress can be cognitive, emotional, behavioral, or physical. *Cognitive coping strategies* change how people interpret stimuli and events. They help people to think more calmly, more rationally, and constructively in the face of stress and may generate a more hopeful emotional state. For example, students with heavy course loads may experience anxiety, confusion, discouragement, lack of motivation, and the desire to run away from it all. Frightening, catastrophic thoughts about their tasks (for example, "What if I fail?") can amplify stress responses. Cognitive coping strategies replace catastrophic thinking with thoughts in which stressors are viewed as challenges rather than threats (Ellis & Bernard, 1985). This substitution process is often called **cognitive restructuring** (Lazarus, 1971; Meichenbaum, 1977; see Chapter 16). It can be done by practicing constructive thoughts such as "All I can do is the best I can." Cognitive coping does not eliminate stressors, but it can help people perceive them as less threatening and thus make them less disruptive.

Seeking and obtaining social support from others are effective *emotional coping strategies.* The perception that one has emotional support, and is cared for and valued by others, tends to be an effective buffer against the ill effects of many stressors (Taylor, 1995). With emotional support comes feedback from others, along with advice on how to approach stressors. Having enhanced emotional resources is associated with increased survival time in cancer patients (Anderson, 1992), improved immune function (Kiecolt-Glaser & Glaser, 1992), and more rapid recovery from illness (Taylor, 1995).

Behavioral coping strategies involve changing behavior in ways that minimize the impact of stressors. Time management is one example. You might keep track of your time for a week and start a time-management plan. The first step is to set out a schedule that shows how your time is now typically spent; then decide how to allocate your time in the future. A time-management plan can help control catastrophizing thoughts by providing reassurance that there is enough time for everything and a plan for handling it all.

Behavioral, emotional, and cognitive skills often interact closely. Discussing stressors and seeking feedback from others help you think more rationally and calmly, and make it easier to develop and use sensible plans for behavioral coping. When behavioral coping eliminates or minimizes stressors, people find it easier to think and feel better about themselves.

Physical coping strategies are aimed at directly altering one's physical responses before, during, or after stressors occur. The most common physical coping strategy is some form of drug use. Prescription medications are sometimes an appropriate coping aid, especially when stressors are severe and acute, such as the sudden death of one's child. But if people depend on prescriptions or other drugs, including alcohol, to help them face stressors, they often attribute any success to the drug, not to their own skill. Furthermore, the drug effects that blunt stress responses may also interfere with the ability to apply coping strategies. If the drug is abused, it can become a stressor itself. The resulting loss of perceived control over stressors may make those stressors even more threatening and disruptive.

Nonchemical methods of reducing physical stress reactions include progressive relaxation training, physical exercise, biofeedback training, and meditation, among others (Carrington, 1984; Dubbert, 1992; Tarler-Benlolo, 1978).

Web-site links are available online.

Computer Projects

Use your computer to make a bar graph of your levels of needs using Maslow's Hierarchy of Needs. For directions, go to: http://www.green-river.com/lesson21.htm

Group Web-Search Activity is available online.

Case Studies are available online.

SUMMARY

- The purpose of highlighting and marking textbooks is to reduce the amount of information that needs to be studied.

- Main ideas (topic sentences) and important supporting details should be highlighted.

- Circling terminology and adding numbers, brackets, abbreviations, and marginal notes can also help to identify important details to learn.

- Punctuation clues (commas, dashes, parentheses, and colons) and word clues (defined, as, means, known as, is, and are) may signal the definitions of key terms to know.

- Three steps may be used to study information that has been highlighted and marked:

  1. Reread the highlighted sentences and key phrases or words.

  2. String the highlighted information together by adding your own words to make complete sentences.
  3. Recite without looking at the printed information. Check your accuracy.

- Writing summaries helps the learning and memory process. Summaries may be written based on:

  1. Stringing highlighted information together in a written form.
  2. Explaining the information in an expanded chapter visual mapping.
  3. Using chapter features as a guide or structure for the summary.
  4. Expanding a chapter outline into full sentences and paragraphs.

OPTIONS FOR PERSONALIZING CHAPTER 7

1. **PROFILE CHART—PERSONAL LOG**   Answer the following questions in your personal log.

   What score did you have on the Chapter 7 Profile? _____

   What did you learn in this chapter that will change the way you previously highlighted or marked textbooks? You may want to refer to the Self-Awareness paragraph you may have completed on page 124 at the beginning of the chapter.

2. **WORDS TO KNOW**   The following terminology is important to know. You should be able to define each of the following terms.

highlighting	word clue	stringing ideas
topic sentence	ordinals	reciting
supporting details	place holder words	paraphrasing
bullets	marginal notes	theories of forgetting
transition paragraph	Maslow's Hierarchy	summaries
punctuation clues	of Needs	chapter outline

3. **EXPAND THE VISUAL MAPPING**   Add supporting details to each of the main branches or main ideas of this chapter. After you have expanded the visual mapping, use your mapping as a guide to write a summary of the chapter.

4. **WRITING ASSIGNMENT 1**   To be a successful student, you must learn how your own memory works. The three aspects of *metamemory* are shown below. For each one, discuss what you already know about yourself. This writing involves *intrapersonal* thought. There are no wrong answers as long as you explain your responses clearly.
   a. What are the *abilities and limitations* of your memory system?
   b. What are some of the *different kinds of memory tasks* you are expected to do in your various courses?
   c. What are some of the *different strategies* you have found yourself using for the different kinds of memory tasks you need to perform? In other words, you do not likely use the same strategy for every learning task. Give examples of different approaches for different tasks.

5. **WRITING ASSIGNMENT 2**   Discuss Maslow's Hierarchy of Needs theory. (See page 131.) Do you agree that "humans are wanting beings who seek to fulfill a variety of needs"? Do you support Maslow's theory that the five basic needs occur in the sequence he gives? Have you ever worked on the five needs levels in a different sequence, or have you found this sequence truly does reflect the pattern of your life? Are there any basic needs that are not mentioned by Maslow and are not included in his five needs levels?

6. **PORTFOLIO DEVELOPMENT**   Use a textbook from another class, and select any chapter to use to demonstrate your understanding and ability to highlight selectively and to use other marking techniques and marginal notes. Photocopy the textbook pages so they can be put into your portfolio. For the same chapter, include a chapter summary. The summary may be based on your highlighting and marking, based on a chapter mapping that you create, based on textbook features provided in the book, or based on a chapter outline that is either in the book or is created by you.

CHAPTER 7 REVIEW QUESTIONS

Multiple-Choice

Choose the best answer *for each of the following questions. Write the letter of the best answer on the line.*

_____ 1. Which of the following is *not* true about writing summaries?
a. Summaries reflect the information that was highlighted in a paragraph.
b. Summaries must be presented in the form of short lists or categories.
c. Summaries include some textbook wording and some of your own wording.
d. Summaries show topic sentences and the supporting details of a paragraph.

_____ 2. Which of the following is *not* true about notetaking in a textbook?
a. It should be done only for textbooks that are difficult to read.
b. It uses selectivity to reduce the amount of information that a student needs to study.
c. It reduces overall reading time so more time can be devoted to the process of learning.
d. It can include highlighting, underlining, or making marginal notes.

_____ 3. When you identify important supporting details in a paragraph, you
a. need to completely underline or highlight the sentence they are in.
b. select key words or phrases to highlight.
c. list each of the details in alphabetical order in the margins.
d. make a mental note to yourself that they support the main idea.

_____ 4. Supporting details
a. can be words, phrases, definitions, or facts that support the topic sentence.
b. can sometimes be marked in the text with the use of bullets.
c. that are words you will need to define should be circled.
d. all of the above.

_____ 5. When careful highlighting and marking are used in a textbook,
a. every single paragraph will have important information marked.
b. approximately 80 percent of the paragraph should be underlined or highlighted.
c. transitional paragraphs are the only paragraphs that will not be marked.
d. all important supporting details will be circled.

_____ 6. If a topic sentence states, "Six strategies can be used to strengthen your vocabulary," the reader
a. should add numbers to his or her marking to indicate each strategy.
b. should watch for ordinals and use the ordinals to number each strategy.
c. needs to be aware of the use of "place holders" that replace ordinals.
d. all of the above.

_____ 7. After the important information in a chapter has been highlighted, the
a. student then needs to practice rereading the highlighted information out loud.
b. student has learned the information and can begin the next chapter.
c. highlighted information needs to be reread, strung together, and recited.
d. highlighted information needs to be copied in an outline form

_____ 8. When highlighted information is "strung together," the student
a. connects the marked words together by adding his or her own words or sentences.
b. rereads aloud all of the information that was highlighted.
c. writes the information in phrases on paper in the same order they were found in the book.
d. connects all of the topic sentences together so they appear one right after another.

_____ **9.** Paraphrasing
   a. is a process that students should use to promote rote memory.
   b. involves restating information in your own words.
   c. involves repeating information in the exact words that were given in the textbook.
   d. all of the above.

_____ **10.** Since many students find that writing reinforces the learning of information,
   a. short notes and lists of information can be written in the margins of the book.
   b. the information highlighted or underlined can be transferred to notes on notebook paper.
   c. ideas can be strung together verbally and then written into the form of a summary.
   d. all of the above.

Short Answers—Case Studies

*Carefully read the following situations. Identify the problem area. Provide
solutions based on the information you learned in this chapter.*

1. Tim gets so frustrated during tests that have essay questions. He feels like he studies hard and knows the information, but it takes him too long to express his ideas on paper. He does well with true-false and multiple-choice questions, but he does poorly on essay tests. What can Tim do to increase his speed for getting ideas out of his head and onto the paper?

2. Janet was so excited with all the colored highlighters she bought, and she used a lot of different colors to highlight almost everything in every paragraph. How can she continue to use a variety of colors but show that she can be more selective? Give her several suggestions that would improve her skills at highlighting.

Learning Terminology

A well-developed vocabulary enables you to explain your own ideas more precisely and comprehend more accurately when you read materials written on higher levels. Do you currently use a system for studying new terms or vocabulary? Do you find that words are "on the tip of your tongue" but that you just can't seem to say or write them when needed? When you read, can you find the meaning of most unfamiliar words without looking in the dictionary? The study tools and strategies in this chapter help you expand your vocabulary.

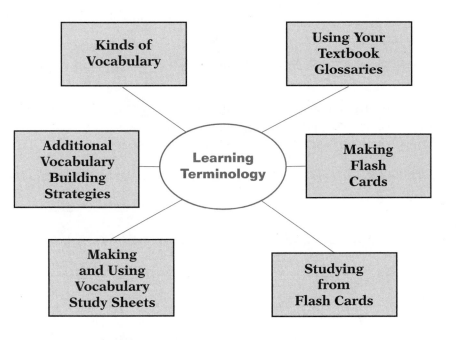

- Kinds of Vocabulary
- Using Your Textbook Glossaries
- Additional Vocabulary Building Strategies
- Learning Terminology
- Making Flash Cards
- Making and Using Vocabulary Study Sheets
- Studying from Flash Cards

CHAPTER 8 **Vocabulary Profile**

DO, SCORE, and **RECORD** your profile before you read this chapter. If you need to review the process, refer to the complete directions given in the Profile for Chapter 1 on page 2.

	YES	NO
1. I actively use methods to increase my vocabulary.	_____	_____
2. I make flash cards that have general lists of related words and cards that give definitions.	_____	_____
3. When I use flash cards, I read only from the front and try to recite what's on the back.	_____	_____
4. I do well on test questions that ask me to write definitions for key words.	_____	_____
5. I review vocabulary words and definitions at least once a week.	_____	_____
6. I have problems finding the definitions of words in paragraphs.	_____	_____
7. I know how to use glossaries in the back of my textbooks.	_____	_____
8. I try to understand a new word by looking at its prefix, suffix, base, or root.	_____	_____
9. I have problems comprehending some textbooks because I don't understand meanings of words.	_____	_____
10. I make an effort to learn unfamiliar words that I hear in conversations, in a lecture, or on television.	_____	_____
11. I always have to use a dictionary to look up meanings of new words.	_____	_____
12. I study vocabulary using techniques that give me immediate feedback.	_____	_____

Self-Awareness: On a scale of 1–10, discuss your opinion about your levels of reading vocabulary, writing vocabulary, and speaking vocabulary. Which level is the most developed? Which is the weakest?

_____

_____

_____

_____

_____

_____

_____

_____

Kinds of Vocabulary

Developing a strong vocabulary is essential for effective communication. A strong vocabulary requires the acquisition of two kinds of vocabularies: receptive and expressive. **Receptive vocabulary** consists of words that you understand when you *hear* them or *read* them. With receptive vocabulary you are *receiving* the words with your eyes or your ears. With a well-developed receptive vocabulary, you are able to read and comprehend more material on higher levels. The following techniques will expand your receptive vocabulary:

1. When you are reading, pay attention to unfamiliar words. Take the time to figure out their meanings by using punctuation or word clues (Chapter 7), using context clues based on the information in the surrounding sentences, using a dictionary or thesaurus, or looking them up in an electronic, handheld spell checker with a **dictionary** or **thesaurus**.

2. In your book where you encountered the word, write the meaning of the word in the margin or substitute the unfamiliar word with a familiar word (Chapter 6). Study the meaning of this word when you study the information on that page.

3. Make your own dictionary or set of flash cards of unfamiliar words that you encountered while reading. Make an *effort* to add these words to your vocabulary.

4. Write down unfamiliar words that you hear. As soon as possible, look the words up in a dictionary. Think back to how the word was used in context when you heard it spoken. Add this word to your own dictionary or set of flash cards.

5. Play word games such as crossword puzzles or Scrabble. Have fun learning new words!

6. Become familiar with the meanings of common prefixes, suffixes, and Greek or Latin roots (word parts). A list of common word parts is online in this book's web site.

7. Consider enrolling in a vocabulary-building class or locate a vocabulary-building self-study workbook. The benefits of having a large receptive vocabulary are many, so the time and effort for independent study will be well spent.

Having a large receptive vocabulary is essential, for it is from this vocabulary that you expand your **expressive vocabulary**. Expressive vocabulary consists of words that you first learn in your receptive vocabulary; you learn them so well that you are able to use them correctly to express yourself when you *speak* and *write*. With a well-developed expressive vocabulary, you are able to use more precise and descriptive words to explain the exact information or images you wish to create for an audience or listener and for the reader of your written work. You become more articulate and your level of communication becomes more sophisticated. In addition to learning the *meanings* of new words taken into your receptive vocabulary, expressive vocabulary requires that you know how to *pronounce* the word correctly, *use* the word in appropriate contexts, and *spell* the word correctly. Because of this additional information that must be learned about a word, the expressive vocabulary is smaller than the receptive vocabulary. You will have many words in your receptive vocabulary that you do not understand sufficiently to use in your own expressive language. You can expand your expressive vocabulary by using the following techniques:

1. Select words that are useful or necessary for you to learn to use to express your ideas. Study these words further by learning how to pronounce them, spell them, and use them correctly in sentences.

2. Frequently use a thesaurus for common words in your writing or speaking. Find words that are more precise and that better describe what you are trying to express.

3. Actively use the new words in your speaking and in your writing. Try to work them into your writing (both personal and academic) and your speaking. As you use the words more frequently, they become more familiar and a part of your accessible vocabulary.

4. Consider enrolling in a vocabulary-building class to learn additional techniques for expanding your expressive vocabulary.

In this chapter, learning the **terminology** (vocabulary words to know) for courses will be emphasized. Since vocabulary is the foundation of understanding any course, you should learn the terminology in each of your classes thoroughly. More than 60 percent of many tests is directly tied to knowing the vocabulary words and their definitions.

Using Your Textbook Glossaries

The **glossary** is a condensed dictionary that gives definitions of key terms in the textbook. When you work with a glossary, keep these three important points in mind:

■ Words that are not key terms for the course, even if they are new words for you, are not in the glossary.

■ The definitions given in the glossary are limited. The words may also have other meanings.

■ If the glossary definition is not clear to you, return to the textbook page to read the word in context or learn more about the word by using a dictionary.

You can also use the glossary as you study. When making flash cards or vocabulary sheets, compare the glossary definition to the one derived from the chapter. Include any additional information or wording that may help you learn the word more accurately. At the end of the term, use the glossary as a review tool: Read through the glossary of terms and then recite the definitions. If the glossary gives page numbers where the terms were used, refer back to those pages for more information as needed. If page numbers are not given, you can use the index in the back of the book to locate page numbers.

If your textbook has no glossary, plan to develop your own glossary or system for listing key terms and definitions, such as using flash cards or vocabulary sheets.

Making Flash Cards

Flash cards are valuable and effective study tools for several reasons. First, when used correctly, they provide you with immediate feedback when you are studying. Second, they are compact and easy to use when you sit down to study or when you have a few extra minutes to review. Third, your set of flash cards can easily be expanded to include information from the textbook as well as the lecture. Fourth, flash cards can be considered an alternative form of notetaking.

How to Make and Use Vocabulary Flash Cards

1. Prepare the flash cards.
2. Make *general category* flash cards.
3. Make *definition* flash cards.

Prepare the Flash Cards

Use three-by-five-inch or five-by-seven-inch index cards to make flash cards (white, colored, lined, or unlined). If you use colored cards, different classes or chapters in the textbook can be assigned specific colors.

Flash cards accumulate quickly, so give some thought to storing them. Several options exist:

- Use recipe boxes to store your cards and dividers to group cards by topics or chapters.
- Punch holes in the cards; use a large metal ring to hold all the cards together.
- Purchase "mini-notebooks" from the college bookstores (dividers are included) for holding flash cards.
- Label envelopes to store your different sets of flash cards.
- Insert small sets of flash cards into "pencil pouches" in notebooks.

Make General Category Flash Cards

Vocabulary terms are often grouped under a larger category. Creating one general card that gives the category on the front and the related terms on the back helps you relate the individual terms to a larger concept (schema). If you know that several terms are related, begin with this **general category flash card**.

Assume you are studying five different theories of forgetting. Your instructor expects you to use the correct terms for these five theories when you speak and write. Before you create the definition cards, develop one general category to help you remember the five theories. A list of related ideas appears on this card.

Category Card

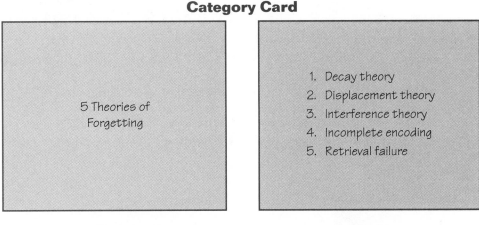

Front

5 Theories of Forgetting

Back

1. Decay theory
2. Displacement theory
3. Interference theory
4. Incomplete encoding
5. Retrieval failure

Notice that the *category is on the front* and the *list of related terms is on the back*. The terms are *not defined* on the back; you want to avoid cluttering the card with too much information. Once you've written the category card, proceed to the definition cards, one for each theory. Your complete set will consist of the number of vocabulary cards plus one general category card.

**Make Definition
Flash Cards**

Individual **definition flash cards** have the term printed clearly on the front of the card. The definition for textbook terminology can be written on the back; the definition should be stated in *three parts*. Using the following three parts to a definition will prepare you to write thorough and accurate definitions on tests. This technique will also remind you to think of both the "big picture" and the "little picture" of words that you study. The **three parts of a definition** are:

1. The *category* (topic) associated with the term (the concept/the big picture).
2. The *formal definition* given by the textbook, glossary, or a dictionary.
3. One *additional detail* (the detail/little picture) to expand the definition. This detail will vary from student to student. Adding one additional detail is your opportunity to show greater understanding of the word. The detail could be a further explanation, an example, or an application.

Definition Card

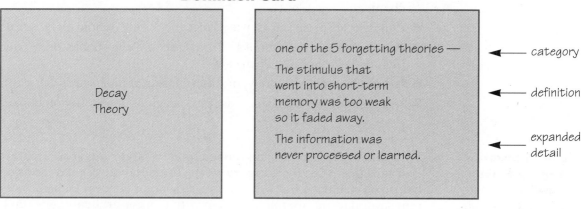

Front   **Back**

Definition flash cards for unfamiliar words that are not textbook terminology may consist mainly of a dictionary definition or a group of synonyms (words with similar meanings) that is taken from a thesaurus. Additional information, such as the pronunciation, **etymology** (word history), or derivatives (related words) may be included on your card.

✎ **EXERCISE 8.1   Making a Set of Flash Cards on Coping Strategies**

Return to Exercise 7.8 on page 138. Review the section "Developing Coping Strategies." Make a category card titled "Four Kinds of Coping Strategies." List the four kinds of strategies on the back of the category card. Then make a definition card for each of the four types of coping strategies. Compare your set of flash cards with those of other students.

✎ **EXERCISE 8.2 Making Flash Cards**

Make a complete set of flash cards (category card and definition cards) for one *of the following:*

1. Maslow's Hierarchy of Needs (page 131)

2. Howard Gardner's Eight Intelligences (page 15)

3. Twelve Principles of Memory (page 34)

4. SQ4R Reading System (page 105)

5. Organizational Patterns in Paragraphs (page 113)

Studying from Flash Cards

Critical thinking and learning occur while you create vocabulary study cards. However, creating the cards is not enough; you need to study and review from the cards. Effective use of your vocabulary cards will occur by involving yourself with the following activities:

> **Learning Activities for Flash Cards**
>
> 1. Study by reciting from the front and the back of the cards.
> 2. Use reflect activities by sorting, summarizing, and grouping.
> 3. Use ongoing review.

Study from Flash Cards

Once you've prepared flash cards, you must use them for studying, or they will have little impact on your learning. To study effectively from flash cards, plan to *study from the front side and from the back side*. The more practice you have working with these words, the more confident you will feel about using the words as you speak and write.

Study from the Front   When you study from the front of the cards, you place the words into your expressive vocabulary. On tests, this will be helpful with true-false, multiple-choice, short-answer, and essay questions. Work from the front of the cards as follows:

1. Begin by stacking the cards with the vocabulary words facing you. Say the word out loud.

2. Recite what you know about the word. Do *not* look at the back of the card.

3. After you have finished reciting, turn the card over for feedback. If you defined the term or gave the correct information for the general category, place the card in a "Yes, I know these" pile.

4. If your feedback indicated that you still don't know the information on the back of the card, read the back out loud slowly. Think about the information. Try to visualize it. Put the card in an "I need to study these more" pile.

5. Review the "I need to study these more" pile once again.

6. Use ongoing review for the complete set of flash cards.

Study from the Back   When you work from the back side of the flash cards, you are challenging your memory in new ways. This method also helps prepare you for fill-in-the-blank questions, which often require you to supply the missing vocabulary word, and for multiple-choice questions, which often give the definition and require you to identify the vocabulary term. To study from the back of the vocabulary cards, use these steps:

1. Read the definition or list of information on the back of the card.
2. Say the vocabulary term that you think is on the front of the card.
3. On a piece of paper, write the term.
4. Check the front of the card to see if you have the correct term and the correct spelling.
5. Once again, make two piles: one pile for cards that were correct and one pile for cards that need more work.
6. Review the cards that need more work.
7. Use ongoing review for the complete set of flash cards.

Reflect with Flash Cards

Many students enjoy working with vocabulary flash cards because they can be used in so many different ways. One obvious advantage is that you can make piles of cards that you know and piles of cards that you need to work with more. A second advantage is that you can use the cards for reflect activities.

The following activities provide you with a multisensory approach to studying vocabulary. You *see* the information, you *recite* the information, and you use a *hands-on* approach to manipulate the cards. You also incorporate critical thinking skills as you creatively find new ways to categorize and organize the information.

1. Shuffle all the vocabulary cards you have. Go through them one by one, sorting the cards into categories that show likeness. Be creative in identifying your categories. For example, if you have made cards all term, you may have the following categories:

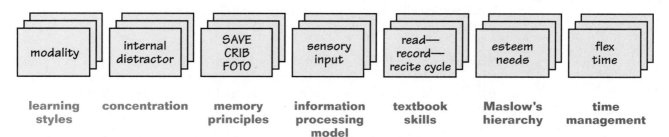

modality	internal distractor	SAVE CRIB FOTO	sensory input	read—record—recite cycle	esteem needs	flex time
learning styles	concentration	memory principles	information processing model	textbook skills	Maslow's hierarchy	time management

2. Select one category of cards above. Lay all the cards in the category word-side up on the table. Try to give a verbal or written summary by using all the words on the cards. This is excellent practice to prepare for essay tests.
3. Shuffle all your cards. Make a mapping on the table similar to the mapping found at the front of each chapter in this book. Again, you will be grouping and categorizing the various cards according to related topics.

✎ **EXERCISE 8.3 Making Flash Cards for Another Class**

Use what you have learned about making flash cards to make a set of flash cards for information that you are studying in another class. Your flash-card set must have at least five cards. Include a category card and definition cards. The definition cards may be for terminology as well as for unfamiliar words that are not vocabulary words for the course. When you turn your cards in, add a card that identifies the course and the textbook used for this assignment.

Making and Using Vocabulary Study Sheets

A second option for creating vocabulary study tools is to use regular notebook paper instead of flash cards. The resulting **vocabulary sheets** contain the same kind of information found on the flash cards. Some students enjoy this option because they prefer having vocabulary work in their notebooks. If you work with a computer, typing your vocabulary sheets provides you with a kinesthetic activity. Set your computer for columns or tables.

How to Make and Use Vocabulary Sheets

1. Prepare a vocabulary sheet with two columns.
2. Include words that describe general categories and words that need definitions.
3. Study by reciting from the left and the right columns.
4. Use ongoing review.

Prepare a Vocabulary Sheet

Begin by drawing a two-and-one-half-inch margin on the left side of the paper. Plan to write only on the front of the paper. Title the top of each page by naming the course, the lecture, or the textbook chapter. This format is the same as the one used for writing questions in SQ4R (see page 106) and for Cornell notes (Chapter 9).

Include Categories and Specific Words

List the general category and the individual terms down the left side of the paper. Write items in the category and the definitions on the right side of the paper. So that your paper isn't cluttered, leave a blank line between each definition and term.

Recite from Both Columns

To get the greatest benefit from your vocabulary sheets, recite and review them frequently. The more often you work with them, the faster the vocabulary words move into your receptive and then into your expressive vocabulary. When you work with your vocabulary sheets, use the following steps to study from both sides of your paper:

Study from the Left-Hand Column Use a piece of paper to cover up the right-hand column. Proceed through these steps:

1. Read the term or category. Recite all the information you can remember about the term. Use complete sentences.
2. Slide your paper down to get feedback. If you were correct, move on to the next term. If you were incorrect, read the definition again. Cover the definition and recite a second time.
3. Put stars by the terms you knew and little checks or symbols by the ones that need more work.

Category	1.
	2.
	3.
	4.
Word	Three-part definition
Word	Three-part definition

Study from the Right-Hand Column   Now reverse the order of studying, just as you did with the flash cards. Different mental operations take place when you reverse the process.

1. Cut or fold the paper so that you have a strip of paper to cover up the left-hand column.
2. Read the definitions or the information on the right-hand side.
3. On the strip of paper, write the term being defined. Continue through the page.
4. Pull the strip of paper away. Compare your answers with the words in the left-hand column. Check your accuracy and your spelling.
5. After you get the feedback about the accuracy of your answers, use a symbol such as a star or highlight the words that need more practice.

Use Ongoing Review

To get the most benefit from your vocabulary sheets, review them frequently. Ongoing review should be a part of your studying strategies. When you first sit down to study, you can review vocabulary sheets as a warm-up activity. When you finish a study block, review the vocabulary sheets. The more you practice, the easier it will be for you to acquire new words for your receptive and expressive vocabularies.

Web-site links are available online.

Computer Projects

1. Scan or copy short passages from your textbooks to use as examples to show different ways terminology is defined. Bring the examples to class. Try to find examples of words defined through punctuation clues, word clues, word structure clues, and context clues.
2. Use the Internet to locate word lists that are valuable for your field of interest. For example, a nursing student may want to find a medical terminology list.
3. Create vocabulary study sheets on your computer. Use either tables or columns or adjust the left margin. Write the terms on the left and the definitions on the right.
4. Look for unfamiliar words in context in magazines, newspapers, or books. Use strategies from this chapter to determine the meanings of the words. Compile a list of words you learned.

Group Web-Search Activity is available online.

Case Studies are available online.

Additional Vocabulary-Building Strategies

Flash cards and vocabulary study sheets are effective study tools for building vocabulary. In Chapter 7, you learned two strategies for identifying definitions within sentences. The first was to use punctuation clues since punctuation marks such as commas, dashes, parentheses, and colons are often used when definitions are given. The second strategy, **word clues**, such as *is defined as, means, is called,* also assist you in locating definitions when they are within the same sentence as the vocabulary word. The following strategies may also be used to help define terminology or unfamiliar words.

**Use Word
Structure Clues**

Words can consist of several structural parts: prefixes, base words, roots, and suffixes. **Prefixes**, often from Greek or Latin, are units of meaning placed before the base word. For example, the prefix *re-* means "again" or "back." The same is true for **suffixes**, the units of meaning placed after the base word to help indicate the part of speech of a word (noun, verb, adjective, or adverb). For example, the suffix *-ness* means "a state, quality, or condition," and it forms a noun. **Base words** are words in English that can stand by themselves. **Roots** are units of meaning, also often from Greek or Latin, that do not form English words until other roots, prefixes, or suffixes are attached to them. For example, *ject* means "to throw"; however, we don't use it as a word until we add another word part (inject, reject, project).

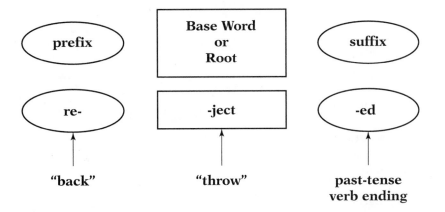

By knowing the meanings of frequently used prefixes, suffixes, and roots, you can figure out the basic definition of many unfamiliar words. **Word structure clues** are helpful tools in the search for word definitions. For example, the word *electroencephalogram* can be broken into its word parts. *Electro* refers to "electrical." *Enceph* refers to the brain, and *gram* refers to a graph. Basically, it is "an electrical brain graph." The glossary definition in a psychology textbook states that an electroencephalogram is "a recording of the electrical signals produced by the nerve cells of the brain, obtained through electrodes attached to the surface of the skull."

Defining a word solely on the structural clues oftentimes does not provide a complete enough definition. After you have the general idea of the word, you can always use a dictionary or the glossary of your book to expand the basic meaning with a full definition.

You can learn hundreds of common word parts to help you determine meanings. Your comprehension of words can be greatly increased by learning the meanings of common prefixes, suffixes, and roots. Check if your college offers vocabulary skill-building courses and if there is a source on campus to obtain lists of structural word parts that you could study and keep in your notebook for quick reference.

✎ **EXERCISE 8.4 Knowledge of the Meanings of Word Parts**

Work with a partner. Together, see how many of the following word parts are familiar to you. Write the meaning of the word part on the line and a word made by using that word part.

Word Part	Meaning	Word
anthro	_____	_____
audio	_____	_____
bio	_____	_____
derma	_____	_____
helio	_____	_____
macro	_____	_____
migra	_____	_____
osteo	_____	_____
pathos	_____	_____
phone	_____	_____
psych	_____	_____
theo	_____	_____
aqua	_____	_____
biblio	_____	_____
cred	_____	_____
graph	_____	_____
hydro	_____	_____
micro	_____	_____
ology	_____	_____
ped	_____	_____
phobia	_____	_____
photo	_____	_____
tele	_____	_____
therma	_____	_____

Use Context Clues   When punctuation clues, word clues, and word structure clues are not provided, try using the **context**—the surrounding words and sentences—to make assumptions about the definition. Because parts of the definition may be scattered throughout several sentences, careful reading is essential. To comprehend sentences and paragraphs, do not skip over words that are unfamiliar to you. Instead, take the opportunity to expand your vocabulary each time you encounter a new word. Use **context clues** to help you understand unfamiliar words even if they are not set off in special print, specified in the margins, or listed as terms to know. If context clues don't provide enough meaning, use a dictionary to find meanings.

The following chart shows common context clues that may appear in your reading.

Context Clue	Definition	Strategy	Example Sentence
Synonyms	words with exact or similar meanings	Try substituting a familiar word (a synonym) for the unfamiliar word.	*probity:* The judge has a keen sense of recognizing a person's honesty and integrity. For that reason, the *probity* of the witness was not questioned.
Antonyms	words with opposite meanings	An unfamiliar word is understood because you understand its opposite.	*impenitent:* Instead of showing shame, regret, or remorse, the con artist was *impenitent.*
Contrast	words that show an opposite or a difference	Look for words such as *differ, different, unlike,* or *opposite of* to understand the differences.	*thallophyte:* Because the fungi is a *thallophyte,* it differs from the other plants in the garden that have embedded roots and the rich foliage of shiny leaves and hardy stems.
Comparison or **Analogies**	words or images that indicate a likeness or a similarity	Look for the commonality between two or more items.	*cajole:* I sensed he was trying to *cajole* me. He reminded me of a salesman trying to sell me a bridge.

Context clues sometimes are not as specific as synonyms, antonyms, or analogies. The meaning of unfamiliar words may simply be "sensed" by relating the information in the surrounding sentences to common sense, personal experience, or a variety of examples. To use these, and all kinds of context clues, the reader must keep a focused mind, concentrate, and search for useful context clues. Reading quickly without time to think, digest the information, and actively be involved with the printed word will leave many unfamiliar words undefined. For this reason, the "read step" of SQ4R encourages the reader to read slowly and to read one paragraph at a time. Use a variety of techniques to understand the full paragraph before moving on. Using context clues is one technique that may be used frequently when careful reading occurs.

EXERCISE 8.5 **Discussing Case Studies**

Work with a partner or a small group to discuss the following case studies.

1. Cecilia is taking a class in medical terminology. She is required to learn approximately fifty different medical terms each week. She has been trying to memorize each word and its definition. The words are grouped according to "word families." For example, one week she had to learn words such as *dermis, epidermis, dermatology,* and *dermatitis.* She is confused and is having difficulty learning all the words each week. What strategies would you recommend that would be more effective than memorizing each individual word?

2. Donnie's public finance book is filled with special terminology that he must learn. The words are in special print and are defined in a glossary. What strategies would you recommend he use at the very beginning of the term to learn and remember the terminology in the textbook?

3. Lisa has difficulty with reading comprehension. She encounters so many words that are unfamiliar to her; she is not able to understand many of the paragraphs she reads. She feels it will take too much time to use a dictionary to look up all the words. For now, she is just getting by but is fearful of what will happen on the first test. What strategies would you recommend Lisa use to begin to deal with her problems?

4. Doris has found that she really enjoys making flash cards for all of her courses. She has started a study group to discuss the course work with other students each week. The members of her study group are impressed with her flash cards and want to use them in the study group. What kinds of activities could the study group members do with Doris's flash cards?

⚙️ Exercise 8.6 LINKS

Work in small groups. Each group should select one of the following discussion questions. As a group, compose an answer or explanation to present to the rest of the class. Each answer should show how the study of vocabulary links to topics that have been previously discussed.

1. How does a strong expressive and receptive vocabulary relate to one or more of Howard Gardner's eight intelligences?

2. Review the processes used to study from flash cards. How are the steps of the Information Processing Model activated by this approach to studying flash cards?

3. Which principles of memory are used when you utilize the methods recommended in this chapter for studying from flash cards or from vocabulary study sheets?

4. Where in the SQ4R reading system is attention given to learning vocabulary?

5. What is the relationship between reading comprehension and vocabulary? Can a person have poor reading comprehension but a strong vocabulary? Can a person have a strong vocabulary but poor reading comprehension?

6. How can all three learning modalities be used to study vocabulary?

SUMMARY

■ Developing a strong vocabulary helps you comprehend what you read in textbooks and hear in lectures (receptive vocabulary).

■ After receptive vocabulary is developed, you can expand your writing and speaking vocabularies (expressive vocabulary).

■ Vocabulary flash cards and vocabulary study sheets should include categories and definitions for key terminology as well as any unfamiliar words you encounter as you read.

■ Studying from your flash cards or vocabulary sheets should include studying from both sides and using reflect activities.

■ The meanings of unfamiliar words can often be learned through punctuation clues, word clues, context clues, word structure clues, glossaries, and reference books (dictionaries or thesauruses).

■ Word structure clues use the meanings of prefixes, suffixes, and roots to understand the general meaning of unfamiliar words.

■ Context clues use the meanings of synonyms, antonyms/contrasts, comparisons/analogies, and similar experiences or common sense to understand the general meaning of unfamiliar words.

OPTIONS FOR PERSONALIZING CHAPTER 8

1. **PROFILE CHART—PERSONAL LOG**   Answer the following questions in your personal log.

   What score did you have on the Chapter 8 Profile? _____

   Which vocabulary, your receptive or your expressive, needs the most improvement? Explain.

   Which specific strategies did you learn in the chapter that you plan to use to strengthen your vocabulary skills?

2. **WORDS TO KNOW**   You should be able to define the following terms.

receptive vocabulary	three parts of a definition	word structure clues
dictionary	etymology	context
thesaurus	vocabulary sheets	context clues
expressive vocabulary	word clues	synonyms
terminology	prefixes	antonyms
glossary	suffixes	contrast
general category flash card	base words	comparison
definition flash cards	roots	analogies

3. **EXPAND THE CHAPTER VISUAL MAPPING**   Expand the chapter visual mapping in the book on page 143 or on your own unlined paper. Use colors and/or pictures to personalize your mapping.

4. **WRITING ASSIGNMENT 1**   Interview two or more people whom you feel have strong vocabularies. Ask them how they acquired such an extensive vocabulary and what strategies they use to learn new words. Summarize your findings in a paper. Devote at least one paragraph to each person you interviewed.

5. **WRITING ASSIGNMENT 2**   Watch a documentary on television or read an informative article in a newspaper or a magazine. Make a list of words that were used that are not in your expressive vocabulary. Discuss strategies you can use to understand the meanings of these words and to add them to your expressive vocabulary. Demonstrate your understanding of the words by using them in original sentences.

6. **PORTFOLIO DEVELOPMENT**   Select one of your courses that has substantial terminology to learn. First, in a short paper, describe a plan for learning the new vocabulary. Implement your plan. In your plan, give examples of your work that show your approach to expanding your vocabulary for at least one chapter of the textbook.

CHAPTER 8 REVIEW QUESTIONS

Multiple-Choice

Choose the best answer *for each of the following questions. Write the letter of the* best answer on the line.

_____ **1.** Provide immediate feedback, are compact to use, and are easy to expand with more words are three reasons
    a. flash cards are effective study tools.
    b. general vocabulary cards should be developed.
    c. definitions should be learned.
    d. vocabulary sheets must have specific definitions.

_____ **2.** When you use vocabulary cards or vocabulary sheets, you should get feedback by
    a. looking at the front of the cards or the left column of the vocabulary sheets.
    b. reciting what is on the back of the cards or what is in the right column.
    c. reciting from both sides of the cards or the vocabulary sheets.
    d. writing down all your answers and checking.

_____ **3.** You can locate definitions of important terms by
    a. using punctuation clues.
    b. recognizing signal words (*is, means, defined as*).
    c. using context clues surrounding the key term.
    d. using punctuation, word structure, and context clues.

_____ **4.** A definition is not directly stated when you have to use
    a. context clues.
    b. punctuation clues.
    c. signal words.
    d. all of the above.

_____ **5.** Receptive vocabulary consists of words
    a. you can understand in context when you read.
    b. you can understand when you read or hear them but you cannot use in your expressive language.
    c. you can use well enough when you read and write them.
    d. that first came out of expressive vocabulary.

_____ **6.** Which of the following is *not* true about flash cards?
    a. Flash cards can serve as a form of notetaking if the set includes definition cards as well as category cards that list important ideas.
    b. Flash cards can provide the student with several kinesthetic learning activities.
    c. Flash cards can be used for reflecting activities when you study.
    d. Studying from flash cards is valuable even though none of the twelve principles of memory are actively involved.

_____ **7.** If you made a set of flash cards and a vocabulary sheet for the exact same group of words, you would likely find that
    a. the same information will appear on both the cards and the vocabulary sheet.
    b. the vocabulary sheets will contain more information.
    c. categories only appear on the flash cards.
    d. reciting from both sides can really only be used with the vocabulary sheet.

Short Answer—Critical Thinking

Write two or three sentences to answer each of the following questions.

1. Explain what will occur with a person's expressive vocabulary if that person's receptive vocabulary is weak.

2. What are at least three ways to make good use of a glossary in the back of a textbook?

3. What is the value of using three parts or levels of information when you write definitions for terminology?

4. Define each of the following terms:
   a. word structure

   b. expressive vocabulary

   c. receptive vocabulary

Making Cornell Notes for Textbooks

Strong notetaking skills are essential for college students, yet many students find good notetaking to be difficult. Do you find your notes difficult to read? Do you take notes but not study from them? This chapter introduces you to the five-step Cornell notetaking system that can be used for all your textbooks.

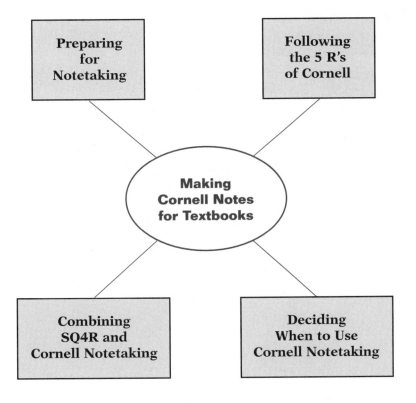

Preparing for Notetaking

Following the 5 R's of Cornell

Making Cornell Notes for Textbooks

Combining SQ4R and Cornell Notetaking

Deciding When to Use Cornell Notetaking

CHAPTER 9   Cornell Notes Profile

DO, SCORE, and **RECORD** your profile before you read this chapter. If you need to review the process, refer to the complete directions given in the Profile for Chapter 1 on page 2.

	YES	NO
1. I take notes only on the front side of my notebook paper.	_____	_____
2. I spend little time studying from my notes.	_____	_____
3. I am selective when I take notes; I write down only the important ideas and details.	_____	_____
4. I take time to study and interpret graphs and charts.	_____	_____
5. I leave a double space in my notes before I begin a new heading.	_____	_____
6. After I take notes on a paragraph, I recite what I wrote before moving on.	_____	_____
7. My notes summarize important charts, graphs, or pictures in the textbook.	_____	_____
8. I practice reciting new information by using a special reduced column of notes.	_____	_____
9. I take time to think about and reflect on the information in the chapter.	_____	_____
10. I use the back side of my notebook paper to make lists of information or questions.	_____	_____
11. I plan time each week to review information that I learned in previous weeks.	_____	_____
12. I always use just one kind of notetaking when I am working with a textbook.	_____	_____

Self-Awareness: How effective is your current notetaking system? Do you understand your notes when you study from them later? Comment on the quality of your notes and then briefly describe the way you study from your notes.

_____

_____

_____

_____

_____

_____

_____

_____

_____

_____

Preparing for Notetaking

This chapter introduces the powerful five-step Cornell notetaking system, which you can use for taking notes from textbooks and taking notes from lectures. The strength of the system is in its steps; if you choose to eliminate any one step, you weaken the system. This notetaking system was designed by Dr. Walter Pauk at Cornell University more than forty-five years ago when he recognized students' need to learn how to take more effective notes. Many college and university teachers consider this system to be the most effective notetaking system for college students.

Effective notetaking is important for several reasons:

1. You become an active learner when you seek out important information and write it down.
2. You focus on organizing the information logically.
3. You select the important information and reduce it to a form that is easy to study and review.
4. You have reduced notes to use for continual review throughout the term.

Setting up your paper:

To begin, you need notebook paper with a *two-and-one-half-inch margin down the left side of the paper.* Many bookstores now carry Cornell notebook paper with this larger margin or a spiral "Law Notebook" with perforated Cornell-style pages. If you are not able to find the Cornell notebook paper for your three-ring notebook, draw a margin on the front side of regular notebook paper (see p. 164). All your notetaking is done on the front side only; the back of the paper is used for other purposes.

At the top of the first page, write the course name, chapter number, and date. For all the following pages, just write the chapter number and the page number of your notes. Later you may want to remove your notes from your notebook; having the pages numbered prevents disorganization.

Following the Five R's of Cornell

The goal of notetaking is to take notes that are so accurate and that have such details that you *do not need to go back to the book to study.* Your studying, your learning, can take place by working with your notes as you use the **five *R*'s of the Cornell system**: record, reduce, recite, reflect, and review.

The Five R's of Cornell

1. *Record* your notes in the right-hand column.
2. *Reduce* your notes into the recall column on the left.
3. *Recite* out loud from the recall column.
4. *Reflect* on the information that you are studying.
5. *Review* your notes immediately and regularly.

Step One: Record

The wider right-hand column is for your notes. In this first step —**record**—read each paragraph carefully, decide what information is important, and then record that information on your paper. Your notes should be a *reduced version* of the textbook. Be selective, or you will wind up wasting your notetaking time and your studying time.

The authors of your textbooks have helped you tremendously by providing you with a structured organization of the information through the use of headings and subheadings. Use these headings and the following suggestions for the first *R* of Cornell.

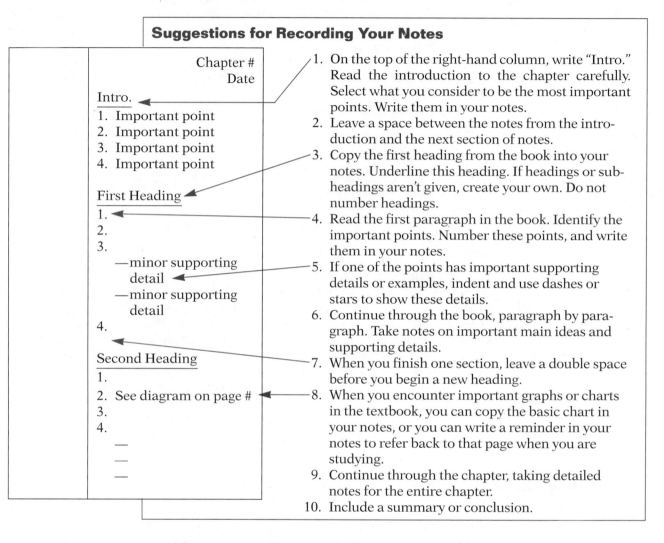

Suggestions for Recording Your Notes

Chapter #
Date

Intro.
1. Important point
2. Important point
3. Important point
4. Important point

First Heading
1.
2.
3.
   —minor supporting
     detail
   —minor supporting
     detail
4.

Second Heading
1.
2. See diagram on page #
3.
4.
   —
   —
   —

1. On the top of the right-hand column, write "Intro." Read the introduction to the chapter carefully. Select what you consider to be the most important points. Write them in your notes.
2. Leave a space between the notes from the introduction and the next section of notes.
3. Copy the first heading from the book into your notes. Underline this heading. If headings or subheadings aren't given, create your own. Do not number headings.
4. Read the first paragraph in the book. Identify the important points. Number these points, and write them in your notes.
5. If one of the points has important supporting details or examples, indent and use dashes or stars to show these details.
6. Continue through the book, paragraph by paragraph. Take notes on important main ideas and supporting details.
7. When you finish one section, leave a double space before you begin a new heading.
8. When you encounter important graphs or charts in the textbook, you can copy the basic chart in your notes, or you can write a reminder in your notes to refer back to that page when you are studying.
9. Continue through the chapter, taking detailed notes for the entire chapter.
10. Include a summary or conclusion.

Take Notes on the Introduction The introduction often provides a brief overview of the content of the chapter. By listing the key ideas in your notes, you will be able to see later if you understood and captured all the key points.

Leave Spaces Between Sections Notes that are crowded or cluttered are difficult to study. By leaving a double space between each new heading or section of your notes, you are visually grouping the information that belongs together. You are also "**chunking**" the information into smaller units, which will help your memory.

Use the Headings The headings are the "skeleton," or outline, of the chapter. Take advantage of this structure by always starting a new section of notes with the heading. Underline the heading so that it stands out from the rest of your notes. If headings or subheadings are not given, look for categories of information. If the information will be clearer to you, create your own headings and group related information under each heading. (See the example on Theories of Forgetting, p. 134.)

Record Important Points   Since you will use your notes for studying, you want to see the big picture and the small pictures (details). *Record enough information to be meaningful later:*

- Avoid using only individual words or short phrases that will lose their meaning when you return to them later.
- Use short sentences when necessary to avoid meaningless phrases.
- Do not copy down information word for word. Shorten the information by rewording or summarizing it.
- If you find some sentences or short sections that are so clearly stated that you want to copy them, omit any of the words that are not essential for your understanding.
- If you have already highlighted the information, move the same information into your notes.
- Number the ideas as you place them into your notes. Numbering helps you remember how many important points are under each heading and breaks the information into smaller, more manageable units.

Record Important Minor Details   You will frequently encounter minor details that belong under an idea that you already numbered. Indicate these details by *indenting* and then using *dashes* or *stars* before writing the details.

Include Graphs and Charts   Visual materials such as graphs, charts, and pictures contain valuable information. Usually you are not expected to know every fact or statistic depicted by the graph, chart, or other forms of visual materials. You are, however, expected to identify important patterns, relationships, or trends shown by the visual materials. Do not overlook these graphic materials when you are taking notes. You can include the information in your notes by *copying* the graphic material into your notes or by *summarizing* the conclusions you make by studying the graphic materials. By taking the time necessary to study graphic materials, you will be able to:

1. Study large amounts of information in a condensed form.
2. Identify patterns, relationships, or trends more easily.
3. Imprint information in a visual form in your long-term memory.
4. Create a visual memory cue to recall information at a later time.

Include a Summary or Conclusion   Summaries or conclusions pull the main ideas together to help you see the "big picture." If a summary is given in the book, include the summary as the last heading in your notes. If there is no summary, you may write your own conclusion to pull the main ideas together.

Highlight the Text First if Necessary   Many students find that highlighting the text helps them identify the most important ideas of the paragraph. The sentences, phrases, or words that are marked consist of the same information you should transfer into your notes. If you have difficulty making detailed notes, try highlighting the text first; then transfer the information into your notes under the appropriate headings.

Step Two: Reduce

After you have finished taking notes for the chapter, you are ready to close the book and begin **reducing**. Now, for the first time, you will be writing in the left-hand column, the **recall column**. Remember, in step one you reduced the textbook information to the most important points and details. In step two, you are going to reduce your notes one step further. These reduced notes will provide you with a feedback system so that you will know what information you have learned well and what information needs more effort. You will also refer to this column frequently for review.

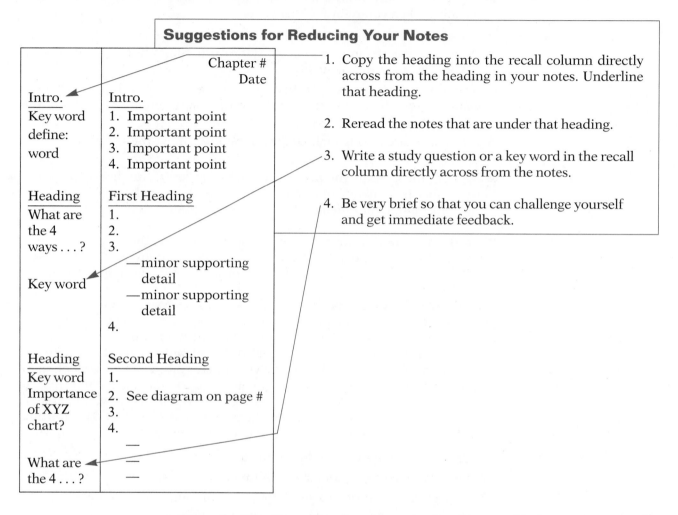

Suggestions for Reducing Your Notes

	Chapter #
	Date
Intro.	Intro.
Key word	1. Important point
define:	2. Important point
word	3. Important point
	4. Important point
Heading	First Heading
What are	1.
the 4	2.
ways ...?	3.
	—minor supporting detail
Key word	—minor supporting detail
	4.
Heading	Second Heading
Key word	1.
Importance	2. See diagram on page #
of XYZ	3.
chart?	4.
	—
What are	—
the 4 ...?	—

1. Copy the heading into the recall column directly across from the heading in your notes. Underline that heading.

2. Reread the notes that are under that heading.

3. Write a study question or a key word in the recall column directly across from the notes.

4. Be very brief so that you can challenge yourself and get immediate feedback.

Copy the Heading   In your notes, the heading provided organization. The same is true in the recall column. To avoid having rambling, unorganized reduced notes, *place the heading directly across from the heading in your notes.* Make it stand out by underlining it.

Reread the Notes   Learning the information continues as you reread your notes. If your notes seem vague, incomplete, or nonsensical, go back to the book and add any necessary details.

Write Study Questions and Key Words   Directly across from each important detail, write yourself a reminder about that detail. You can write it as a *brief study question.* You do not need to use complete sentences; abbreviated forms, such as the following, work: Why? How many kinds of ...? Name the 6 ... Related to *X* how? Another option is to simply write *key words.* These may be words that you will need to define or relate to other ideas.

Be Brief   You will be using this recall column for the next step of studying. It is important that the column not be cluttered with too much information. If you give yourself all the answers, you will end up reading the information and not challenging your memory. *Remember to be selective by focusing only on key words or study questions.* Do not give all the answers!

	5 Forgetting Theories
Intro principles—forgetting	Intro 1. Even when use principles of memory, info can be forgotten.
Decay Where in Info Proc. Model? What happens?	Decay Theory 1. Occurs in STM 2. Stimuli are too weak so info fades before it is processed
Displacement Theory Which memory? What happens with info? Why?	Displacement Theory 1. Occurs in STM 2. Too much info comes in too quickly, so some info is shoved aside 3. Not enough time given to process
Interference Theory LTM—What happens?	Interference Theory 1. In LTM 2. New and old info interfere with each other 3. Happens when new and old info are similar
Incomplete Encoding Happens where? Describe what happens	Incomplete Encoding Theory 1. Happens when info is rehearsed 2. Info is only partially learned or learned inaccurately 3. Info cannot be recalled because it was never imprinted in LTM
Retrieval Failure Which memory? Why can't info be found? Schemas	Retrieval Failure Theory 1. Info learned but can't be found in memory bank —weak organizational or filing system used in memory —lack of use—no ongoing review —not associated with schemas
Summary model—strategies—eliminate	Summary Info can be forgotten during several different stages of the Info Processing Model. Effective strategies can reduce/eliminate effects of forgetting theories.
Name the 5 theories of forgetting (D-D-I-I-R)	5 theories: decay, displacement, interference, incomplete encoding, and retrieval failure

Step Three: Recite

Reciting is a powerful tool for learning information and strengthening memory. If you are able to recite information accurately, you are learning. If you are not able to recite information accurately, you immediately know that more time and attention are needed. This **immediate feedback** is the strong benefit of this third step of Cornell.

Suggestions for Reciting

Chapter #
Date

Intro.
Key word
define:
word

Heading
What are
the 4
ways . . . ?

Key word

Heading
Key word
Importance
of XYZ
chart?

What are
the 4 . . . ?

1. Cover up the notes on the right.

2. Start at the top of the recall column. Read the heading and the first key word or question.

3. Talk out loud in complete sentences. Explain the information.

4. If you don't remember the information, uncover the right-hand column. Reread the information. Cover it up and try reciting it again.

5. Move through your notes in this manner.

6. Adjust the recall column as needed.

Cover the Notes   Use a blank piece of paper to cover the notes on the right-hand side. Since you see only the recall column, you can now understand the importance of placing the headings in the recall column to help you remember the overall organization.

Read and Then Recite   Read the headings and the key words or questions. Without looking at your notes, answer the questions and tell what you remember about the key words. Pretend you are explaining the information to a friend. *Talk out loud in complete sentences.*

■ If you can verbalize the information accurately, you probably understand it.

■ If you "go blank," that is valuable feedback that you are not yet ready to move on. Simply pull the paper down, read the information, cover it up, and try again. Reciting after you reread enables your memory to begin processing the correct information.

■ If you are not sure if you recited the correct information, also pull the paper down to check your accuracy. The positive feedback you receive for correct answers will strengthen your memory of them.

Continue Reciting   Move through your entire set of notes by reciting, checking accuracy, and reciting again. Remember to take full advantage of this system by using the feedback to look at your notes and recite again.

Adjust the Recall Column   Sometimes it is difficult to know how much and what kind of information to put in the recall column.

■ If you found that you did not give yourself enough cues to recite important points, add more key words or study questions to the recall column.

■ If you found that you wrote all the important information in the recall column and you ended up reading what was there, you had nothing left to recite from memory. Cross out (or white out) some of the details before you recite again.

■ Star the information you did not recall the first time. Pay extra attention to these areas the next time you recite.

Step Four: Reflect   To **reflect** means to "think or consider seriously." The reflect step can be individualized and can include a wide variety of activities and study tools. Several reflect activities are listed here:

Suggestions for Reflecting

1. Take time to think about the information in your notes.
2. Line up your recall columns to see the overall structure of the chapter.
3. Write your own summary at the bottom of your notes.
4. Use the back side of your notepaper to make lists of information or questions.
5. Make your own study tools such as flash cards, visual mappings, or pictures for later reviews.

Take Time to Think   Reflecting lets the information register and settle in your brain. It also allows you to look at the information from your own perspective and experiences, to look for connections or relationships between ideas, and to think of ways to extend the information beyond its original context. The process of reflecting is a process of using a wide variety of critical thinking skills.

Line Up the Recall Columns   To gain an overview of the entire chapter, remove your notepaper from your notebook. Arrange your notes on a table so that you can see all the recall columns lined up in sequence from left to right. By looking at the headings and the details, you will see the entire outline for the chapter. If you enjoy studying from outlines, you could convert this information into outline form to use for review.

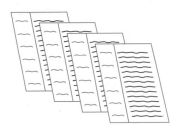

Write a Summary   Look only at the information in the recall columns. Write a summary that explains the important points. Your summary should include the main ideas and brief statements of major supporting details. Your summary should be written in full sentences and paragraphs. Save this summary because it is a good review tool to use before tests.

Write on the Back Side of Your Notepaper   The back of your notepaper is now available for you to make additional lists of information or reminders. You can also include diagrams or charts to show how different ideas are related. If you have questions that you would like to ask the instructor, jot them down on the back, too. The backs are convenient and available, so use them as needed.

Make Your Own Study Tools for Later Review   The reflect step is a creative and highly individualized step. No two students will do the exact same activities in the reflect step. This is the time for you to decide *what will work best for you*. Consider the many different kinds of study tools you know how to make (or will be learning how to make). Select one or more that would help you learn the information more thoroughly as well as provide you with study tools to use as you review throughout the term. Here are just a few options:

■ Make flash cards of all the key vocabulary terms.

■ Make a visual mapping, hierarchy, or outline of the chapter or parts of the chapter.

■ Practice drawing or copying diagrams from the chapter.

■ Add pictures, cartoons, or stick figures that can serve as memory triggers for parts of your notes later.

■ Make study tapes that review the recall column or that list the important points you want to remember.

■ Use any of the study strategies described for each of the three learning styles (visual, auditory, kinesthetic).

■ Write a summary that follows your visual mapping.

Step Five: Review

This last step of the Cornell system keeps the information active in your memory. Review provides the repetition you need to retrieve information quickly and accurately from your long-term memory.

Suggestions for Reviewing

1. Plan time for immediate review.
2. Plan time weekly for ongoing review.

Do an Immediate Review   Reviewing actually begins when you are working at the fourth step. In the reflect step, you take time to think about the information you have covered, and you take time to create additional study tools. However, **immediate review** goes one step further. Before you close your book and quit studying, take a few additional minutes to review your recall columns. This provides one final opportunity to strengthen your memory for the organization and content of the material.

Ongoing Review   **Ongoing review** means reviewing previous work so that you are continually practicing learned information. Ongoing review is necessary because you will be storing more and more information in your long-term memory as the term progresses, so you must make sure that "old" information is practiced. In addition, by including ongoing reviews in your weekly study schedule, you save time in the long run. When tests, midterm exams, or final exams approach, you won't need to cram, for you will have kept the information active.

Several activities can take place during ongoing review:

■ Review the recall columns of your notes. The more frequently you review these, the faster you can move through the columns. Also, as the term progresses, you will find that information placed in your notes early in the term is now clear and easy to understand.

■ Review any reflect or review materials that you created earlier.

■ If you have a list of questions from the second step of SQ4R or your own written summary, review these.

■ Review chapter introductions, summaries, and lists of vocabulary terms for the chapter.

Now that the five *R*'s of the Cornell system have been discussed, take time to learn to use each of the steps. Remember, omitting any one step will weaken the system. The following pictures may help you learn and remember the steps more quickly.

1. Record	2. Reduce	3. Recite	4. Reflect	5. Review

🔗 Exercise 9.1 **LINKS to Maslow's Hierarchy**

Return to Maslow's Hierarchy of Needs in Exercise 7.3 (page 131). If you have already highlighted and marked this excerpt, you are ready to begin taking Cornell notes. If you have not read or highlighted this excerpt, read and highlight before you begin taking Cornell notes. Complete each of the following steps on your own paper.

1. Draw a two-and-one-half-inch margin down the left side of your notebook paper.

2. Use the strategies presented in this chapter for taking notes in the right-hand column.

3. Reduce the notes in the left-hand column. Write the heading and the key words or very brief study questions. Do not write too much information.

4. Cover up the right side of your notes. Practice reciting your notes out loud and in complete sentences. Check your accuracy.

5. Do one of the following reflect activities:
   a. THINK about the information and the following questions. Then summarize your ideas in a short paper.

   Do I believe that people are "wanting beings" who seek to fulfill needs?

   Do I believe this is really how needs we want to fulfill are arranged?

   Could emphasis on the various needs occur in a different order?

   Do my needs fall into this sequence? How?

    b. The article suggests ways the business world can meet the different levels of needs of their employees. Brainstorm how colleges and universities strive to meet the different levels of needs of students. Summarize your ideas in either a chart or in paragraph form.

    c. If you were in marketing or sales, how could you advertise in different ways to meet different levels of need? What would advertisements look like for each of the five kinds of needs?

    d. Make vocabulary cards or a visual mapping of the information.

    e. Use the highlighting as a guide to write a summary. Use full sentences and write in paragraph form.

6. Review your work so that you will be prepared to discuss this in class.

✎ **EXERCISE 9.2   Cornell Notetaking Practice**

Practice taking Cornell notes on the section in this chapter titled, "Following the Five R's of Cornell," pages 163–171. Begin by taking notes in the right-hand column. Then reduce your notes by making the recall column. The Cornell Notetaking Assessment Form on page 174 may be used to evaluate your notes.

Deciding When to Use Cornell Notetaking

There are five main textbook notetaking options: highlighting, marginal notes, separate notes using the Cornell system, visual mappings or hierarchies, and flash cards. You can select these options based on the course, the level of difficulty of the material, and your own preferences.

> **Choosing the Most Appropriate Notetaking System**
>
> 1. Use *one* form of notetaking for easy textbooks.
> 2. Use *two* forms of notetaking for textbooks with larger amounts of information.
> 3. Use *three or more* forms of notetaking for textbooks that are difficult and challenging for you.

Use One Form of Notetaking

If the course and the textbook are relatively easy for you, *one form of notetaking* is sufficient. In other words, you can select marking important information, making notes in the margins, taking Cornell notes, making visual mappings, or making flash cards. Your choice of methods can be based on the following:

    1. If I am going to use only one form of notetaking, which method will best help me clearly see the main ideas and important supporting details when I study?

    2. If I decide to take only Cornell notes or visual mappings, is this choice made simply to avoid writing in my book? If the answer is yes, consider the benefits of being able to write directly in the book. The time saved and the benefits of choosing the method that works best for you may outweigh your reservations.

Use Two Forms of Notetaking

If the course and the textbook have large amounts of important ideas, facts, and supporting details that are new to you, using two forms of notetaking may bring better results. Consider several common combinations:

    1. Mark main ideas and important details that support the main idea. Move this information into your Cornell notes.

2. Mark main ideas and supporting details. Make marginal notes or flash cards.

3. Make Cornell notes for the chapter. Convert the Cornell notes into visual mappings to study and review.

Use Three or More Forms of Notetaking

When you take a course that is very difficult or challenging, you may feel that you need "all the help you can get." Using three or more forms of notetaking allows you to work with the information in more than one way; this added variety and exposure often provide the practice, thinking, and memory work needed to learn thoroughly. Because of the time involved, you would not want to use this intensive approach for every course, but recognize that it is available. Experiment to find the combinations best suited for the material and for your learning strategy preferences.

Combining SQ4R and Cornell Notetaking

You have now learned two very powerful study methods for mastering learning. SQ4R (Chapter 6) is a six-step system for reading a textbook; Cornell is a notetaking system that can be used with textbooks. Consider how these two systems can be combined effectively.

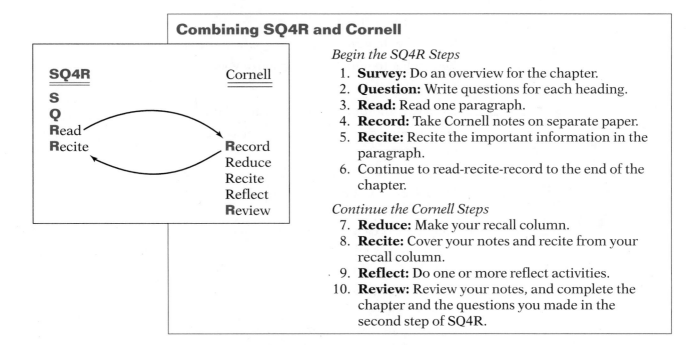

Combining SQ4R and Cornell

SQ4R   Cornell
S
Q
Read
Recite
      Record
      Reduce
      Recite
      Reflect
      Review

Begin the SQ4R Steps

1. **Survey:** Do an overview for the chapter.
2. **Question:** Write questions for each heading.
3. **Read:** Read one paragraph.
4. **Record:** Take Cornell notes on separate paper.
5. **Recite:** Recite the important information in the paragraph.
6. Continue to read-recite-record to the end of the chapter.

Continue the Cornell Steps

7. **Reduce:** Make your recall column.
8. **Recite:** Cover your notes and recite from your recall column.
9. **Reflect:** Do one or more reflect activities.
10. **Review:** Review your notes, and complete the chapter and the questions you made in the second step of SQ4R.

Note that you begin with the first three steps of SQ4R: survey, question, and read. The Cornell system then merges with the reading system for the record step. (Record is step four of SQ4R and step one of Cornell).

Once you have completed the reading and have taken the notes, put the book aside. Focus your attention on the Cornell notes you have taken and the remaining steps of Cornell: reduce, recite, reflect, and review. Join the review steps in SQ4R with the review step in Cornell. You have now successfully combined two powerful systems for learning.

Cornell Notetaking Assessment Form

Name _____   Date _____

Topic of Notes: _____

Record Step

_____ You clearly showed and underlined the headings. Well done!

_____ You need to identify and underline the headings.

_____ Your notes will be easier to study because you remembered to leave a space between headings.

_____ Your notes will be less crowded or cluttered if you leave a space before you begin a new heading.

_____ Your notes show accurate and sufficient details. Good work.

_____ Consider using numbering to show the different details under a heading.

_____ You need to write more; some important details are missing.

_____ Phrases often lose meaning over time. Try to use more complete sentences to explain details.

_____ You either copied or referred to specific page numbers to remind yourself of important graphs, pictures, or charts. Good!

_____ Be sure to include information about graphs, pictures, or charts in your notes.

_____ Strive for neater penmanship.

_____ Remember to write on only one side of the paper.

_____ Remember to number each page of your notes.

Reduce Step

_____ Use a two-and-one-half-inch recall column.

_____ Your headings and questions are placed directly across from the same information in your notes. Well done!

_____ Remember to move the heading into the recall column.

_____ Try placing questions or key words directly to the left of the information in your notes.

_____ Your key words or questions are effective.

_____ You are giving yourself too much information or all the answers. You will end up reading the information rather than reciting.

_____ You will need more key words or questions in the recall column to guide you when you recite.

_____ Try using your recall column to see if the key words or questions you wrote are sufficient to help you recite.

_____ Remember that you can add information to the recall column if you feel more is needed when you are reciting.

Other

_____

_____

_____

Photocopy this form before you use it.

EXERCISE 9.3 Applying Cornell Notetaking

Locate one or two pages in this textbook or in any other textbook you are currently using this term. Photocopy the pages. Select pages that begin with a new heading rather than selecting information that started on previous pages. Take Cornell notes on the two pages you selected. Turn in your photocopied pages and your Cornell notes.

Web-site links are available online.

Computer Projects

1. Select a historical event, a geographic location, the name of an inventor, or a geological or meteorological topic (volcanoes, earthquakes, hurricanes, comets). Use the Internet to locate an informative article on your topic. The article needs to be two or more pages long. Print the article. Then take Cornell notes on its content.

2. Check out all the writing topics via the Internet on this web site:

   http://longman.awl.com/englishpages/basic_wkbk_write. htm

3. Use your computer to take Cornell notes for a textbook chapter or a lecture. Use columns or set a two-and-one-half-inch left margin. If you set the margin, take your notes in the right-hand column. Handwrite the questions later in the left-hand column.

4. Use your graphic functions. Try to make a bar graph to show your assessment of your level of talent/intellect for Gardner's eight intelligences *or* your level of need fulfillment of Maslow's hierarchy of needs.

5. Use your graphic functions. Make a linear chart of your homework grades for any class this term.

6. Make a pie chart to show the major categories that represent how you spend your time each week. You may divide the pie beyond the three basic areas of school, work, and leisure.

Group Web-Search Activity is available online.

Case Studies are available online.

SUMMARY

■ The Cornell system provides you with a five-step method for recording and learning information accurately and thoroughly.

■ You will become an active learner when you use all five *R*'s of Cornell:

1. Select the important information and record it in the right-hand column of your note-paper.
2. Reduce the information to key terms or study questions; write this reduced information in the left-hand column.
3. Cover up the right-hand side of your notes while you recite information in complete sentences; use the left-hand column as a guide for reciting.
4. Reflect on the material, finding relationships and creating study tools.
5. Use immediate and ongoing review to rehearse information.

■ The Cornell notetaking system can easily be incorporated into the SQ4R reading system; thus, two powerful study systems are combined to increase your learning potential.

OPTIONS FOR PERSONALIZING CHAPTER 9

1. **PROFILE CHART—PERSONAL LOG**   Answer the following questions in your personal log.

   What score did you have on the Chapter 9 Profile? _____

   How do you feel about your overall notetaking skills? Discuss the strengths and the weaknesses in notes you have previously taken for textbook chapters.

   What advantages do you see in using the Cornell notetaking system?

2. **WORDS TO KNOW**   Knowing the following vocabulary terms is important.

   five *R*'s of the Cornell system   reciting
   record   immediate feedback
   chunking   reflect
   reducing   immediate review
   recall column   ongoing review

3. **EXPAND THE CHAPTER VISUAL MAPPING**   Expand the chapter visual mapping on page 161 by adding details to each of the main heading boxes. If you wish, you may use the chapter mapping to guide you in writing your own chapter summary.

4. **WRITING ASSIGNMENT**   Compare your old notetaking system to the Cornell system. How are they alike? How are they different? What differences will you see in your level of understanding and your overall grade when you begin using the Cornell system consistently?

5. **PORTFOLIO DEVELOPMENT**   Take a complete set of Cornell notes for any chapter in any one of your textbooks. Do a self-evaluation by using the Cornell Notetaking Assessment Form that is on page 174. Your portfolio project should also include an example of a *reflect activity*. In a short paper, briefly summarize how you used each of the 5 *R*'s of the Cornell notetaking system.

CHAPTER 9 REVIEW QUESTIONS

True-False

Carefully read the following sentences. Pay attention to key words.
Write T *if the statement is TRUE. Write* F *if the statement is FALSE.*

_____ **1.** The majority of your review time should be spent working with your notes.

_____ **2.** Cornell notes are a reduced version of textbook information.

_____ **3.** It is best to read the whole chapter first and then go back to take notes.

_____ **4.** It is not necessary to take notes on graphs, charts, or pictures since they are always easy to remember.

_____ **5.** Graphic materials are included in textbooks to help the reader memorize all the details, facts, or statistics.

_____ **6.** Too much information in the recall column causes you to read and not do much reciting.

_____ **7.** More questions or key words can be added to the recall column if there are too few cues to help you recite.

_____ **8.** If you are short on time, it is best to always skip the fourth step of Cornell.

_____ **9.** Ongoing review gets you in the habit of using repetition as a regular part of studying.

_____ **10.** If you highlight your textbook and take Cornell notes, basically the same information will appear in both notes.

Short Answer

Complete the following chart by listing the five steps of the Cornell system in order and explaining the purpose *of each step.*

Steps of Cornell	The *purpose* of this step is to:
R	
R	
R	
R	
R	

Application

Take a complete set of Cornell notes on the following information from a psychology textbook. Organize your notes neatly and logically. Be sure to develop the recall column.

Basic Memory Processes

We know a psychologist who sometimes drives to work and sometimes walks. On one occasion, he drove, forgot that he had driven, and walked home. When he failed to find his car in its normal spot the next morning, he reported the car stolen. The police soon called to say that "some college kids" had probably stolen the car because it was found on campus (next to the psychology building!). What went wrong? There are several possibilities, because memory depends on three basic processes—encoding, storage, and retrieval (see Figure 8.1).

First, information must be put into memory, a step that requires **encoding.** Just as incoming sensory information must be coded so that it can be communicated to the brain, information to be remembered must be put in a form that the memory system can accept and use. In the memory system, sensory information is put into various *memory codes,* which are mental representations of physical stimuli. For example, **acoustic codes** represent information as sequences of sounds. **Visual codes** represent stimuli as pictures. **Semantic codes** represent an experience by its general meaning. Thus, if you see a billboard that reads "Huey's Going Out of Business Sale," you might encode the sound of the words as if they had been spoken (acoustic coding), the image of the letters as they were arranged on the sign (visual coding), or the fact that you saw an ad for Huey's (semantic coding). The type of coding used can influence what is remembered. For example, semantic coding might allow you to remember that a car was parked in your neighbors' driveway just before their house was robbed. If there was little or no other coding, however, you might not be able to remember the make, model, or color of the car.

The second basic memory process is **storage,** which refers to the maintenance of information over time, often over a very long time. When you find it possible to use a pogo stick or to recall a vacation from many years ago, you are depending on the storage capacity of your memory.

The third process, **retrieval,** occurs when you find information stored in memory and bring it into consciousness. Retrieving stored information such as your address or telephone number is usually so fast and effortless it seems automatic. Only when you try to retrieve other kinds of information—such as the answer to a quiz question that you know but cannot quite recall—do you become aware of the searching process. Retrieval processes include both recall and recognition. To *recall* information, as on an essay test, you have to retrieve it from memory without much help. *Recognition* is aided by clues, such as the alternatives given in a multiple-choice test item. Accordingly, recognition tends to be easier than recall.

Basic Memory Processes
Remembering something requires, first, that the item be encoded—put in a form that can be placed in memory. It must then be stored and, finally, retrieved, or recovered. If any of these processes fails, forgetting will occur.

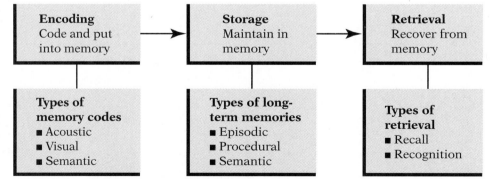

Bernstein, Douglas A., Thomas K. Srull, Christopher D. Wickens, and Edward J. Roy, PSYCHOLOGY, Fourth Edition. Copyright © 1997 by Houghton Mifflin Company. Used with permission.

Using Cornell Notes for Lectures

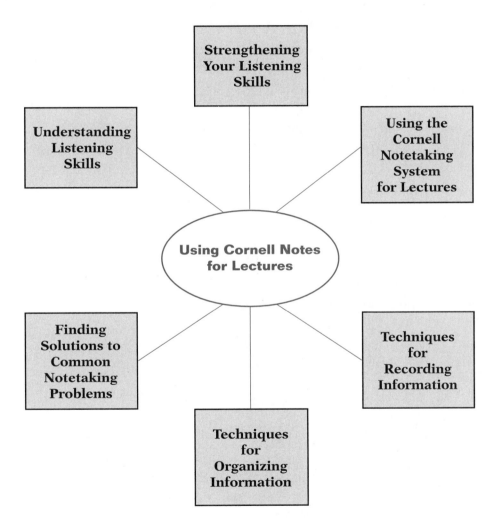

Strengthening Your Listening Skills

Understanding Listening Skills

Using the Cornell Notetaking System for Lectures

Using Cornell Notes for Lectures

Finding Solutions to Common Notetaking Problems

Techniques for Recording Information

Techniques for Organizing Information

Capturing important information given during lectures is essential, yet without specific strategies, it can be difficult to do effectively. Do you have trouble writing fast enough to keep up with the speaker? Do part of your notes make no sense when you reread them? Do you ever decide to just listen because notetaking is too frustrating? Do some of your instructors seem to get off track and discuss information out of sequence? This chapter explores methods to help you reduce your notetaking frustrations and improve the quality of notes you take during lectures. Strategies for strengthening your listening skills, which are essential for good notetaking, are also provided.

CHAPTER 10 Lecture Notes Profile

DO, SCORE, and **RECORD** your profile before you read this chapter. If you need to review the process, refer to the complete directions given in the Profile for Chapter 1 on page 2.

	YES	NO
1. I have problems knowing what information to put into notes.	_____	_____
2. My notes are too confusing to use for studying.	_____	_____
3. I stop taking notes when the speaker sidetracks from the topic.	_____	_____
4. I spend time going over my notes and filling in missing information as soon after the lecture as possible.	_____	_____
5. The main ideas and important details are easy to identify in my notes.	_____	_____
6. Internal and external distractors often interfere with my ability to concentrate during a lecture.	_____	_____
7. If I get behind and can't keep up, I stop writing and start listening more carefully.	_____	_____
8. I frequently use symbols, abbreviations, and shortened sentences in my lecture notes.	_____	_____
9. I try to reword (paraphrase) what is said so I don't write word for word.	_____	_____
10. I practice reciting important information in my notes.	_____	_____
11. I use the instructor's verbal and nonverbal communication patterns to help me identify what information is important.	_____	_____
12. I can usually take notes that are adequate and easy to use for studying.	_____	_____

Self-Awareness: Describe your reaction and concerns to taking a class that requires extensive notetaking for lectures. What do you know about your notetaking skills?

_____

_____

_____

_____

_____

_____

_____

_____

_____

Understanding Listening Skills

Of the four verbal communication skills (listening, speaking, reading, and writing), listening skills are often the weakest. You may think that as long as you have ears that work, you can listen. If your auditory channels are functioning, you can *hear*, but that does not necessarily mean that you are *listening*. Listening requires more than taking in the sounds and being aware that words are being spoken.

Listening involves understanding what you are hearing and having the ability to attach meaning to the words and to interpret what the speaker is saying. Frequently, people incorrectly perceive *speaking* as an active process and *listening* as a passive process. The truth is that *listening is an active process that engages the listener in a variety of mental processes*. The poor listening habits that many people have tend not to come from the training given in schools; instead, the poor listening habits often are learned because of the *lack* of training or instruction. Poor listening habits may appear in many forms. The following chart categorizes other types of poor listeners based on the primary behavior shown when effective listening is not occurring:

Why We Don't Hear Others

If you want to listen so you really hear what others say, make sure you're not a:

Mind reader. You'll hear a little or nothing as you think, "What is this person really thinking or feeling?"

Comparer. When you get sidetracked assessing the messenger, you're sure to miss the message.

Rehearser. Your mental tryouts for "Here's what I'll say next" tune out the speaker.

Derailer. Changing the subject too quickly soon tells others you're not interested in anything they have to say.

Filterer. Some call this selective listening—hearing only what you want to hear.

Sparrer. You hear what's being said but quickly belittle it or discount it. That puts you in the same class as the derailer.

Dreamer. Drifting off during a face-to-face conversation can lead to an embarrassing "What did you say?" or "Could you repeat that?"

Placater. Agreeing with everything you hear just to be nice or to avoid conflict does not mean you're a good listener.

SOURCE: *Communication Briefings*, as adapted from *The Writing Lab*, Department of English, Purdue University, 1356 Heavilon Hall, West Lafayette, IN 47907.

Berko, *Communicating*, p. 53

Identifier. If you refer everything you hear to your experience, you probably didn't really hear what was said.

A person may begin listening to a speaker with the complete intention to "stay tuned in," listen attentively, follow the ideas, and make every effort to understand the information. However, good listening is similar to concentration: It's here one second and then it's gone. All of the following factors can influence your ability to be a good listener.

- interest in the topic
- attitude toward the subject
- attitude toward the speaker
- tone of voice
- rate of speech
- speech patterns and mannerisms
- degree of organization of the lecture
- teaching/lecture style
- distractions from people nearby
- room temperature or lighting
- number of interruptions in the speech
- degree of insulation from outside sounds
- familiarity with the words or terminology
- familiarity with the topic

- length of time required to remain seated
- level of difficulty of the course
- quantity of information presented
- sitting posture during the lecture
- seating location in relation to the speaker
- personal physical level (tired, sick)
- personal emotional level at the time
- personal background experiences
- learning style
- cultural background

Notice that the first few items are related to *attitude*. A positive attitude toward the topic, the subject or the class, and the speaker lead to positive listening. A negative, disinterested, judgmental attitude will bring negative results by putting up barriers or shutting down your auditory channels that are required for good listening. Some of the factors above are directly related to the speaker. Ideally, all speakers should automatically use an appropriate tone of voice, rate of speech, pleasing speech patterns and mannerisms, and be well-organized. However, this sometimes is not the case. You, the listener, need to find ways to overcome the barriers that are directly related to the speaker and his or her form of delivery of information. External distractors that were previously discussed in Chapter 5 that occur while you are studying also occur while you are listening. Many of the same techniques for improving concentration can be applied to improving your listening skills. The factors listed at the top of the right column relate to your level of understanding of the course work. The time-management, goal-setting, and reading techniques learned in previous chapters will result in greater familiarity and understanding of the course work so these factors do not become barriers to good listening. The remaining factors are all related to *you* on a personal level.

✎ EXERCISE 10.1 Recognizing the Relationship of Learning Styles and Listening

Read the following excerpt from a communication textbook. Practice your highlight and marking skills. Then proceed to Exercise 10.2.

The Role of Global/Linear Thinking/Listening   We are unique in the way we listen and learn. Part of the differences among us is based on the way our brain works. The human brain is divided into two hemispheres, and research shows that some people are prone to use one side of the brain more than the other. This **brain dominance** accounts for learning and listening in patterned ways.

The left hemisphere of the brain is most responsible for rational, logical, sequential, linear, and abstract thinking. People who tend to be left-brain dominant listen and learn best when materials are presented in structured ways. They tend to prefer specifics and logic-based arguments. Because they tend to take information at face value, abstractions and generalizations don't add much to their learning. Because they are so straight-line in their learning preferences, they are often referred to as **linear learners/listeners**.

The right hemisphere of the brain is responsible for intuitive, spatial, visual, and concrete matters. It is from the right side of the brain that we are able to visualize. Those with this listening/learning dominance prefer examples rather than technical explanations. They prefer knowing the information can be useful and applied. The right-brain dominant person tends to be creative and rely on intuitive thinking, can follow visual/pictographic rather than written instructions, likes to explore information without necessarily coming to a conclusion, and enjoys interaction rather than lecturing. Because of their preference for a generalized rather than specific description, right-brain dominant persons are often labeled as **global listeners/learners**. Many global learners find much of the traditional lecture method of teaching in U.S. schools and universities, a linear methodology, to be dull and frustrating.

Most people are a combination of global and linear learner/listeners. If you fall into this classification, you can be more flexible in how you listen and learn than those with extreme style preferences.

It is important for you to recognize your listening/learning style; it can make a difference in the way you approach the listening/learning environments. If you know that you need examples and the speaker is not giving them, you should ask for them. If the speaker is not drawing specific conclusions and not speaking in a structured format, and these are necessary for your understanding, then you must probe for information that will allow you to organize the ideas. Don't assume that the speaker knows how you need to receive information; he or she doesn't. Many classroom instructors teach based on their own listening/learning style, forgetting that all students don't learn that way. If you are a global listener/learner, this may account for why you had trouble with some math or science classes. On the other hand, if you are a linear listener/learner, literature and poetry classes may have been difficult for you.

Berko, *Communicating,* pp. 58–59

✎ **EXERCISE 10.2   Dominance Inventory—Left/Right, Linear/Global Dominance**

Answer all of these questions quickly; do not stop to analyze them. When you have no clear preference, choose the one that most closely represents your attitudes or behavior.

1. When I buy a new product, I

   A. _____ usually read the directions and carefully follow them.

   B. _____ refer to the directions, but really try and figure out how the thing operates or is put together on my own.

2. Which of these words best describes the way I perceive myself in dealing with others?

   A. _____ Structured/Rigid

   B. _____ Flexible/Open-minded

3. Concerning hunches:

   A. _____ I generally would not rely on hunches to help me make decisions.

   B. _____ I have hunches and follow many of them.

4. I make decisions mainly based on

   A. _____ what experts say will work.

   B. _____ a willingness to try things that I think might work.

5. In traveling or going to a destination, I prefer

   A. _____ to read and follow a map.

   B. _____ get directions and map things out "my" way.

6. In school, I preferred

   A. _____ geometry.

   B. _____ algebra.

7. When I read a play or novel, I

   A. _____ see the play or novel in my head as if it were a movie/TV show.

   B. _____ read the words to obtain information.

8. When I want to remember directions, a name, or a news item, I

   A. _____ visualize the information, or write notes that help me create a picture, maybe even draw the directions.

   B. _____ write structured and detailed notes.

9. I prefer to be in the class of a teacher who

   A. _____ has the class do activities and encourages class participation and discussions.

   B. _____ primarily lectures.

10. In writing, speaking, and problem solving, I am

   A. _____ usually creative, preferring to try new things.

   B. _____ seldom creative, preferring traditional solutions.

Scoring and interpretation:

Give yourself one point for each question you answered "b" on items 1 to 5 and "a" on 6 to 10. This total is your score. To assess your degree of left- or right-brain preference, locate your final score on this continuum:

Left _____ Right
       1   2   3   4   5   6   7   8   9   10

The lower the score, the more left-brained tendency you have. People with a score or 1 or 2 are considered highly linear. Scores of 3 and possibly 4 show a left-brained tendency.

The higher the score, the more right-brained tendency you have. People with scores of 9 or 10 are considered highly global. Scores of 7 and possibly 6 indicate a right-brained tendency.

If you scored between 4 and 7 you have indicated you probably do not tend to favor either brain and are probably flexible in your learning and listening style.

Please bear in mind that neither preference is superior to the other. If you are extremely left- or right-dominant, it is possible to develop some of the traits associated with the other hemisphere, or you may already have them.

Berko, *Communicating*, p. 75–77, 1998.

Web-site links are available online.

Computer Projects

1. If you have a laptop computer and you have relatively fast typing speed, experiment taking notes during a lecture or while watching an educational program on television. Recognize that many times you will abbreviate, misspell, or not have the best organization for your notes. Revise later.

2. Revise a set of your lecture notes *if* you actually learn from typing or rewriting.

Group Web-Search Activity is available online.

Case Studies are available online.

Strengthening Your Listening Skills

Now that you have a better understanding of the many factors involved in listening, the next step is to begin applying strategies that strengthen your listening skills and assist you in becoming a good (or better) listener. The following strategies promote **focused listening**. Focused listening is the process of concentrating intently on what is being communicated. Your attention is placed on the information coming into your short-term memory. The intent is to receive the information, understand it, and begin the task of processing its meaning. Focused listening requires effort and mental discipline. The following twelve strategies are keys to strengthening your listening skills and becoming a more effective listener:

Twelve Strategies for Strengthening Listening Skills

Strategy	Further Explanations
Eliminate distractors	Use the Chapter 5 techniques to eliminate internal and external distractors. Take charge by selecting a location away from external distractors (specific individuals, window, door, and so on).
Pay attention to levels of information	Capturing only the main ideas is not sufficient; capturing every detail is not possible or recommended. Strive to follow the speaker's ideas by seeing the relationships between the information presented. Identify the "big picture" and recognize the important details that develop the big picture or main idea. Think in terms of "levels" of information.
Stay tuned in	Resist the temptation to tune out when information is too technical, difficult, unclear, or boring. Force yourself to listen more intently to identify trends or the sequencing used with the information. Work hard to achieve the mental discipline required to stay tuned in with the speaker.
Monitor your emotional response	Emotions can interfere with listening, distort the information, and set up barriers to understanding. Push yourself to put your own emotions aside so you can give the speaker the opportunity to develop his or her ideas. Jot your emotional responses on a piece of paper; save the discussion of your point of view for an appropriate time after the presentation or lecture.
Create an interest	The attitude you bring with you will affect your ability to listen. Genuine interest occurs when you are familiar with the topic, have an existing interest or curiosity about the topic, or have an excellent motivational speaker. When these situations do not exist, the responsibility to create an interest lays on your shoulders. Relate the topic to your overall goals, write questions that may generate your curiosity, or involve yourself in discussions with people who already have a genuine interest in the topic.
Ask questions	Many teachers and students value questions that ask for clarification or additional information when the questions are asked at appropriate times and are related to the topic being presented. If the speaker prefers not to address questions until the end of the lecture, jot questions on the side of your paper so you can ask them at the appropriate time. Asking questions is a sign of interest and a desire to learn; do not hesitate to ask questions when the time is appropriate.
Be non-judgmental	Paying too much attention to a speaker's clothing, mannerisms, speech patterns, or appearance can be a major distraction from hearing and understanding the content of the message. Strive to focus on the information, not the person. Avoid criticism or judgments about the person. If for some reason the physical presence of the person is too great of a distraction, focus your eyes on the chalkboard or on your notes.
Posture and position yourself for listening	Body postures and position affect the quality of your listening and your level of attentiveness. Slouching conveys an image of disinterest; sit straight in the chair or lean forward slightly with your pen in hand ready to take notes. The back of the room tends to have more distractors, and seeing the overhead transparencies or the chalkboard tends to be more difficult; position yourself closer to the front of the classroom where concentration, attention, and interest often increase.
Visualize the topic and the content	Connecting visualization to the listening process helps imprint information into your memory system and makes retrieval of information more efficient and accurate. Strive to "make a movie in your mind" of the information presented by the speaker.

Paraphrase the speaker	For effective notetaking, understanding the information presented in a lecture and then quickly rephrasing it for your notes is essential. Rephrasing (paraphrasing) results in a shorter, more condensed form of an idea. Practice paraphrasing and condensing rather than attempting to write word for word what the speaker says.
Pay attention to nonverbal clues and body language	Listening also involves picking up nonverbal messages presented through a speaker's gestures, mannerisms, stance, facial expressions, and pauses in verbal presentation. Carefully watch the speaker for nonverbal clues or body language clues that signal important ideas, shifts in ideas, or important supporting details. Many people give nonverbal clues without being aware of this behavior; however, you as a listener should strive to detect the nonverbal patterns used.
Enroll in a listening class	Check to see if your school has a listening class. When listening courses are available, they often focus on critical listening skills which increase a person's auditory memory and expand the ability to remember verbal information more accurately.

EXERCISE 10.3   You as a Listener

Answer the following questions on your own paper.

1. Recall the last time you were in a large group and were required to listen to a speaker or a presenter. Refer to the "Twelve Strategies for Strengthening Listening Skills" on pages 186–187. Which of the techniques would have been effective for you to use so you could have been a more attentive listener?

2. Refer to the descriptions of different kinds of listeners on page 181 under the section, "Why We Don't Hear Others." Which of these descriptions describes you? Explain.

3. Do you see yourself more as a "global listener" or a "linear listener?" Explain.

4. On a scale of 1 to 10, how would you rate yourself as an effective listener in a large group or lecture situation? Explain.

Using the Cornell Notetaking System for Lectures

Many classes will require you to have strong listening skills in order to understand the lectures you will hear and to capture the information to place in your notes for future studying. Capturing the information from lectures is important for several reasons:

■ Lectures help you understand the course content better.

■ Lectures often clarify or expand textbook information.

■ Lectures help identify and emphasize the important course information that you are expected to learn.

■ Lectures provide additional information or points of view that are not included in the textbook.

The Cornell notetaking system presented in Chapter 9 is the same notetaking system you will use to take effective lecture notes. For many students, taking notes from a textbook is not too difficult because the information is printed and the pace for taking notes is controlled by you. During lectures, however, you do not have the advantage of controlling the pace, and you often do not have the advantage of knowing the overall organization that will be presented in the lectures. Some teachers do provide students with an outline for the lecture or begin the lecture by telling the main topics that will be covered. Even with an initial outline, you will need to learn new skills that will allow you to keep up with the lecture and select the appropriate information for your notes. You will also need several new techniques for organizing notes during a lecture. Begin by reviewing the five *R*'s of Cornell that you will be using for your lecture note-taking: **record**, **reduce**, **recite**, **reflect**, and **review**.

1. Record	**2. Reduce**	**3. Recite**	**4. Reflect**	**5. Review**

✎   **EXERCISE 10.4   Brainstorming about Lecture Notes**

Brainstorming is a process of generating as many ideas as possible. Each group member freely contributes ideas and all ideas are accepted by the group and included on a list. Work with a partner or in the group to complete the following directions.

On your paper, compile a list of notetaking difficulties you have experienced. After you have compiled a list of problems, categorize them. Two common categories are "Problems Keeping Up" and "Problems Organizing the Information." Add other categories that are needed to organize your information. Plan to share this list with the rest of the class.

Techniques for Recording Information

The following techniques are designed specifically for taking lecture notes. When used properly, you will have less difficulty "keeping up" and will be able to capture the most important information in your notes. These techniques are needed to deal with the discrepancy between rate of speech and rate of writing. The average **rate of speech** during a lecture is 100–125 words per minute. Rates of speech that are higher than 125 words per minute do create some additional notetaking problems that will be discussed later. The **rate of writing** is about 30 words per minute. Noticing the discrepancy between the rate of speech and the rate of writing makes it apparent that you will not be able to write word for word. The following techniques will help you modify your writing so that you will be able to "keep up with the speaker":

Techniques for Recording Information

1. Paraphrase the speaker by shortening and rewording.
2. Use abbreviations to reduce the amount of writing.
3. Create a set of common symbols.
4. Use a modified form of printing/writing.
5. Practice often.
6. Keep writing when the information is difficult or confusing.

Paraphrase

Paraphrasing means to reword information into your own words. By paraphrasing, you will be able to shorten the information. Paraphrasing is a mental process that must be done quickly. As soon as you capture the speaker's words and interpret the message, write the information in a shortened form. Your sentences do not need to be grammatically correct. Words such as *the, an, and, there,* and *here* may be left out of your sentences, for they do not add to the overall meaning. Paraphrasing is perhaps one of the most difficult parts of notetaking, but with practice and familiarity with different teachers' lecture styles, your skills at paraphrasing will improve.

Use Abbreviations

Many words can be abbreviated to reduce the amount of writing. When you find content-related words that are frequently used, create your own abbreviations for the terms. Other common abbreviations, such as the following, can also be used.

BC. for because	**PRES.** for president
EX. for example	**SOC.** for social or sociology
IMP. for important	**SOL.** for solutions
POL. for politics	**W/OUT** for without

Use Symbols

Frequently used words can also be represented by symbols. The following symbols are often used in notes to reduce the amount of writing.

&	and	→	leads to/causes
@	at	<	less than
↓	decreases	>	more than
≠	doesn't equal	#	number
=	equals	+/−	positive/negative
↑	increases	∴	therefore

Use Modified Printing

It is not uncommon to hear a person say that his or her handwriting was ruined in college. Lecture notetaking requires quickness; time is of the essence. As a result, many students move toward a style of handwriting that is functional without great emphasis on style, neatness, or consistency. One way to increase your writing speed is to use a modified form of writing that consists of a mixture of cursive writing and printing. Feel free to experiment with this mixture of cursive writing and printing to see if it increases your speed. Of course, when you are required to handwrite a personal letter or a job application, return to your neater, more consistent style of writing. Since your notes are usually only for you to see, relax your handwriting standards (but not to the degree that your writing is illegible).

Practice Often

Notetaking gets easier if you practice often. You can practice Cornell notes in every class and also at home. Practice taking notes as you watch educational television, attend meetings, listen to a sermon, or even talk on the phone! Many situational opportunities are available to practice your skills. Practice will increase your ability to paraphrase quickly and capture the speaker's main points.

Keep Writing

One of the most common mistakes students make when information is difficult, confusing, or unorganized is to stop writing and just listen. In actuality, this is the time that writing is more important than ever. If you can write down the information, even if you are not understanding what is being said and have difficulties paraphrasing, the information you write will provide you with material to look over later, to ask other students or the teacher about, and to compare to the information in the textbook. So, when the task gets difficult, *keep writing.* You can sort it out later.

Techniques for Organizing Information

Knowing how to structure notes sometimes is difficult because you do not have a clear sense of the overall organization of the content of the lecture. Most lectures are organized with headings (main ideas) and supporting details; the problem is that you don't usually have access to the instructor's notes that show this outline. Sometimes instructors provide students with an outline or may provide students with an outline if it is requested or suggested. If no outline is available, you will need to listen carefully for the main headings or shift of ideas. In all situations, you will then need to listen and select the important details.

Selecting the important information and the right amount of information can be challenging. If your notes are too brief and lack sufficient details, they will not be very helpful when you need to study the information or prepare for tests. Notes that are too detailed can always be reduced during the reduce step of Cornell, so don't worry about having too many notes. More is better than too little. Selectivity is the key. If you know some information is not essential, do not add unneeded information to your notes. If you are not sure if some information is going to be meaningful or essential, to be safe, try to include it in your notes. The following techniques will help you organize your notes in meaningful ways:

Techniques for Organizing Your Notes

1. Listen for key words that signal headings and main points.
2. Listen for terminology and definitions.
3. Listen for important details (dates, names, facts, and statistics).
4. Listen for ordinals (number words).
5. Listen for examples.
6. Use verbal and nonverbal clues as signals.

Listen for Key Words

The words in the following list often signal a new heading or a new supporting detail. As soon as you hear these key words, ask yourself if the topic (heading) has shifted in the lecture, or if the instructor shifted to a new supporting detail.

advantages	effects	parts	stages
benefits	factors	principles	steps
causes	findings	purposes	techniques
characteristics	functions	reasons	types of
conclusions	kinds of	rules	uses
disadvantages	methods	solutions	ways

Listen for Terminology

In Chapters 8 and 9 you learned the importance of identifying and taking notes on terminology you encounter when you read. For the same reasons, getting terminology and definitions in your notes is important: understanding the terminology lays a strong foundation for learning course content. Word clues often signal definitions and signal you to get the information in your notes:

X *means* . . .	X *is defined as* . . .	*The definition of* X *is* . . .
X *is also called* . . .	X *also referred to as* . . .	

When you hear these words, use the abbreviation *DEF,* to signal you are writing a definition. Or, you may want to use the equal sign (=) as your own symbol to connect a word to a definition. *X* = definition. . . .

Listen for Details

As was also discussed in Chapters 8 and 9, supporting details are dates, names, facts, statistics, definitions, and examples that develop or "prove" the main idea. Notes with sufficient details for future use need to include the above kinds of information. If you find yourself only writing headings or just listing a few points and writing very little, chances are you need to start adding more supporting details to strengthen your notes.

Listen for Ordinals

When you hear "first," make that point number 1 in your notes. Each **ordinal** (number word) helps you organize the details in your notes and confirm that you are selecting the correct number of separate points for your notes. In addition to the ordinals that are number words, there are also *place holders,* or words that *represent* a number. The following words are examples of ordinals and place holders:

first	next	in addition
second	also	last
third	another	finally

Listen for Examples

Examples often serve as vivid triggers or reminders about a specific main idea or point that is being developed. Frequently, examples are informative and interesting; association between the example and what you are expected to learn is easier. For that reason, reference to the example should be in your notes. Sometimes, however, a considerable amount of time is spent on the example, especially if it is an anecdote of a personal experience. Your notes only need to show the basic idea of the example as a reminder of the placement of the example in the lecture; your notes do not need to "retell the whole story."

Use Verbal and Nonverbal Clues

Key words such as *kinds of, steps, advantages of,* and so forth are verbal clues that signal the information is important. The following **verbal clues** are even stronger signals of information that should be included in your notes:

"This is important. You need to know and understand this."

"This will be on the next test."

"As I have already said . . ." (ideas are repeated).

"Be sure you copy this information (from the overhead or chalkboard)."

"If you haven't already done so, be sure you read carefully the information on pages . . ."

"I can't emphasize enough the importance of . . ."

A person's intonation (pitch of his or her voice), volume of voice, and rate of speech can also be considered verbal clues. Listen to your instructor's patterns carefully. Does he or she speak louder, more enthusiastically, faster, slower, or at a different pitch when giving important information? Many speakers may not even be aware of the verbal patterns they use to emphasize important points, but focused listeners can identify the patterns and use the information to help select the ideas that are important for notes.

Information that is written on the chalkboard or charts or graphs that are displayed on an overhead projector are actually visual clues that information is important. As the information is discussed, you have another verbal clue that the chart, graph, or information on the board is important. If it weren't, why would time be spent displaying it? Information on the board or on overheads should appear in your notes on a regular basis.

Watch your instructor's **nonverbal clues** or patterns as well. Body stance, hand gestures, and facial expressions (forehead wrinkles, eyebrows rise) are nonverbal clues that communicate to observant listeners. If the instructor pauses to look at his or her notes or simply pauses to allow you time to write, the pauses are nonverbal clues. Writing information on the board, pointing to parts of it over and over, or circling words on the board are also nonverbal clues indicating that information is important.

Finding Solutions to Common Notetaking Problems

Learning to take effective lecture notes occurs through experience with different teachers, lecture styles, and content; lots and lots of practice; and application of the techniques previously discussed. You may encounter some additional problems with lecture notes; fortunately, there are techniques to solve or reduce these problems. The following problems that you may encounter in a few classes are common for many college students. Solutions for these problems follow.

- Difficulty taking notes on unfamiliar material
- Problems "keeping up" even after using the techniques previously discussed
- Problems with a wandering mind because of a slow lecture style
- Sidetracking by the instructor
- Spelling problems
- Poor concentration and inattentiveness
- Disorganized notes
- Lectures follow the book exactly and move too quickly

Solutions to Common Notetaking Problems

1. Become familiar with the material before the lecture.
2. To help you "keep up," leave a gap and continue, or shift to paragraph form.
3. Use active listening techniques when the rate of speech is too slow.
4. Take notes on "sidetracking."
5. Spell as it sounds and check the spelling later.
6. Use focused listening techniques to combat inattentiveness and poor concentration.
7. Work to better organize your notes immediately after the lecture.
8. Highlight and take notes in the book instead of on paper when the lecture follows the book.

Become Familiar with the Material

When lecture notetaking is difficult due to the use of unfamiliar terms and concepts, the best solution is to refer to the course syllabus of reading assignments. Preview (survey) the material before the lecture. If you have time, use the SQ4R system to read the chapter. A sense of confidence is gained because you know the information is presented in the book and can be reviewed outside of class.

**Leave a Gap or Shift
to Paragraphs**

If you fall behind, do *not* stop writing and decide to just listen. Instead, leave a gap in your notes and start taking notes again for as long as you can keep up with the instructor. After class, ask another student or the instructor to help fill in the gaps. The more you practice and use the strategies in this chapter, the less frequent and the smaller will be the gaps in your notes.

You can also shift to paragraph form. Notes are definitely easier to work with when they are clearly organized. However, you will encounter times when you simply cannot keep up with the instructor and organize your notes at the same time. If you find yourself slowing down by trying to decide if a detail is a supporting detail or one that should be indented, shift to writing in paragraph form. Simply keep writing what you hear; paraphrase by restating the information in your own words or write abbreviated sentences. Later, when you have more time, you can reread the paragraph and organize it in a more meaningful way when you make the recall column.

Paragraph Form ⟶

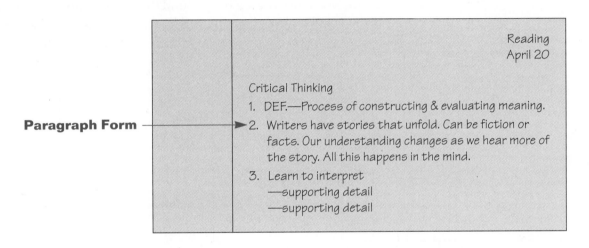

Reading
April 20

Critical Thinking
1. DEF.—Process of constructing & evaluating meaning.
2. Writers have stories that unfold. Can be fiction or facts. Our understanding changes as we hear more of the story. All this happens in the mind.
3. Learn to interpret
   —supporting detail
   —supporting detail

Use Active Listening

There are times that you may find your mind wandering because the speaker is talking too slowly. Again, the problem is attributed to a discrepancy between rates. The *rate of speaking* may be one hundred words or less or an example may go on too long to be meaningful. The **rate of thinking** is about four hundred words per minute. Your mind is moving much more quickly than the words of the speaker. The result is often daydreaming, doodling, or losing focus. In addition to the listening techniques covered at the beginning of this chapter, the following techniques can help you become an active listener:

Keep Writing   Even if the details don't seem vital to your notes, write them anyway. They can always be eliminated later by not including them in the recall column of your notes. By continuing to write, you remain actively involved with the lecture.

Mentally Summarize   In your mind, run through the main ideas and the supporting details that have been discussed. Try to mentally review and summarize them.

Anticipate the Next Point   With focused listening, you can often tune in to the speaker's outline. Keeping in mind the points that have already been discussed, anticipate or guess the next point. Then listen carefully to determine whether your prediction was correct.

Mentally Question the Information   Ask yourself several basic questions. Do you agree with the information? Does it agree with the textbook? Does it go beyond the textbook? How does it relate to other areas previously presented?

Take Notes on Sidetracking

Some organizational problems occur because the instructor **sidetracks** by discussing something that does not seem to fit the outline of the lecture. When you know this has happened, continue to *take notes on any of the "sidetracked" information* that may be important. Try to organize this information under headings with main ideas and important supporting details. Where should you place this information in your notes? There are two options that work well:

■ Since you are taking notes on only one side of the paper, use the back side of the previous page of notes. Record your sidetracked notes here.

■ Continue to take notes in the Cornell column. When you finish taking the sidetracked notes, draw a box around this information to set it off from your regular set of notes.

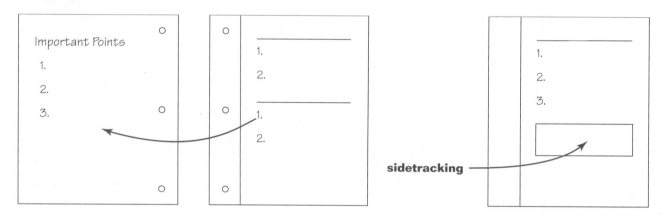

Spell What You Hear

Write what you hear, even if you know it is not correct. As soon after class as possible when you develop the recall column, correct the spelling by any of the following methods:

■ Use a portable spell checker or language master for quick correcting.
■ Enter the word on a computer and run the spell checker command.
■ Check the textbook chapter, index, or glossary.
■ Use a reference book of common misspellings and correct spellings.
■ Ask another student for the correct spelling.
■ Use a dictionary. (This is the most lengthy process if your spelling is too far from the correct spelling.)

Many strategies are available to help you, an adult, learn to be a better speller and "sound words out" more accurately. You may shudder at the thought of a spelling class if you remember the problems you had in your younger years. Good news! Approaches in teaching spelling have changed drastically over the years, so explore the new strategies and take the initial steps to become a stronger speller.

Use Focused Listening Strategies

Inattentiveness and poor concentration were discussed at the beginning of this chapter. Exercise 10.1 also introduced you to the concept of global and linear listeners and strategies that each might use to improve listening skills during lectures. Review the section on listening and then identify specific strategies that deal with your reasons for inattentiveness or poor concentration. Set goals for yourself to begin using specific strategies during lectures. Listening and concentration both require an interest, commitment, and mental discipline on your part. To make the changes, take the time to identify the specific issues involved, and then take the responsibility to create a plan of action for change.

Work with Your Notes

Notes that appear to be disorganized can be organized more effectively shortly after the lecture. In Chapter 3 for time management, a recommendation was made to schedule a study block immediately after a lecture class if possible. Right after a lecture class, the information is still fresh in your mind. During this time you can add missing details, confer with other students about your notes, and create your recall column. Before you begin the recall column, take time to highlight the important information in your notes. Highlighting the meaningful information is one way to "reorganize" your notes without rewriting them. Then, take time to create your recall column. The recall column can now be organized neatly and logically since you are not under the pressure of time and do not have to think and write quickly. Remember that the majority of your time will be spent reciting from the recall column, so if the recall column is well organized, unorganized notes do not become detrimental.

Some students insist on rewriting their notes or typing them on a computer. Some teachers will advise *not* to do this because of the time that is involved. For many students, the advice is good; time can be better spent on reflect and review activities. However, students who are kinesthetic or highly visual may find value in rewriting or typing notes. The physical process of rewriting becomes a review and a memory-building technique. If this is the case for you, rewrite the notes, reorder the information, and add a more meaningful structure to your notes. If you want to rewrite simply so your notes "look better," the perfectionist in you needs to "lighten up" and make use of your precious study time for other learning activities.

Highlight and Take Notes in the Book

A wide variety of lecturing styles will be encountered in college. Lecturing straight from the book is not very common, but it does occur. If you try taking notes from a teacher who lectures from the book, the rate of speech is too rapid. When this occurs, save the Cornell notetaking for later. Instead, follow along in the book. Highlight the points as they are mentioned in class. Make marginal notes throughout the book. After class, if you want to have Cornell notes as one of your methods of studying for the class, use the highlighting, the marginal notes, and the organizational structure (headings and subheadings) to guide you in making Cornell notes.

✎   **EXERCISE 10.5 Taking Lecture Notes**

Select any one of your classes. Use the Cornell system to take notes from one of the lectures. On your own paper, identify the class, the topic, and the instructor's name. Answer the following questions. Turn your answers in with your lecture notes. (Your lecture notes may be evaluated by using the assessment form on page 196.)

1. What problems did you have taking notes from this lecture?

2. What are possible solutions for the problems you had?

3. How soon after the lecture did you work on the recall column? Did this seem effective? Why or why not?

4. Did the recall column work for you? Did it give you enough or too much information to help you with reciting? Explain.

Notetaking Assessment Form for a Lecture

Name _____   Date _____

Lecture _____   Course _____

Record Column for Notes

_____   You identified and underlined the main headings. Well done!

_____   You need to listen for key words that indicate a new heading. Write the heading and underline it.

_____   Your notes are clear, well organized, and detailed.

_____   Your notes appear to be crowded or cluttered. Try spacing your notes apart more; leave spaces between new sections.

_____   Try using numbering to separate each new supporting detail.

_____   Your notes lack some important details. Try to write more.

_____   You are using too many short phrases that will lose meaning after time. Try to write more complete ideas or sentences.

_____   Your notes are very lengthy. Try to paraphrase and write shorter sentences. Be selective.

_____   Include information that was presented on the overhead or was written on the chalkboard.

_____   Strive to improve legibility and neatness.

_____   Be sure you fill in the gaps after the lecture.

_____   Try to correct spelling errors after the lecture.

_____   See the instructor to discuss your notes together.

Recall Column

_____   The organization and content of your recall column are well done.

_____   Copy the heading from your notes into the recall column.

_____   Use a wider recall column so that you have more room to write.

_____   Try including more key words or questions so that you have clues for reciting.

_____   Put fewer key words and/or information in your recall column. With this much information, you will likely read, not recite.

_____   Align your recall column so that the key words or questions are directly across from the related information in the notes.

_____   Try using the recall column. Add or delete key words or questions to make it more effective.

Other

Photocopy this form before you use it.

⊖⊖ Exercise 10.6 LINKS

Practice your notetaking skills by taking Cornell notes on any *one* of the following sections from this chapter:

1. Understanding Listening Skills (pages 181–182).

2. Exercise 10.1, Recognizing the Relationship of Learning Styles and Listening (page 183).

3. Strengthening Your Listening Skills (pages 185–187).

4. Techniques for Recording Information (pages 188–190).

5. Techniques for Organizing Information (pages 190–192).

6. Finding Solutions to Common Notetaking Problems (192–195).

SUMMARY

■ Listening is an active process that involves understanding and attaching meaning to what you hear.

■ A wide variety of factors influences a person's ability to be a good listener. They include attitudes, interests, environment, experiences, learning styles, and personal background.

■ Twelve different strategies can be used to strengthen your listening skills.

■ The same five steps of the Cornell notetaking system are used for lecture notes: record, reduce, recite, reflect, and review.

■ Discrepancies in rate of speech (100–125 words per minute) and rate of thinking (400 words per minute) create notetaking problems. Strategies exist to overcome the problems.

■ Recording techniques include paraphrasing, abbreviating, using symbols and modified writing, practice, and the suggestion to keep writing through difficult material.

■ Techniques for organizing information involve listening for key words, terminology, important details, ordinals, and examples.

■ Verbal and nonverbal clues may also help signal important information to put into notes.

OPTIONS FOR PERSONALIZING CHAPTER 10

1. **PROFILE CHART—PERSONAL LOG**   Answer the following questions in your personal log.

   What score did you have on the Chapter 10 Profile? _____

   What did you learn about yourself as a listener and a notetaker? Give specific examples or explanations.

2. **WORDS TO KNOW**   Knowing the following vocabulary terms is important.

listening	recite	ordinal
linear learners/listeners	reflect	verbal clues
global listeners/learners	review	nonverbal clues
focused listening	rate of speech	rate of thinking
record	rate of writing	sidetracks
reduce	paraphrasing	

3. **EXPAND THE CHAPTER MAPPING**   Because there are six main categories, you may want to work on legal-sized paper or sketching paper that is large enough to expand the map. If you would like to create a condensed mapping of key details, you may expand the map in the book on the first page of this chapter.

4. **WRITING ASSIGNMENT 1**   Discuss the inventory score you had for Exercise 10.2 (pages 184–185). Do you agree with the score? Which kind of learner/listener are you? What are some of the characteristics common to this kind of learner/listener? How can you use this information to improve your listening skills during lectures?

5. **WRITING ASSIGNMENT 2**   Conduct a short survey among students who are not enrolled with you in this class. Prepare a questionnaire based on categories given on page 181 under the section "Why We Don't Hear Others." Summarize your findings.

6. **PORTFOLIO DEVELOPMENT**   Analyze one set of the notes you took at the beginning of the term. Make copies of the Notetaking Assessment Form for Lectures found on page 196. Use the form to complete an assessment of your earlier notes. Discuss the weaknesses and strengths of the notes you created before you learned about the Cornell notetaking system. Then provide a set of more recent lecture notes taken in any one of your classes. Use another Notetaking Assessment Form to assess these notes. Summarize the changes and improvements you have seen in your notes since using the Cornell notetaking system.

CHAPTER 10 REVIEW QUESTIONS

True-False

Carefully read the following sentences. Pay attention to key words.
Write T *if the statement is TRUE. Write* F *if it is FALSE.*

_____ 1. You should leave one or more blank lines before you begin to take notes on a new heading or main idea.

_____ 2. An average lecturer speaks at a rate of 200–250 words per minute.

_____ 3. Speaking is an active process, but listening is a passive process.

_____ 4. Major ideas or headings should be underlined so that they stand out from the supporting details.

_____ 5. Words such as *advantages, purposes, uses, kinds of,* and *steps* are signals that can help you organize your notes.

_____ 6. You should copy most of the information written on the chalkboard into your lecture notes.

_____ 7. Good listening also involves the ability to interpret nonverbal communication.

_____ 8. When you fall behind and miss information, it is recommended that you stop writing and rely on your auditory memory skills.

_____ 9. A person's attitude is one factor that influences whether a person is a good listener or a poor listener.

_____ 10. The recall column should be developed during the lecture.

_____ 11. You can increase your speed of writing by paraphrasing, using abbreviations, writing sentences that are not grammatically correct, and using modified printing.

_____ 12. Take notes, summarize, anticipate, and question are strategies to use when you begin to lose concentration because the instructor is speaking too slowly.

_____ 13. Rehearsers, filterers, derailers, and placaters have acquired the necessary skills to be good listeners.

_____ 14. Some notetaking problems may occur when the student and the teacher have different learning/listening styles.

_____ 15. The Cornell steps for lecture notes are different from the Cornell steps for textbook notes.

Short Answer—Critical Thinking

For each of the student situations below, discuss specific strategies from this chapter that could be used to reduce or eliminate the problem. Briefly explain how the strategies would be solutions.

1. Calib has learned the five *R*'s of Cornell. His notes are well organized; his recall columns give complete lists or complete sentences to summarize the notes. He reads the recall column and usually thinks about the information. When he reviews, he rereads the recall column. Calib usually does well on all the test questions that cover the textbook information, but he frequently misses questions that come from lectures. He doesn't understand why, since he thinks his notes are thorough. What else can he do?

2. Kimberly is very uncomfortable sitting in a classroom. She often feels like other students are watching her so she sits in the back corner. She has a lot of problems taking notes. Her notes are too brief and impossible to use for studying. Sometimes she has problems with her notes because she can't clearly see what is written on the board. Other times she simply loses her concentration by watching other students. When she does try taking notes, she can't write fast enough to get all of the teacher's words on her paper. What would you recommend?

Essay (Express your answer in several paragraphs.)

Select one *of the following topics to discuss. Use your own paper for your answers. Your answer should not be more than one page.*

1. Discuss a variety of factors that influence a person's ability to listen effectively. Your discussion may include factors that contribute to good listening, factors that contribute to poor listening, and factors that affect the way a person has been trained or conditioned as a listener.

2. Summarize the brain dominance theory by summarizing the characteristics of "right-brain and left-brain" learning.

Using Visual Notetaking Systems

Visual notetaking offers you an opportunity to use originality, creativity, pictures, drawing, and colors to help you learn and retrieve information from memory. Do you find it is easier to remember information presented in pictures, graphs, or diagrams? Do you know how to create visual mappings, hierarchies, comparison charts, and time lines? Do you often draw or sketch information on paper that was originally written in paragraph form? In this chapter you learn to organize and utilize visual notes to process new information for memory and make learning even more fun!

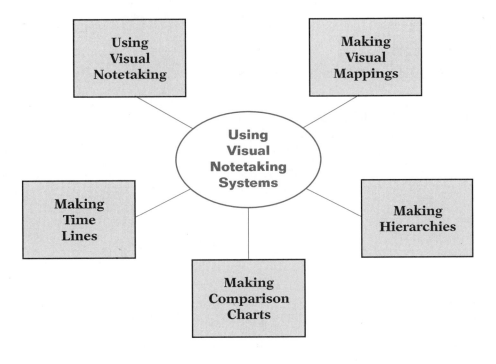

- Using Visual Notetaking
- Making Visual Mappings
- Using Visual Notetaking Systems
- Making Time Lines
- Making Hierarchies
- Making Comparison Charts

CHAPTER 11 Visual Notetaking Profile

DO, SCORE, and **RECORD** your profile before you read this chapter. If you need to review the process, refer to the complete directions given in the Profile for Chapter 1 on page 2.

		YES	NO
1.	I am comfortable reorganizing or rearranging information instead of studying it in the same order it was presented.		
2.	I use reciting frequently when I study.		
3.	I draw various kinds of pictures to help me remember what I've read.		
4.	I understand the concept of different levels of information.		
5.	I learn main ideas well but I often overlook important details.		
6.	I use these two principles of memory frequently when I study: recite and review.		
7.	I close my eyes or look up into the air to visualize or picture charts.		
8.	When I recite, reflect, and review, I stop to get feedback so that I know if I am remembering information correctly.		
9.	I know how to make mappings, hierarchies, comparison charts, and time lines.		
10.	I am eager to try creative ways to take notes.		
11.	I know how to convert visual notes into printed summaries.		
12.	When I make drawings, I experiment with layout and use of colors.		

Self-Awareness: Are you uncomfortable with the idea of taking notes in a visual form that involves pictures, colors, and a reorganization of the information? Why or why not?

_____

_____

_____

_____

_____

_____

_____

_____

_____

Using Visual Notetaking

In Chapter 1 you explored your learning styles or learning preferences. If you have strong visual skills, visual notetaking such as visual mappings, hierarchies, comparison charts, and time lines may become your preferred methods for learning new information.

Although visual notetaking is generally used to create reflect activities, some students become so proficient with visual notetaking that it can replace the Cornell notetaking system. The goal of this book is to help you find the methods that work best for you. Use visual notetaking as your main system of notetaking if it helps you learn and remember new information more easily.

Visual notetaking offers you an opportunity to organize and record information in *creative* ways. Because it draws on your originality, there is more than one way to correctly present information. You do not need to be artistically talented to use visual notes; stick figures or basic sketches are sufficient as long as you understand the pictures you create. Because visual methods involve a relatively new form of notes, you may at first feel uncomfortable with these methods. Give yourself time and practice to learn these tools; they just may be your key to a stronger memory and system for recalling information quickly.

Students with weak visual skills may want to adapt some of the steps used to study from visual notes. If picturing or visualizing information is a struggle, the following suggestions are recommended; they help transfer the visual aspects of the study tools in this chapter to an auditory approach:

1. Complete the visual notes as discussed in this chapter.

2. Turn on a tape recorder. Look at the visual notes you created.

3. Follow the recommended steps for studying the information. Instead of visualizing, verbalize. Discuss the information out loud and speak in complete sentences.

Making Visual Mappings

You have already had some experience with **visual mappings** if you have completed the Options for Personalizing the Chapter exercise at the end of each chapter.

Mappings can be used in a variety of ways. You can make a visual mapping of

■ A paragraph or a group of paragraphs under one heading.

■ A topic or a subject presented in several chapters and lectures.

■ Your lecture notes (in addition to Cornell or an alternative notetaking method).

■ Information to review for a test.

■ Each chapter you have covered.

■ Ideas brainstormed for a paper or a speech.

How to Create Mappings

Four basic steps are involved in creating visual mappings. Your choice of borders, shapes, pictures, and colors in each step gives you the opportunity to be creative.

How to Create Mappings

1. Write the topic in the center of your paper.
2. Write the main ideas or the main headings; use lines to connect them to the topic.
3. Add major details to support the main ideas.
4. Add any necessary minor details.

Write the Topic   In the center of your paper, write the **first level of information**—the topic. The topic can be the title of a chapter, the name of a lecture, or the subject you wish to map. For example, SQ4R is a subject, not the name of a chapter or a lecture.

Border   The border can be a box, a circle, or even a picture. If you are making a mapping of types of real estate investments, you may want the center picture to be a house or a building. If you are making a mapping on memory, you may want the center picture to be a person's head.

Paper size   If you know that your mapping will include many details, you may want to work on legal-size paper (eight-and-a-half by fourteen inches) or drawing paper that is even larger. If your mapping is on a smaller topic, notebook-size paper is sufficient.

Write Main Ideas   Next add the **second level of information**, the main ideas of the topic. For a visual mapping of a chapter, use the main headings found in the chapter. For a visual mapping of a subject, show the main categories of information related to the subject. (See sample mapping on p. 205.)

Borders, Shapes, or Pictures   To make the main ideas or categories stand out, place a border or shape around each item on level two. You may want to use a different shape than was used for the topic. Pictures can be used instead of geometric shapes or pictures can be placed inside shapes.

Colors   Some people's memories are strengthened with the use of color. Experiment with colors by shading in the main ideas. Use different colors for each level of information.

Spacing   Visually appealing and uncluttered mappings are easier to visualize or memorize. Before you begin adding the level-two information, count the number of main ideas to decide how to space them evenly around the page. Place them relatively close to the topic so that you'll have room to add details later.

Organization   The most common organization for this level-two information is clockwise, beginning at the eleven o'clock position. If there is a definite sequence to the information, such as steps that must be learned in order, you may want to add numbers to the lines that extend from the topic or inside the borders.

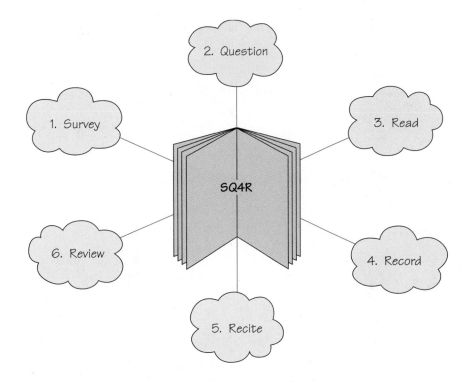

Connections   Draw a line from each main idea to the topic. This gives a visual representation of their relationship. Each main idea is thus represented as a subtopic of the topic in the center of the paper.

Add Major Details   Now add the major supporting details for each main idea. This is the **third level of information**. Write only key words that serve as "triggers" for you to recite in full sentences. Avoid the tendency to write long phrases or full sentences; your mapping will become too cluttered. Draw lines from these key words to the main ideas they support. Level-three information does not need to be in clockwise order or start at the eleven o'clock position.

Quantity of Details   Be selective. Include only as many major details as you need to help you remember the important information. You do not need to have the same number of details for each main idea. It is up to you to determine how many details will help your memory.

Horizontal Writing   To make your mapping easy to read, keep all your writing horizontal. Avoid writing at a slant, sideways, or turning the paper as you write, resulting in words written upside down.

Borders   If the mapping details stand out clearly without borders (as shown in the SQ4R mapping), don't include any. If you are color-coding levels of information, you also may want to enclose these major details within a border.

Personalize with Pictures   Pictures help imprint the information in your visual memory. Many times pictures are easier to recall than words, so include pictures when appropriate.

Add Minor Details   If you need some minor details, use the same guidelines as for major details. (Note the minor details for the record step in the following example.) If you find that you need one or more levels of information beyond the minor details, such as may be the case with a long chapter, consider reorganizing the information into several different topics and creating several mappings. You may find that narrowing or limiting the topic of a mapping will be more beneficial for visualizing and studying. By reorganizing, you chunk

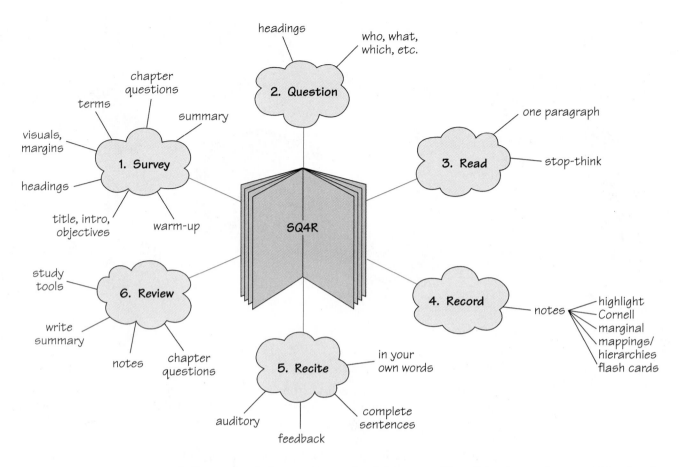

information into more meaningful groups. Your big picture is not so big that it is difficult to memorize, visualize, or comprehend.

The following mapping on a lecture about vocabulary skills is an example of converting your notes into a mapping. Assume the instructor first discussed two kinds of vocabulary (receptive and expressive) and then discussed six strategies for finding definitions, providing details and examples for each of the strategies. Your visual mapping of the lecture would look something like this:

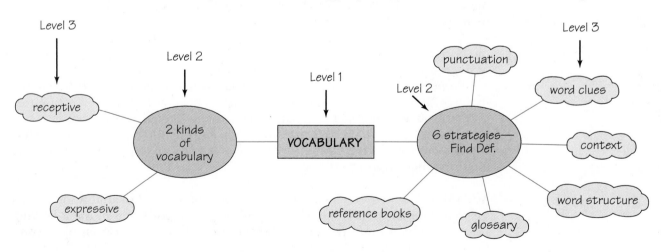

✎ **EXERCISE 11.1 Making a Visual Mapping for Textbook Information**

Return to Exercise 7.8 on page 138. Make a visual mapping of the four kinds of coping strategies. In your visual mapping, include three or more levels of information.

How to Study from Visual Mappings

Visual mappings are powerful and work effectively because they are based on memory principles that boost your ability to learn new information. The information in mappings is organized logically, shows relationships, and helps you associate one idea with another. Concentration and interest increase as you work to present information creatively. As you recite, review, receive feedback, and visualize, the process of learning is enhanced.

> ## How to Study from Mappings
>
> 1. Look intently (stare) at your visual mapping until you think you have it in your memory.
> 2. Close your eyes or look away. Visualize and recite the topic.
> 3. Visualize and recite each main idea. Check your accuracy.
> 4. Visualize one main idea at a time. Recite the details. Check your accuracy.
> 5. Use reflect activities.
> 6. Use ongoing review.

Look Intently at Your Mapping   Stare at the visual mapping you created. Pay attention to the words, shapes, and colors; try to engrain in your memory the locations of the level-two information. Your goal is to carve a mental image of *the level-one and level-two information.* You do *not* need to attempt to visually remember the level-three information. Move to the next step when you feel you have the mental image learned.

Visualize and Recite the Topic   Close your eyes, look away, or look "up and to the left" toward the ceiling. Try to picture only the topic of your mapping. Practice seeing the words, the shape, and the color (if any was used). Recite what is written in the center of your mapping (the topic).

Visualize and Recite the Main Ideas   Strengthen the visual image of the skeleton of the mapping by picturing only the topic and the number of main ideas or categories directly connected to the topic. Now recite by naming the topic and each of the main ideas. Your reciting may *sound* like this: "In SQ4R there are six main ideas branching off the topic SQ4R. They are survey, question, read, record, recite, and review."

Check your accuracy   Refer back to your mapping to verify that you recited correctly. If you were correct, move on to the next step. If you were not correct, study the skeleton with the topic and the main ideas. Look away to visualize and recite again. Get more feedback.

Recite Main Ideas and Details   Now that you can clearly picture the skeleton, return to the first main idea. Without looking, try to tell all that you remember about this main idea. Your goal is to include all the key words (major and minor details) that were shown on your mapping. Talk to yourself in complete sentences.

It is not necessary to visualize all major and minor details written on your paper. It is important, however, that you include these details in your reciting.

Check your accuracy   Refer to your mapping to see if you included all the major and minor details for the main idea you just recited. Did you forget to include some information? If yes, try reciting and including the information as you look at your mapping. The major and minor details can be visual clues for you. Then look away and recite. Get feedback again to be sure that this time you incorporated the details in your reciting.

Continue this process for each of the main ideas. Don't rush the process; work through each category in a careful, thoughtful way. When you are finished with the entire mapping, move on to a reflect activity.

Use Reflect Activities   You can reflect several ways:

1. Copy the skeleton of your mapping on paper. Then, without referring to the mapping, fill in the words for the topic and the main ideas.

2. Try to redraw the mapping with as many major and minor details as possible without looking and without first giving yourself the skeleton.

3. Repeat the process of visualizing and reciting the entire mapping. Turn on a tape recorder as you recite. The tape can become auditory notes for review.

4. Convert the visual information back into print form by summarizing. Use the main headings of the visual mapping as your guide and the structure for your summary. Write one paragraph (or more) for each heading. Summarize the details related to that heading. Writing summaries from visual mappings begins to prepare you for essay writing and short-answer questions that may appear on future tests.

Use Ongoing Review   Since visualizing does not require you to have materials such as notebooks, paper, or pencil available, you can review any time you have a few available minutes. As you wait in between classes, ride a bus, take a shower, or wash dishes, try to reconstruct the mapping in your mind.

You may want to make a smaller version of your mapping to place on flash cards for review. These cards can also be placed around your house where they are easy to see and quick to review.

As you remember, the final step of the Information Processing Model is retrieval. To access this mapping from your long-term memory, practicing retrieval is essential. With more practice, you'll see the picture more sharply and more readily.

Making Hierarchies

Hierarchies are a form of visual mapping in which information is arranged in levels of importance from top down. If visualizing mappings with lines extending in all directions was difficult for you, you may prefer the organized structure of hierarchies. Three different hierarchies for SQ4R could look like this:

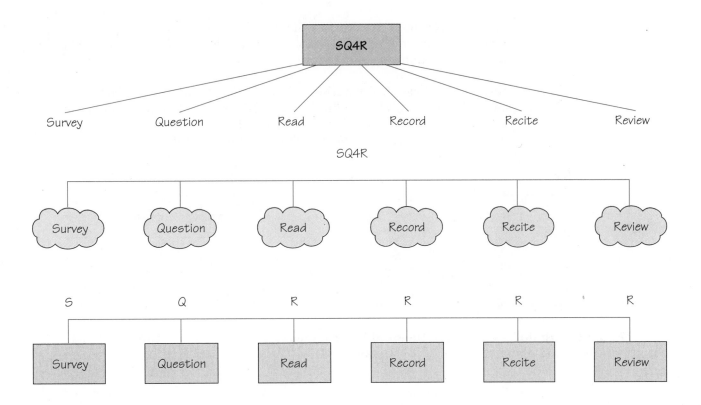

How to Create Hierarchies					

The steps for creating hierarchies are similar to the steps for mappings. The same levels of information are used: topic, main idea, major details, and minor details.

How to Create Hierarchies

1. Write level-one information (the topic) on the top line of the hierarchy.
2. Draw lines downward from the topic to show level-two information (the main ideas).
3. Under each main idea, branch downward again for level-three information (major details).
4. Add level-four information (minor details) under the major details if needed.

Write Level-One Information   Place the topic or the subject on the top line. You do not need to put a box or border around the topic, but you can if you wish.

Show Level-Two Information   When hierarchies are created for textbook chapters, the headings in the book become level-two information. When you create a hierarchy for a general topic such as SQ4R, level-two information represents general categories.

Determine the number of main ideas to be placed under the topic. Branch *downward* to level two to write the main ideas. Consider using legal-size paper for more extensive hierarchies. Space the main ideas evenly on the paper to avoid a cluttered or crowded look. Always write horizontally. Try adding color-coding and various shapes or pictures to strengthen the visual image.

Many textbooks provide informative introductions; these can be included in your hierarchies under a category labeled "Intro." Key words, concepts, or objectives can now be added to the hierarchy. Another category can also be included, if needed, to show graphs, visual aids, lists of terminology, or any other information you want to remember.

Add Level-Three Information   Because level three often has numerous supporting details, you need to consider how you will place the details on the paper. To avoid a cluttered or crowded look, the details can be staggered or arranged in a variety of layouts as shown in the illustrations.

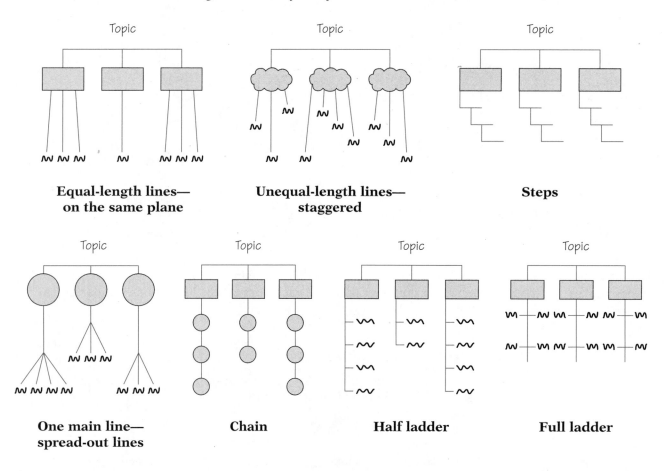

**Equal-length lines—
on the same plane**

**Unequal-length lines—
staggered**

Steps

**One main line—
spread-out lines**

Chain

Half ladder

Full ladder

Provide Level-Four Information   Minor details can be added by branching *downward* from level three. Be selective. Include only essential key words that you feel you need to help you remember the information. Again, select a layout that will organize the details clearly. Borders, pictures, and color-coding can also be used.

✎ **EXERCISE 11.2 Making a Hierarchy for Textbook Information**

Read the following excerpt from a business textbook. Create a hierarchy (which will look very much like a flow chart) to show this information. Create your hierarchy on your own paper.

Kinds of Managers

Managers can be classified two ways: according to their level within the organization and according to their area of management. In this section we use both perspectives to explore the various types of managers.

Levels of Management

For the moment, think of an organization as a three-story structure. Each story corresponds to one of the three general levels of management: top managers, middle managers, and first-line managers.

Top Managers A **top manager** is an upper-level executive who guides and controls the overall fortunes of the organization. Top managers constitute a small group. In terms of planning, they are generally responsible for developing the organization's mission. They also determine the firm's strategy. It takes years of hard work, long hours, and perseverance, as well as talent and no small share of good luck, to reach the ranks of top management in large companies. Common job titles associated with top managers are president, vice president, chief executive officer (CEO), and chief operating officer (COO).

Middle Managers Middle management probably comprises the largest group of managers in most organizations. A **middle manager** is a manager who implements the strategy developed by top managers. Middle managers develop tactical plans and operational plans, and they coordinate and supervise the activities of first-line managers. Titles at the middle-management level include division manager, department head, plant manager, and operations manager.

First-Line Managers A **first-line manager** is a manager who coordinates and supervises the activities of operating employees. First-line managers spend most of their time working with and motivating their employees, answering questions, and solving day-to-day problems. Most first-line managers are former operating employees who, owing to their hard work and potential, were promoted into management. Many of today's middle and top managers began their careers on this first management level. Common titles for first-line managers include office manager, supervisor, and foreman.

Areas of Management

Organizational structure can also be divided into areas of management specialization. The most common areas are finance, operations, marketing, human resources, and administration. Depending on its mission, goals, and objectives, an organization may include other areas as well—research and development, for example.

Financial Managers   A **financial manager** is primarily responsible for the organization's financial resources. Accounting and investment are specialized areas within financial management. Because financing affects the operation of the entire firm, many of the CEOs and presidents of this country's largest companies are people who got their "basic training" as financial managers.

Operations Managers   An **operations manager** manages the systems that convert resources into goods and services. Traditionally, operations management has been equated with manufacturing—the production of goods. However, in recent years many of the techniques and procedures of operations management have been applied to the production of services and to a variety of nonbusiness activities. Like financial management, operations management has produced a large percentage of today's company CEOs and presidents.

Marketing Managers   A **marketing manager** is responsible for facilitating the exchange of products between the organization and its customers or clients. Specific areas within marketing are marketing research, advertising, promotion, sales, and distribution. A sizable number of today's company presidents have risen from the ranks of marketing management.

Human Resources Managers   A **human resources manager** is charged with managing the organization's human resources programs. He or she engages in human resources planning; designs systems for hiring, training, and evaluating the performance of employees; and ensures that the organization follows government regulations concerning employment practices. Because human resources management is a relatively new area of specialization in many organizations, few top managers have this kind of background. However, this situation should change with the passage of time.

Administrative Managers   An **administrative manager** (also called a *general manager*) is not associated with any specific functional area but provides overall administrative guidance and leadership. A hospital administrator is a good example of an administrative manager. He or she does not specialize in operations, finance, marketing, or human resources management but instead coordinates the activities of specialized managers in all these areas. In many respects, most top managers are really administrative managers.

Whatever their level in the organization and whatever area they specialize in, successful managers generally exhibit certain key skills and are able to play certain managerial roles. But, as we shall see, some skills are likely to be more critical at one level of management than at another.

Pride, *Business*, pp. 180–182.

**How to Study
from Hierarchies**

As with mappings, hierarchies need to be visualized, recited, and reviewed to work as effective study tools. Since the study techniques are the same as those used with visual mappings, they are summarized, rather than detailed, here.

How to Study from Hierarchies

1. Look intently (stare) at your hierarchy until you think you have it in your memory.
2. Close your eyes or look away. Visualize the topic on the top line.
3. Visualize and recite each main idea that drops down from the topic. Check your accuracy.
4. Visualize one main idea at a time. Recite the details. Check your accuracy.
5. Use reflect activities.
6. Use ongoing review.

Reciting, reflecting, and reviewing are essential. In Chapter 2 you learned that short-term memory can handle only a limited amount of information at one time. If your hierarchy has more than seven main ideas on level two, you are wise to divide your reciting, reflecting, and reviewing into smaller sections.

For example, if you are studying a mapping or a hierarchy for the twelve principles of memory, find ways to divide the information into smaller parts. Visualize and recite the first section; then continue to work with additional sections. Your reciting may sound like this: "There are twelve principles of memory. The first four are selectivity, association, visualization, effort; they spell the word *SAVE*. The second four spell the word *CRIB:* concentration, recitation, interest, and big picture–little pictures. The last four (*FOTO*) are feedback, organization, time on task, and ongoing review. Selectivity means . . .

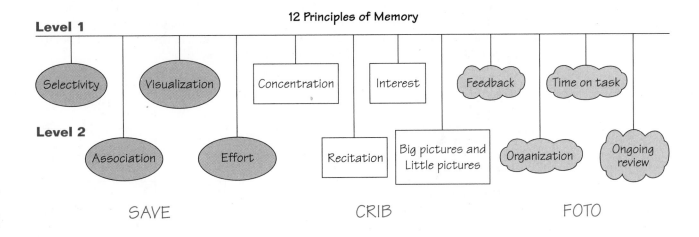

⊖⊖ Exercise 11.3 LINKS

Work with a partner to complete this exercise. Select one of the following items to develop into a visual mapping or a hierarchy. If possible, do not duplicate; there are sufficient choices so that each set of partners will be able to work on a different assignment.

Use your own paper or overhead transparency. Develop a visual mapping or a hierarchy that has at least three levels of information. Personalize your work by adding shapes, colors, and pictures when appropriate.

1. Howard Gardner's Eight Intelligences (Chapter 1, pages 15–17).

2. Expand the Chapter 3 Visual Mapping (page 51).

3. Steps for Writing Goals and Tips for Reaching Goals (Chapter 4, pages 76–79).

4. Techniques for Reducing Internal and External Distractors (Chapter 5, pages 95–97).

5. Organizational Patterns *or* Comprehension Strategies (Chapter 6, pages 113–115).

6. Theories of Forgetting (Chapter 7, page 134).

7. Four Context Clues (Chapter 8, page 155).

8. Kinds of Listeners (Chapter 10, page 181).

9. Global and Linear Thinkers/Listeners (Chapter 10, page 183).

10. Twelve Listening Strategies (Chapter 10, pages 186–187).

Making Comparison Charts

Comparison charts (also known as matrixes, grids, or tables) are designed to organize a large amount of information into a format that is visual and easy to use to compare and contrast information. Comparison charts are organized with columns and rows. The category or characteristics that are being compared or contrasted are placed at the top of each column. The subjects that are being compared or contrasted are placed at the beginning of each row. Whenever you are working with several related subjects that each have specific characteristics, this form of visual notetaking is useful.

Categories → Subjects ↓	Column 1	Column 2	Column 3
Subject A			
Subject B			
Subject C			

How to Create Comparison Charts

In a comparison chart, *columns* run up and down, and *rows* run across the page. Important information about each subject is written inside the boxes (cells). The number of columns and rows is determined by the amount of information being covered. The following steps show how to organize information for matrixes. If you use a computer, matrixes can be made through "table" commands.

How to Create Comparison Charts

1. Identify the number of subjects to be compared or contrasted. Write one subject on each row.
2. Identify the categories of information to be discussed. Write one category at the top of each column.
3. Complete the comparison chart by writing key words in each box where columns and rows intersect.

Identify Subjects and Label Rows   Since comparison charts are designed to compare or contrast information for two or more subjects, begin by identifying the number of subjects. Many times the number of subjects (topics) are grouped together in the printed text information. Once you have identified the number of subjects, you can begin to make the rows for your comparison chart. If you have two subjects, your chart will have only two rows. Write the names of the subjects on the row.

As you become more familiar with visual materials and recognize different kinds of visual materials from your textbooks, you will note that some tables or informational charts in textbooks place the subjects at the top of the columns instead of at the beginning of the rows.

Identify Categories and Label Columns   Identifying categories requires you to think carefully about the information you have read. What categories of information were discussed for all or most of the subjects? You can almost always use a general category titled "Characteristics," but more specific categories are more useful. The number of categories you select determines the number of columns in your comparison chart. Label the top of each column.

If you have difficulties finding appropriate labels for the columns, try using this approach to help you organize important information for the chart:

1. List each of the subjects across the top of a piece of paper.
2. Under each subject, list important details associated with that subject.
3. Look at your list of details. Can the details be grouped into larger categories?
4. If you see a logical category of information under one subject, is that same kind of information also given for other subjects? If so, you have discovered an appropriate title for a category.

Complete the Comparison Charts   There are two ways to complete the boxes in the chart. Complete one column at a time by providing essential details for each subject that is listed down the side of the chart.

The second way to complete the comparison chart is to complete all the boxes in one row at a time. With this method, all the essential details about one subject are given before working with the details of the other subjects.

✎ EXERCISE 11.4   Creating a Comparison Chart for Levels of Management

Part I:
Refer back to Exercise 11.2 (pages 211–212). Create a chart for the three kinds of managers. Label the rows: top managers, middle managers, and first-line managers. You will need to seek out labels for each of the categories.

Part II:
Use the same process as above to create another comparison chart for the "Areas of Management" information in Exercise 11.2. You will need to decide on the number of columns and rows, the labels for the columns and rows, and the important supporting details for each cell.

How to Study from Comparison Charts

When you are the creator of comparison charts, you need to ask yourself, "What information am I expected to know?" For some comparison charts, the most valuable information to know will be patterns or trends. For other comparison charts, you will be expected to know the details within each cell of the chart. Once you are able to identify the information that you are expected to know, you will be able to select the most appropriate methods to study the information.

Reciting and visualizing from comparison charts can be more demanding than reciting and visualizing from mappings or hierarchies because you are telling about more than one subject or main idea. You are also comparing or contrasting it to other subjects or main ideas. If you are expected to know the specific details inside the cells, use the following steps to recite and learn the information:

How to Study from Comparison Charts

1. Name and visualize the topic, the subjects in the rows, and the categories across the top of the comparison chart.
2. Recite information by moving across the rows or down the columns. Get feedback.
3. Use reflect activities.
4. Use ongoing review.

Name and Visualize the Rows and Columns   The skeleton of the chart includes the title, the subjects written down the side (labels of the rows), and the categories written across the top of the chart (labels of the columns). Take time to create a strong visual image of this chart before reciting information inside the boxes. Explain the chart to yourself as you try to restructure it visually without looking.

Recite and Get Feedback   Recite in a logical order. Decide if you want to recite row by row, telling everything about one subject at a time, or column by column, telling how one specific category is used for each of the subjects. After you recite either a row or a column, refer back to the chart to check your accuracy. Immediate feedback is important; recite again if you found that you made mistakes. Continue until you can recite the entire chart.

Use Reflect Activities   If adding pictures to visual notetaking helps you remember information, add pictures inside each box. If color helps you remember visual information more easily, add color. You can use colored pencils to shade each subject (each row) in a different color (or to complete the boxes of the chart so that the key words appear in different colors).

There are three basic reflect activities that are effective for comparison charts. The first two can be done by looking at the chart.

■ Read through the chart row by row. Turn the key words in the boxes into complete sentences. Speak so that the information is clear and organized. Use a tape recorder to record your presentation. Listen to the recorder several times for review. Visualize each part as you hear it on the recorder. Use the same process reading and speaking in full sentences as you explain each column.

■ With the chart in front of you, write a summary that includes all the key points. First write a summary that explains all the categories one row at a time. Then write a summary that explains one category at a time as it relates to each subject. This activity is basically the same as the first activity above, except that it is a written, rather than a verbal, exercise.

■ Try to redraw the entire chart without looking at your original. First label your rows and then your columns. Go back to each box and fill in the key words.

Use Ongoing Review   As with any form of notetaking, comparison charts need to be reviewed often so that they stay fresh and accessible in your mind. Because a comparison chart contains so much information, practice retrieving it frequently.

Making Time Lines

The last visual notetaking system is the time line. A **time line** is a visual representation of a series of events in chronological order (time sequence). Time lines are used most frequently in history courses because the events within a chapter are often written in a time sequence. Events in later chapters may cover the history of another part of the world during the same time period. A time line can help you get a clear picture of the years specific events happened and what events occurred in the same time period.

How to Create Time Lines

Time lines vary in length. They can be made for sections of a chapter, a full chapter, a lecture, or an entire course. Use the following steps to create time lines that show the chronological sequence of important events:

How to Create Time Lines

1. Select appropriately sized paper for your time line.
2. Draw a horizontal line and label it with dates.
3. Write events above their dates.

Select Paper   For shorter sections of a chapter or for one lecture, regular notebook paper can be used. If you plan to make an ongoing time line for a full chapter or a course, expect to create a lengthy time line. For example, you may want to begin a time line for an entire history course. You will add information to the time line after each lecture and as you work through each chapter. Because of the length of this time line, you may want to use the following options:

■ Tape pieces of blank paper together, or use computer paper that has not been separated.

■ Use a roll of adding machine tape.

■ Tape a long piece of butcher paper to a wall.

Draw and Label a Horizontal Line   Draw a solid line across the middle of your paper. Divide the line into equal size segments. Below the line, label each segment with dates. You may want to label year by year, five years at a time, or even longer, depending on the length of the time period you are covering.

Add Events   Each time a new event is introduced in the book or in the lecture, add it to the time line. Locate the correct date on the horizontal line; draw a line upward and name the event. You can also use the following options for adding events to your time line:

■ Add pictures for greater visual impact.

■ When you have more than one event for a time period, write the events in a column above the date or "branch them upward."

■ Color-code or draw boxes around events to separate them.

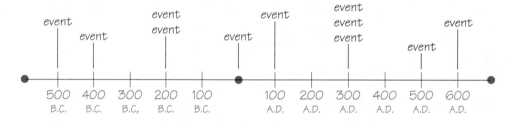

Time periods in equal intervals

How to Study from Time Lines

Become familiar with each event on the time line; take time to picture the event occurring. Then ask yourself questions related to the chronological order of the events: What came before this? How did the previous events influence this event? How did this event influence the following events? What events happened at the same time? Visualize the sequence of events unfolding through time.

The following suggestions can also be used to study from your time lines:

Make Flash Cards   Make a set of question cards as you look at the time line. Write the answer on the back of each card. Use the cards the same way you use vocabulary flash cards. Sometimes you can study by looking at the questions and referring to the time line for answers. Other times you can refer to the backs of the cards for feedback.

Recite Dates   Use your hand, arm, or paper to cover the bottom half of the time line. All you will see are events. Recite the dates for each event.

Recite Events   Reverse the process. Cover up the top of the page. All you will see are dates. Recite which events occurred on each date.

Write Summaries   Look at the beginning section of your time line. Use complete sentences to write a summary that includes the main events and their dates. As you complete one section of the time line, continue to the next section until you have a summary of all the dates and events on your time line.

Use Ongoing Review   Ongoing review is always necessary. Recite from your flash cards, your time lines, and your summaries throughout the term. Each time you add new information to your time line, spend some time reviewing the information that is already there.

 EXERCISE 11.5   **Creating a Time Line**

Select one of the following topics to use to create your own time line. Begin by drawing a line across your paper, dividing the line into units of time, and then labeling the time line with dates and events.

Option 1: Select a magazine or newspaper article that shows the development of events over a time period of more than one month.

Option 2: Use a history textbook. Select a section in one of the chapters to represent in a time line.

Option 3: Create a time line that shows the major events in your lifetime.

Web-site links are available online.

Computer Projects

1. Explore the graphic capabilities of programs you have access to. Try to create at least three different kinds of visual notetaking examples (pie chart, bar graph, mapping, hierarchy, time line, line graph, comparison chart).

2. Use a tables format on your computer to complete Exercise 11.4.

Group Web-Search Activity is available online.

Case Studies are available online.

SUMMARY

- Visual mappings, hierarchies, comparison charts, and time lines are all visual representations of information.

- Use visual mappings and hierarchies to show the relationships between main ideas and supporting details.

- Use comparison charts to compare or contrast two or more subjects.

- Use time lines to present chronological information.

- Visual notetaking tools must be studied thoroughly after they have been created. Steps for studying include:
  1. Visualize the image you drew without looking at it.
  2. Recite the topic and the main ideas. Then recite the details for each main idea.
  3. Get feedback to check your accuracy.
  4. Reflect by reproducing the visual notetaking tool on paper, by writing summaries, or by working with the information in other ways.
  5. Review the image frequently to keep it active in your memory.

OPTIONS FOR PERSONALIZING CHAPTER 11

1. **PROFILE CHART—PERSONAL LOG**   Answer the following questions in your personal log.

   What score did you have on the Chapter 11 Profile? _____

   What advantages and disadvantages do you see in using visual notetaking instead of or in addition to Cornell notetaking?

2. **WORDS TO KNOW**   Knowing the following terms is important.

visual mappings	hierarchies
first level of information	comparison charts
second level of information	time line
third level of information	

3. **EXPAND THE VISUAL MAPPING**   Expand the visual mapping on page 201 by adding level-three information. Personalize the mapping by adding colors and pictures.

4. **WRITING ASSIGNMENT 1**   Discuss ways you can begin to incorporate more visual notetaking into your method of studying. Which courses and textbooks are appropriate for this visual presentation of materials?

5. **WRITING ASSIGNMENT 2**   Many students are excited to learn about visual forms of notetaking and find that this approach to capturing information on paper is creative, less restrictive, and easier to use to learn and recall information. Discuss the relationship of this notetaking approach to the three main modalities, multi-sensory learning, and the theory of multiple intelligences.

6. **PORTFOLIO DEVELOPMENT**   Compile samples of visual notetaking for materials in any of your classes. Strive to demonstrate your understanding of visual mappings, hierarchies, comparison charts, and time lines. Your work may be completed on a computer using graphic software.

Chapter 11 Review Questions

Multiple-Choice

Choose the best answer *for each of the following questions. Write the letter of the best answer on the line.*

_____ **1.** Mapping can be used to
   a. take lecture notes.
   b. take textbook notes.
   c. make reflect activities.
   d. all of the above.

_____ **2.** Hierarchies
   a. use rows and columns.
   b. show only the main ideas of what you read or heard.
   c. contain the same information found on visual mappings.
   d. always arrange information chronologically.

_____ **3.** Visual notetaking requires the use of
   a. visualization.
   b. creativity.
   c. recitation.
   d. all of the above.

_____ **4.** If you have large amounts of information for a mapping,
   a. use complete sentences.
   b. use larger paper.
   c. omit some ideas.
   d. all of the above.

_____ **5.** If a mapping shows specific steps or a specific order of information,
   a. remember the order.
   b. don't use mappings.
   c. add numbers to the lines.
   d. none of the above.

_____ **6.** It is acceptable to
   a. write full sentences in each cell of a comparison chart.
   b. write sideways if needed.
   c. put more than one event on a time line date.
   d. none of the above.

_____ **7.** When you visualize your notetaking, you should
   a. try to see the skeleton first.
   b. be creative and make changes as you go.
   c. stare at the paper for five minutes.
   d. add new information that you forgot to put in the original mapping.

_____ **8.** Feedback
   a. is nonessential when you work with visual notetaking.
   b. lets you know how well you are learning.
   c. comes only in auditory form.
   d. is characterized by none of the above.

_____ **9.** Reflect activities often include
   a. making tapes as you recite in full sentences.
   b. reproducing the visual notes from memory.
   c. summarizing the information in new ways.
   d. all of the above.

_____ **10.** Students with weak visual processing skills
   a. shouldn't try visual notetaking because it's too frustrating.
   b. can develop visual notetaking and then incorporate auditory systems for reviewing.
   c. should use mappings and hierarchies for class notes.
   d. should ask a notetaker to make the visual notes.

_____ **11.** To avoid having cluttered hierarchies,
   a. stagger the information on lower levels.
   b. write more complete sentences.
   c. eliminate some main ideas.
   d. eliminate some key words.

_____ **12.** If your mapping or hierarchy has more than seven main ideas,
   a. chunk the ideas so that you study sections at a time.
   b. consider making two hierarchies or mappings.
   c. use boxes and/or color to separate each part.
   d. all of the above.

_____ **13.** On a time line, the
   a. earliest date is on the right.
   b. earliest date is on the left.
   c. number of years is hard to see immediately.
   d. dates are written above the line.

_____ **14.** The columns on comparison charts
   a. show the percentages to use.
   b. show the categories, characteristics, or traits that will be compared and contrasted.
   c. cannot contain more than five cells.
   d. label the rows to be studied.

_____ **15.** When reciting is done with visual notetaking, it should
   a. begin from the bottom up.
   b. move counterclockwise.
   c. go from details, to main ideas, to topic.
   d. go from topic, to main ideas, to details.

Short Answer—Critical Thinking

1. On your own paper, convert the visual mapping for this chapter (page 201) into a hierarchy. Your hierarchy must show three or more levels of information. You may add color and/or pictures to your hierarchy if you wish. If you have a computer program that makes hierarchies, you may use it.

2. Compare the visual mapping to the hierarchy. In a paragraph, briefly explain which visual notetaking system is easier for you to use.

Preparing for Tests

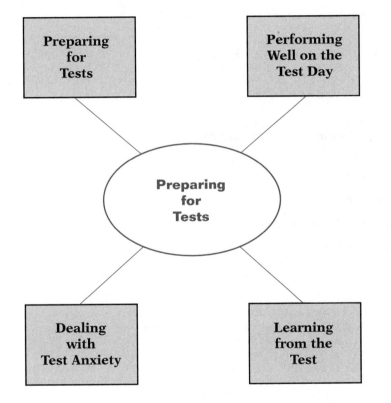

Preparing
for
Tests

Performing
Well on the
Test Day

Preparing
for
Tests

Dealing
with
Test Anxiety

Learning
from the
Test

Many students experience strong physical, emotional, and behavioral reactions or anxieties when they are faced with taking tests. Do you get headaches, stomachaches, anxiety, or short-temperedness in testing situations? Does your mind go blank in the middle of a test? Do you often feel underprepared for tests? Does your performance on tests reflect the amount of studying and learning you have accomplished? In this chapter, you learn test-taking techniques that diminish or eliminate test anxiety and help you perform more effectively each time you are required to complete a test.

CHAPTER 12   Test Strategies Profile

DO, SCORE, and **RECORD** your profile before you read this chapter. If you need to review the process, refer to the complete directions given in the Profile for Chapter 1 on page 2.

	YES	NO
1. Even though I know the material, my mind goes blank when I take tests.		
2. I usually feel prepared for tests.		
3. I am often nervous, feel sick, or have physical problems (headache, stomachache, clammy hands) right before a test.		
4. I am able to go into tests with an attitude of confidence.		
5. I am so relieved when I finish a test that I leave as soon as I answer the last question.		
6. If I run out of time, I just leave blanks for the questions I don't have time to answer.		
7. I try to find out as much information as possible about a test before it is given.		
8. I spend time analyzing my answers and study techniques after the test is graded.		
9. I make special summary notes before every major test.		
10. I make a five-day study plan before major tests.		
11. I use the survival technique of cramming for most tests.		
12. I practice predicting and writing test questions as one way to prepare for tests.		

Self-Awareness: Describe your current attitude toward tests. How do you respond when you hear there will be a test? How would you rate your test-taking skills?

_____

_____

_____

_____

_____

_____

_____

_____

_____

Preparing for Tests

Tests in college are a reality. Grades are *earned,* not just "given." Tests are one method of assessing your level of understanding and determining the information that you have learned. Tests are basically "check points" of your progress. To reduce anxiety and stress related to tests, you can begin by being well prepared for tests.

Tests concern some students because they know they are underprepared. Students who are underprepared often find a solution in **cramming**. Cramming is an attempt to learn large amounts of information in a short period of time. As discussed in the Information Processing Model and with the Twelve Principles of Memory, the brain needs time to process information accurately. Cramming may put some information into memory, but it will not lead to thorough understanding or confidence. Cramming is a "survival technique" that may backfire and create even more stress or anxiety about an upcoming test because students who cram become aware of how much *they don't know.* The most basic solution is to study and learn on a consistent basis, week by week. This is most likely to happen when you have a well-designed time management schedule, use the 2:1 ratio, use effective study methods, and use ongoing review.

In addition to the basic study skills you have learned throughout this textbook, the following techniques will also help you be better prepared for tests:

Test Preparation Strategies

1. Make a five-day time management plan to prepare for major tests.
2. Make summary notes as you review chapters and sections of materials.
3. Find out as much as you can about the upcoming test.
4. Predict test questions and practice writing test questions.
5. Participate in a review session.

Five-Day Plan

Review the **five-day study plan** to prepare for tests (Chapter 4, page 81). For smaller tests, use the same steps but shorten up the time period. Perhaps you will do all of the steps in two days instead of five days. The important point is to allow some time to review the information and then some time the night before the test and the day of the test to review summary material one last time.

Make Summary Notes

Summary notes are a special set of notes that you create specifically to study for tests. These are the notes that you will review the day before the test (day 5) and immediately before the test. Frequently when you begin the review and test preparation process, you become aware of how much you have learned. Information that was once foreign now seems to be "obvious, logical, or common sense." After reviewing this information and feeling confident that you know it, you do not need to spend any more time reviewing it. Move on to the next set of information. The information that you identify that needs to be reviewed further should be placed in some form of summary notes. Summary notes are also valuable if you know specific kinds of questions that will appear on the test. For example, if the teacher clearly tells you that there will be an essay on a specific topic, as you review, you will want to create summary notes that pull information together that can be used in that essay. The following formats all work effectively for summary notes:

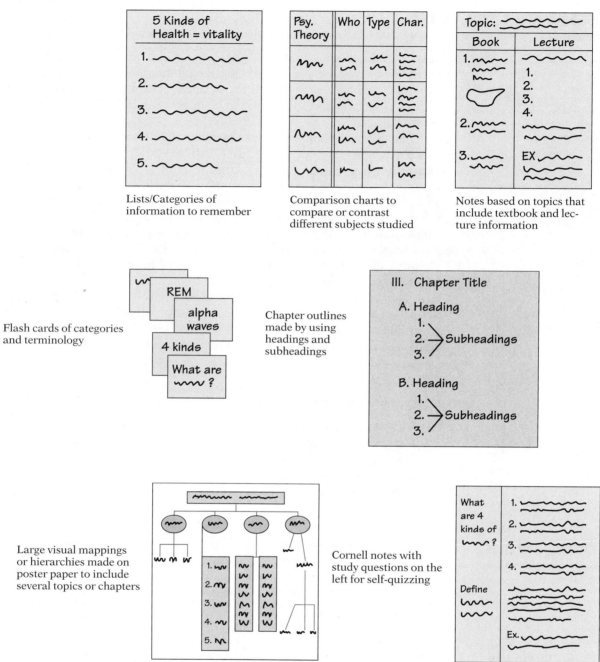

Lists/Categories of information to remember

Comparison charts to compare or contrast different subjects studied

Notes based on topics that include textbook and lecture information

Flash cards of categories and terminology

Chapter outlines made by using headings and subheadings

Large visual mappings or hierarchies made on poster paper to include several topics or chapters

Cornell notes with study questions on the left for self-quizzing

Find Out About the Test

Take the time and effort to find out as much as you can about the upcoming test. Some teachers make previous tests available for review. Some teachers will provide you with details about the types of questions and which areas to study. Knowing the kinds of questions, the number of questions, and the areas of emphasis often have a calming effect because you are better able to predict what you will encounter when you receive the test. Sometimes talking to students who previously completed the course is helpful, especially if the teacher provides you with little information. Former students may be able to give you suggestions for ways to study for a particular teacher's test and the kind of test to expect. However, teachers change their tests and their test formats, so do not become over-confident based on the information received from former students.

Predict Test Questions

Predicting test questions is an excellent method for preparing for tests and reducing test anxiety. Predicting test questions is even easier to do after you have taken one or two tests from a specific teacher and have a sense of the types of tests he or she uses. Understanding types of test questions is the first step. The following chart shows test formats that are common in college courses:

Kind of Question	Level of Difficulty	Includes	Requires
Recognition (objective)	Easiest	True-False Multiple-Choice Matching	Read and recognize whether information is correct; apply a skill and then recognize the correct answer.
Recall	More demanding	Fill-in-the-Blanks Listings Definitions Short Answers	Retrieve the information from your memory.
Essay	Most difficult	Essays	Retrieve the information from memory, organize it, and use effective writing skills.

Effective test preparation should include studying all the important material thoroughly so you are well prepared for any type of test question. However, many students prefer to modify their test-preparation strategies to reflect specific testing formats when the formats are announced in advance. If you know you will be taking a test with **objective questions** or **recall questions**, the following chart provides you with a summary of the types of material you should focus on and practice strategies to build into your review time.

If You Predict . . .	Study This Kind of Information:	Practice May Include:
Objective Questions	• Definitions of key terms • Category flash cards • Details: names, dates, theories, rules, events	• Writing true-false questions • Writing multiple-choice questions • Writing matching questions • Working with a study partner to exchange practice questions
Recall Questions	• Information presented in lists • Definition cards —say and spell words on the front for fill-in-the blank tests —three-part definitions on the back of cards for definition and short-answer tests • Category cards • Cornell recall columns • questions created in the Q step of SQ4R • Summaries at the end of chapters	• Reciting information in full sentences and in your own words • Short summary writing to practice expressing ideas on paper • Writing answers to the questions created in the Q step of SQ4R • Writing your own questions for fill-in-the-blank questions, listings, words to define, and short answers • Working with a study partner to exchange practice questions

Essay questions sometimes are more difficult to predict. Essay questions cover larger topics, so one way to predict essay questions is to actively identify the "big picture" ideas or concepts that were covered. Essay tests and the types of essay questions you may encounter will be discussed in more detail in Chapter 14.

Participate in Review Sessions

Review sessions are a powerful way to receive immediate feedback about the topics you understand clearly and the ones that need further review. Review sessions often provide you with the opportunity to verbalize information, which again is an excellent form of feedback. Actively listening to other students explain information or answer practice test questions can be a rewarding learning experience. If the teacher has not organized a review session, take the initiative to invite another student or a small group of students to meet with you to review. Frequently review sessions are more productive if one person suggests a review approach to use. Here are a few possibilities:

- Each member writes a specific number of practice test questions to bring to the group.
- Each member is responsible for summarizing a specific chapter and facilitating a discussion on that chapter.
- Each member brings some type of study tool to the group to use for reviewing. This may be a set of flash cards, Cornell notes, or visual notes.

EXERCISE 12.1 Academic Preparation Questionnaire

*What was the last test you took in one of your classes?*_____
Think back to the days prior to that test. Check YES or NO to the following statements. Be honest with your answers.

	YES	NO
1. I had all the reading assignments done on time.	_____	_____
2. I had all the homework assignments done on time.	_____	_____
3. I reviewed the work on my homework assignments when they were returned.	_____	_____
4. I asked questions about information I didn't understand.	_____	_____
5. I worked with a tutor or a study partner for review.	_____	_____
6. I recited information that I was studying on a regular basis.	_____	_____
7. I followed my time management schedule and used the 2:1 ratio.	_____	_____
8. I spent time reviewing each week.	_____	_____
9. I attended classes regularly.	_____	_____
10. I was an active learner and used a variety of methods to study.	_____	_____
11. I used active reading techniques and the SQ4R method.	_____	_____
12. I created study tools that I have found to be effective for me.	_____	_____
13. I found enough time to read the textbook carefully and highlight.	_____	_____
14. I made a special study schedule for the days prior to the test.	_____	_____
15. I used study techniques that gave me feedback.	_____	_____
16. I was an active listener and participant in class.	_____	_____
17. I was able to stay fairly motivated about the class and the work.	_____	_____
18. I was organized and was able to find the materials I needed to study.	_____	_____
19. I avoided cramming the night before the test.	_____	_____
20. I can honestly say that I gave it my best.	_____	_____

If you answered yes *to all or most of the above questions, you used effective study techniques and should have been well prepared for the test. All of the* no *answers indicate a need to improve your study methods. Analyze the* no *answers to determine which study techniques need to be strengthened. Review the specific skills you need to learn to utilize more effectively.*

EXERCISE 12.2 Predicting Test Questions

*Assume that you will soon have a test in this class that will cover three chapters.
If an actual test is not scheduled within the next week, you may identify any three
chapters for this exercise.*

Which chapters will be your focus for this exercise? _____
*Assume that you asked about the type of test that will be given. You were told that
the test will have true-false, listings, definitions, and short answers. There will be
a total of 100 points.*

Write five good true-false questions.

1. _____

2. _____

3. _____

4. _____

5. _____

Write two questions that require an answer that is in the form of a list of information.

1. _____

_____

2. _____

_____

Write three questions that ask for a definition of a specific vocabulary word (terminology).

1. _____

_____

2. _____

_____

3. _____

_____

Write two short-answer questions that will require two or three sentences to answer.

1. _____

_____

2. _____

_____

*Bring these questions to class. You may be asked to exchange your test questions
with another student or to share your questions in class.*

Performing Well on the Test Day

After days of preparation and anticipation, the day of the test arrives. The following techniques will help you perform at your very best and reward you for your efforts:

Techniques for Performing Well

1. Be physically ready before entering the classroom.
2. Use four "Smart Start" tips the first three minutes of the test.
3. Read directions carefully and circle key words.
4. Direct your thoughts outward toward the test.
5. Ignore other students.
6. Use test time wisely.
7. Use the four levels of response for answering questions.

Be Physically Ready

Before a test, getting ready physically is also of primary importance. You can *physically get ready* for a test in several ways:

1. Get a good night's sleep the night before a test. Do not stay up too late studying; if you have used effective study techniques, you won't need to cram. You want to have minimal fatigue and an alert mind, both of which can come through a restful sleep.

2. Allow time for a healthy breakfast. A nutritious breakfast begins your day with a high energy level that is maintained for several hours. Avoid sugary foods such as doughnuts—they may give you an "energy boost" but will wear off quickly and leave your energy level lower than before you ate.

3. Check that you have all the necessary supplies such as paper, pencils, pens, calculator, spell checker, and review notes.

4. Allow extra time to get to school early so that you don't feel the need for last-minute rushing. Take care of basic needs (restroom, drink of water) before you go into the classroom. Then sit in your usual place unless you get too distracted by friends sitting near you. Use your time right before class productively:

   ■ Get your necessary supplies ready on your desk.

   ■ Take a few minutes to focus on the subject. Mentally rehearse some of the information you have reviewed.

   ■ Use a familiar relaxation method, or visualize yourself successfully completing the test.

Use Four Smart Start Tips

The four **"Smart Start" tips** should begin the minute you receive the test. Make these Smart Start tips a habit; they have a calming effect, get your mind focused, and get you off to a positive start. The four Smart Start tips are:

1. *Jot Down Important Information*   As soon as you get the test, on the side or back of the test jot down any information you want to be sure to remember. This may include formulas, mnemonics, lists, or facts. If you are not allowed to write on the tests, ask if you may have blank paper available for organizing ideas.

2. *Listen to Directions*   As the teacher begins to talk, pay close attention to the directions. There may be changes on the test, corrections, or suggestions.

3. *Survey the Test*   Take a quick look through the test to find out:

- The types of questions
- If questions are printed on the back of pages
- Where to place your answers
- The point value of questions
- The length of the test

4. *Budget Your Time*   Once you have surveyed, make a quick plan to budget your time. This is especially important if you have essay questions. Next to each major section of the test, estimate and jot down how much time to spend on each section so that you have time to complete the entire test. Be sure to leave enough time to write and proofread essay answers.

Read Directions Carefully

Read all the directions carefully. Before you begin answering questions, get a clear picture of what is being asked. In Chapter 14 you will learn the meanings of different direction words; pay close attention to these words to assure that you are giving an answer that matches the question. For multiple-choice questions, note whether or not more than one letter answer can be used. For matching, note whether or not a letter answer can be used more than once. For listings, pay attention to the number of items you are expected to include in your answer. For short answers, circle the words that indicate what is expected in your answer. Regardless of the question format, if the directions are long or confusing, take time to circle all the key words that will help you focus on what is expected from you. Ask for clarification if the directions are not clear.

Direct Your Thoughts Outward

Sometimes when students start to feel pressure during a test, a negative inner voice starts interfering with thoughts such as "I can't do this. I am not going to pass this test. I want to quit." In addition to the negative "chatter," eyes stop focusing and students may find themselves reading carelessly, skipping words, or misreading words. Some of the physical symptoms of test anxiety (which are discussed later) may begin. In the above situations, attention is shifted off the test; the challenge now is to get the attention focused back to the test. Quick relaxation techniques, positive self-talk, and positive visualization can be used as soon as you sense that you are shifting focus off the test. The following techniques can also be used to get your focus outward and back on the test:

- *Become a more active learner.* Circle direction words and underline key terms in directions and in questions. These markings help keep your eyes and your mind focused on the task at hand.
- *Mouth the questions* or even read them in a whisper. This activates your auditory channel and asks one more of your senses to help you out.
- Use a blank paper or your arm to *block off the rest of the test.* Since anxiety often results in the eyes jumping around or moving randomly, this method helps keep your eyes focused on one question at a time and produces a calming effect.

Ignore Other Students

Sometimes a relaxed attitude can be altered or influenced by other students or friends. Do not watch others to see if they are farther ahead than you or are working more easily than you. The first students to leave do not necessarily know the information best; they may in fact not know the information at all, which is why they left early. Try very hard not to compare yourself or your performance to others. Work at your own pace, always doing the best you can with your answers. Keep your mind and your eyes on your test. Avoid looking at someone else's desk; your glances may be interpreted as attempts to cheat or get answers from someone else. Every minute during a test is valuable time; don't waste it by getting sidetracked worrying about others.

Using Test Time Wisely

Students with effective test-taking skills do not finish a test and then rush out of the room; instead, they use the extra time to review all the answers on the test, proofread for mistakes, and strengthen short-answer or essay questions by adding more information.

The following questions about using test time wisely are frequently asked by students:

1. *Should I change answers while I'm reviewing the test?* Do not change answers if you are panicking and feel time running out. Change answers only if you can justify the change; perhaps other questions on the test gave you clues or helped you recall information necessary to answer the question.

2. *Are there any other reasons to stay longer?* Yes. Some students feel more comfortable asking questions about the test when fewer students are present. The teacher's response to a question may trigger your memory or give you a needed clue.

3. *What if I don't have time to finish the test?* If you run out of time, guess at answers rather than leaving them blank. A blank space can only be wrong; an educated guess can add a few more points if it is correct. For essay questions, take a few minutes to list the points you would have included in your essay if you had had more time. Listing your main points usually leads to some test points.

If you often have problems finishing tests on time, *before* the day of the test ask if more time will be allowed if it is needed. Some teachers will make arrangements for extended time on tests if the request is made prior to the day of the test.

Use the Four Levels of Response for Answering Questions

The reward of effective studying is to be able to read a question and immediately respond with the correct answer. All students wish this could happen all the time, but in reality, there will be times in which the immediate response is not available. When this occurs, learn to work through the question by using **four levels of response**. The levels are shown below.

Immediate response is what you hope happens for each question. This is the payoff for effective studying. After carefully reading the question, you are immediately able to provide the correct answer. The question automatically triggers associations, and the information from long-term memory is available. Immediate response boosts your confidence and moves you through the test more quickly.

Delayed response occurs when you read the question but are not sure of the answer. Read the question *twice*. Do a quick **memory search** by trying to recall the information by linking or associating the key words in the question to clusters of information in your memory. For example, if the true-false question reads, "Metacognition involves knowing a wide variety of strategies and being able to choose the correct strategy for the learning task involved," try recalling the definition you learned for metacognition. Do the learned definition and this statement mean the same thing? Or try to visualize the notes that you made on metacognition or hear the teacher discussing metacognition. If you are still not sure of the answer, delay your response. *Skip the question for now.* Return to it after you have answered as many questions as you can using immediate response. *Make a small check next to the question or on your answer sheet.* This serves as a reminder to return to the question later. Move to the next question.

Assisted response occurs when you return to the unanswered questions. Now you use the rest of the test to help you find a possible answer. Look at the key words in the question. In the preceding example, the key words would be *metacognition* and *strategies.* Skim through the test looking for these words. The information used in other questions may assist you in finding the correct answer. It may be that as you worked through the test, you found information that triggered your memory and enabled you to answer a question that you had left unanswered. During assisted response, utilize whatever you can to produce an answer.

Educated guessing strategies can sometimes be used when all else fails. Chapter 13 provides you with some strategies for educated guessing. These strategies improve your odds at guessing correctly, but they are not foolproof. Educated guessing strategies are *never* more effective than knowing the answers. Educated guessing can be used for true-false and multiple-choice questions.

EXERCISE 12.3 **Using Levels of Response**

In Exercise 12.2, to practice predicting test questions, you wrote your own true-false, listing, definition, and short-answer questions. Work with a partner. Read your questions to your partner. Keep track of the number of immediate responses your partner was able to give for your questions. If your partner doesn't immediately know the answer, allow your partner to use delayed response techniques. Keep track of the number of delayed responses used by your partner. This exercise gives your partner feedback on topics that he or she needs to study further. Reverse roles so you have the same opportunity to use immediate or delayed responses for your partner's questions.

Learning from the Test

Tests are valuable learning tools. Right after a test, make a list of the questions that confused you. Write down topics that you did not study thoroughly enough; return to your notes or your book to look up answers or information that is still on your mind.

When the test is returned, analyze it:

- What kinds of questions did you miss the most? Do you see a pattern? For example, if you missed the most points on fill-in-the-blank questions, that's a signal that you need to learn better strategies for that kind of question.
- Did you make any careless mistakes? Which ones and how?
- What was the source of the information you missed? Was it discussed in a lecture, was it from the textbook, or was it on a handout or an overhead?
- Which parts of the test had the best scores? Why?

Learn the information that was incorrect on the test. You don't want the incorrect answers to stay in your memory. Make notes or flash cards with the correct answers. Discuss any of the questions you missed with your teacher if you still don't understand the information. On your final exam you will likely see these questions again, so learn from your mistakes right away.

Adjust Your Study Strategies Take a careful look at the study strategies you used to prepare for the test. Identify which strategies are effective and proving to be powerful for your memory system. Review the Principles of Memory checklist in Exercise 2.7. Identify the principles that were not utilized sufficiently. Spend time planning ways you can strengthen your memory and your academic performance by using more of the memory principles.

Adjust Any Negative Response If you did not score as well as you had hoped, don't be too hard on yourself. This is just one test. Use it as motivation to improve your studying and test-taking techniques. Give yourself credit for the parts that you did well on. Discuss your progress with your teacher. Find out if there are options to retake the test or if any extra credit can be undertaken to improve the grade. Be willing to ask for help and listen to suggestions. Learning is a lifelong process; you won't master it all at once. You can, however, continue searching for new keys to success and new strategies that are right for you.

EXERCISE 12.4 Analyzing Results

Answer the following questions on your own paper.

1. What was the last test score you received in any course this term?

2. Were you pleased with the results? Why or why not?

3. Were all your assignments done before the day of the test?

4. How much time did you spend reviewing for the test? Was it sufficient or was it too little?

5. Did you study alone or with a partner?

6. How did you organize yourself to review? What visual notetaking or study tools did you make or use?

7. What kinds of patterns of error did you notice on your test? Were some kinds of questions more difficult for you? Which kinds? Did many of your mistakes come from the same chapters?

8. What adjustments will you make in your study strategies for the course being discussed?

EXERCISE 12.5 Test Anxiety Indicator

Check the response that seems to best *describe you this term.*

	NEVER	SOMETIMES	ALWAYS
1. I procrastinate so much about studying that I am always behind in my assignments.	❑	❑	❑
2. I found it necessary to cram for the last test I took.	❑	❑	❑
3. I read the textbook, but I do not highlight or take any other kind of textbook notes.	❑	❑	❑
4. I have trouble sleeping the night before a test.	❑	❑	❑
5. I fear the consequences of failing the test.	❑	❑	❑
6. I can't help but remember what happened on the last test: I really blew it.	❑	❑	❑

	NEVER	SOMETIMES	ALWAYS
7. My negative voice is quick to tell me what I can't do.	❒	❒	❒
8. I can feel a lot of tension in my shoulders, arms, or face on the day of a test.	❒	❒	❒
9. My heart beats fast during a test.	❒	❒	❒
10. I feel hot, clammy, or downright sick during a test.	❒	❒	❒
11. I am much more hesitant to enter the classroom on a test day.	❒	❒	❒
12. I try to find excuses not to go to school on the day of a test.	❒	❒	❒
13. I am irritable, snappy, impatient, and sometimes even rude right before a test.	❒	❒	❒
14. I make careless mistakes on the test. Sometimes I can't believe the answers that I marked.	❒	❒	❒
15. As soon as I leave the classroom after taking a test, I remember answers that I didn't know during the test.	❒	❒	❒
16. My mind goes blank, but I know that I know the answers.	❒	❒	❒
17. I get distracted and annoyed by the littlest things others do in class during a test.	❒	❒	❒
18. I always worry about not having enough time to complete tests.	❒	❒	❒
19. Without knowing why, I panic and start changing answers right before I turn the test in.	❒	❒	❒
20. I get stuck on one question and become stubborn. I don't want to move on until I remember the answer.	❒	❒	❒
21. I hurry to get out of the room and out of the test as quickly as possible.	❒	❒	❒
22. Enough is enough. I don't even want to think about going back to check my answers or proofread.	❒	❒	❒
23. I turn in tests that are incomplete even when I have more time.	❒	❒	❒
24. I find myself blaming the teacher, my family, or my friends for the fact that I am not prepared for this test.	❒	❒	❒
25. I did not find time to make summary notes or review effectively.	❒	❒	❒

Answers in the NEVER column = No problem; not indicators of test anxiety
Answers in the SOMETIMES column = Possible indicators; seek ways to alter your behavior
Answers in the ALWAYS column = Sources of test anxiety; seek strategies to reduce these

Dealing with Test Anxiety

Understanding anxiety begins by first understanding stress. **Stress** is defined as your reaction or response to events or situations that threaten to disrupt your normal pattern or routine. You may experience stress because of a job interview, financial problems, an argument with a friend, a relationship problem, or a test. Stress occurs with many situations in which you must perform or make a decision. Stress in each of these situations is natural and actually can be beneficial. Stress often gives that extra bit of adrenaline that helps a person perform *better*.

With normal stress, a person is aware of the stress and aware of the source of the stress. The person is also still able to control his or her reaction or responses. A student may feel stress related to an upcoming test. That stress actually helps to motivate the student to work hard to try to do his or her best. **Anxiety** occurs when the level of stress is excessive to the point that it hinders the ability to perform well. During a bout with anxiety, a person no longer recognizes the source of the excessive stress, no longer has control of the situation, and is reactionary rather than problem-solving oriented.

Test anxiety is excessive stress that may occur before a test or during a test. Performance is hindered and thinking abilities are immobilized. A student may "go blank," make excessive careless mistakes, mark answers in the wrong place, or quit due to frustration. Symptoms of test anxiety may appear in physical or emotional forms as shown in the chart below:

Physical Symptoms of Anxiety	Emotional Symptoms of Anxiety
Rapid heart beat	"Going blank"
Increased blood pressure	Sense of confusion, disorientation
Upset stomach, nausea	Panicky feelings
Shakiness	Depression
Abnormal nervousness	Procrastination
Headaches	Short temper
Tight muscles, tension	Continuous negative self-talk
Clammy palms, sweating	Crying, sobbing
Blurred vision	Misdirected attention, focus on other things
	Feelings of "fight or flight"
	Fixating on one item too long
	Exaggeration of consequences
	Feelings of frustration, anger

During test anxiety, the person's thoughts and reactions are focused *inward* both physically and emotionally. The focus on the task to be done and the focus on the test itself have been replaced by combinations of reactions that are listed in the chart above. On page 232, "Direct Your Thoughts Outward" techniques were given for performing well on tests. When "test stress" starts to accelerate during the test, this technique of directing thoughts outward should be started immediately before the stress becomes excessive. Remember that during feelings of normal stress, you are still able to control your reactions and make decisions; therefore, one way to control test anxiety is to recognize when stress is building and take action! You can be better prepared to take action by taking the following two steps:

Steps to Eliminate Test Anxiety

1. Identify the source of your test anxiety. Different sources have different solutions.
2. Identify and use anxiety-reducing strategies appropriate to the source of your anxiety.

Sources of Test Anxiety

Test anxiety is a *learned behavior.* You are not born with test anxiety. Since test anxiety is a learned behavior, it can be unlearned. The first step is to analyze the situation and your feelings to identify where this behavior began or what triggered the anxiety in the first place. These are four common sources of test anxiety:

1. Underpreparedness
2. Past experiences
3. Fear of failure
4. Poor test-taking skills

Underpreparedness   Knowing that you are not prepared and knowing that you did not put enough time or effort into the learning process is often one source of test anxiety. Unfortunately, when you recognize that you really are not ready for a test and it is close to test time, the "solution" is to cram. However, cramming may actually increase a person's test anxiety by drawing attention to the amount of information that has not been understood or learned. The following student scenarios illustrate situations of test anxiety:

■ Joe has not studied much for his communications class because he was "only taking it on a pass/no pass basis."

■ Mark has not had his reading or homework assignments done on time all term. Some of the reading may not even be done by the test day.

■ Kim finds a lot of the information in the course confusing. She never was able to understand the book or the lectures.

■ Lisa had some personal and work-related problems that disrupted her study schedule. She simply did not have the time or the energy to study as thoroughly as she usually does.

■ Kyle knew what he could and should have done, but he did not follow through with the review work he needed.

■ Pat was slowed down by sickness and was not able to do much studying.

The solution for test anxiety based on underpreparedness is obvious: *Use the techniques presented throughout this textbook.* Consistent, effective study strategies will make an enormous difference. You will be able to go into tests with some feelings of stress, but the stress level will be a motivator, not a hindrance.

Past Experiences   Some anxiety stems from past experiences that affected one's belief system, self-esteem, and confidence. There's the belief that what happened in the past will occur again in the present. Many belief systems are strong and firmly planted in one's personality; for cases that are tied back to years of childhood experiences, traumas, abuse, or extreme emotional distress, the help of a certified counselor or therapist is highly recommended.

As already mentioned, test anxiety is focused *inward*. It is not surprising, then, that our inner voice will begin its negative self-talk and remind us about past experiences. The following student situations may be similar to your own experiences. The statements in italics are typical kinds of negative self-talk that demonstrate false beliefs held by the students.

■ The last time Ray took a test in one of his classes, he did not do very well even though he studied and thought he was ready. *I just don't know what this teacher wants. I just know the same thing will happen. I am not going to pass this test either.*

■ Jimmy has always had problems taking tests. He dreads getting back the results. *I can't pass this even if I try. I've never been any good at taking tests. I hate them!*

■ Kathryn had problems learning as a child. She was influenced by the negative comments made by her parents, teachers, and friends throughout her school years. She can still hear their words. *You just aren't trying hard enough. Why can't you be more motivated? You're just lazy, but I know you can do better if you try.*

■ Dale "suffers" from perfectionism. He has studied and he is ready, but he doesn't believe that because there are more details that he doesn't know to perfection. He takes great pride in getting the highest grade in the class. *I wish there was more extra credit. I'm really going to need it. I knew I shouldn't have gone golfing on Saturday. It serves me right for not studying more. I know better.*

Test anxiety that is rooted in past experiences sometimes can be difficult to diminish because of the complexity and the dynamics of belief systems, established behaviors, and the power of emotions. For more severe test anxiety based on past experiences, the best strategy may be to work with a counselor, therapist, or psychologist to get to the root of the belief system and learn ways to alter your beliefs. For milder cases, techniques that you have learned such as affirmations, positive self-talk, seeing success, and goal setting may be the key to changing your belief systems and attitudes about yourself and your ability to succeed on tests. Use of effective study strategies, working in study groups, using ample feedback, and successful completion of daily assignments will also build your confidence level and reduce your test-anxiety level.

Fear of Failure   Fear of failure is a third source of test anxiety. For a variety of possible reasons, over-emphasis is placed on the importance of one test. Following are a few of the characteristics related to the fear of failure:

1. You may fear that someone else will be disappointed in you. Perhaps it is a family member, a personal friend, or an employer. You don't want to let them down or embarrass yourself by reporting your grades or performance.

2. You equate your grades to your level of self-worth or self-esteem. If you do well on a test, you are a "good person." If you do poorly on a test, you are a "dumb person" or "no good." With this fear of failure, the person fails to see that one test or one grade is only a measure of performance *at that one moment in time* and *for that specific material*. It is not a test of everything you learned or everything that you are.

3. The test is given much greater value in your mind than it is worth in reality. You over-exaggerate the importance of the test to the point where the test "will determine everything: whether or not you pass the class, whether or not you can stay in school, whether or not you will ever be able to have the career you want, whether or not you will succeed in life." Because you see so much riding on the test, you fear not doing well. It is true that some tests are of more value than others, but to keep the true perspective, refer to your course syllabus to be reminded of the actual value of one given test to your overall score. For most courses, there are a variety of opportunities during the term to earn a grade; the final grade may be calculated on several tests, quiz scores, lab projects, group projects, attendance, participation, papers, or extra credit.

4. Fear of losing a scholarship, financial aid, athletic eligibility, insurance eligibility, and other benefits are closely tied to test anxiety based on fear of failure. These consequences are real and sometimes there are severe consequences to pay for not performing well. However, *one test* is not what put students in these predicaments. Remember, test anxiety is a learned behavior, and so are study methods. Students who are "down to the wire" and students whose academic performance will determine the continuation of sources of funding or eligibility for various programs are students who have established a variety of academic-related patterns over the course

of one term or more. If you are in this situation, using what is presented in this book is more important than ever! You need to make the decision to break the negative patterns, set goals, and make new commitments. In addition, close communication with school counselors, advisors, and teachers is essential to learn about possible options or procedures that can assist you with your situation.

Poor Test-Taking Skills   A student who is well prepared and who feels in control of the subject matter may still experience text anxiety. The source this time is lack of knowledge on how to take tests. Learning *how* to take tests is all the student needs to learn. (Test-taking strategies will be discussed in Chapters 13 and 14.) The following situations demonstrate this source of test anxiety:

■ Adolpho has not been in school for fifteen years. He was never taught how to take tests. He studies effectively, knows the information, and can answer questions easily during class or during study groups. However, he does not perform well on tests.

■ Cynthia does very well on essay tests. She is able to write extensively and is able to organize her thoughts effectively. She fails miserably on objective tests. True-false and multiple-choice questions are where she invariably loses the most points.

■ Lee does well on the parts of the test that he completes. However, he never seems to finish a test. He almost always loses all the points for essay questions because he doesn't have enough time to write the answers.

■ Daniel does well on objective-test questions, but he misses a lot of possible points on short answers and essays. He has not yet taken any college writing classes, and writing skills have always been weak for him.

■ Chelsea does fairly well on paper-pencil tests. However, many of her classes require that tests be done in a computer lab. She has a lot of difficulty with computer tests and tends to easily get frustrated and distracted.

Web-site links are available online.

Computer Projects

1. Explore some of the web sites above. Create a brochure or flyer for specific techniques that you feel would be valuable for you to use consistently.
2. Predict test questions. Create a test that can be distributed to other students for practice work.
3. Use your computer to create at least one kind of summary material for an upcoming test.

Group Web-Search Activity is available online.

Case Studies are available online.

🔗 Exercise 12.6 **LINKS**

You have already learned a variety of strategies from other chapters that can be used to reduce or eliminate test anxiety. Work in a small group to brainstorm as many different strategies as possible to reduce test anxiety according to its source. You may use your textbook. Use large chart paper to record your answers. Use the format shown below:

Source of Anxiety	Strategies and Solutions
Underpreparedness	
Past Experiences	
Fear of Failure	
Poor Test-Taking Skills	

Use Anxiety-Reducing Strategies

In addition to the strategies you identified in Exercise 12.6, many other strategies are available to help you unlearn test-anxiety behaviors. Take time to try using the strategies that relate specifically to your source of test anxiety.

Self-Fulfilling Prophecy   There is a saying, "What you see is what you get." The **self-fulfilling prophecy** is based on a modification of that saying: "What you *say* is what you get." If you find yourself involved in negative self-talk, remind yourself that your belief system may in fact affect the outcome. Consider what you will get when you say negative statements such as "I won't pass." "I am going to fail this test." "I am too dumb to do this." The self-fulfilling prophecy can work *for you* by changing your sentences to positive sentences that focus on *what you have achieved*. For example, wouldn't you prefer to get what you say with the following saying? "I have been in every class. I have understood the work. I did well on homework assignments. I studied for this test. I am ready! I will show what I know! I am relaxed."

Seeing Success   This is a visualization exercise that needs to be repeated several times a day for several days before the test day. "**Seeing success**" is a technique that was first introduced to you in Chapter 5 for shorter visual images. Seeing success may help alter the image you have about yourself and your abilities. The visual image can also be recalled right before the test or during the test if you start to feel excessive stress building. To do this, close your eyes and picture yourself going through the steps of test preparation. Make the pictures clear and believable.

Internal Locus of Control   The term *locus of control* refers to the location or place of control. An **internal locus of control** means that the individual feels he or she has the power to control circumstances. An **external locus of control** means that the individual relinquishes control and sees other people or other situations as having the power. Low self-esteem, low confidence in one's abilities, and high levels of frustration blamed on what other people are doing to cause a person's situation are results of an external locus of control. To reduce test anxiety, the locus of control needs to shift to the individual, to become an *internal* locus of control. A person who has an internal locus of control has self-confidence and perceives that he or she has the capability to perform well and to succeed. The central focus or source of power is in accepting responsibility for events. Notice the difference in power between external and internal centers of control in the following chart:

External Locus of Control	Internal Locus of Control
I didn't do well because the teacher doesn't like me.	My negative attitude is affecting my work.
This test is totally unfair.	I wasn't very prepared for this test.
I couldn't study because of my children.	I didn't remember to study the charts.
All the questions were trick questions.	I need to find more time to myself to study.
I failed the test because it was poorly written.	I need to strengthen my test-taking skills.
The teacher doesn't even take the time to try to understand what I wrote.	I need to add more review time.
	I need to improve my writing skills.
The teacher didn't understand my situation.	I didn't know the answer to the essay question.
	I should join a study group.

Systematic Desensitization   Behavior research deals with understanding and changing people's behavior. With some behaviors, such as test anxiety, strong feelings and reactions are associated with specific situations. For test anxiety, just the thought of a test can trigger feelings of anxiety. **Systematic desensitization** involves a series of exercises or activities designed to reduce the strong reaction to a specific thought or event. *Seeing success* is one type of systematic desensitization. Recalling a test in which you were well prepared and did perform well and then reliving the sequence of events in your mind is another form of desensitization. The fear-based thoughts are replaced with the positive thoughts as a way to desensitize your reaction to the word *test*. Following are two additional ways systematic desensitization can be used.

1. Make a list of specific situations or words that trigger your anxiety toward tests. Your goal is to change your perception of those words or situations. Visualize yourself reacting to them differently. Practice and repetition with this visualization are important. For example, you might hear a teacher say, "There will be a test on these chapters in one week." If your initial reaction is nausea and tension, picture yourself hearing the teacher's announcement again, only this time you react by saying to yourself, "Good. I have time to make a five-day plan." By using this technique, you are substituting a negative reaction or behavior with a constructive, positive behavior. The constructive behavior now focuses on a plan and a self-talk script to repeat and practice.

2. Systematic desensitization can be taken one step further. Predict and write out practice test questions. Act out taking the test with less stress. Decide on an appropriate amount of time for your self-made test. Work through the test in a way that is similar to the test-taking situation. If the classroom in which you will take the test is empty later in the day, go into the classroom to take your practice test. You want to create a belief system that you are able to take tests without all the emotional, reactionary responses involved.

These new test-anxiety reducing techniques, plus the many techniques you have used throughout this course, will reduce your negative response to tests and improve your overall performance on tests. Knowing about the techniques is not enough; full responsibility and commitment to changing your test-anxiety behavior are essential. You can learn to take tests with only the normal levels of stress present, and you can perform well to demonstrate how much you really have learned.

Test preparation involves academic and emotional preparation. The following chart summarizes some of the techniques that you have already learned that apply directly to being prepared for tests. If you have been using these techniques throughout the term, preparation for tests involves refining or honing your memory. If you have not been using some of these techniques, one excellent way to begin to prepare for future tests is to activate the knowledge that you have learned in these chapters.

Academic Preparation	Make use of your learning modality preferences.	Chapter 1
	Use the Twelve Principles of Memory when you study.	Chapter 2
	Schedule your study times throughout the term.	Chapter 3
	Schedule ongoing review time each week.	Chapter 3
	Avoid procrastination by setting goals.	Chapter 4
	Use goal-setting for your study blocks.	Chapter 4
	Create a five-day plan prior to major tests.	Chapter 4
	Create a physical stage conducive to studying.	Chapter 5
	Use active reading and effective reading techniques.	Chapters 6–9
	Use highlighting and effective notetaking techniques.	Chapters 9–11
Emotional Preparation	Use visualization to "see success."	Chapter 5
	Use positive self-talk and affirmations to boost confidence.	Chapter 5
	Learn to reduce or eliminate distractions.	Chapter 5
	Learn to use relaxation techniques to calm your mind.	Chapter 5

✎ **EXERCISE 12.7   Discussing Case Studies**

Work with a partner or in a small group. Read the following case studies; discuss possible test-preparation and test-taking strategies each student could begin to use to improve performance.

1. Melanie: "I get so worked up the night before a test that I am a total wreck by the time I get to school. My stomach is upset, my hands sweat, and I feel a total state of panic. I tried relaxing by watching a movie. I tried to get to bed early. I tried talking to a friend. Nothing seemed to help. I am so exhausted before I have even taken the test."

2. Robert: "I get so nervous before the first test in a class. I don't know if I am studying the right information. I have no idea what kinds of questions will be used or what this teacher's test will even look like. I am so afraid of not studying the right information, so I end up spending incredible amounts of time studying everything. I just don't know what to expect."

3. Jane: "I really think I study effectively. I always feel like I know all the information that I need to know. It usually doesn't take me long to finish a test. I go through all the questions, just the way they are presented, and write what I really believe is the right answer. I usually leave the test feeling like I have done well. Then the surprise! I always seem to make a lot of careless mistakes. I don't understand how I can miss questions on the tests when I know the answers."

4. Simon: "I often get called in to work at night, so my study time is really sporadic. For that reason, I decided to take this class for a pass/no-pass grade so I don't need to study as much. I counted on the tests being true-false and multiple-choice. I just found out that this teacher doesn't use those kinds of tests. All the test questions are short-answer or essays. Since I can't bluff my way through those very well, I am going to have to do some serious reading and cramming for the test in two days. I don't think I'll do very well. In fact, chances are pretty good that I am going to fail. Maybe I should just drop the course all together so it doesn't hurt my GPA. I kind of don't want to though because I like the class. I haven't missed a class yet. I guess I better decide and then start making some changes."

SUMMARY

- Many techniques that have been presented in previous chapters will help students be well prepared for tests and avoid the need to cram.

- To prepare for tests, students can make a five-day study plan that includes making summary notes.

- To prepare for tests, students should try to find out as much information as possible about the test, predict and write practice test questions, and participate in review sessions.

- When students predict test questions, they should practice using recognition, recall, and essay questions.

- Four "Smart Start" tips are to jot down reminder notes on your tests, listen to directions carefully, survey the test, and budget your time for the parts on the test.

- Other test-taking techniques include reading directions carefully, circling key words in directions, ignoring other students in the class, changing answers when the change can be justified, and spending the extra time at the end of a test rechecking answers.

- Shifting inward thoughts to outward thoughts and to the test can help performance and reduce test anxiety.

- The four levels of response for answering questions are
  1. Immediate response
  2. Delayed response
  3. Assisted response
  4. Educated guessing

- Students should learn from tests when they are returned. Study strategies should be adjusted accordingly.

- Stress is normal; excessive stress is called anxiety. Anxiety produces both physical and emotional symptoms.

- There are four main sources of test anxiety:
  1. Underpreparedness
  2. Past experiences
  3. Fear of failure
  4. Poor test-taking skills

- There are many strategies to use to reduce test anxiety. Four new ones are self-fulfilling prophecy, seeing success (in a longer version), inner locus of control, and systematic desensitization.

- Test anxiety is a learned behavior that can be unlearned.

OPTIONS FOR PERSONALIZING CHAPTER 12

1. **PROFILE CHART—PERSONAL LOG**   Answer the following questions in your personal log.

   What score did you get on your Chapter 12 Profile? _____

   What are the most important changes you need to make in preparing for tests and taking tests?

2. **WORDS TO KNOW**   Knowing the following vocabulary terms is important.

cramming	immediate response	test anxiety
five-day study plan	delayed response	self-fulfilling prophecy
summary notes	memory search	seeing success
objective questions	assisted response	internal locus of control
recall questions	educated guessing	external locus of control
Smart Start tips	stress	systematic desensitization
four levels of response	anxiety	

3. **EXPAND THE CHAPTER MAPPING**   On your own paper or on page 223, expand the chapter mapping by adding level-three information. Personalize your visual mapping by adding colors or pictures.

4. **WRITING ASSIGNMENT 1**   Discuss how you feel in general about tests and what the test scores mean to you. On what kind of tests do you usually perform better? What test-preparation or test-taking strategies in this chapter will be most useful for you?

5. **WRITING ASSIGNMENT 2**   Describe the differences between internal and external locuses of control. Give examples of situations in which you were operating from an external locus of control. Then discuss ways you could shift that external locus of control to an internal locus of control.

6. **PORTFOLIO DEVELOPMENT**   For your portfolio, prepare a detailed five-day plan to use prior to a major test or final exam. Discuss how much information you were able to gather about the kind of test that will be given. Prepare for the test by predicting test questions, writing practice test questions, and preparing a special set of summary notes. Include all of the above in your portfolio.

CHAPTER 12 REVIEW QUESTIONS

Multiple-Choice

Choose the best answer *for each of the following questions. Write the letter of the best answer on the line.*

_____ **1.** Test anxiety can stem from
   a. fear of failure.
   b. underpreparedness and past experiences.
   c. poor test-taking skills.
   d. all of the above.

_____ **2.** Being underprepared can create
   a. panic and concern.
   b. the need to cram.
   c. test anxiety.
   d. all of the above.

_____ **3.** Cramming
   a. is a survival technique used for underpreparedness.
   b. uses most of the memory principles.
   c. processes large amounts of information efficiently.
   d. can be effective when done correctly.

_____ **4.** Test anxiety can be reduced by
   a. ignoring other students in class.
   b. focusing on outward thoughts and actions.
   c. recognizing your strengths and accomplishments.
   d. all of the above.

_____ **5.** Before a test, it is important to get ready
   a. physically by having a good night's sleep and an energy-producing breakfast.
   b. mentally by reciting, reflecting, and reviewing.
   c. physically, emotionally, and mentally.
   d. emotionally by thinking positively and securing support from others.

_____ **6.** A student who uses a wide variety of study techniques to learn thoroughly should be able to answer most questions on a test by using
   a. educated guessing.
   b. delayed response.
   c. assisted response.
   d. immediate response.

_____ **7.** When you skim through the test looking for clues to questions, you are using
   a. educated guessing.
   b. delayed response.
   c. assisted response.
   d. immediate response.

_____ **8.** On tests, you should keep your original answer
   a. no matter what.
   b. unless you find a valid reason for changing it.
   c. because your first "hunch" is always the best.
   d. unless you get a sudden impulse to change it.

Definitions

In two or three sentences, write a definition for each of the following terms.

1. Summary Notes

2. Systematic Desensitization

3. Locus of Control

4. Self-Fulfilling Prophecy

Short Answer—Critical Thinking

Use your own paper to write answers to the following questions. Answers should be in paragraph form.

1. Summarize the four sources of test anxiety.

2. Discuss the important strategies you should use during the first five minutes of a test.

3. Discuss common physical and emotional symptoms of test anxiety, and then discuss any specific symptoms you experience prior to or during a major test.

4. Discuss the difference between stress and anxiety.

Developing Strategies for Objective Tests

Learning to read and answer objective test questions (true-false, multiple-choice, and matching) is essential for college students. Do you have difficulties understanding exactly what is being asked on tests? Do you treat each part of a multiple-choice question as a true-false question? Do you often miss points on matching questions because you get confused about which answers you already used? The strategies in this chapter provide you with step-by-step methods for answering objective questions and improving your test scores. A section is also included for educated guessing and taking computerized tests.

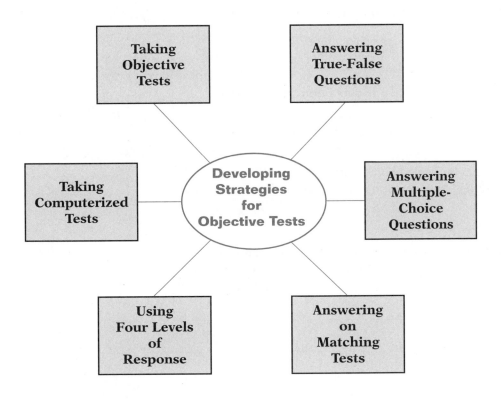

Name _____ Date _____

 CHAPTER 13 Objective Test Profile

DO, SCORE, and **RECORD** your profile before you read this chapter. If you need to review the process, refer to the complete directions given in the Profile for Chapter 1 on page 2.

	YES	NO
1. I am able to answer true-false questions without making many mistakes.	_____	_____
2. True-false questions are confusing for me because I don't understand what they are asking.	_____	_____
3. I have problems selecting the right answer on multiple-choice questions.	_____	_____
4. I have a system for answering matching questions so that I don't use an answer twice.	_____	_____
5. I watch for modifiers in questions because they can affect the meaning of the question. (Modifiers include words such as *no, never, some, few, always, often.*)	_____	_____
6. I can tell when a question is testing a definition or a cause/effect relationship.	_____	_____
7. I make too many careless mistakes on tests.	_____	_____
8. I turn each part of a multiple-choice question into a true-false question before I answer.	_____	_____
9. The first time I work through a test, I leave blank the answers that I don't know and then return to them when I have time.	_____	_____
10. I use other parts of the test to help me find answers I don't immediately know.	_____	_____
11. I read both columns of items on a matching test before I even begin answering.	_____	_____
12. If I see an unfamiliar term in a multiple-choice option, I usually choose that option because I feel I must have overlooked that term when I studied.	_____	_____

Self-Awareness: Describe your general performance level and confidence level on objective tests that include true-false, multiple-choice, and matching questions.

_____

_____

_____

_____

_____

_____

Taking Objective Tests

Objective tests involve questions that are presented in the form of true-false, multiple-choice, or matching. Objective test questions are also called *recognition questions* because you are basically required to recognize the correct answer from the choices that are given. Objective questions do require that you do **memory searches** to use associations and retrieval skills to relate the questions to the information that you learned. Because the information is presented to you rather than requiring you to recall the information on your own from memory, objective questions are often considered the easiest to answer. Study the following chart to gain a greater understanding of the three kinds of objective test questions. Notice that the four levels of responses can be used for each of the objective formats.

Objective Questions

Kind of Question	General Format	Key Elements	Levels of Response
True-False	One statement is given. The statement is completely true or one or more parts of the statement make the complete statement false.	negatives modifiers definition clues relationship clues	immediate delayed assisted educated guessing
Multiple-Choice	A statement is started with a stem and is followed by options. Usually only four options are given and only one option is correct. Multiple-choice questions can be done as four true-false questions.	stem options distractors negatives modifiers definition clues relationship clues	immediate delayed assisted educated guessing
Matching	Two columns of information need to be matched. The length of the columns does not need to be equal. Usually each item in the right column can be used only once.	left column right column word clues grammatical clues	immediate delayed assisted educated guessing

Answering True-False Questions

True-false questions are one of the most basic forms of objective questions, for they take less time to read and can easily be scored by hand, by Scantron (the tests in which you fill in the numbered bubbles to indicate your answer), or by computer. Students sometimes feel that some true-false questions are "trick questions" mainly because they do not know how to read and interpret the questions correctly. The following guidelines can help you improve your performance on true-false tests:

- Read the statement carefully. If you tend to misread questions, point to each word as you read the statement. *Circle key words used in the question.*

- Be *objective* when you answer. Do not personalize the question by interpreting it according to what you do or how you feel. Instead, answer according to the information presented by the textbook author or your instructor in class.

- The statement must be *completely true* in order for you to mark it *True*. Check *items in a series of items* very carefully. Every item must be true in order to mark *T*. If any one part of the statement is inaccurate or false, you must mark the entire statement *False*.

- Do not take the time to add your reasoning or argument to the side of the question. Frequently, the only information that will be looked at is the *T* or *F* answer, so other notes, comments, or clarifications will be ignored during grading.

- If you are taking a true-false test using paper and pencil (instead of a Scantron or computerized version), make a strong distinction between the way you write a *T* and an *F.* Trying to camouflage your answer so it can be interpreted as a *T* or an *F* will backfire. Answers that cannot be clearly understood are marked as incorrect.

In addition to the above guidelines, it is important that you pay close attention to four key elements of true-false questions. Learning to identify these key elements will result in more careful reading of true-false questions and more accuracy in your choice of answers.

Key Elements in True-False Questions

1. Negatives in the form of words or prefixes
2. Modifiers in the form of 100-percent modifiers and in-between modifiers
3. Definition clues signaling the definition of a term is being tested
4. Relationship clues signaling the relationship between two items is being tested

Watch for Negatives   As you read true-false questions, pay close attention to any negatives. **Negatives** are words or prefixes in words that carry the meaning of "no" or "not." *Negatives do not mean that the sentence is going to be false.* Instead, negatives affect the meaning of the sentence and require you to read and think carefully. Watch for the following negatives in questions:

Negative Words	Negative Prefixes
no	dis (disorganized)
not	im (imbalanced)
but	non (nonproductive)
except	il (illogical)
	in (incomplete)
	ir (irresponsible)
	un (unimportant)

Sentences with negatives can be confusing and can leave you wondering what is really being asked. One method of working with statements that have a negative word or a negative prefix is to *cover up the negative* and read the sentence without it. If you are able to answer *true* or *false* to the statement without the negative, the correct answer for the statement with the negative will be the *opposite* answer.

Watch for Modifiers

Modifiers are words that tell to what degree or frequency something occurs. There is a huge difference between saying that something *always* happens and saying that something *sometimes* or *often* happens. You must learn to pay close attention to these words to determine how often or how frequently something actually occurs. As you notice in the following list, there are other kinds of modifiers, too. Words such as *best* or *worst* show the extremes and indicate that there is *nothing* that is greater or better.

Modifiers can be shown on a scale. The **100-percent modifiers** are on the extreme ends of the scale. They are the absolutes with nothing beyond them. The **in-between modifiers** are in the middle of the scale. They allow for more flexibility or variety because they indicate that a middle ground exists where situations or conditions do not occur as absolutes (100 percent of the time).

Modifiers

100 Percent	In Between	100 Percent
all, every, only	some, most, a few	none
always, absolutely	sometimes, often, usually, may, seldom, frequently	never
everyone everybody	some people, few people, most people	no one nobody
best	average, better	worst
Any adjective that ends in *est*, which means "the most" (largest)	Any adjective that ends in *er*, which means "more" (larger)	least fewest

Watch for Definition Clues

A test-writer must find ways to create false statements for true-false tests; one common way to develop false statements is by testing your understanding of the definition of a specific term. The following words, called **definition clues**, often signal that a question is evaluating your understanding of a definition:

Definition Clues	
Clues that Signal Definitions	Sentence Pattern Used
defined as also known as are/is means states that which is referred to as involves are called	word ———— def. clue ———— definition *check carefully*

For definition questions, circle the clue words that signal definitions. Underline the key term that is being defined. Then, ask yourself, "What is the definition I learned for this word?" Once you can recall the definition you learned, compare it to the definition that is given. If your definition and the test question definition are the same, the statement is *true*. If there is a discrepancy, analyze the test question definition carefully because it may be saying the same thing but simply using different words. If the definitions are not the same, the answer will be *false*.

Watch for Relationship Clues

Some true-false questions test whether a certain relationship exists. Relationships often show cause/effect—one item causes another item to occur. Become familiar with the following words for relationships. When you see these **relationship clues** in true-false sentences, think carefully about the relationship being discussed before you decide whether the statement is true or false.

Relationship Clues	
Clues that Signal Relationships	Sentence Pattern Used
increases result produce since reason so, so that affects creates because decreases causes effect	Subject A ———— rel. clue ———— Subject B *check carefully*

In relationship questions, circle the relationship clues. Underline the key terms that are involved in the relationship. Then, ask yourself, "What do I know about how these two terms are related or associated to each other?" Once you have a relationship idea in your mind and before you mark true or false, compare your idea with the one presented in the question.

✎ **EXERCISE 13.1 Careful Reading of True-False Questions**

Read the following true-false questions, which test information learned in previous chapters. Pay close attention to items in a series; when you find negatives, definition and relationship clues, or modifiers, circle them. Write T for true and F for false.

_____ 1. The three areas of life that need to be balanced are school, leisure, and studying.

_____ 2. You can increase your speed in notetaking by paraphrasing, using abbreviations, and writing sentences that are not grammatically correct.

_____ 3. The recall column in the Cornell system should have the headings, key words, study questions, and all the answers.

_____ 4. The use of music, rhymes, and tunes is unacceptable as a learning strategy.

_____ 5. Ongoing review is essential in the Cornell system but is optional in the SQ4R system.

_____ 6. Anxiety is never based on irrational fears and old belief systems.

_____ 7. Reciting is important because it utilizes the auditory channel and provides feedback for understanding.

_____ 8. Spaced practice is preferred so that the student can usually avoid rote memory and cramming techniques.

_____ 9. Too much information in the recall column of Cornell causes you to read instead of recite.

_____ 10. The amount of time spent on social or leisure activities should always be more than the total hours for work.

_____ 11. Concentration is defined as the ability to focus on two or more things at one time without being distracted.

_____ 12. Time lines are graphic materials used to organize information chronologically.

_____ 13. *Schema* is another term for the feedback loop.

_____ 14. Everyone should always try to divide her or his "life's pie" into three equal parts.

_____ 15. It is always best and most productive to study late at night when there's no one around to bother you.

_____ 16. Always begin by studying your favorite subject first so that you can get motivated.

_____ 17. Reading and speaking are active processes, but listening is an inactive process.

_____ 18. Most people are a combination of global and linear learners and thinkers.

_____ 19. Nonverbal, spatial, intuitive, and holistic are characteristics of right-mode thinking.

_____ 20. All cultures place a high premium on the same good listening behaviors.

_____ 21. A disorganized desk is not an external distractor.

_____ 22. The process of selectivity is not used during the fourth step of SQ4R.

_____ 23. Students should use every concentration technique during a study block.

_____ 24. Cramming can frequently be avoided if ongoing review is used each week.

_____ **25.** Test anxiety may stem from being underprepared or lacking test-taking skills.

_____ **26.** Semantic encoding is defined as the process of coding words for long-term memory.

_____ **27.** The Interference Theory of Forgetting states that information in short-term memory is confused because too much information enters the system too quickly.

_____ **28.** Increasing the amount of information in a schema often makes learning information on that subject easier to do.

_____ **29.** Spaced practice is preferred for studying because it encourages students to avoid marathon studying.

_____ **30.** Because test anxiety is a learned behavior, it can be unlearned through the use of strategies, practice, and willingness to change.

Answering Multiple-Choice Questions

Careful reading is also essential for answering multiple-choice questions correctly. For multiple-choice questions, there are two parts to the question: the stem and the options. The **stem** is the beginning part of the statement. The **options** are the choices for the correct answer. Usually there are four options, and only one of the options is the correct answer. Your goal is to eliminate the options that are incorrect. These incorrect options are referred to as **distractors**. The following guidelines will help you improve your performance on multiple-choice questions:

- Read the directions carefully. Usually the directions say to choose *one answer*. However, variations of this do exist; you may find directions that say you may use more than one answer. If no mention is made about the number of answers to choose, always select only one.

- The directions often say to choose the *best answer*. One or more of the answers may be correct, but the answer that is the most inclusive (includes the most or the broadest information) is the best answer.

- Read all of the options before you select your answer. Some students stop as soon as they find a good answer. It is important to read all the options so you are sure you are finding the best option.

- Write your letter answer on the line. Some students make careless mistakes writing the correct answer on the line. If this is a tendency of yours, first *circle* the letter answer and then write the letter on the line. Using this method, you are able to quickly check that you wrote what you circled and what you believe is the correct answer.

The following steps will guide you through the process of answering multiple-choice questions. Use each step before you write your final answer:

Steps for Answering Multiple-Choice Questions

1. Read the stem, finish the statement in your mind, and check to see if the answer is one of the options.
2. Read the stem with each option as a true-false statement.
3. Eliminate the distractors and select from the remaining options.

Finish the Stem

The first step with a multiple-choice question is to read the stem and finish the stem in your mind. This helps you "get into the correct memory schema" and relate the rest of the question to something you already know. The answer that you get may or may not be one of the answers given as an option, but you will be thinking along the same channels. For practice, how would you complete each of the following stems in your mind?

_____ 1. The principle of Big Picture–Little Pictures _____

_____ 2. Expressive vocabulary refers to _____

_____ 3. Howard Gardner's eighth intelligence is called _____

Read as Four T-F Statements

When you read the stem of a multiple-choice question with just one of the options, the result is a one-sentence statement that can be treated as a true-false statement. This process can continue until each of the options has been analyzed as a true-false statement. The strategies you learned above for true-false statements will be used in exactly the same way for multiple-choice questions. Here is the process:

1. Read the stem with the first option.
2. If the statement is false, *cross off the letter of that option.* This is a distractor and will not be the correct answer.
3. If the statement is true, *it may be the correct answer.* You won't know for sure until all the options have been read with the stem. If you would like, you may write a *T* at the end of all the options that make a true answer when they are added to the stem.

Web-site links are available online.

Computer Projects

1. Use your computer to create true-false or multiple-choice questions for specific chapters in this text or for a final exam.
2. Use a columns format to create matching questions for the final exam.
3. Explore some of the sites on the web site. Create a brochure for objective test-taking strategies.

Group Web-Search Activity is available online.

Case Studies are available online.

Name _____   Date _____

✎ **EXERCISE 13.2 Answering Multiple-Choice Questions**

For each of the following questions, read the stem and answer the question in your own words. Look to see if your answer matches one of the options. Then make a true-false statement by reading the stem with each of the options. Write T or F at the end of each option. Cross off the false statements. Select the best answer from the remaining options.

_____ **1.** Maslow's hierarchy of needs is a theory that explains
    a. people's needs.
    b. how people are motivated by their needs.
    c. why needs are sustained over time.
    d. universal behaviors that exist in all cultures.

_____ **2.** Mapping can be used to
    a. take lecture notes.
    b. take textbook notes.
    c. make review study tools.
    d. all of the above.

_____ **3.** It is acceptable to
    a. put many key words in each cell of a comparison chart.
    b. write sideways on visual mappings if needed.
    c. put more than one event on a time line date.
    d. none of the above.

_____ **4.** When you visualize a mapping, you should
    a. try to see the skeleton first.
    b. always be creative and make changes as you go.
    c. never stare at the paper for as long as five minutes.
    d. add new information that you forgot to put in the original mapping.

_____ **5.** When making a hierarchy of information from a chapter, level-two information
    a. should reflect only the chapter headings.
    b. should show all important terminology.
    c. should always include pictures.
    d. may include your own categories and chapter headings.

_____ **6.** Cramming
    a. is one of the most effective short-term memory processing strategies available.
    b. uses all the memory principles.
    c. processes large amounts of information efficiently.
    d. is not a technique used by prepared students.

_____ **7.** Anxiety refers to
    a. controlled stress.
    b. uncontrolled stress.
    c. a natural form of stress.
    d. motivational stress used to be productive.

_____ **8.** Test anxiety can be reduced by focusing on
    a. test-taking tasks and ignoring others.
    b. outward thoughts and actions.
    c. your strengths and accomplishments.
    d. all of the above.

_____ **9.** The principle of Big Picture–Little Pictures
  a. encourages you to memorize individual facts and details.
  b. is based completely on rote memory.
  c. recommends that you process information only in clusters.
  d. recommends that you try to "see the trees" *and* "see the forest" when you study.

_____ **10.** Expressive vocabulary refers to understanding words
  a. that you read.
  b. well enough to use them when you speak.
  c. that you hear in conversations.
  d. well enough to use them to communicate verbally and in writing.

Answering on Matching Tests

Matching questions are based on paired associations. **Paired associations** are items that were linked together when you learned the information. For example, a word is linked or paired to its definition. When you think of the word, you associate it with the definition. When you think of the definition, you pair it with the word. Paired associations for matching may include:

- Words and their definitions
- People and what they did
- Dates and events
- Terms and their function or purpose
- Problems and their solutions

When you are faced with matching questions on tests, you will see a list of words on the left and their paired association on the right. The key to answering matching questions is to work through them in a systematic way. The following steps will help you avoid confusion and perform better on tests that have matching questions:

Four Steps for Working Through Matching Questions

1. Read the directions carefully.
2. Count the number of items in each list to see if the lists are equal.
3. Begin by reading the column that has the shorter entries.
4. Use the four levels of response to answer the questions.

Read the Directions

Begin by reading the directions carefully. Usually each item on the right can be used only once; if an item can be used more than once, the directions will probably say so.

Count the Items

Count the number of items in the left column and then the number of items in the right column. If the lists contain an equal number of items, each item will be used once. Sometimes the list on the right is longer, indicating that some of the items will not be used. Extra items make matching questions a little more difficult because you cannot automatically match up whatever is left over.

Read the Shortest List

Usually the column on the left will have the shortest entries. These may be words (terminology), names, dates, or events. Read these so that you are aware of the choices that are available. Also notice what types of pairing will be used. Are these people, events, dates, or vocabulary terms? Below, the list on the left has shorter entries; read this list first.

_____ 1. intrinsic rewards   **a.** a technique used to switch the time blocks of specific activities

_____ 2. trading time   **b.** material items or activities used when goals are met

_____ 3. motivation   **c.** a feeling, emotion, or desire that moves a person to take action

_____ 4. extrinsic rewards   **d.** feeling proud, relieved, or satisfied

Use the Levels of Response

Now that you are familiar with the items on the left, begin reading the first item on the right. Read the item carefully, and quickly search your memory for an association to that item. Look on the left to see if the associated word is on the list. For example, if the item on the right is a definition, search your memory for the vocabulary term. Then use the **four levels of response**:

Immediate Response   Immediate response can be used when you immediately know the answer. Once you see a definite match, write the letter on the line and *cross off the letter you used so you do not reuse it again.* If you do not immediately know the answer, move to delayed response. Do not guess or write any answer that you are not absolutely certain is correct.

Delayed Response   Delayed response is needed when you do not immediately know the answer. Try one or more of these techniques for identifying the answer:

■ Reread the item of information one more time, but read more slowly. If it helps, "mouth" what you read or read with a whisper. Circle key words.

■ Do a *memory search*. Ask yourself what you remember about this information. What is it connected to? Where did you first learn it? Use associations to try to recall more about the item. Is there anything similar to this in the other column?

■ Use **word clues** and **grammar clues**. Key words in the information may help you figure out where that item belongs. For example, if you see the word *system*, *technique*, or *rule*, you would narrow your focus by looking for choices in the shorter list that are dealing specifically with a system, a technique, or a rule. When you read and connect the item on the left with the item on the right, a meaningful "thought unit" or sentence should emerge. To find this meaningful connection, *mentally chatter your way* to the answer.

If none of these techniques work, do *not* guess. If you are not able to identify the correct answer after trying one or more of the above techniques, *leave the answer space blank.* Use some type of symbol, like a checkmark, in the left margin as a reminder that you need to return to this question later. Move on to the next item. Always work your way from the top down to the bottom of the list.

Assisted Response   Assisted response means that you will look for assistance from other parts of the test. Scan through the test to look for any of the key words used on either side of your matching list. Other parts of the test may have information that helps you recall associations or jogs your memory about the information in the matching questions. Use the other test questions as a resource! If you cannot find any clues in other parts of the test, move to the last kind of response.

Educated Guessing If you have exhausted the above techniques and still have not come up with the correct answer, educated guessing is usually recommended. Some teachers will dock points for incorrect answers, but that is less common. You know if you put nothing on the line, it will be wrong; you might as well take the remaining items that couldn't be matched and fill in any empty lines with any of those remaining letters. Then be sure to make a mental note of those items so you can check your book and notes right after class.

The following example shows how a student tackled a matching section on a mid-term exam. Refer to the blue numbers below to follow the student's thought process.

① Directions say to use each answer once.

② Two answers are extra and won't be used.

Matching

Match the items on the left to the items on the right. Write the letter of each answer on the line. Each item on the right may be used only one time.

③ Read the shorter list.   ④ Start with "a." Do only ones I know.

_h_	1. circadian rhythms	a. creating a border for visualization
___	2. motivation	b. associating items together
_a_	3. framing	c. short-term memory and feedback loop
_j_	4. affirmations	d. feeling, emotion, or desire that elicits an action
_f_	5. chunking	e. feedback
___	6. sensory stimuli	f. breaking tasks into more manageable units
_b_	7. linking	g. procedural memory
_i_	8. memory storage centers	h. body's natural patterns and rhythms
___	9. active memory paths	i. long-term and short-term memory
___	10. result of self-quizzing	j. positive statements written in present tense
		k. rehearsal and retrieval
		l. words, sounds, pictures, tactile sensations

⑤ I need to use helper words to try to connect the items I don't know really well. Use delayed response.

⑥ I need to use the rest of the test to assist me to find more answers. Use assisted response.

⑦ I need to fill in any remaining blanks with letters I didn't use. I need to guess.

✎ **EXERCISE 13.3 Matching Problems and Solutions**

Read the problem on the left. Find the solution on the right. Write the letter of the solution on the line. You can use each answer only once.

_____ **1.** I highlight too much.

_____ **2.** I don't know how to study from underlining.

_____ **3.** When I read, I need to find a way to make important terminology stand out more clearly.

_____ **4.** I have trouble finding the topic sentence.

_____ **5.** I have problems finding definitions for key words in the book.

_____ **6.** I don't feel like I really understand how to use the textbook features very well.

_____ **7.** I need a fast way to look up page numbers to find information in my book.

_____ **8.** The teacher said to check our work with the answer keys in the book, but I can't find any answer keys in my chapters.

_____ **9.** I have trouble getting started when I have a reading assignment. I'm just not motivated to "dig right in" and do the serious reading.

_____ **10.** I go into "automatic pilot" every time I try to read pages in my textbook.

_____ **11.** I can't write fast enough to write down everything the teacher says in a lecture.

_____ **12.** When the teacher talks so slowly, my mind wanders to other things.

_____ **13.** My notes are a jumbled mess. All the information is all run together.

a. Circle the words that you need to be able to define.

b. Survey the book at the beginning of the term.

c. Use punctuation, word clues, word structure clues, and context clues.

d. Try to organize with headings and numbered details. Leave spaces between headings.

e. Only mark the main idea and the key words for details.

f. Read one paragraph at a time. Stop. Take time to comprehend what you read.

g. Use your own words to string together the ideas you marked.

h. Use the index.

i. Survey the chapter first as a "warm-up" activity.

j. Paraphrase with shortened sentences. Abbreviate. Use symbols.

k. Check the first and the last sentences to see if one has the main idea that controls the paragraph.

l. Keep writing, anticipate new points, question ideas, or mentally summarize.

m. Check the appendix of the book.

⊖⊖ Exercise 13.4 LINKS

Assume that you are told to study for a test in this class and that the test will consist mainly of matching questions. You are told to spend ample time studying the terminology for the course. Write your own practice matching test. You may use any of the terminology discussed so far in this class. Remember to scramble the order of the definitions!

_____ 1.   a.

_____ 2.   b.

_____ 3.   c.

_____ 4.   d.

_____ 5.   e.

_____ 6.   f.

_____ 7.   g.

_____ 8.   h.

_____ 9.   i.

_____10.   j.

_____11.   k.

_____12.   l.

_____13.   m.

_____14.   n.

_____15.   o.

Using the Four Levels of Response

Chapter 12 discussed the four levels of responses for answering questions. In this chapter, you have already seen how the four levels of response, including educated guessing, were used for matching questions. Before we discuss educated guessing, review the following information about the first three levels of response.

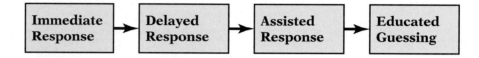

Immediate response is the first step and the goal of students who are prepared and have used effective study strategies throughout the term. If you read the question and do not immediately know the answer, move to the next level of response.

Delayed response is the second level of response. This is the time to reread the question carefully and more slowly. Look for clues to help you; these may be word clues, grammar clues, items in a series, in-between and 100-percent modifiers, negatives, or definition or relationship clues. Analyze or circle key words in the sentence and do a memory search. Try to "chatter your way" to the answer by talking through associations and answering questions you formulate in your mind. After this applied effort, if you still do not know the answer, leave the answer line blank and move to the next step. Do not spend too much time struggling with one question when there are many more questions on the test. To remind yourself that you left this question unmarked, put a checkmark or symbol in the left margin.

Assisted response occurs when you scan through the rest of the test looking for reminders or clues that will help you answer a question. Sometimes similar information is included elsewhere in the test in a different test question format. Other times, when you reread one question and answer, it triggers the association needed to find the missing answer. As you work through the test the first time, sometimes you encounter information that helps you answer a question you had left unanswered. Assisted response involves a serious effort to make associations, link information together, and find correct answers. If you come up empty in your search for the answer or if you run out of time, your last resort is to use educated guessing.

Educated guessing involves using specific strategies to improve your odds at guessing the correct answer. These strategies are not foolproof; they will not always lead to the correct answer. *Do not rely on these strategies* for good grades. Use them only when all other strategies have not produced the correct answer.

The following chart shows ten educated guessing strategies for true-false and multiple-choice questions. Use these strategies only as a last resort when nothing else seems to work.

Ten Educated Guessing Strategies

1. Guess *false* if there is a 100-percent modifier.
2. Guess *true* if there is an in-between modifier.
3. Guess *false* if there is a relationship clue.
4. Guess *false* if the statement is ridiculous, foolish, insulting, or has unfamiliar terms.
5. Guess *true,* the wild-shot guess, if there are no other clues in a true-false question.
6. If there are numbers as options, eliminate the highest and the lowest; guess one of the options that remain.
7. If there are multiple-choice options that are almost identical (look alike), choose one of those two options.
8. If one multiple-choice option is longer in length or more inclusive in content, choose it.
9. If the last option is "all of the above" and this option is not used throughout the test, choose it.
10. Guess *c,* the wild-shot guess, if there are no other clues in a multiple-choice question.

100-Percent Modifiers (False)

The *100-percent modifiers* are the *absolutes,* meaning that they are the extremes and no exceptions are allowed. Few things happen or exist without exceptions, so the odds are in your favor that questions with 100-percent modifiers will be false. Guess *false.* (See page 253 to review the modifiers.)

Notice how the 100-percent modifiers make the following statements false:

_____F_____ **1.** Attendance in college is required in every class.

_____F_____ **2.** Always begin by studying your favorite subject first.

_____F_____ **3.** Never use a tape recorder in class.

When a multiple-choice option with a 100-percent modifier is added to the stem, a true-false question is created. The true-false guessing strategy for 100-percent modifiers is to guess *false.* Notice how this same strategy is used in the following example:

_____ **1.** The prefix *intra-*
   a. is never used in English words.
   b. always means "between."
   c. means "within" or "inside of."
   d. none of the above.

_____F_____ **a.** The prefix *intra-* is never used in English words.

_____F_____ **b.** The prefix *intra-* always means "between."

_____T_____ **c.** The prefix *intra-* means "within" or "inside of."

In-between Modifiers (True)

The *in-between modifiers* make room for exceptions or for the statement to sometimes apply and sometimes not apply. If you are using educated guessing, when you see an in-between modifier, guess *true.* Odds will be in your favor. Notice how the in-between modifiers make these examples true:

_____T_____ **1.** Reviewing notes from a previous paragraph can sometimes be used to help understand a difficult paragraph.

_____T_____ **2.** In a sole proprietorship, the person who owns the business is usually the one who also operates it.

The same is true for multiple-choice since each option can be converted to a true-false statement when it is added to the stem. If more than one option is *true,* remember to then select the answer you believe is the *best* answer.

_____ **1.** Intrapersonal intelligence is an intelligence that
    a. <u>always</u> shows leadership and group charisma.
    b. <u>often</u> involves a special interest in personal growth and insights.
    c. <u>seldom</u> is combined with linguistic or interpersonal intelligence.
    d. is <u>never</u> taught in schools.

Notice how option *a* and option *d* have 100-percent modifiers. If guessing strategies are used, these would be marked *false.* Both option *b* and option *c* have in-between modifiers. For a guessing strategy, guess one of these two options. However, before you purely guess, think it through more carefully. Option *c* is not accurate information; option *b* makes sense and is the correct answer. If you didn't know this, by reducing the choices to two options, you have a fifty-fifty change of guessing correctly. (Needless to say, *knowing* the correct answer is always preferred!)

Relationship Clues (False)

True-false questions often test your knowledge of facts; on a higher level, true-false questions can test your understanding of relationships. Two common kinds of relationships questioned on tests are cause/effect and explanation through reason. When you see one of the common relationship clues (*because, since, so, cause, effect,* or *reason*), first try immediate, delayed, and assisted responses. If you cannot figure out the answer, guess *false.* Why? These higher-level thinking skills questions can easily be written to show false relationships. Notice how the two parts of the following questions do not show a true relationship.

____F____ **1.** Lack of motivation is the <u>reason</u> unsuccessful students avoid using time management.

____F____ **2.** Cramming is not recommended <u>because</u> it uses only eight of the twelve principles of memory.

This same strategy can be used for multiple-choice questions. After each option below, you will see the true or false answer that would be used for that option.

_____ **1.** Systematic desensitization
    a. <u>causes</u> a person to react more mildly to criticism. (F)
    b. works <u>because</u> the immune system is strengthened. (F)
    c. should <u>never</u> be used to avoid undesirable situations. (F)
    d. helps a person change his or her negative reaction to specific events. (T)

Ridiculous, Foolish, Insulting, Unfamiliar (False)

If you see statements that are meant to be humorous, ridiculous, or unreasonable, mark them false for true-false questions, and mark them as distractors in multiple-choice questions. If you have attended class regularly and have done all the reading assignments, if you encounter unfamiliar terms, odds are in your favor that the statement is false or it is a distractor in a multiple-choice question. Notice how this works in the following examples.

____F____ **1.** Howard Gardner's multiple intelligences theory applies only to people with IQ's over 175. *(ridiculous)*

_____F_____ **2.** Howard Gardner's multiple intelligences theory added an eighth intelligence called psychic/intuitive. *(unfamiliar terms)*

_____F_____ **3.** Interpersonal intelligence is shown by those who party instead of study. *(ridiculous)*

_____d_____ **4.** When you don't know the answer to a test question, you should
   a. try using the rest of the test to trigger your memory. **(T)**
   b. try looking at another student's answers. *(ridiculous)* **(F)**
   c. cry. *(ridiculous)* **(F)**
   d. use delayed or assisted response before educated guessing. **(T)**

_____a_____ **5.** Interpersonal intelligence is
   a. seen in people with social and leadership skills. **(T)**
   b. associated to immaturity. *(ridiculous)* **(F)**
   c. not a useful quality in school beyond the first grade. *(silly)* **(F)**
   d. a form of type B behavior. *(unfamiliar term)* **(F)**

Wild-Shot Guess (True)

If there are no modifiers to use and there is no relationship shown, you will need to take a **wild-shot guess**. If you run out of time on a test and simply must guess, *guess true*. There is a logical reason for this. When teachers write tests, they usually prefer to leave the correct, accurate information in your mind. They know that you are likely to remember what you read. Therefore, they tend to write more true statements than false statements.

Eliminate the Highest and Lowest Numbers

When the options are numbers, chances are better that the correct answer is one of the numbers in the middle range. Therefore, treat the highest and the lowest numbers as distractors. That leaves you with two options. Try to reason through to make the better choice. If any one of the other guessing strategies apply (such as choose *c*), incorporate that strategy as well to choose your answer.

_____ **1.** An average rate of thinking speed is
   a. 800 words per minute. (Eliminate the highest.)
   b. 600 words per minute. ⎡Choose between these
   c. 400 words per minute. ⎣two options.
   d. 200 words per minute. (Eliminate the lowest.)

Choose One of the Look-Alike Options

Some questions have two options that look almost the same. Perhaps only one or two words are different. Chances are good that the correct answer is one of these two. Eliminate the other options and focus on these two look-alikes. Carefully think through and associate the information with what you have learned. If you can't decide, choose either one.

_____ **1.** Compared to the left hemisphere of the brain, the right hemisphere of the brain
   a. understands spoken language better.
   b. has better logical abilities.
   c. perceives words better.
   d. perceives emotions better.

Focus on *c* and *d* because they are look-alikes. Now try to reason your way through this. You have already eliminated *a*, which deals with language.

Because *c* also relates to language, it, too, must be incorrect. This leaves you with *d* as the correct answer, which it is. (Notice in this case how the guessing strategy to use *c* does not work—there are no guarantees!)

Choose the Longest or Most Inclusive Option

This guessing strategy is based on two premises. First, sometimes more words are needed to give complete information to make a correct answer. Second, an answer that covers a wider range of possibilities is more likely correct.

You can begin by looking at the *length* of the answer. If one option is much longer than the others, choose it. Also look at the content of the answers. Sometimes two or three answers may be correct to some degree, but one answer contains more information or a broader idea. This answer is the most inclusive. Notice how the *most inclusive answer* in the following is the best answer.

_____ **1.** Test anxiety can be reduced by focusing on
   a. yourself and ignoring others.
   b. outward thoughts and actions.
   c. your strengths and accomplishments.
   d. the four strategies to reduce test anxiety.

All of the answers are correct to some degree. However, *d* is the longest and includes a wider range of information. The answers *a*, *b*, and *c* fit under the information given in *d*.

Choose "All of the Above"

If you know for sure that two options are correct, but you are not sure about the third option and the fourth option is "all of the above," choose it. This is a safe guess since you can choose only one answer and you know that two are correct. If you do not know for certain that two are correct, and you have tried each option in a true-false form and don't know the answer, go ahead and choose "all of the above." This strategy is not a very reliable one, especially if "all of the above" is used throughout the test. Be sure to check out all other possibilities before you decide to use this strategy.

_____ **1.** Cramming is
   a. the result of being underprepared.
   b. a frantic attempt to learn a lot of information in a short amount of time.
   c. a method that does not use very many memory principles.
   d. all of the above.

Your first reaction might be to choose *b* because it is the longest answer. However, if you know that at least two of the choices are correct, your only choice then is to choose *d*, which is correct.

Choose C as a Wild-Shot Guess

Many teachers favor the *c* answer for the correct answer. If you try writing some of your own multiple-choice questions, you may find that you too tend to put more correct answers in the *c* position than in any other position. Here are a few explanations for why *c* is the most common answer:

■ *A* is not used as often because many students would stop reading the questions and stop thinking about the answer if the correct answer was given first.

■ *B* is not used as often for the same reason that *A* is not.

■ *C* seems to hide the answer best and force the reader to read through more of the options.

■ *D* seems to be too visible because it is on the last line.

✎ **EXERCISE 13.5 Having Fun with Educated Guessing**

This exercise has test questions on topics that may not be familiar to you.
However, if you apply the educated guessing strategies to answer these questions,
you will be correct. Work with a partner and discuss your answers.

_____ **1.** In 1913, President Woodrow Wilson believed that concentrated economic power threatened individual liberty and the monopolies had to be broken up to open up the marketplace.

_____ **2.** All matter exists in only one of three physical forms: solid, liquid, or gas.

_____ **3.** The liquid form of a given material is always less dense than the solid form.

_____ **4.** Prolonged overuse of alcohol can result in life-threatening liver damage, vitamin deficiencies that can lead to irreversible brain disorder, and a host of other ailments.

_____ **5.** Rome's early wars often gave plebeians the power to demand that their rights be recognized, but their demands were seldom met.

_____ **6.** Because monasteries believed in isolation, they never conducted schools for local people.

_____ **7.** In 1013, the Danish ruler Swen Forkbeard invaded England.

_____ **8.** The only objective of medieval agriculture was to produce more cattle for meat and dairy products.

_____ **9.** Historians have determined for certain that the bubonic plague originated in southern Russia and was carried to Europe by traveling soldiers.

_____ **10.** Economic growth was rapid during the Italian Renaissance.

_____ **11.** The first movies, which began in the late 1880s, were slot-machine peep shows in penny arcades.

_____ **12.** The Warren Court in 1962 declared that schools would always have the right to require prayers in public schools, but students had the right to refrain from praying.

_____ **13.** The world's population has more than doubled since 1950.

_____ **14.** The behavioral theory suggests that people learn to use alcohol because they want to become more sensitive to others.

_____ **15.** Alcoholic parents, hyperactivity, and antisocial behavior in childhood are reasonably good predictors of alcoholism in adults.

_____ **16.** The Dow Jones Industrial Average, established in 1897, is a stock index still in use today.

_____ **17.** The Standard & Poor's 500 Stock Index and the New York Stock Exchange Index never include more stocks than the Dow Jones averages.

_____ **18.** The Securities and Exchange Commission (SEC) was created in 1934 because stockbrokers wanted access to a compiled list of all trading.

_____ **19.** The Abolitionist newspapers frequently attacked the Fugitive Slave Act as a violation of fundamental American rights.

_____ **20.** In the 1970s, unemployment was high due mainly to the oil embargo.

Use the educated guessing strategies for the following multiple-choice questions. Remember to convert each option into a true-false question before you select the best answer.

_____ **1.** A response pattern known as *cynical hostility*
   a. is linked to coronary heart disease and heart attacks.
   b. develops in childhood years.
   c. is characterized by resentment, frequent anger, and distrust.
   d. all of the above.

_____ **2.** Signs of post-traumatic stress disorder are
   a. never being able to sleep.
   b. shown in a frequency histogram.
   c. poor concentration, anxiety, and nervousness.
   d. apparent at the time of the trauma.

_____ **3.** The domestication of plants and animals began around
   a. 7000 B.C.
   b. 4000 B.C.
   c. A.D. 1200.
   d. 9000 B.C.

_____ **4.** The mental shortcuts called *heuristics* are
   a. informal reasoning based on which events or hypotheses are likely.
   b. informal reasoning based solely on using a given algorithm.
   c. formal reasoning based on the use of an algorithm and logic.
   d. required in at least one stage of every scientific model.

_____ **5.** With a *balloon automobile loan,* the
   a. buyer feels stupid when the balloon payment is due.
   b. buyer must sell the car back to the lender at the end of the loan.
   c. first six monthly payments are large but later payments are reduced.
   d. monthly payments are lower but the final payment is much greater.

_____ **6.** Reinforcement theory is
   a. based on giving rewards for behavior you want repeated.
   b. based on forcing issues.
   c. never to be used by effective managers.
   d. the very best training to use for infants.

_____ **7.** In business, the agency shop
   a. never charges dues.
   b. charges annual fees of $10 or less.
   c. requires employees to pay dues even if they don't join.
   d. requires employees to always be union members.

_____ **8.** Volcanic mountains are formed from
   a. cinder piles and ash.
   b. cinder piles, lava rock, ash, and shields of magma.
   c. erosion.
   d. sandstone and shale.

_____ **9.** Consumer spending reports have shown that _____ percent of American's disposable income in 1994 was spent on food.
  a. 5
  b. 9
  c. 15
  d. 28

_____ **10.** World population estimates show the population in the year 2000 will be at least
  a. nine hundred million.
  b. twenty-three billion.
  c. six billion.
  d. ten billion.

Taking Computerized Tests

Computerized tests usually consist of multiple-choice questions. Frequently, computerized tests are based on test banks that are provided by the textbook publisher. Some of the test banks randomly assign test questions that will be different for each student or different each time the test is taken. Students encounter problems with the randomly assigned test questions because the questions given are testing content from the book, and sometimes the content was not covered in class. In addition, there is not always equity from one student to another. One student may by chance be given more difficult questions while another student is given relatively easy questions. Some of the computerized test-bank programs allow the instructor to tag the questions to be used so the questions reflect more of the course content that was discussed in class.

Computerized tests are marketed for teacher convenience and speed in grading, which are seen by some teachers as important when class sizes or workloads are high. Students do get immediate feedback as to whether or not their answers are correct. The methodology used assumes that students will take the time to learn from their mistakes. Some students prefer computerized tests because time limits are less rigid than taking tests in the classroom. Since they are in control of the pace, they feel less stress.

Several disadvantages also exist for computerized testing. The immediate feedback can be rewarding when the answers are correct, but emotional stress and frustration levels may increase and self-confidence may decrease when negative feedback flashes on the screen that an answer is wrong. A second disadvantage is that most computerized programs do not let you go back to change answers or go back to look at previous questions. Therefore, the strategy of using assisted response is eliminated. A final disadvantage is that you do not get a paper copy of the test so you can study the information you missed and learn from the test. You do not have the tests to use as part of the review process for later tests or the final exam.

If you have the option of taking paper-pencil tests instead of computerized tests, you may want to try a computerized test to see how you respond and perform. Once you have had a few experiences with computerized tests, you will be in a better situation to decide which format you prefer. Be prepared, however, for the fact that sometimes you do not have the option of deciding whether or not to take a test on paper or on a computer.

When you are assigned the task of taking a computerized test, allow yourself ample time to take the test. Avoid going into the lab when you are rushed. For some students, the careful thought that is needed for computerized tests requires more time than regular tests. Select a time of the day when you are feeling mentally sharp, alert, and ready for applying your concentrated effort. In addition to these general suggestions, the following strategies will help you perform more effectively on computerized tests:

Strategies for Taking Computerized Tests

1. Read the directions carefully so you understand the program and how to respond.
2. Use the multiple-choice test taking strategies previously discussed in this chapter.
3. If you give an incorrect answer, study the question before you move on.
4. Use strategies to stay relaxed, positive, and focused.
5. Explore options that may be available to you after you have taken the test.

Read the Directions

Computerized programs vary, so it is very important to read the directions carefully. Learn the basic options or commands that are available for the program you will be using. Frequently asked questions are: How do I log on? Is there a time limit? How do I delete an answer before entering my choice? Can more than one answer be correct? May I have a blank paper with me to work out problems or jot down ideas as I think? Is there a way to see all the questions before I start answering? Is a screen reader program with voice (and earphones) available for this program? Is there a practice test I can do first? May I take the test a second time?

Use the Multiple-Choice Strategies

Use the same multiple-choice strategies that were presented earlier in this chapter. Read the stem and try to complete the stem with your own words. Look to see if one of the options matches your words. Then read the stem with each option and convert each option into a true-false question. Eliminate any of the options that would be false. Remember that you are doing this *with your eyes*. Pay close attention to key words, modifiers, negatives, and relationship and definition clues. Once you have decided on an option, reread the question with your option one more time. This is important because you do not usually have the opportunity to return to change your answer.

Study the Question After an Incorrect Answer

If you answer incorrectly and the screen tells you that you have made a mistake, avoid the tendency to get away from that question and to move quickly to the next question. If the test questions are given randomly, it is possible that a future question on the same material may be given. Take time to reread the question and understand your error. If the question gives the correct answer, learn the information with that answer. The information may also help you later with another closely related question. Taking the time to learn from the question helps to keep your mind focused on the material and reduce the tendency to move to the next question too hastily and with a negative attitude.

Use Stress-Reducing and Concentration Strategies

If you find yourself tensing up, feeling discouraged, impatient, angry, or irritated, stop for a few short minutes to do a relaxation technique. Breathe by threes, use the relaxation mask, or give yourself some positive self-talk. Stretch your arms, roll your head around, shake out your hands, roll your shoulders around, or even stand up for a minute to reduce the building stress. If you are finding yourself losing concentration, try to identify the distractors. Use any of the concentration strategies to get your mind on track and back to the task at hand. If the location of your computer station is a distractor, remember the next time to select a computer that is removed from the steady flow of traffic. Your goal is to work as much as possible with the relaxed, "Ahhhhh" state of mind.

Explore Options

If you are uncomfortable taking computerized tests or find computerized tests a difficult format to use to perform well, communicate your concerns with your instructor. Perhaps he or she will be able to provide you with additional suggestions for effectively taking computerized tests. The following are other options you may want to explore. After all, it never hurts to ask.

1. Ask the lab assistant if a *hard copy* (printed copy) of the test questions can be made available while you take the test. Explain that sometimes you find it helpful to be able to write on the test, circle words, and see all the questions as you work.

2. Ask your instructor if tests can be taken a second time. If you can, ask if you may take notes during the first test.

3. Ask your instructor or the lab assistant if you may have a hard copy of the test questions so you can study and learn from the errors.

4. Try to remember questions that puzzled you or that you didn't think were discussed much in class. Talk to your instructor about these questions.

5. Ask if there are other options available instead of taking the computerized tests. Could essays or short answers be done on paper instead? Could a project or portfolio assignment be used in lieu of a computerized test?

Computerized tests will likely become more interactive and more sophisticated as technology advances. Learning to be comfortable working on a computer is essential. Learning to take computerized tests may also be essential if the trend to assess student performance continues in the direction of computerized testing. Be an active learner by asking lab assistants, instructors, and other students for additional strategies that can help you with computerized tests for specific classes. You may end up being a member of the group of students who prefer computerized testing!

SUMMARY

■ Recognition questions, also called objective questions, include true-false, multiple-choice, and matching.

■ Words used in objective questions must be read more carefully:

1. Definition clues
2. Negatives
3. 100-percent and in-between modifiers
4. Relationship clues

■ Both the stem and all the options in a multiple-choice question should be read as true-false statements before they are answered.

■ A three-step strategy can enable you to answer multiple-choice questions.

■ Objective questions utilize the steps of immedi- ate response, delayed response, assisted response, and educated guessing.

■ A four-step approach is recommended when you are answering matching questions.

■ Some strategies can be used to increase your odds at guessing on true-false and multiple-choice questions.

■ Do not become falsely confident because you know educated guessing strategies; the best approach is to be prepared and learn as much information as possible so that you do not need educated guessing on a regular basis.

■ Special strategies can be used to increase your performance on computerized tests.

OPTIONS FOR PERSONALIZING CHAPTER 13

1. **PROFILE CHART—PERSONAL LOG**   Answer the following questions in your personal log.

   What score did you have on the Chapter 13 Profile? _____

   Which of the three kinds of objective question formats do you prefer? Why? Which do you tend to have more difficulties using? Why?

   What strategies did you learn in the chapter that will help you perform better on objective tests?

2. **WORDS TO KNOW**   Knowing the following vocabulary terms is important.

objective tests	definition clues	four levels of response
memory searches	relationship clues	word clues
negatives	stem	grammar clues
modifiers	options	wild-shot guess
100-percent modifiers	distractors	
in-between modifiers	paired associations	

3. **EXPAND THE CHAPTER VISUAL MAPPING**   Add level-three details on the Chapter 13 visual mapping. You may expand the mapping in your book or on your own paper. For additional practice, convert the visual mapping into a summary written in paragraph form.

4. **WRITING ASSIGNMENT 1**   Teachers many times have preferences for certain kinds of tests. Discuss the kinds of tests that you have experienced in each of your classes. What is each teacher's style of testing?

5. **WRITING ASSIGNMENT 2**   Chapter 12 discussed four different sources of test anxiety. Summarize each of those sources and then discuss how the information in this chapter can reduce test anxiety.

6. **PORTFOLIO DEVELOPMENT**   Create a chart that shows all of your classes this term, the test grades you have received, and the types of tests that were used. Then select any three tests that have been graded and returned to you. "Analyze" your errors. Report on the kinds of errors you have made and the test-taking skills you have now learned that can correct each type of error.

CHAPTER 13 REVIEW QUESTIONS

True-False

Carefully read the following sentences. Pay attention to key words.
Write T *if the statement is* TRUE. *Write* F *if the statement is* FALSE.

_____ **1.** In matching tests, you always have two columns equal in length.

_____ **2.** The words *reason, because,* and *since* are often relationship clues.

_____ **3.** All items listed in a series must be false before you can use a false answer.

_____ **4.** True-false statements that use negatives are always false.

_____ **5.** The most inclusive option in a multiple-choice question is often the best answer.

_____ **6.** A distractor in a multiple-choice question is the correct answer.

_____ **7.** If a multiple-choice question has four options, the question should be read as four true-false statements.

_____ **8.** If you can't give an immediate response, you should use educated guessing.

_____ **9.** In matching questions, an item from each column can be formed into a sentence by using helper words during the delayed response step.

_____ **10.** For most students, computerized tests are easier because questions can be answered and scored quickly.

Multiple-Choice

Write the letter of the best answer on the line.

_____ **1.** Guess *false* on a true-false question when the question has a(n)
   a. 100-percent modifier or a relationship clue.
   b. in-between modifier and a negative word or prefix.
   c. in-between modifier and a definition word clue.
   d. all of the above.

_____ **2.** The _____ of a multiple-choice question should be used with each option.
   a. distractors
   b. directions
   c. stem
   d. all of the above

_____ **3.** Educated guessing should be used after
   a. the recall step of response.
   b. the immediate response step.
   c. all other options have been tried.
   d. the delayed response step.

_____ **4.** When you first read the stem of a multiple-choice question, you should
   a. decide you really don't like the question.
   b. turn it into a true-false question.
   c. finish the stem with your own words then see if an option matches your words.
   d. identify the distractors immediately by using educated guessing strategies.

_____ **5.** When you are told your answer is incorrect on a computerized test, you should
   a. take a deep breath, relax, and try to not get irritated.
   b. try to remember the test question so you can discuss it later.
   c. take a little bit of time to learn the information with the correct answer.
   d. all of the above.

Matching

Match the items on the left to the items on the right, writing the letter answer on the line. Each answer can be used only once.

_____ **1.** Paired associations

_____ **2.** 100-percent modifiers

_____ **3.** In-between modifiers

_____ **4.** Relationship clues

_____ **5.** Prefixes with negative meanings

_____ **6.** Recognition questions

_____ **7.** Delayed response

_____ **8.** Assisted response

_____ **9.** Stem

_____**10.** Distractors

a. words such as *sometimes, often, some, perhaps*

b. units of meaning that are attached to the beginning of words and have the meaning of "no" or "not"

c. guessing true or the letter C

d. the linking of two ideas together

e. the beginning part of a multiple-choice question

f. answers that are known immediately

g. options that are incorrect answers

h. involves rereading, looking for clues, and doing memory searches

i. words that are absolutes

j. objective questions

k. a response given after you skim the test for clues

l. words that often show cause-effect

Short Answer—Critical Thinking

Answer one *of the following questions on your own paper. Your answer should be written in paragraph form.*

1. Discuss the differences between taking a paper-pencil multiple-choice test and a computerized multiple-choice test.

2. Discuss the situations when educated guessing is appropriate and situations when it is not.

Developing Strategies for Recall and Essay Tests

Recall and essay questions require students to retrieve information from memory, apply it, and express the answer in well-written sentences, paragraphs, or essays. Do you sometimes feel that you know the information but that you just can't seem to get it written on paper? Does your written response not really answer the question? Do you have difficulties organizing your ideas clearly? Do you run out of time and leave essay questions unfinished? This chapter provides you with valuable strategies for answering fill-in-the-blank, listings, definition, short-answer, and essay questions.

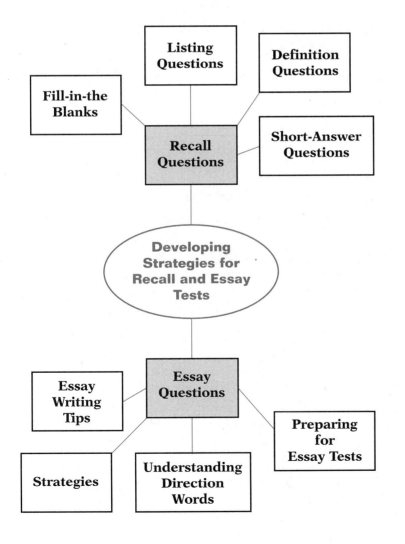

CHAPTER 14   Recall and Essay Profile

DO, SCORE, and **RECORD** your profile before you read this chapter. If you need to review the process, refer to the complete directions given in the Profile for Chapter 1 on page 2.

	YES	NO
1. I go blank when I have to come up with exact words to fill in the blanks of sentences.	_____	_____
2. Open-ended questions that have many possible answers are difficult for me to answer.	_____	_____
3. When I am asked to define a word, my definition is usually one sentence long.	_____	_____
4. I make a quick outline, mapping, or plan before I begin writing an essay answer.	_____	_____
5. I understand the different answers needed for questions that require me to define, explain, discuss, or compare.	_____	_____
6. I often lose points on essays because I don't include enough details.	_____	_____
7. I often get off track and don't answer the question that is being asked.	_____	_____
8. If I have to list specific details, I usually am not able to remember all the items in the list.	_____	_____
9. I often try to "bluff" my way through essays because I don't know how to write them or because I don't know the information.	_____	_____
10. When there is time during a test, I proofread my answers.	_____	_____
11. I use my course syllabus and class notes to predict themes that might be used in essay questions.	_____	_____
12. As I prepare for essay tests, I create special summary sheets for major categories, trends, patterns, or relationships.	_____	_____

Self-Awareness: What are some of the most common problems you encounter on tests that require you to retrieve information from your memory? What are common problems on tests that require essay answers?

_____

_____

_____

_____

_____

_____

_____

Recall Questions

The four most common types of **recall questions** are fill-in-the-blank questions, listing questions, definitions, and short answers. Elaborative rehearsal, thorough learning, and efficient long-term memory retrieval techniques are essential for answering such questions. No educated guessing strategies are available for these questions; however, you can learn to answer recall questions more effectively by using the following strategies.

Fill-in-the-Blank Questions

A **fill-in-the-blank question** is a sentence with one or more words missing. You must read the sentence carefully and decide which key words will complete the sentence correctly. If you know a test will have fill-in-the-blank questions, you can predict that the majority of the answers will relate to terminology. The following strategies provide you with methods for studying and completing this kind of recall question.

Strategies for Fill-in-the-Blank Questions

1. Study from the back of your flash cards.
2. Use immediate response.
3. Use delayed response; search your memory for the category and ask questions.
4. Use assisted response by skimming the rest of the test.
5. Substitute a related synonym or phrase.

Study from the Back of Your Flash Cards   Many fill-in-the-blank questions are based on key vocabulary terms. Spend extra time studying from the *back* of your flash cards so that you can readily recall the terms on the front. If you are studying from vocabulary sheets, cover up the left column. Read the definitions and practice reciting and spelling the terms in the left column. Your flash cards or vocabulary sheets should include all the key terms in the chapter and other terms given in lectures.

Use Immediate Response   If you created, recited, and reviewed vocabulary cards or vocabulary sheets using the method just described, you can often get an **immediate response**. The following points are important to remember when you fill in the blanks:

■ Unless the directions say otherwise, place only one word on each blank line.

■ The length of the line is not an automatic clue to the length of the word that will fit on the line.

■ The completed sentence should make sense and be grammatically correct.

■ Blanks that are separated with commas indicate a series of items.

■ Several blank lines without commas between them indicate that you will be completing a phrase with a specific number of words.

Use Delayed Response   To use **delayed response**, search your memory for the general category or topic related to the information in the sentence. Once you identify the category, search your memory for the details. Try to recall a specific chapter, a specific visual mapping, a study tool, or a mnemonic you rehearsed for the category. Then ask yourself questions, such as *What is . . . What do we call . . . Where is . . . When . . . Who . . . ?* "Talk" your way to the answer.

This **memory search**, or process of thinking back and connecting to information learned, needs to be done quickly. If you have difficulty identifying the category, recalling the study tool used, or answering the questions you formulate, delay your response. Do not spend too much time on one question. If you need to leave the question blank, put a checkmark next to the question so you remember to come back to it later. Move on to the next question.

Use Assisted Response   After you have answered all the questions you can on the test, return to the unanswered ones and apply **assisted response**. Since fill-in-the-blank questions are usually key vocabulary terms, use the rest of the test to look for the terms or their categories. For example, if you know the term belongs to the category "test anxiety," skim through the test looking for other questions about test anxiety. Sometimes you will find the word or an item on the test that will trigger an association to the missing word.

Substitute a Synonym or Related Phrase   You may be able to pick up partial points by writing something in the blank even though you know it is not the correct term. Try one of the following possibilities:

■ Use a **synonym** (a word with a similar meaning) or a substitute word. You may not get full points for your answer, but you may be given partial credit.

■ If necessary, write a short phrase. Some teachers (not all) will recognize your effort.

Filling in the blank using synonyms, substitutions, or phrases does show an effort on your part. Realize, however, that you may put effort into using this approach but that your answer may still be marked wrong because the *exact* answer was needed. Make a mental note to find the correct answers after the test.

✎ EXERCISE 14.1 **Filling in the Blanks**

Work with a partner. Read the following questions carefully. They are all review questions based on key terms from previous chapters. First try an immediate response; then try a delayed response by doing a memory search and posing a question.

1. The _____ _____ technique is a concentration technique for letting other people know that you do not want to be disturbed.

2. The beginning part of a multiple-choice question is called the _____.

3. _____ time consists of a few hours each week added to your time-management schedule to allow for any extra study time beyond your regular study blocks.

4. Howard Gardner's _____ intelligence refers to a person's ability to work cooperatively, understand people, and demonstrate leadership skills.

5. The second step of the Cornell system uses the memory principle of selectivity when information is selected to put in the _____ column.

6. The memory principle of _____ is used when two items are linked together in memory so one can trigger the recall of the other.

7. _____ are units of meaning that are added to the endings of words.

8. Maslow's highest level of needs in his hierarchy is called _____

    _____.

9. _____ are clusters of related information that are imprinted in long-term memory.

10. Excessive stress is called _____.

11. _____ are number words such as *first, second,* and *third.*

12. _____ vocabulary refers to words you understand when you read them or when you hear them.

13. The process of understanding your memory system and knowing how to select appropriate strategies for different kinds of learning tasks is called _____.

14. An _____ is a "memory trick strategy" that involves making up a word by using the first letters of each of the key words that need to be remembered.

15. A _____ _____ describes a person who is a "right-brain dominant person" who tends to be intuitive, creative, and visual.

Listing Questions

Listing questions require you to recall a specific number of ideas, steps, or vocabulary words. The answers are usually key words; full sentences are not generally required. Listing questions often begin with the direction word *list* or *name*. Using the following strategies will improve your performance on listing questions:

Strategies for Listing Questions

1. Predict listing questions when you study.
2. Underline key words and determine whether the question is closed or open-ended.
3. Use immediate response.
4. Use delayed response; do a memory search and ask questions.
5. Use assisted response.
6. Substitute a related synonym or phrase.

Predict Listing Questions When You Study   You can **predict listing questions** as you read, take notes, and create study tools by recognizing or anticipating possible items for listing questions. Lists to study can be found:

■ On vocabulary category cards (see Chapter 8, page 147)

■ In questions created for headings in the SQ4R system

■ In Cornell recall columns

■ In chapter objectives and introductions

■ In level-one and level-two information in mappings or hierarchies

■ In paragraphs that use ordinals (number words)

■ In marginal notes written in your textbooks

Underline Key Words and Determine Whether the Question Is Closed or Open-ended   By underlining the key words in the question, you will be able to focus specifically on the information being asked. Notice how the underlining in the following question helps you focus:

> **1.** Lining up the Cornell columns is one reflect activity you can do during the fourth step of the Cornell notetaking system. List five other study tools that you can make during the reflect step to reinforce the learning process.

Now decide if the question has specific answers or if there are a variety of possible answers. **Closed questions** require very specific answers and often the answers must be in a specific order. **Open-ended questions** can have many possible answers. You can pull related ideas and information from throughout the term to develop your answer for an open-ended question. The above question about study tools during the reflect step of Cornell is an open-ended question. Any five of the following answers would be correct: visual mappings, cartoon/pictures, acronyms, time lines, study tapes, written summaries, predicted test questions, vocabulary flash cards, or hierarchies.

Notice the difference between closed questions and open-ended questions in these examples:

These are closed questions:

1. List the five *R*'s of the Cornell notetaking system in the order in which they occur.

2. What are the steps for the SQ4R textbook reading system?
3. Name the four levels of response that can be used for answering test questions.
4. List the four steps, in order, for writing effective performance goals.

These are open-ended questions:

1. List at least five strategies that can be used to reduce test anxiety.
2. List six concentration strategies to reduce external distractors.
3. List five traits of good, effective listeners.
4. List six common characteristics of the linear thinker/learner in the brain dominance theory.

Use Immediate Response   After you have underlined the key words in the directions, you may be ready with the answer. Being able to give an immediate response is the reward for effective studying. Immediate response indicates that you organized and rehearsed information effectively, which enabled you to quickly retrieve from long-term memory what was needed.

Use Delayed Response   If immediate response wasn't available, move to delayed response. Association triggers are needed to help you connect the key words in the directions to the information you want to find in your memory bank. Use the following technique:

- Focus on the key words you underlined in the directions. These will help you identify the category.

- Search your memory for study tools that you created to rehearse the information. Try to picture the flash cards, the Cornell recall column, or the introductions in the chapter headings.

- Turn the information into a new *question*. In the preceding example, you might pose the question "What study tools help me reflect on information that I am learning?"

Because you probably have many other questions to deal with on the test, memory searching and questioning must be done relatively quickly. If you are able to retrieve an answer, or part of an answer, write it down. If you are not able to complete the listing, *place a checkmark next to the question.* You can come back to it later after you have completed as many questions as possible.

Use Assisted Response   When you return to the unanswered or partially answered questions, skim through the rest of the test for possible clues. Many times important information appears in the test in more than one place but in a different questioning format. Focus on the key words that you underlined in the directions. When you find a possible answer, check it against the question that you posed earlier.

Substitute Synonyms or Short Phrases   If you were not able to locate the exact terms for the listing, use synonyms or short phrases. These answers are not as accurate, yet they show your effort and general understanding. An empty space can bring only one result: no points. You may receive full points or partial points for using synonyms or short phrases.

Notice how synonyms or short phrases were used for *d* and *e* to complete the following answer in a listing question.

1. List the five theories of forgetting.
   a. Decay theory
   b. Displacement theory
   c. Retrieval failure theory
   d. Encoding—only partially recorded in memory
   e. Old and new information get confused

EXERCISE 14.2 Predicting Listing Questions

Work in groups. Each group selects one of the chapters in this textbook to use to predict questions that may appear on a test as listing questions. Each group will report back to the class. The predicted listing questions may be compiled for future reference to study for the final exam.

Definition Questions   Any question that asks you to "define" a term is a **definition question**. This kind of question asks you to retrieve specific information from your memory and organize the information into sentences. Paired association is required and achieved if you have studied from vocabulary cards or vocabulary sheets. You can predict that these questions will come from the course-specific terminology that was defined in your textbook and in lectures. The following strategies will result in well-developed definition answers:

Strategies for Definition Questions

1. Read the question carefully. Underline the term to be defined.
2. Use the three steps for writing definitions.
3. Use delayed response and assisted response if necessary.

Identify the Term   For a short definition question, the term is easy to identify. Underline the term to help you keep your focus on that one word. Sometimes definition questions begin by giving background information. Read all of the information carefully and then underline the term to be defined. The following examples both are definition questions.

1. Define the term *neurons.*
2. The human nervous system is comprised of two primary types of cells, the neurons and the glial cells. Glial cells provide physiological support to neurons. Define *neurons* in the central nervous system.

Use the Three Steps for Writing Definitions   In Chapter 8 (page 148), you learned three steps for writing definitions. First, you name the category associated with the term. Second, you give the formal definition. Third, you expand the definition with one more detail. Use this same technique to define words in a definition question. The following examples show a weak answer and a strong answer.

Question:	Define the term *distributed practice.*
Weak Answer:	It means you practice at different times.
Strong Answer:	Distributed practice is a time-management strategy that is also related to the memory principle of time on task. It means that study blocks are spread or distributed throughout the week. Distributed practice is the opposite of marathon studying.

Expanding your definition is the open-ended part of a question that gives you the opportunity to show you know more about a word than just its definition. The following chart shows seven methods, followed by an example, that are commonly used to expand a definition:

Method	Example
Add one more fact.	*Distributed practice often occurs when the 2:1 ratio is used.*
Give a synonym.	*Distributed practice is the same as spaced studying.*
Give an antonym, a contrast, or a negation.	*Distributed practice is the opposite of marathon studying or massed practice.*
Give a comparison or analogy.	*Distributed practice is like working on a goal a little every day instead of trying to complete all the steps in one block of time.*
Define the structure of the word.	*The root of <u>neuron</u> is "neuro," which means <u>nervous system</u>.*
Give the etymology.	*The term <u>locus</u> comes from the Latin "loci," which means <u>place</u>, so locus of control refers to a place where there is the control.*
Give an application.	*Metacognition is used any time a person faces a new task and needs to decide on the best method for him or her to do the task efficiently.*

Use Delayed and Assisted Response if Necessary   If you are not able to give an immediate response, the questions given for identifying the general category may help you with the delayed response. If your mind is blank and you can't write the definition or expand the definition, place a checkmark next to the question and move on. After you have answered all the questions you can, skim through the rest of the test to search for additional clues or details to complete your answer. Remember that key terms are frequently used or referred to in other parts of the test in other questioning formats.

✎ EXERCISE 14.3 Answering Definition Questions

Work with a partner. Select any one chapter from this textbook. Refer to the "Words to Know" in the Options for Personalizing the Chapter. Predict two vocabulary terms that might appear on a test. Write a definition question, and then write a three-sentence answer to your question. Your work may be shared in class.

Short-Answer Questions

Short-answer questions usually require a short paragraph of three-to-seven sentences for the answer. Sometimes they look like "mini-essays" and other times they look like expanded "listing questions" that use sentences to explain the items in a listing. With short answers, both the content of your answer and your writing skills are important. Some teachers will grade higher when you use correct grammar, punctuation, and spelling.

As with listing questions, short-answer questions may be *closed questions* in which very specific answers are expected. They may also be *open-ended questions* that require you to connect or relate ideas from different parts of the course, or they may require you to apply your knowledge to new situations. Both types of short-answer questions require sufficient details to show that you know the information. The following steps can help you write an effective answer:

Strategies for Answering Short-Answer Questions

1. Identify the direction word and underline the key words.
2. Make a mental plan or short list of key ideas to use in your answer.
3. Write a strong, focused opening sentence.
4. Add additional sentences with specific details.
5. Use delayed and assisted response if necessary.

Identify the Direction Word and Underline Key Words   The first step is to pay attention to the **direction word** in each question. Each type of direction word requires a specific kind of answer. To get full points for your work, your answer must match the question. The following direction words are common for short-answer questions:

Direction Word	What Is Required
Discuss/Tell	Tell about a particular topic.
Identify/What are?	Identify specific points. (This is similar to a listing except that you are required to answer in full sentences.)
Describe	Give more specific details or descriptions than are required by "discuss."
Explain/Why?	Give reasons. Answer the question "Why?"
Explain how/How?	Describe a process or a set of steps. Give the steps in chronological (time sequence) order.
When?	Describe a time or a specific condition needed for something to happen, occur, or be used.

Circle the key direction word when you first read the question. Review in your mind what is required by this direction word. Because you want to respond quickly, become very familiar with the preceding descriptions of direction words. Then underline key words that will be used in your answer.

Each of the following test questions has the same subject: visual mappings. However, because of the different direction words, each answer will be slightly different.

(Why) is recitation important to use while studying a mapping?

(Explain how) to create a visual mapping.

(How) should you study from a visual mapping?

(When) should visual mappings be used?

Make a Mental Plan or a Short List of Ideas   Look at the key words underlined in the step above. These words should be included in your answer. Pause and do a *memory search* for appropriate details for your answer. Either make a mental plan or jot down a short list of points that you will want to present in sentence form. Do only what is expected; do not pad the answer with unrelated information.

Write a Strong Opening Sentence   Since you will not have much space to write a long answer, begin your answer with a sentence that is direct and to-the-point. Your first sentence should include the key words of the question and show that you are heading in the direction required by the direction word. Do not beat around the bush or save your best information for last. The first sentence, when well written, lets the teacher know right away that you are familiar with the subject.

Notice the difference in quality in the following opening sentences. The first one does not get to the point. The second and third examples are direct and show confidence.

Question:	Why is recitation important in the learning process?
Weak:	Recitation is important because it helps a person learn better.
Strong:	Recitation, one of the twelve principles of memory, is important to use for studying for three reasons.
Strong:	Recitation is important for studying because it involves the auditory channel, feedback, and practice expressing ideas.

Add Sentences with Details   After you write your opening sentence, expand your answer with more information. Give appropriate details to support your opening sentence; try to use course-related terminology in your answers.

Notice the difference in the weak answer and the strong answer in the following example.

Weak:	Recitation is important because it helps a person learn. Everyone wants to do the very best possible and recitation helps make that happen. When you recite, you talk out loud. You practice information out loud before a test.
Strong:	Recitation is important for studying because it involves the auditory channel, gives feedback, and provides practice expressing ideas. When a person states information out loud and in complete sentences, he/she activates the auditory channel, which results in a stronger imprint in long-term memory. Reciting also gives feedback so a person knows immediately whether or not the information is understood on the level that it can be explained to someone else. Taking time to recite also provides the opportunity to practice organizing ideas so they can be clearly expressed.

Use Delayed and Assisted Response if Necessary   If you are unable to write a strong opening sentence for your short answer, do a memory search for the topic. Frequently students are able to write the opening sentence, but they have difficulty with the necessary details to expand the opening sentence. If the delayed response and the memory search do not result in sufficient information or details, place a checkmark next to the question and move on. After all other questions have been answered, skim through the test for related details that can be added to your short answer. Expand your answer with these details.

EXERCISE 14.4 Predicting Short-Answer Questions

Short-answer questions are designed to assess if you understand information well enough to express it, if you understand relationships, and if you can apply the information to given situations. Select any topic discussed so far in this course that you think would be a possible short-answer question for the final exam. **Use your own paper.** *First, write the question, and then write a three-to-seven sentence answer. Your work may be shared in class, and your question may be used on a test or final exam.*

Question: _____

Answer:

EXERCISE 14.5 Writing Answers to Short-Answer Questions

Select one *of the following short answer questions. Write a three-to-seven sentence answer. Use the techniques and steps discussed above. Write your answer on your own paper. Proofread it for correct grammar, punctuation, and spelling.*

1. Discuss the differences between *hearing* and *listening*.

2. Explain why *rote memory* is not a reliable method for studying in college.

3. Explain how *locus of control* affects a person's perception of his or her life.

4. Discuss any one strategy that can be used to comprehend a difficult paragraph.

5. Describe a *five-day study plan* for a major test.

6. Tell the process that stimuli go through to be imprinted in long-term memory.

7. When should educated guessing be used on tests?

8. Explain how the *Decay Theory of Forgetting* works.

9. Briefly discuss ways to keep your mind on the speaker when the rate of speech is very slow and your rate of thinking is very fast.

10. What is the strategy *self-fulfilling prophecy* and how is it related to positive self-talk?

Exercise 14.6 LINKS

Assume you are in a health class and are preparing for a test that includes the coping strategies presented in Exercise 7.8, page 138. Write the following kinds of practice questions on your own paper. Then present your questions to a partner to answer while you practice answering your partner's questions. Try answering these recall questions without looking back at the passage.

1. Write three fill-in-the-blank questions.

2. Write one listing question.

3. Write one definition question.

4. Write one short-answer question.

Essay Questions

Essays are demanding. They require that you know the information thoroughly, be able to pull the information from your memory, and write about relationships rather than individual, isolated facts. The way you express the information and the relationships needs to follow a logical line of thinking. Essays also require a sound grasp of writing skills (grammar, syntax, and spelling) as well as a well-developed expressive vocabulary. If essay writing is intimidating to you, be assured that you can strengthen your essay-writing skills by using the following strategies and, if you feel it necessary, by enrolling in writing or vocabulary courses.

Preparing for Essay Tests

Preparation for essay tests involves gathering information about "the big picture" concepts, trends, and relationships and then associating supporting details to be used within the essay. The strategies used to prepare for essays vary based on the type of essay test that will be used:

Strategies for Different Kinds of Essay Tests

1. Predict and organize for essay tests when the topics are unknown.
2. Organize and practice writing essays when a choice of topics is known in advance.
3. Organize materials when the essay is an open-book test.
4. Organize and develop essay answers for take-home tests.

Predict and Organize for Essay Tests When the Topics are Unknown   The most challenging type of essay test is the one in which the topics for the essay questions are not announced in advance. For this type of test, your study strategies throughout the term need to include *elaborative rehearsal* of both the textbook and the lecture material. Elaborative rehearsal occurs when you work with the information; rearrange it; look for relationships, patterns, and trends; and work to recognize key concepts, main ideas, and themes as well as significant supporting details for the "big pictures." The following strategies will help you prepare for essay exams when the topics are not announced in advance.

Use the course description and course syllabus to identify major themes that are used. The course syllabus states the purpose of the course and the information that you should know by the end of the term. Use this to help predict test questions. Use the direction words (page 292) to write "big-picture" questions, and then use the techniques discussed later in the chapter to write answers to your essay questions.

Study visual materials that you have created throughout the term. Visual mappings, hierarchies, time lines, pie charts, tables, and comparison charts are ideal study tools to create and learn to prepare yourself for essay questions. These visual forms of notetaking include, in a concise manner, the main ideas and the significant supporting details. Practice visualizing the *skeleton* of each visual study tool; the skeleton consists of the topic (level-one information) and the main components or main ideas (level-two information). Then practice level-three information (the details) through reciting information about each part of your visual study tool. Use these visual notes as the basis for writing practice essay test questions. Write answers to your questions without referring to your written notes (but do refer to your visual memory notes).

Create summary sheets for major themes. Look at your textbook and your class lecture notes to identify major topics or themes that were developed throughout the last few weeks or throughout the term for final exams. These **summary sheets** will help prepare you for essay questions that require you to compare, contrast, summarize, describe, explain, discuss, tell, or state about major themes. The summary sheets may simply list key details for two or more themes, or they may be set up as comparison charts with subjects listed down the left side and categories of information across the top. (Review comparison charts on pages 215–217.)

Predict test questions and practice writing answers. In addition to using your course syllabus, your visual notes, and your summary charts as sources for predicting test questions, also analyze your lecture notes for themes or large categories of information that were discussed in class. What topics seemed to be given the most lecture or discussion time in class? Write a series of practice questions. Consider working with a study partner so that each of you can create practice essay questions to give to each other. Set a time limit to compose an answer to the practice questions. Use the strategies discussed later in this chapter to compose your answers. If you practice expressing your ideas *before a test*, dealing with essay questions on a test is much less stressful and intimidating.

Organize and Practice Writing Essays When Topics Are Known in Advance
Some teachers will give you the topics for the essay questions, the exact essay questions, or a group of essay questions from which the test questions will be selected. The advance notice offers you the opportunity to prepare thoroughly and practice developing a comprehensive answer. When essay questions are given in advance, the expectation is that your answer or answers will be better organized, developed, and supported with relevant supporting details than they would have been if the questions were not announced in advance. You are expected to have an answer already formulated; however, usually *you are not allowed to bring a completed essay, notes, or an outline with you to the test.* To prepare for this approach to an essay test, schedule sufficient time prior to the essay test to use the following strategies.

Organize materials for the known topic. If the topic is given but the actual questions are not given, begin by generating a set of notes related specifically to the topic. Use the *index* in the back of your book for page references related to the topic. Reread each of the pages listed in the index; make your preferred style of *summary notes* for the information. Then review your lecture notes and homework assignments for additional information related to this topic. Compile all the information that you can relate to the topic. Refer once again to your course syllabus for general themes. What general themes relate specifically to this topic? How could this relationship be worded in an essay question? Predict and write several possible essay questions. Use the strategies presented later in the chapter to write answers to your own questions, or exchange practice questions with a study partner and write answers to your study partner's questions.

Organize materials and your answer when you are given the exact question. Use the same techniques for organizing materials that were given above. Then create either an outline or a visual mapping or hierarchy for each part of your essay. This outline or visual form of notetaking should be memorized so it can guide you when you write the essay in class. Practice writing the essay answer several times and during several different study blocks; include specific details and course terminology in your answer. Use the other essay writing techniques discussed later in the chapter.

Organize materials and answers for all the questions given to you in advance. Sometimes you will be given a group of questions and told that the actual questions used on the test will be selected from this group. Your task now is larger than if you were given one exact question in advance. For this approach, you will need to complete the process explained above for *each essay question.* Needless to say, scheduling sufficient time to study and write essay answers is essential. An outline or set of visual notes should be memorized for each essay question. For each of the questions, practice writing an answer without referring to an outline or notes. If you practice writing the answer on several different occasions, you will feel well prepared, confident, and ready to repeat the performance in the classroom on the day of the test.

Organize Materials for an Open-Book Test   Students are often excited and relieved to learn that an essay test will be an open-book test. However, the previous strategies for preparing for tests by anticipating test questions, preparing summary sheets, and practicing writing answers should still be used. In addition, the following strategies should also be used so you are not wasting valuable test time searching for needed information:

- **Become very familiar with the index of your book** so you can look up the topic quickly.

- **Use a special highlighter for important facts** (significant dates, names, events, statistics, or terminology) **and quotations** you predict may be needed on the essay.

- **Use tabs to mark significant pages** such as important summary charts, tables, lists or steps, or visual materials.

Organize and Develop Answers for Take-Home Tests   Expectations for a polished essay are higher when the essay questions are given as a take-home test. The major problem many students face with take-home tests is not allowing enough time to develop essay answers. Use the steps presented in Chapter 4 (page 82) for a term-project goal.

Take-home essays, which are written in untimed situations, use basically the same steps used in classroom tests with a few modifications in the first and last paragraphs. In an essay test, the first paragraph is very brief; it basically gives the thesis sentence. In an untimed essay, this first paragraph can be written to create a stronger interest for the reader. The paragraph may begin with a captivating introduction, called a *lead-in,* and end with your thesis sentence. Introductions or lead-ins may include:

- A short personal experience, an incident, or an event from the text or an analogy that is closely related to the thesis

- Factual information from your text or from library research

- Brief background information that prepares the reader for your thesis

- A fictitious situation that introduces the thesis

The last paragraph continues to serve as a summary or conclusion. The first part of the paragraph will still echo your thesis sentence. However, it can also include implications or applications of the topic of your essay. This closing paragraph can be written to leave the reader with some new angles or thoughts to consider.

If you decide to use these variations for your introductory and concluding paragraphs, remember to be concise. Lengthy variations shift the focus away from your thesis and body, and that is not your intention.

Understanding Direction Words

Some of the direction words used in short-answer questions also appear in essay questions. Understanding the direction words is essential for your essay to address the question that was posed. Study the following direction words so that you will know the kind of information that is expected in your answer:

Direction Word	What Is Required
Compare	Show the similarities and differences between two or more items.
Contrast	Present only the differences between two or more items.
Define	Expand the definition with more examples and greater details.
Trace/Outline	Discuss the sequence of events in chronological order.
Summarize	Identify and discuss the main points or the highlights of a subject. In-depth details are not expected.
Evaluate/Critique	Offer your opinion or judgment, and then back it up with specific facts, details, or reasons.
Analyze	Identify the different parts of something. Discuss each part individually.
Describe	Give a detailed description of different aspects, points of view, parts, characteristics, or qualities.
Discuss	Tell about the parts or the main points. Expand with specific details.
Explain/Explain Why	Give reasons. Tell why. Show logical relationships or cause-effect.
Explain How	Give the process, steps, stages, or procedures involved. Explain each.
Illustrate	Give examples. Explain each example with details.

The following example will show the significance of understanding the direction word. One essay question on a literature test stated "Compare the writing style of Homer in *The Odyssey* and John Milton in *Paradise Lost*." According to the chart, *compare* means to show the similarities and the differences between Homer and Milton. You would need to ask yourself, "What things can I compare?" Because this is a literature class, you can compare the kind of structure each writer used, the themes, the characters and how they were developed, the plots, the settings, the tones, and the style and vocabulary used. In your essay, you would want to focus on the similarities or differences between the two authors in respect to the various elements of literature you chose to include. A student who doesn't understand the significance of the direction word "compare" may simply write one paragraph about Homer and another paragraph about Milton. This student would assume that the teacher could infer the differences by reading the two paragraphs. However, writing essays doesn't work that way. You need to clearly show the relationships in your writing. The student mentioned earlier made the mistake of treating the question as if it simply asked him or her to "describe" the two writers. To avoid similar errors, learn the meanings of each of the common direction words.

✎ **EXERCISE 14.7 Discussing Expectations for Answers**

Work with a partner or in a small group. Follow the directions below for each essay question. Circle the direction word. Underline the key words that would be used in your answer. Decide if the question is an open-ended or closed question. Jot your answer in the margin. Discuss the kind of answer that is expected based on the meaning of the direction word.

1. Discuss this statement: Business competition encourages efficiency of production and leads to improved quality control.

2. Is gross national product really a reliable indicator of a nation's standard of living? Explain.

3. Why should business take on the task of training the hard-core unemployed?

4. What are the major differences between the economic model of social responsibility and the socio-economic model?

5. Define the goal of affirmative-action programs and tell how the goal is achieved.

6. Explain the differences between general partners and limited partners.

7. Trace the incorporation process and describe the basic corporate structure.

8. Discuss the changes made in Washington in the post-Watergate years to place greater restrictions on the executive power of the President of the United States.

9. Contrast the opinions and sentiments expressed by the people of Panama and the American people in 1977 in regard to the ownership and rights to the Panama Canal.

10. President Clinton's 1998 visit to China brought the Tiananmen Square event back into the public's awareness. Trace the events in China that led up to and followed the massacre in Tiananmen Square.

11. In the late 1990s, environmental issues remained high on the international list of global problems. Summarize the global environmental issues that may have the greatest impact on the welfare of the world's population.

12. Which leadership style or styles most closely conform to supportive communication? Explain.

13. Think of and then discuss three examples of positive ethnic stereotypes.

14. Compare the thinking styles of vertical thinkers and lateral thinkers. Include the characteristics of each type of thinker and give examples to clearly show the differences in the way each would operate in daily life situations.

15. What are Piaget's stages of human development? Summarize each stage of his theory.

16. Trace the path of blood in the circulatory system of mammals.

Strategies for Answering Essay Questions

The following strategies for answering essay questions are very similar to the strategies used for short-answer questions (page 286). The procedures have been expanded to meet the essay requirement that full paragraphs be used to communicate the information. Understanding the general structure of an essay and using the following strategies will result in better performance on essay tests.

> ### Strategies for Answering Essay Questions
>
> 1. Identify the direction word and underline the key words.
> 2. Write a strong, focused opening sentence called a *thesis sentence* or *thesis statement*.
> 3. Plan your answer before you begin writing. Make a brief outline, visual mapping, hierarchy, or list of ideas to develop the body of your essay.
> 4. Develop the body of the essay. A common format to use is the five-paragraph essay.
> 5. Summarize your main ideas in a short, concluding paragraph.
> 6. Proofread and revise.

Identify the Direction Word   As discussed in the previous section, the beginning step in writing an essay is knowing what kind of answer is expected. The direction word indicates what is expected and should guide the direction of your answer.

Write a Strong Thesis Sentence   A **thesis sentence** directly states the main point you want to make in the entire essay. The thesis sentence for an essay test should be the first sentence on your paper. This sentence should:

■ Clearly state the topic of the essay

■ Include key words that are a part of the question

■ Show that you understand the direction word

■ Indicate a given number of main ideas you will discuss

The thesis statement is important to you and to your teacher. For you, it serves as a guide for developing the rest of your essay. It provides the basic outline of main ideas to develop with important supporting details. For the teacher, it serves as an immediate indicator that you understand the question and know the answer. Because of the significance of the thesis statement, take time to create a strong, direct, confident opening sentence.

In the following chart, notice how the questions are analyzed. The direction word is identified and circled. Key words are underlined. Thought is given as to the type of answer that is expected, based on the direction word. Finally, a possible thesis statement, which would help guide the direction of the body of the essay, is given.

Question	Direction	Possible Thesis Statements
(Discuss) the characteristics of each of Howard Gardner's multiple intelligences.	Discuss = tell about What are the eight intelligences?	*Each of Howard Gardner's eight intelligences has clearly recognizable characteristics.*
(Explain why) elaborative rehearsal is more effective for college learning than rote memory strategies.	Explain why = give reasons What are the reasons? How many reasons?	*Elaborative rehearsal is more effective than rote memory because more of the memory principles are used and information in memory is in a more usable form.*

Plan Your Answer Before You Begin Writing   Organizing information for many students is the most difficult part of writing essays. Many students wander off course or are at a loss for ideas to write in essays without first making a plan. Outlines, visual mappings, hierarchies, or basic lists that are not as detailed as outlines are three common plans used to organize information for an essay. Explore the different formats and then decide which works best for you. The following examples show the use of a plan in outline form, visual mapping form, and hierarchy form.

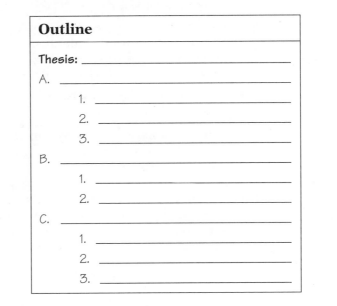

MAPPING

HIERARCHY THESIS

Develop the Body of Your Essay   A strong thesis statement and a plan for the information you want to include in your essay lead naturally into the next step, the actual writing of the essay. *Each category or section* of information in your outline, visual mapping, or hierarchy can be expanded into sentences and developed into *one paragraph*. Each additional category or section would thus become another paragraph. Remember, however, that a person with strong writing skills is capable of combining ideas in a variety of ways, so devoting one paragraph to each section of your plan is one possible way to develop the body of the paragraph, but other options may also exist.

The following suggestions will help you develop a more effective essay answer:

■ Limit each paragraph to one main idea. Shifting to a new main idea is the signal to move to the next line, indent (about five spaces), and begin a new paragraph.

- Complete sentences need to be used to express your ideas and present your information. Short phrases, charts, or lists of information are not appropriate for an essay.

- Supporting details are essential or your essay will be underdeveloped. Include facts such as names, dates, events, statistics; include definitions, examples, or appropriate applications of the information you are presenting. Do not make the mistake of assuming that information is obvious and your teacher knows what you are thinking or clearly sees the connection. Write as if your reader is *not knowledgeable* about the subject.

- Use course-specific terminology. You spent time studying all the vocabulary words, so strive to include them in your answers as much as possible. Use other words that you learned from class or the textbook and words you have added to your expressive vocabulary.

- Use the basic five-paragraph essay format or a variation of the format as discussed below.

The **five-paragraph essay format** is a standard format that can be used effectively for most essay tests. It begins with the thesis statement, which is then followed by the **body of the essay**. The body often consists of three paragraphs developing three main ideas. Each paragraph includes specific supporting details that show your understanding and knowledge. (Additional paragraphs can be added for longer essays.) A short summary or **concluding paragraph** ends the essay. The following chart shows the five parts of this format for a sample essay question.

Q: *Summarize strategies to use to strengthen a person's vocabulary, textbook reading, and test-taking skills.*

Thesis: _____

_____

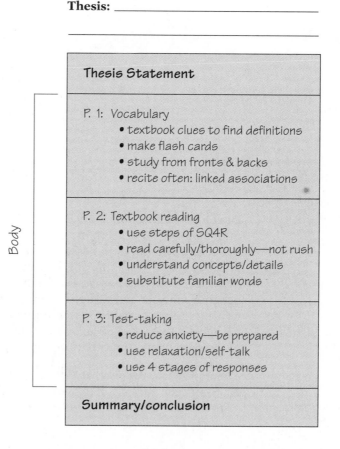

Thesis Statement

Body

P. 1: Vocabulary
- textbook clues to find definitions
- make flash cards
- study from fronts & backs
- recite often: linked associations

P. 2: Textbook reading
- use steps of SQ4R
- read carefully/thoroughly—not rush
- understand concepts/details
- substitute familiar words

P. 3: Test-taking
- reduce anxiety—be prepared
- use relaxation/self-talk
- use 4 stages of responses

Summary/conclusion

Summarize Your Main Points   Finish your essay with a short summary sentence or paragraph. Summarizing leaves a clear picture of your main points in the reader's mind and signals that you have finished with your thoughts. Your summary should reflect the same information you used in your thesis sentence. If your summary and thesis sentence do not focus on the same subject, check to see where you got sidetracked when you developed the body of your essay.

Proofread Your Work   After you have completed your essay, take a few minutes to *proofread* for mechanical errors such as spelling, grammar, word usage, or sentence structure. Many teachers try to grade mainly on the content, but mechanical errors are distracting, and maintaining a focus on the ideas is therefore more difficult.

If your writing skills are still weak for college-level writing, consider enrolling in writing skill-building courses to improve your spelling, grammar, punctuation, and organizational skills. Also, ask your instructor if you can use a dictionary, thesaurus, spell checker, or laptop computer when you write essays.

> Q: *Many study skills were discussed this term to help you become a successful college student. Select any four skills that you feel are most important for your personal success in college. Discuss the importance of those skills to you.*

Thesis: _____

_____

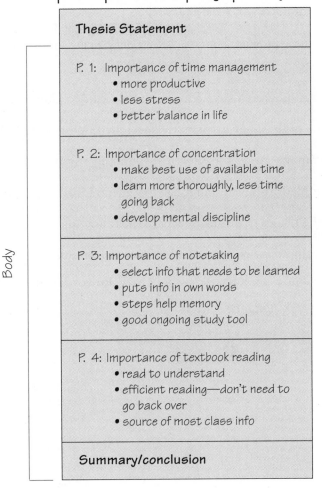

Example of a plan for a six-paragraph essay

Name _____   Date _____

✎ EXERCISE 14.8 Strengthening a Weak Essay

Read the following essay question and one student's answer. Then work with a partner to discuss answers to the questions that follow the essay.

Question: *Discuss the parts of the Information Processing Model.*

> There are six main parts to the Information Processing Model.
> The first part of the model is the input. This is where we use our senses to get information. The information then starts into our memory system.
> Short-term memory is the next part of the model. It really is short! It doesn't hold much here. Sometimes, in fact, information gets shoved out or forgotten here because it can't hold much.
> If it makes it out of short-term memory, the information goes on the practice path. This is also called the rehearsal path. This is where a lot of practice takes place until ideas are learned. Rehearsal can include reading carefully, quizzing yourself, going over flash cards, or working on recall columns of notes. Any kind of activity that helps you work with the information and lets you know if you are learning works here.
> Next, information goes into long-term memory. Well, not really all the time. If you rehearse and can't answer, you don't know it. It isn't in long-term memory. The information can go back up on this loop. Try again.
> When you're successful in learning, the information goes into long-term memory. Somehow it finds its way around the brain and gets plunked in the right place. It is permanent. It's always in there. When you want to use it, you send yourself a message to get it out. The information you learned then goes out on the retrieval path. This is the path that leads to you being able to give an answer, show you know something or use the information in some way.
> Those are all the parts of the Information Processing Model. The model takes you from the sensory input all they way through to the output. That's how we learn.

Questions:

1. Is the thesis statement strong, neutral, or weak? Explain your answer.

2. Is the body of the essay sufficiently developed? What details would you want to add?

3. Is the summary paragraph effective? Explain your answer.

4. Give examples of slang or language that is too informal for an essay.

5. Identify the places in this essay where the following writing tips could be used:

   ■ Avoid using the word *you*. Reword so *you* is not used.

   ■ Avoid vague pronouns such as *it* or *they*. Reword by using the noun word.

   ■ Avoid "weak sentence starters" such as: *There is . . . There are . . . Here is . . .* Reword.

✏ EXERCISE 14.9 Enough Talk! Let's Write!

Select one of the topics below. Use your book and your notes to gather information for your answer. Organize the information. Write a thesis statement and a plan (an outline, mapping, or a hierarchy). Then develop your essay; proofread your work. Essays may be shared in class.

1. Summarize the relationship of the twelve principles of memory to one of the following: SQ4R, Cornell notetaking, or visual notetaking.

2. Contrast the capabilities and the functions of short-term memory and long-term memory.

3. Discuss specific strategies that can be used to deal with the four sources of test anxiety.

4. Identify the study skills areas in which you feel you have made the most progress this term. Tell about the strategies or techniques you learned to use which can be attributed to your success.

5. Outline the study strategies you will use within the first three weeks of the next term you are enrolled in school.

6. Illustrate common examples of three students you know who have difficulties in school due to procrastination, test anxiety, lack of time management, or weak vocabulary skills. Discuss strategies each of the three students would benefit learning in order to reduce or eliminate their academic difficulties.

7. Define one of the four forgetting theories and discuss learning strategies that can be used to combat the forgetting process.

8. Contrast the way you were before you enrolled in this class and the way you see yourself now in terms of your attitude toward learning, your learning environment, and your study strategies.

Additional Essay Writing Tips

Writing strong essay answers becomes easier with practice. When you receive your essay tests back, take time to read the comments and suggestions. You can learn to improve your essay writing skills by analyzing your essays. Your analysis can also include looking for patterns to the kinds of questions your teacher tends to assign. Are the questions mainly from information in the textbook, in lectures, or both? Then look at other essay test-taking skills. Were you effective in predicting essay test questions? When you wrote your essays, did you answer the questions directly? Were your answers well organized? Did you provide sufficient details?

The following tips will also strengthen your essay-writing skills:

- If you are given several choices of questions to answer, look at the choices carefully. The majority of students tend to choose the question that is the shortest and looks the easiest. However, these questions are usually more general and sometimes more difficult to answer. Questions that "look the most difficult" because they are longer may actually be more specific and easier to answer. Consider your choice of questions carefully.

- If you are required to do more than one essay question, begin with the one that is most familiar and easiest for you. Your confidence will be boosted and your mind will shift into the essay-writing mode.

- Strive to write as neatly as possible. Illegible handwriting will hurt your grade. If you need to delete some of the information, delete it by crossing it out with one neat line.

- Consider writing on every other line so you have room to revise or add information if time permits before the test time ends.

■ If you were not able to budget your time sufficiently, turn in your plan (outline, mapping, hierarchy, or list). You may earn some additional points for showing you knew the information and would have included it if you hadn't run out of time.

■ If you have more than one essay to complete on a test, be sure to write something on each question. You will lose too many points by totally leaving out one question. It is usually better to turn in some work on two essays versus only one essay completely developed.

■ Weigh the value of different questions. If one question is worth more points, take more time to develop that answer or to return to that answer later and add more information to strengthen your answer.

■ If your keyboarding skills are good and you have a laptop computer, ask if you can write your essay on the computer and turn in the disk. Work tends to appear neater, easier to read, and void of spelling errors.

Web-site links are available online.

Computer Projects

1. Use an outlining program or a graphic program to create summary charts, an outline, or a plan for an essay question.
2. Create a brochure that features what you consider to be the most helpful test-taking tips.
3. Predict an essay question for an essay test in any one of your classes. Plan the essay and write the essay using your computer. Ask a classmate to critique your essay.

Group Web-Search Activity is available online.

Case Studies are available online.

SUMMARY

- Fill-in-the-blank questions often require one vocabulary word for each blank.

- Listing questions often begin with the words *List* or *Name*. Answers do not need to be in full sentences.

- A three-part answer can be used to write thorough definitions: (1) name the category, (2) define the word, (3) expand with one more detail.

- Three-to-seven complete sentences are used for short-answer questions. The answer must follow the direction word in the question.

- Predicting test questions and writing your own practice questions and answers is one way to prepare for upcoming tests.

- The four levels of response are used in recall questions. However, educated guessing is replaced by substituting words or synonyms when exact information cannot be recalled.

- Recall questions and essay questions may be open-ended or closed questions.

- Different strategies can be used for essay questions based on whether or not you are given the topics or the questions in advance, in an open-book test, or in a take-home test.

- Summary notes made before an essay test is one way to compile information about "big pictures," trends, patterns, or major relationships.

- Understanding the direction words in short-answer and essay questions is essential to move the answer in the required direction.

- A basic essay structure includes a thesis statement, several paragraphs in the body of the essay, and a concluding paragraph.

- Outlines, visual notes, or lists may be used as a plan to organize an essay before the writing begins.

OPTIONS FOR PERSONALIZING CHAPTER 14

1. **PROFILE CHART—PERSONAL LOG** Answer the following questions in your personal log.

   What score did you have on the Chapter 14 Profile? _____

   Which specific strategies did you learn in this chapter that will help you improve your performance on tests with recall and essay questions?

2. **WORDS TO KNOW** Knowing the following terms is important.

   recall questions
   fill-in-the-blank question
   immediate response
   delayed response
   memory search
   assisted response
   synonym
   listing questions
   predict listing questions
   closed questions

   open-ended questions
   definition question
   short-answer questions
   direction word
   summary sheets
   thesis sentence
   five-paragraph essay format
   body of the essay
   concluding paragraph

3. **EXPAND THE CHAPTER VISUAL MAPPING**   For this chapter, the mapping already shows levels one, two, and three information. Expand the mapping by adding level-four details. You will need to work on a larger piece of paper. Personalize your mapping with colors, pictures, or other shapes.

4. **WRITING ASSIGNMENT 1**   Summarize the most valuable study skills you learned this term. Focus on the study skills that are increasing your performance in college and increasing the image you have of yourself as a successful college student.

5. **WRITING ASSIGNMENT 2**   Write a thank-you letter to another classmate, your teacher, a study group leader, a study buddy, or a tutor who helped you succeed this term.

6. **PORTFOLIO DEVELOPMENT**   Throughout the term you have read about and possibly selected portfolio activities that demonstrate your skills and application of the strategies in this course. Now take time to organize your portfolio so that your projects can be presented in an organized manner. Consider creating an introductory page to discuss the goals and organization of your overall portfolio projects. Consider creating a table of contents. Be sure that your name is visible on the cover and the inside of your portfolio.

CHAPTER 14 REVIEW QUESTIONS

*The following questions will provide you with practice using the test-taking tech-
niques from Chapter 14 as well as provide you with the opportunity to review
material from throughout the term.*

Fill-in-the-Blank

Write one word on each line to correctly complete each sentence.

1. A _____ is defined as a word that has the same or similar meaning.

2. _____ questions on tests are questions that require very specific answers and the answers often must be given in a specific order.

3. A _____ sentence is the main idea for an entire essay.

4. A _____ sentence is the main idea for one specific paragraph.

5. _____ are words used in objective tests that indicate how frequently or how completely something occurs. Examples are *sometimes, seldom, always,* and *never.*

6. An _____ _____ of control means that a person takes responsibility for his or her life and feels an ability to control many of life's situations.

7. Students who have test anxiety due to _____ often find the need for last-minute massed practice or cramming.

8. A _____ _____ is a type of visual graphic that organizes information to be compared by using columns, rows, and cells.

9. The _____ step of the Cornell notetaking system is designed for the student to practice information by talking out loud and in complete sentences.

10. _____ can be eliminated by using goal setting and time-management techniques that encourage a person not to put things off for a later time.

11. The three basic learning modalities are _____ , _____ , and

    _____ .

12. When using the SQ4R textbook reading system, the first *R* of the Cornell system would begin during

    the _____ step of SQ4R.

Definitions

Write a complete definition for the following terms.

1. Listening

2. Define *one* of the following kinds of poor listeners: the rehearser, the filterer, the identified, the derailer, the sparrer, or the placater.

3. active learning

4. elaborative rehearsal

Listing

Use your own paper to write the answers to the following questions.

1. Name the eight intelligences as defined by Howard Gardner.
2. List the five forgetting theories that were discussed in this course.
3. List the steps involved in effective goal setting.
4. Name any six concentration strategies to deal with internal or external distractors.
5. List the Twelve Principles of Memory.

Short-Answer Questions

Write the answers to the following questions on your own paper.

1. Explain how to study from the highlighting done in your textbook.
2. What is the relationship between receptive vocabulary and expressive vocabulary?
3. How do the discrepancies between the rate of speech, the rate of writing, and the rate of thinking affect a person's notetaking skills?
4. Tell how highlighting or a chapter visual mapping can be used to write summaries.

Essay

Select one *of the following to develop into an essay. Write your answer on your own paper.*

1. Summarize the techniques that can be used to improve comprehension of a difficult paragraph.
2. Compare and contrast right-brain learners from left-brain learners.
3. Discuss four main sources of test anxiety and the strategies that can be used to overcome test anxiety.
4. Define active learning as it relates to a college student.
5. Identify and describe the notetaking options that can be used in college courses.

Appendixes

APPENDIX A

Chapter Profile Materials

APPENDIX B

Portfolio Assessment Form

APPENDIX C

Library Projects

Name _____ Date _____

APPENDIX A
Chapter Profile Materials

Master Profile Chart

Learning Styles	Processing Memory	Time Management	Setting Goals	Concentration	Reading	Textbook Information	Terminology	Cornell Textbooks	Cornell Lectures	Visual Notes	Test Preparation	Objective Tests	Recall & Essay Tests
1	2	3	4	5	6	7	8	9	10	11	12	13	14
12	12	12	12	12	12	12	12	12	12	12	12	12	12
11	11	11	11	11	11	11	11	11	11	11	11	11	11
10	10	10	10	10	10	10	10	10	10	10	10	10	10
9	9	9	9	9	9	9	9	9	9	9	9	9	9
8	8	8	8	8	8	8	8	8	8	8	8	8	8
7	7	7	7	7	7	7	7	7	7	7	7	7	7
6	6	6	6	6	6	6	6	6	6	6	6	6	6
5	5	5	5	5	5	5	5	5	5	5	5	5	5
4	4	4	4	4	4	4	4	4	4	4	4	4	4
3	3	3	3	3	3	3	3	3	3	3	3	3	3
2	2	2	2	2	2	2	2	2	2	2	2	2	2
1	1	1	1	1	1	1	1	1	1	1	1	1	1
0	0	0	0	0	0	0	0	0	0	0	0	0	0

Beginning-of-the-Term Profile

1. As you begin a new chapter, complete the chapter-profile chart.
2. Score your profile. (See Chapter 1, page 2.) Find the chapter number above. Circle your score to show the number correct.
3. Connect the circles with lines to create a graph (your Master Profile Chart).

Profile Answer Keys

1: Learning Styles	2: Processing/ Memory	3: Time Management	4: Setting Goals
1. **Y** N	1. **Y** N	1. **Y** N	1. **Y** N
2. **Y** N	2. Y **N**	2. Y **N**	2. Y **N**
3. **Y** N	3. **Y** N	3. Y **N**	3. Y **N**
4. **Y** N	4. Y **N**	4. **Y** N	4. **Y** N
5. Y **N**	5. **Y** N	5. **Y** N	5. **Y** N
6. **Y** N	6. Y **N**	6. Y **N**	6. **Y** N
7. **Y** N	7. **Y** N	7. **Y** N	7. Y **N**
8. Y **N**	8. Y **N**	8. Y **N**	8. Y **N**
9. **Y** N	9. Y **N**	9. Y **N**	9. Y **N**
10. **Y** N	10. **Y** N	10. Y **N**	10. **Y** N
11. **Y** N	11. **Y** N	11. **Y** N	11. Y **N**
12. **Y** N	12. **Y** N	12. Y **N**	12. **Y** N

5: Concentration	6: Reading	7: Textbook Information	8: Terminology	9: Cornell— Textbooks
1. **Y** N	1. Y **N**	1. Y **N**	1. **Y** N	1. **Y** N
2. Y **N**	2. **Y** N	2. **Y** N	2. **Y** N	2. Y **N**
3. Y **N**	3. **Y** N	3. Y **N**	3. Y **N**	3. **Y** N
4. **Y** N	4. Y **N**	4. **Y** N	4. **Y** N	4. **Y** N
5. **Y** N	5. Y **N**	5. **Y** N	5. **Y** N	5. **Y** N
6. **Y** N	6. **Y** N	6. **Y** N	6. Y **N**	6. **Y** N
7. **Y** N	7. Y **N**	7. **Y** N	7. **Y** N	7. **Y** N
8. Y **N**	8. Y **N**	8. **Y** N	8. **Y** N	8. **Y** N
9. **Y** N	9. Y **N**	9. **Y** Y	9. Y **N**	9. **Y** N
10. Y **N**	10. **Y** N	10. Y **N**	10. **Y** N	10. **Y** N
11. **Y** N	11. **Y** N	11. Y **N**	11. Y **N**	11. **Y** N
12. Y **N**	12. **Y** N	12. **Y** N	12. **Y** N	12. Y **N**

10: Cornell— Lectures	11: Visual Notes	12: Test Preparation	13: Objective Tests	14: Recall/ Essay Tests
1. Y **N**	1. **Y** N	1. Y **N**	1. **Y** N	1. Y **N**
2. Y **N**	2. **Y** N	2. **Y** N	2. Y **N**	2. Y **N**
3. Y **N**	3. **Y** N	3. Y **N**	3. Y **N**	3. Y **N**
4. **Y** N	4. **Y** N	4. **Y** N	4. **Y** N	4. **Y** N
5. **Y** N	5. Y **N**	5. Y **N**	5. **Y** N	5. **Y** N
6. Y **N**	6. **Y** N	6. Y **N**	6. **Y** N	6. Y **N**
7. Y **N**	7. **Y** N	7. **Y** N	7. Y **N**	7. Y **N**
8. **Y** N	8. **Y** N	8. **Y** N	8. **Y** N	8. Y **N**
9. **Y** N	9. **Y** N	9. **Y** N	9. **Y** N	9. Y **N**
10. **Y** N	10. **Y** N	10. **Y** N	10. **Y** N	10. **Y** N
11. **Y** N	11. **Y** N	11. Y **N**	11. **Y** N	11. **Y** N
12. **Y** N	12. **Y** N	12. **Y** N	12. Y **N**	12. **Y** N

End-of-the-Term Profile

1. Cut a two-inch wide strip of paper to cover up the original answers on the profile questions at the beginning of each chapter. Re-do all the profile questions so you can see changes that you have made this term. Write Y or N *next to the number of each profile question.*

2. Score your profile answers by using the answer key on this page.

3. Chart your scores on the Master Profile Chart. Use a different color ink so you can compare these scores to your original scores.

Name _____ Date _____

APPENDIX B
Portfolio Assessment Form

Portfolio Project for Chapter _____

■ Write a short introduction that states your goals for this project.

Required Element:

_____ Sufficient details included

_____ Accurate information presented

_____ Neatness, clarity of presentation demonstrated

_____ Originality, critical thinking demonstrated

_____ Skill requirement demonstrated

_____ Other _____

Required Element:

_____ Sufficient details included

_____ Accurate information presented

_____ Neatness, clarity of presentation demonstrated

_____ Originality, critical thinking demonstrated

_____ Skill requirement demonstrated

_____ Other _____

■ Write a short self-assessment conclusion that states your personal view on the value and the quality of your project.

Evaluation Comments:

Photocopy this form before you use it.

APPENDIX C
Library Projects

Exploring Your Library

Your school's library is an extremely valuable resource that you will use throughout your college years. Visit your library to find the answers to the following questions. If you are not able to find answers by exploring on your own, ask the reference librarian for assistance.

1. What are the library hours this term?
2. Are library tours available to help you learn more about your library? If yes, when are they scheduled?
3. Is a library class offered to help you learn more about using the library? If yes, what is the name of the class?
4. What are the procedures for checking out a library book?
5. Does your library have the following resources?

_____ magazine subscriptions   _____ CD-ROM databases

_____ video and audio tapes   _____ online (computer) databases

_____ newspaper files   _____ microfilm/microfiche readers

_____ card catalogs   _____ interlibrary loan privileges

6. Where are the reference materials located?
7. What are the most common reference materials in your library?
8. What library call number system is used to organize the books in your library?
9. How can you find out if your library subscribes to a specific magazine?
10. Where is the "reserve section" for books reserved for class use by instructors?

Library Projects

Application Exercise

Use your library skills to begin researching a topic of your choice. The objective of this exercise is for you to show you understand how to access different kinds of information in your library. You will not be asked to do complete research or to write a research paper.

Follow each step of these directions:

1. Select a study skills topic from the list below. If you have another subject that is related to study skills that is not shown below, discuss the topic with your instructor first. Circle the topic you wish to research:

time management	any aspect of memory
forgetting	listening skills
brain/cognitive research	ADD
self-esteem	Howard Gardner's multiple
motivation	intelligences
Maslow's hierarchy	metamemory
self-talk	metacognition
mnemonics	textbook reading

punctuation skills	neurotransmitters
vocabulary development	test anxiety
Greek/Latin roots	alpha waves in learning
word etymology	goal setting
Cornell notetaking	learning styles/learning modalities
brain dominance theory	effect of (you decide) on the brain
assertiveness	visualization
test-taking skills	stress
essay writing	learning disabilities
concentration	right-brain thinking
relaxation techniques	long- or short-term memory

2. Before you begin the next two steps, ASSUME that you are actually going to write a research paper. Since the above topics are broad topics, you will need to NARROW your topic so that all the resources you locate focus on the same aspect. For example, if you decide to research "motivation," you may want to specifically find resources that discuss *motivation in adult students*. This would be your narrowed topic. You would, therefore, disregard resources that talk about motivation in research rats, motivation methods for toilet training a toddler, or motivation in the corporate world. SELECT resources that are compatible and focus on the same issue or narrowed topic.

   Some students use the online periodicals cataloging system to get ideas for narrowed topics. For example, if you look up magazine articles on "stress," you will find subcategories for stress. The subcategories are narrowed topics that may be useful for a paper.

3. Use your library system to locate the following resources that could be used for a paper on your narrowed topic. Be sure to write down the location of the material or print a copy of the site information so you can document that you identified the required sources of information. Your information should show the author, title, copyright date, and other bibliographic information.

   ■ Two books, tapes, or videos related to your narrowed topic

   ■ Two magazine articles related to your narrowed topic

   ■ Two web site addresses or CD-ROM sites related to your narrowed topic

4. Compile your resources. Attach a summary sheet on the front of your work that identifies your topic, your narrowed topic, and the names of your two books/videos/tapes, two magazine articles, and two web site or CD-ROM documents.

Extra Credit: Do ONE of the following:

1. Check out one of the books, tapes, or videos. If you select a book, read one chapter and write a summary of important information learned from the chapter. If you select a tape or a video, listen to or view it. Write a summary of important information learned.

2. Locate and photocopy one of the magazine articles. Use your textbook marking skills to highlight important information. Write a summary of the important points in the article. Turn in both the article and your written summary.

3. Print one document from the Internet and one document from a CD-ROM database. Write a summary that compares and contrasts the information from these two different sources of information.

Index